*Site Planning*

Kevin Lynch

*Site Planning*

Second Edition

The M.I.T. Press
*Cambridge, Massachusetts, and London, England*

*It was set in Linofilm Palatino*
*by Southern New England Typographic Service, Inc.*
*printed on Finch Filmtext, 60 lb.*
*by The Colonial Press Inc.*
*and bound by The Colonial Press Inc.*
*in the United States of America.*

*ISBN 0 262 12050 X (hardcover)*

*Library of Congress catalog card number: 75-158161*

# Contents

# List of Illustrations

# List of Tables

# Preface to the First Edition

$S$ite planning is the art of arranging buildings and other structures on the land in harmony with each other. This book is intended to be an introduction to the art, an exposition of its principles, and a condensed technical reference. It will be of interest to students and to professional city planners, architects, landscape architects, and civil engineers. But those who enjoy the urban landscape or who are concerned with the social issues which it generates may also find some pleasure in it.

There is not much that is original in these pages, except perhaps for the way they are put together. The ideas come from many sources and have been so condensed, reorganized, and interpreted that they can rarely be referred to a single source. My education in architecture and its roots in the land began with Frank Lloyd Wright, who opened my eyes. Since then, I have been able to work or to teach with skilled men and to learn thereby: Lawrence Anderson, Robert Woods Kennedy, Ralph Rapson, John Myer. Gyorgy Kepes and his ideas are present as always.

Several expert site planners have made important comments on early drafts of this text: Hideo Sasaki, Julian Whittlesey, Ralph Eberlin. Mark Sagal of the Perini Corporation was helpful in checking my cost figures and Robert Newman in advising me on exterior acoustics. Rodney Freebairn-Smith took on the demanding task of searching for photographic illustrations. The text has grown gradually out of notes for a course in site planning, beginning with an original nucleus by Draveaux Bender on sewer and water systems. Here and there he will find fragments of his original work.

My best teachers have been the students of architecture and city planning at M.I.T.

*Cambridge, Massachusetts*　　　　　KEVIN LYNCH
*March 1962*

# Preface to the Second Edition

This book has remained in continuous use as a reference and a teaching textbook, but it became obsolete in several ways. Serious gaps in its coverage appeared, and peculiar errors floated up to the surface. It had been organized in two distinct parts — one on fundamentals and the other on detailed techniques — in the hope that while techniques would change, fundamental ideas would persist. While some new technical procedures developed, the great majority remained remarkably stable. Contrary to prediction, the important changes occurred in the fundamentals: the ways of looking at site problems, of analyzing values, and of connecting values and solutions. So much, then, for prophecy.

The book has therefore been completely reorganized and rewritten. The division into parts has been abolished, and technical chapters have been placed with the general chapters to which they relate, where they may be either read or passed over. A discussion of particular kinds of site planning has been put at the end. Presumably, then, a consecutive reading of Chapters 1, 2, 3, 6, 9, 10, and 11 together will give the reader a comprehensive view of the art of site planning.

Many changes have been made in the original material and some foolish errors corrected. New illustrative material has been introduced, and the use of the margins as a cross-reference system has been amplified. A great amount of new material has been added, particularly in regard to ecology, psychosocial analyses, and design method. Most important, perhaps, the original idea of environmental design as a continuous process involving many participants has been much more systematically developed. This point of view is summarized at the end of Chapter 11.

Many people have helped me to make this revision. Robert Rau, drawing on his long professional experience and on the experience of the Rouse Corporation, has been my major support in questions of site engineering and the design of shopping centers. He has consulted with me on so much of the text that he is almost a joint author for sections of it, without, however, incurring any of the guilt of that post. Peter Hornbeck has made many useful suggestions to me about site analysis. Stephen Carr reviewed the section on psychological analyses, and William Porter the section on design method. Tunney Lee made trial use of the new text in his site-planning studio at M.I.T. The firm of Sasaki, Dawson, and DeMay has been most generous with material on landscape construction and design, as well as on institutional site planning. Frederick H. Bair, Jr., gave me some useful material on the site planning of mobile home parks. It would have been difficult to do without this help.

I hope this new text may be useful for another decade.

*Cambridge, Massachusetts*         KEVIN LYNCH
*April 1971*

*Chapter* 1

# The Art of Site Planning

The handsome places we know seem to have grown naturally, while recently planned areas are ugly and uncomfortable. If that is true, why do we make site plans?

Roads, buildings — even gardens — do not grow and organize themselves. They are placed and shaped by someone's decisions, however limited or careless, however obscured by the passage of time. The real issue is not whether sites should be planned but rather how systematic and extensive that planning should be. We are driven, in part willingly, in part anxiously, to organize sites in a comprehensive and conscious way. The economic advantages of large-scale development, the more rapid evolution of technology and greater conflict of purpose, the growing complexity of site facilities, and the tempting possibilities of comprehensively designed environments are some of the motives that drive us. As more building is done with standardized units on a large scale and at a rapid rate, a formal design process becomes imperative. The ultimate consumer becomes more and more difficult to reach. There is less opportunity for that gradual adjustment of use and structure that guided older site organizations. But regardless of scale or deliberation, any human site is somehow planned, if only by piecemeal decision.

Site planning may have attained a new importance, but it is an old art. One thinks of such magnificent places as

## 2

*Normal site design is careless and ugly*

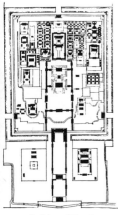

*Peking: The Inner City*

the Imperial Palace of Peking, the center of Pergamum, the Katsura Palace, the crescents of Bath, the Italian squares, the small New England settlement. By contrast, site design in the United States today is monotonously conventional, careless, shallow, and ugly. In part this reflects a lack of skill, which this book seeks to remedy. But there are other problems, as we shall see. In common practice, siting is a hurried layout, in which details are left to chance, or it is an abstract subdivision to which buildings are later mechanically attached, or it is a last-minute effort to fit a previously designed building into some piece of available land. Site planning is thought to be a minor, independent adjunct to the more important decisions of developers, engineers, architects, or builders.

Unfortunately, the site is a crucial aspect of our environment. It has a biological, a social, and a psychological impact that goes far beyond its accepted influence on cost and technical function. It limits what people can do and at the same time opens new opportunities for them. For some groups — for children as an example — it may be the dominant feature of the environment. Its influence outlives that of the individual structure, since site organization usually persists for generations.

FIGURE 1 *The Royal Crescent at Bath, with wartime allotments occupying part of its great lawn. Common upper-class values permitted the formal order and a relation to open space at a noble scale.*

Aerofilms Ltd.

FIGURE 2    *The Inca settlement of Machu Picchu, marvelously fitted to its precipitous site high in the Peruvian Andes.*

It was once thought that the physical environment determined the character of life. When that view collapsed, the natural reaction was to insist that environment had no consequence whatever. But each view rests on the fallacy of the other. Organism and environment interact; environment is both social and physical. One cannot predict the nature of a man from the landscape he lives in, but neither can one foretell what he will do or feel without knowing the landscape. Man and habitat work together. As men multiply and their technology comes to dominate the earth, the organization of the land becomes more important to the quality of their lives. Now there is fear that technology may threaten even the continuance of life. Pollution impairs the living system. Careless disturbance of the landscape is harmful to us; skilled siting enhances us. Well-organized, productive living space becomes a critical resource for humanity, like energy, air, and water.

*Man and environment work together*

*References 5, 9, 16, 20*

Site planning is the art of arranging the external physical environment to support human behavior. It lies along the boundaries of architecture, engineering, landscape architecture, and city planning, and it is practiced by members of all these professions. Site plans locate struc-

*A definition of site planning*

tures and activities in three-dimensional space and, when appropriate, in time. The differences that arise from that spatial and temporal arrangement are the meat of the matter: they include differences in proportion, density, shape, duration, grain, rhythm, pattern, succession, or linkage. Other aspects of site planning follow after these considerations. No important element can be changed without widespread effects. The site is not simply a collection of buildings and streets but a system of structures, surfaces, spaces, living things, climates, and details.

Site planners normally deal with a particular contiguous area under the control of one agency. They may be concerned with a small cluster of houses, with a single building and its grounds, or with something as extensive as a small town that is to be built in one operation. Site planning is distinct from city design, which proposes environmental policies for large areas, undefined time scales, and many clients. Site planning can also be separated from the design of objects such as bridges or buildings, from interior design, from the layout of small and isolated exterior settings such as gardens, and from the design of things to be used in scattered places. Site plans are prepared whenever substantial groups of buildings are erected: houses, factories, shopping centers, institutions, cultural centers. But they can also involve the development of larger landscapes: parks, farms, forests, highways, and urban settings.

*The site-planning process* The formal process begins with an understanding of the persons for whom the site is being planned and a definition of what their role will be in creating or deciding the features of that plan. Next comes an analysis of the situation: a study of the site itself and also of the whole structure of power, value, and technology within which the work must be carried out. The purposes of the plan are stated in concrete terms leading to a program that details the behavior that the plan will support, the required physical characteristics, and expected costs. Finally a design is created — a form that the site will be given to fulfill the program.

Reciting these stages makes them sound logical and linear, as though each directly followed the preceding one. But in fact the process is looping and cyclical. Purpose cannot be precisely stated until site limitations are known. The site cannot be thoroughly analyzed until purposes are set forth. Clients set the purpose, but purpose also helps to determine the relevant clients. Previous experience and the previous history of the problem are used to make the first entry into these circles. From that point on, site design is a learning process, in which a coherent system of form, client, program, and site gradually emerges. Even after a decision is made and building begins — even after the site is occupied — the feedback from experience continues to modify the plan.

Designers of environment tend to overemphasize the importance of the physical setting they are currently proposing. They think that their personal addition will have an overwhelming influence on all those who will later come to use it. It is more accurate to describe any new site form as only a further modification of a prolonged interplay between inhabitants and their surroundings. Sporadic site manipulation becomes continuous site management.

Every site, natural or man-made, is to some degree *Site* unique, a web of things and activities. That web must be understood: it imposes limitations; it contains new possibilities. Any plan, however radical, maintains some continuity *See Chapter 2* with the preexisting locale. Understanding a locality demands time and effort. The site planner properly suffers a chronic anxiety about this "spirit of place."

The human purposes to be met by any site plan are in *Purpose* practice strangely distorted. Stated objectives are usually a mixture of a few explicit and measurable ends, such as cost and capacity, numerous important but ill-defined values that lurk behind "reasonableness" and "good practice," a disconnected set of detailed standards based on unconsid- *See pages 37–43* ered assumptions, and a flourish of noble ends that have no meaningful application. As a result, many important ends are not served; others, including trivia, are overemphasized. Freedom of solution is restricted, and unforeseen consequences may develop. Inarticulate criteria cannot be designed for, tested for, or rationally weighed and compromised.

Objectives, like the site itself, are always specific and particular. They depend on the situation and the values of the client. Who sets those objectives? Ideally, it will be the user of the site, but there are problems of absent, voiceless, or uninformed clients, of user complexity and conflict, and of distinctions between users and nominal clients that make a rational program difficult to achieve. In any case the designer has clear responsibilities to clarify objectives, to raise them for debate, to reveal new possibilities or hidden costs, and to speak for the absent or voiceless client. Designers often assume their own values and disregard those of the future inhabitants. Since most designers are members of a particular social class, the error may be aggravated. Even where the site planner hopes to modify existing values, he must at least understand the situation from which he hopes to depart. Later chapters will examine these puzzles in more detail.

Direct functional goals and limits are easy to state and test: "to house 100 families," "to allow a flow of 2000 cars per hour," "not to cost more than $50,000." Objectives that deal with the quality of a place are harder to assert. The level of generality is one difficulty. Shall it be "a comfortable environment" or "all south and west facades to be shaded by trees"? The first is too general to test; the second dictates the solution before the design process has begun. "To maintain indoor summer temperatures within the comfort range" might be a better statement of the objective, as it is testable and can be accomplished by various schemes. Generally, it is preferable to express objectives in as concrete a form as possible, short of fixing a physical solution. Quite often the best form is one that specifies the human behavior desired in the locality, along with its necessary supporting qualities: "a street that allows a pedestrian to cross at any point with safety, with no more than an average delay of four seconds."

Objectives should be significant and worthy of our attention in applying them, and they should help us to discriminate between alternative solutions. "All houses must be oriented to the cardinal directions" may discriminate between plans but have little real importance, while "all houses must be accessible on foot" may be important but not discriminating. The set should be complete: when a plan meets the stated objectives, all its major purposes should have been fulfilled.

Part of a site designer's expertise is his accumulated experience in the achievement of objectives. He constantly checks his environment and the performance of realized site plans: Did that device in fact encourage social communication? How did the microclimate actually change? Has the plan been adapted easily? Like the old-fashioned craft that site planning still is, most of its knowledge is personal or learned from colleagues. We are only now beginning to get systematic analyses of past work, which should in time become a constantly developing body of data on the relation between purpose and form. It is still a moot point whether these data are best organized as an array of form types with their typical results, or as an array of purposes with effective forms for achieving them, or more loosely as a set of good case histories, or perhaps as a series of changeable manuals of form and purpose for typical general situations and functions. Meanwhile, we most often still proceed on the basis of the way we did it before. Novel forms are tried out on hunches and then imitated elsewhere without any study of actual results. The professional uses his own eyes and ears as best he can. Indeed, even when we have systematic data, personal observation will still be necessary. Every site plan should have learning built into it: a way of comparing observed results with the original program.

As our knowledge grows, the material in this book will lose its relevance, just as parts of the earlier edition have lost relevance in ten years' time. Moreover, the techniques and principles to be discussed later are based on present technology and present social organization in this country. As technology and society change, site planning must change with them. Values will shift more slowly, but they will affect design more radically.

*Future obsolescence of this text*

The designer begins by assuming that he is ignorant of his site and the group for whom he is designing, that his previous standards cannot be applied, and that whatever he does will soon undergo the first of a long series of modifications. His plan foresees those changes as far as possible, and beyond that he provides for adaptation. Every site has a long history, which bears on its present. Every site will have a long future, over which the designer exerts only slight control. He peers into that future as far as he can but realizes that others will adjust his plan to new demands.

Site planning, then, is the organization of the external physical environment to accommodate a variety of human behavior. It deals with the location and nature of structures, land, activities, and living things. It creates a possible pattern of these elements in space and time, which will be subject to continuous future management and change. The technical output of site planning — grading plans, utility layouts, structure locations, activity diagrams, planting plans, sketches, specifications — are simply conventional ways of recording this complex organization and of guiding its realization.

In the text to follow, Chapters 1, 2, 3, 6, 9, 10, and 11 deal with the fundamentals of site planning: the analysis of locality, the technique of organizing places and activities to fit human purpose, the design of the movement sys-

*Outline of the book*

tems and the sensuous form, problems of control, and the process of site design and site management itself. These six chapters may be read as a single connected whole, a synopsis of the art. Interspersed in this sequence are three pairs of chapters — 4 and 5, 7 and 8, 12 and 13 — which deal with technical issues: site and social analysis, streets and utilities, design methods and costs. They expand on the chapters that precede them. Finally, Chapters 14 and 15 discuss particular kinds of site planning — for housing in particular but also for commercial centers, industrial estates, institutions, recreational areas, parks, and renewal areas. The book may therefore be read in several sequences or degrees of completeness, although the six chapters of the main sequence are written to be read in that order. Marginal references and diagrams supplement the text, refer to relevant material in other chapters, or lead to other sources. The brief concluding list of references is selected and annotated.

*Chapter* **2**

# Analyzing a Locality

The existing site and the purpose for which it is wanted, which are the two sources of the design, are curiously interrelated. Purpose depends on the limitations that the site will impose, and site analysis depends on purpose. The same piece of ground will be seen quite differently by a quarryman, a biologist, a fortifications engineer, a farmer, and a building contractor, or even by builders using different technologies or serving different markets. Each view is correct but partial.

The site is analyzed for fitness to our purposes but also in its own right as a living, changing community of plants and animals. This community has its own interests in the site. In our anthropocentric way, we want our human interests to prevail, yet we must at least consider those of the existing occupants. Such consideration is vital even in selfish terms, since if we know the interconnections of this existing system, we are less likely to set off some inadvertent disaster: severe erosion, an explosive invasion of weeds, or a drop in the water table. Thus site analysis has two elements — the one oriented to human purpose and the other to the site itself as an ongoing system.

*The site itself*

Experience allows us to set realistic purposes before a particular site has been analyzed or to judge a site before detailed purposes are known. There are site factors that are influential in most building developments, but an unusual purpose may invalidate them. No site is studied pedantically by describing all the factors in some standardized list. The purpose of the reconnaissance and the nature of the site determine what to look for.

*Past sensitivity*     In the past, sites were often well understood. Earlier people had less power to change the land, although they were quite capable of destruction in the course of many generations — witness the degradation of the Mediterranean world by poor agricultural management since classical times. Yet since preindustrial people had little power to change a place in the short run, they were perforce keenly aware of the limitations it presented. Magical beliefs also had an influence on them. If a locality was the home of a local spirit, people avoided disturbing that home without due precaution, including a careful study of local configuration and the anxious introduction of artificial structures. In consequence, development was closely tied to site. In most cultures land is sacred, not to be violated by mere human beings. It is enduring, powerful, extensive, the home of spirits and the dead, the productive mother on whom human life depends. As we discard these religious ideas and increase our power to impose site changes, we lose these restraining attitudes. We no longer unconsciously achieve development in harmony with its setting, nor de we achieve structures expressive of locality.

Although the completely harmonious and mature site is unusual (and had best be left alone), the completely chaotic and meaningless one is nonexistent. Every site, however disturbed, has had some time to experience the mutual adjustment of its elements. The surface flow of water has created a drainage pattern, plant and animal life has formed an ecological system, neighboring structures lean against each other, shops have arranged themselves in relation to the resident population, and climate has weathered all alike. Any site is composed of many factors — above, below, and on the ground surface — but all these factors are interrelated and have achieved some sort of balance, whether it is static or moving toward another equilibrium.

*Site equilibrium*

*Unique character*     Because of the complexity of parts and their intricate patterning together, we find that each site is in some measure unique. The words *site* and *locality* should convey the same sense that the word *person* does: a complexity so closely knit as to have a distinct character, worthy of interest, concern, and often of affection. These interrelations and this essential character must be understood by the site designer. Understanding will indicate the practical limits imposed upon him, as well as the damage that he may inflict by careless interference. More important, it will reveal the hidden potentialities of the place, the points where his design can clarify its character, build new connections, or develop deeper meanings. Analysis of site is not only a technique for conservatives; it is also a prelude to successful revolution.

Site development can have unexpected — often undesirable — effects that pass along the whole chain of living things. A new road may block drainage, induce erosion, overturn soil horizons, kill plants and animals, dispossess human residents, introduce new species, bring in hunters, litterers, or builders, scar the hillsides, pollute air and water, or import exotic chemicals. The entire living community, men included, must adjust to this new situation. We now dominate the earth. Earlier men could cut or burn a forest, wash away a field, foul a river, exhaust a mine, or extinguish a local species. Today we can pollute great lakes and even the ocean, dirty the global air, and diffuse chemicals throughout the living world. Even if we walk softly, we shall reshape the land, and the quality of that man-formed surface may come to be one of the crucial scarce resources for our continued existence.

*Unintended effects*

Critics, rightly fearful, deplore all new development and wish that the land might be as it once was. But how was it? Chaotic or brutal, often enough, and certainly never the same for very long. Environment changes steadily, even without our interference: new species crowd out old ones, climates shift, geological processes continue. Living organisms are self-generating, competitive, interacting, evolving. Decay, waste, entropy, and change are all part of the natural order. The past cannot be fully restored, nor can the present be fixed.

Man is himself a part of nature, and his cities are as natural as his fields. We inevitably upset the ecology of a site. We cannot preserve a preexisting balance, although occasionally we may intervene to restore in some degree a state that has since disappeared. More often, we try to create a new balance, as stable as the old one but better suited to our purposes. Our true anxiety is that we may let slip some irreversible change that we cannot later recall or deflect. Our task is the more difficult because changes occur more rapidly now, falling upon us before we recognize them.

*Creating a new balance*

The ecological system — particularly that fraction

which is the human behavioral system — is the key aspect of any site. The diverse living species, which capture the energy of the sun, prey and are preyed upon, exist in fine balance with their immediate setting of water, air, and earth. On this system we also depend for survival. Its balance and its stability are fundamental indexes of the quality of a place.

*Ecology*

*Reference 26*
*See pages 45–47*

Ecology is the study of the dynamic relations between a community of organisms and its habitat. When applied to systems as large as those which we consider here, the study is imprecise but useful as a point of view. Self-reproducing, evolving, competing, and cooperating organisms interact with their changing spatial environment to form a community that persists but also gradually changes. Individuals come and go, while the forest remains but gradually expands or undergoes a shift in species. If men cut the forest, the new species colonize the cutlands, but the new community is less stable and less diverse than before and tends toward the forest once more. But if the soil has washed away or if the climate has shifted, then the forest may never return. In so changing, communities are said to "improve" or "deteriorate," but the basis for judgment differs between designer and scientist. Ecological communities are not moral, and to us they may appear ugly or wasteful. For example, they must contain much dying and decaying material. Optimum net production, for human purposes, is usually achieved in communities that are below their biological optimum. A lovely meadow or an orchard, a clean pond or field of wheat is maintained only by constant human interference.

Nor do ecological processes seem inexorable, at least to our present state of knowledge. Processes continue within ranges of tolerance, disturbed ecologies can be restored, although long periods of time may be required to do so, and only occasionally does some irreversible event occur: a permanent loss of soil cover, the eutrophication of a lake, the introduction of a new and aggressive species. Nevertheless, most large-scale human interventions have been dysfunctional, if not always disastrous. Stable, man-made regional landscapes are rare. They exact unremitting human effort and concern. Eighteenth-century England, Moorish Spain, or Japan come to mind, but not many other "civilized" landscapes. The importance of understanding the ecological relationships in a place is clear enough if we want to avoid irreversibilities, sudden jumps, or unpredictable side effects, or if we want our designs to be as nearly self-maintaining as possible.

While "improvement" for the scientist refers to the maturity and stability of the system, the diversity of its species, and the level of yield in terms of energy exchange or biomass, "improvement" for the site designer refers to overlapping but not identical ends: stability and predictability, human comfort and usefulness, interesting diversity, sensuous beauty, self-maintenance. Scientific and design criteria will often partially coincide, but not always. With further understanding and after a revolution in our values, we may find a more consistent ethic that embraces all living organisms. Meanwhile, we are at least concerned with preserving the preconditions for life on earth.

How human beings act toward one another and toward other living things is for us the most critical aspect of all. This can best be described in terms of *behavior settings*, or small localities bounded in time and space within which there is some stable pattern of purposeful human behavior. Physical setting and behavior are mutually adapted to each other. A teen-age hangout, a hunt, a church service, a repair garage in operation are examples of behavior settings. Ecological systems and behavior settings are organized complexities in which many elements work together. They normally change slowly but can shift in unexpected ways if disturbed. They are in part self-regulating: changing their surroundings and also adapting to their surroundings. One unit is linked to the next. Changes will be propagated through the entire system, sometimes reaching catastrophic dimensions, but normally damping out. How these two systems are presently working and how they may be modified to human advantage are usually our key questions.

*Behavior settings*

*Reference 10*

Knowledge of the site is essential to design, but information is expensive to gather and expensive to use. As site data are potentially infinite, a thorough survey can paralyze action. One plans initial data gathering as carefully as development itself, estimating the time and resources needed to acquire and to use each item at the specified level of detail. Will knowing something affect a decision sufficiently to justify the cost of learning? Can the data be gotten in time to be useful? It is efficient to confine the initial survey to bare essentials and gather special data later in the design process as new questions arise. The data store must therefore be organized to receive a steady stream of new information.

*Gathering data*

Past experience indicates the categories of data most likely to be useful. For example, foundation conditions and the water table are the key subsurface conditions. The rock and earth below ground level have practical importance primarily for the way in which they can be excavated, their characteristics of drainage, and the manner in which they will support structures and plants. The engineering characteristics of soil depend on type and moisture content. Critical problems must be studied by laboratory methods, but a surprisingly good picture, if we are concerned with local roads and low buildings, can be gained from a field reconnaissance. Other sources of information include small test pits, agricultural and geological maps, existing cuttings and foundations, the type of vegetation on the site, and the experience of previous builders and engineers. Soils may be divided into basic groups; these classifications and their significance are described in Chapter 4. Lying over the subsoil is a relatively thin layer of organic topsoil, the essential medium for the growth of plants. Centuries are required to produce it. It is of value not only for any particular development but as a part of our general heritage. It must be conserved.

At some greater depth is the water table: the line below which the interstices between the soil grains are permanently full of water. Where this groundwater table is less than 6 or 8 feet below the surface, all development costs are increased: excavations must be braced with sheeting and pumped out, and utilities and basements must be waterproofed. Some soils are untrustworthy foundation material when wet. In particular, one avoids building over a subsurface watercourse or filling in surface drainage without providing for the resulting underground flow.

Therefore certain subsurface conditions are danger signals calling for more detailed and expert attention: rock lying close to the surface; a high water table or an underground stream; the appearance of soft clay, loose silt, or fine water-bearing sand; any evidence of slides or subsidence; an area that has been a dump or is newly filled; or the presence of swamps, peat, or muck in more than small isolated pockets.

The topographic surface, the boundary between earth and air, is the zone richest in living things. It has particular implications for site development. The topography itself sometimes determines a plan. The gradient of paths, the flow of utilities, the use of areas, the disposition of buildings, and the visual aspect are all affected by it. The designer must grasp the characteristic of the landform as a whole and identify its key points for the purpose he has in mind. He must have a sense of its scale, of the meaning of various slopes, and of the relation of its plan shape to its perspective shape. In most cases the existing topography has an underlying order brought about by the flow of surface water. Thus the basic modeling of the ground can usually be analyzed by locating the ridge and drainage lines.

*Slope*

Slopes can be classified according to their potential use: the flat ground, usable for intensive activity; the easy grades, suitable for movement and informal activity; and the steep land, difficult to use or to move over. Topography can be analyzed piecemeal, outlining the areas suitable for intensive use, the badly drained portions, and so on. Regions where the surface is difficult and tends to determine the layout of circulation may be distinguished from gentler regions where the paths can be disposed in many different patterns. There may be "passes," restricted localities that offer the only opportunity to cross some rough terrain, or there may be lines along which an approach would develop a very special visual sequence. Moreover, there may be points that have commanding views, areas that are distinct visual units, or localities that are well oriented to the sun. At times some of these characteristics may be dominant and practically inalterable. Thus a design may have to take for granted the necessity of developing a particular view, avoiding a certain ground, preserving a special tree, saving a piece of water.

On the ground surface there will be a particular association of plants and animals, all dependent on one another and on the way that human beings use the site. Together with the topography, this living community gives the site its essential character. There are landscape families that have a common pattern, a common history, and typical associations of detail: the bushy pasture of New England, the American ribbon shopping street, the coastal mangrove swamp, or the intricate farming pattern of Tuscany. But each site must be studied individually. Tough, resilient communities must be distinguished from delicate ones, which can be easily destroyed. One looks for signs of change: erosion, muddy water, empty stores, or dying trees. What further changes will occur as the site is more intensively developed? Any existing landscape is an equilibrium of surface and drainage, use, and cover. In geologic time all surfaces are changing, but within a human generation these natural shifts are usually slow. Wherever the ground is disturbed by man, or even where the intensity

*Landscape families*

FIGURE 3 *A fine rural landscape has an obvious harmony and character.*

of use changes, the plant cover and surface form must be modified to attain a new balance.

*Climate*

*See pages 60–78*

Each site has a general climate, which it shares with the surrounding region, and a series of microclimates, which may be peculiar to very small areas. The general climate is expressed in a set of average data for the region: solar angle, days of sunlight, ranges of temperature and humidity, precipitation, wind direction and force. This information will influence the orientation of structures, their shielding or exposure to sun, the equipment for cooling or heating, the fenestration, the building materials, the cover and planting in general. Furthermore, the typical light conditions will affect the visual form.

Human beings are comfortable at certain optimum ranges of daylight, of air movement and purity, and of temperature and humidity. The site plan modifies the existing climate to approximate this optimum condition. The means for this approximation will vary with each climate. It is unfortunately commonplace to import forms suitable for one climate into a completely different one: to plant lawns in the desert, to build North American houses in the tropics or to use stuccoed half-timber in the New England wilderness.

Within the general climate, there are surprising varia-tions in the microclimate of a site due to cover and topog-raphy. Wind speed and temperature vary markedly within a few feet of elevation or from spot to spot. The site planner pays close attention to these effects, since they are not recorded in official data and since he can take excellent advantage of them. The form of the topography, the surface materials, the plant cover, the location of structures, the presence or absence of water, all have a striking impact on the microclimate, on the quality of light, and on the propagation of noise. The designer learns about this by direct reconnaissance, by talks with local people, by the way in which older structures have weathered, or by the type, condition, and budding time of existing plants. Plants are particularly good indicators: they speak not only of the climate but of the soil, the water, even the history of the place.

*Microclimate*

*Reference 37*

The designer must observe in detail how the area is ac-tually used by its human inhabitants, identifying the timing

*Human use*

FIGURE 4 *But the character of an urban landscape must also be understood.*

*Walker Evans*

and extent of the behavior settings and noting their characteristics. Watching truck movements and the walk to work and spotting the local hangout or the sled run will be more informative than pages of statistics. Unfailingly, one needs to know the pattern of activity within the site and on its borders. Then it is important to discover the access to destinations outside the site, as well as the relation to the general circulation system: the highways, footpaths, railroads, transit lines, and airports. The type and condition of structures and the location, elevation, and capacity of any technical facilities in or near the site must also be mapped: roads, power lines or water supply, disposal systems, communications lines. The more developed a site becomes, the more these man-made features of use, structure, circulation, and utilities become predominant over the factors of soil, topography, and cover.

*Intangible qualities*
*See Chapter 9*

One is also interested in the sensuous form of a place: the way a locality looks and smells and sounds, as well as other intangible features that must be reckoned with. There will be public controls that affect it: zoning or subdivision regulations, building codes, and official maps. There will be rights that persons hold in the area: ownerships, tenancies, rights-of-way, easements of various kinds, liens, restrictions due to private covenants, mineral rights, and so on. There will be economic and political relations and certain institutions that underlie its structure. The place will have a history, and there will be plans for its future. People will have attached personal meanings to it: memories, expectations, its sacredness, the fact that it is the focus of a larger area.

*Looking for a coherent pattern*

All of these factors — the conditions below ground, the surface form activity and life, the structures and facilities, the visual character, the bath of air that envelops them, the meanings, rights and regulations — make up the nature of a site. This is always a complex and often a confusing picture. The designer sifts through the mass of data to find the elements that are decisive for his purpose, and then he tries to fit these elements into some kind of pattern on which he can base his design. He separates transitory or disappearing features from more permanent or emergent ones; he discounts the fine old decaying trees in favor of new growth or distinguishes the form of a hill from the scars of recent excavation.

It is only after repeated analysis and the trial of many plans that a stable site pattern appears — a certain configuration of area line and point, a basic set of landscape forms, which is the essence of the place for the purpose in mind. Yet the designer must not be so strongly directed toward his purpose or so intent on finding a coherent pattern that he misses the facts that might begin to change his purpose or that do not fit his pattern.

Therefore it is advisable to study a site in several different ways. One begins by searching rather aimlessly, forgetting the use to which the area is to be put, looking directly at the site itself, and watching for interesting features and revealing clues. This unsystematic, almost subconscious, reconnaissance produces information that would otherwise be missed. It will at least serve as a general orientation. It is useful now to look briefly at the history of the site, its natural evolution, its former use and association. It is equally useful to inquire into its image in the minds of users and decision makers; how they characterize it, how they feel about it, and what they expect of it. Much of the flavor and structure of a place, as well as its present direction of change, is thereby revealed.

*Preliminary reconnaissance*

Then more systematic surveys can be undertaken, guided partly by the purpose to be served, partly by the desire to predict how the site will react to the disturbances of development and occupation. For the latter reason, one always investigates how the site presently maintains itself as an ongoing ecological system and where the most vulnerable points in that system are. No information should be sought unless it appears that it will later influence the design in some significant way. Some types of information, such as a topographic map, ecological and climatic data, and a survey of activity and circulation, are almost always required.

*Systematic analysis*

Some data continue to be useful during construction and subsequent operation and so justify substantial expense. One example is a base map showing the legal lines such as boundaries and easements; the location of existing utilities, roads, paths, buildings, and walls; the local activities and circulations; the presence of swamps, streams, and water bodies; the general vegetative cover, including its condition and the precise locations of large trees or unique species; a notation of rock outcrops and other visible geologic features; contours and the spot elevations of key points; compass directions; and the character of the site environs. A planner will take copies of this map into the field for personal annotation, to get a "feel" for the site by analyzing its character, its views, its approaches, its problems, and its possibilities. He should visit the locale many times, under varied circumstances of weather, season, light, and activity.

*Base maps*

Before the systematic survey begins, it is useful to pre-

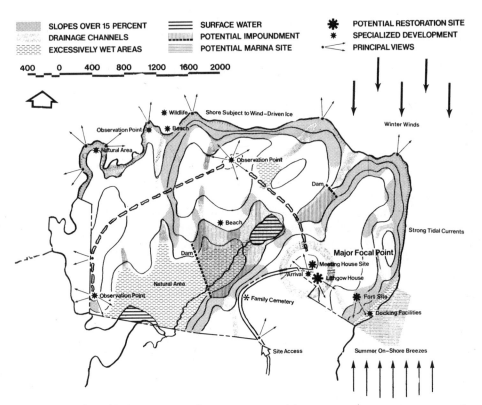

SLOPES OVER 15 PERCENT
DRAINAGE CHANNELS
EXCESSIVELY WET AREAS

SURFACE WATER
POTENTIAL IMPOUNDMENT
POTENTIAL MARINA SITE

POTENTIAL RESTORATION SITE
SPECIALIZED DEVELOPMENT
PRINCIPAL VIEWS

400   0   400   800   1200   1600   2000

Wildlife
Shore Subject to Wind–Driven Ice
Winter Winds
Observation Point
Beach
Natural Area
Observation Point
Dam
Strong Tidal Currents
Beach
Dam
Major Focal Point
Meeting House Site
Arrival
Lithgow House
Natural Area
Observation Point
Family Cemetery
Fort Site
Docking Facilities
Site Access
Summer On–Shore Breezes

FIGURE 5   *A preliminary site evaluation, prepared by Design-Science International, compared with an aerial photograph of the same locality.*

pare a complete schedule of the data to be gathered. A typical checklist of this kind is given in Chapter 4 as an example. However, any standard schedule of information must be viewed with suspicion as there simply is no universal list. The data gathered and the form into which they are put depend on the purpose of the development, the nature of the place, and the resources available to make the survey. An adequate reconnaissance may consist of a single freehand sketch made on the site, or it may require an elaborate technical organization. In either case it should be as spare and succinct as possible and flexible enough to receive new information. It must always include personal observation, obtained perhaps partly by car or helicopter, but always to some degree on foot.

Once the information is assembled, it must be sifted, organized, and put into concise and usable form. It will thus be brought to a final point: a graphic and written statement describing the essential nature of the site for the purpose at hand, how it is changing and is likely to change. The principal constraints and problems of the location are set down, as well as its basic potentialities and values.

This is the basis on which the design is developed. It will be found that this concept of the site will be modified as the design unfolds and that further information always comes to light or must be sought. Site analysis is not a self-contained step that is completed before design begins. First thoughts on design accompany and guide the original reconnaissance. Since the analysis must be in a form that can accept new information, recurrent monitoring should be planned. Analysis continues as long as the design is being created.

The image of the site guides the design. It does not dictate the design, however, nor is there any unique solution latent in the site, waiting to be uncovered. The plan develops from the creative effort of the designer himself. But it must respond to the site, and not disregard it. Often the designer will be working with the grain of the locality, treating it delicately, emphasizing its strong points and teasing out its potentialities. Sometimes he will dramatically cut across it or oppose its nature. This, too, can succeed only if the site is thoroughly understood.

Analyzing a site will vary considerably depending on its character: whether it is clear of intensive human use or heavily occupied; whether it is a mature, stable landscape or one that is changing rapidly; whether it is dominant or recessive, intended for conservation or for radical renewal. In

*Concept of site as a basis for design*

the case of urban renewal, for example, the site planner is working over ground occupied by many human and physical assets, all entangled in the great urban spider web. The area is dotted with structures and activities of continuing utility, seemingly dispersed at random but actually according to some social and economic ordering. The impulse of a designer trained to order and pattern is to sweep all this aside, just as a bulldozer blade sweeps away a wood. But a more sympathetic analysis of these features would reveal their function and meaning, like the hidden order of a forest community. If it has already been decided that the area will be restructured for some entirely new purpose and for some entirely new client, then these features may not warrant recording in any detail. Even then, they may point to some persistent conditions of site or culture which must be reckoned with.

Site Selection

It sometimes happens — and it should happen more often — that the site is not fixed before the designer is brought in. In this case, having been given the general objectives, he is involved in the process of site selection, which may be a narrow weighing of two alternatives or a broad area-wide search. Site selection uses the same techniques as any site analysis, but a broad search will most often begin by the reduction of possibilities to a manageable handful of alternatives. This is usually done by screening: blocking off on an area map the regions that, in the light of objectives, are unacceptable for such reasons as excessive grade or cost, poor soil, small size, previous development, or lack of access.

The remaining lands not blocked off are then reconnoitered to eliminate any other obviously unacceptable localities, and the surviving plots of adequate size are treated as alternative sites, each of which is analyzed in some depth for the most critical factors. Analyses are arranged comparatively, and preliminary layouts are made on each site, since nothing illustrates the character of an area so well as its influence on the layout itself. From these comparative displays an informed choice can be made. This method is preferable by far to the normal process of calling in the planner only after a site selection has been made.

*Use of a given
site*

Occasionally the designer may be called upon to make just the opposite analysis: given a site, what is its best use? This is a vaguer and more difficult question. It requires a very careful analysis of the place as an ongoing social and ecological system, since the values internal to a site may in this case be expected to have greater weight. The site is reconnoitered thoroughly, clues and hints being sought for in the ground itself. Chinese garden designers sat quietly for days in a place, meditating on its character before they even began to consider its possibilities. The regional context of the locality must also be examined: the surrounding system of circulation and of neighboring use and settlement. Possible markets will be explored. A broad social framework of objectives will be established and, within that, a choice of possible alternate sets of more specific objectives that might govern the use of that particular piece of land. The possible uses are then narrowed to those most feasible, and a comparative set of analyses, including sketch layouts, market analyses, and a schedule of probable costs and benefits, is made for each set of purposes. The choice can then be made from these comparisons, by using judgments of ecological stability, market, and social purpose.

Most site analyses are conducted for some single purpose and lose their utility once site development is carried through. Planners' files are full of outmoded information. Even the documents intended for more lasting use, such as the U.S. Geological Survey topographic maps, city base maps, or the "land use" records of planning agencies, always record the landscape at some particular point in time and are not easily kept up to date. It should be evident that much of the character of the site depends on factors that change continuously: ecology, behavior, climate, man-made structures. What is more, sites have long futures, and site planning must increasingly be seen as a continuous stream of modifications applied to a changing landscape, rather than as a convulsive creation imposed on a static world. Site analysis should be a continuous process on which a continuing design process can be based.

*Continuous site analysis*

There have been attempts to make all-purpose surveys, which will have permanent usefulness or which may even serve to fix permanently the proper use of an area. These eternal surveys founder on a series of difficulties: (1) even "natural" conditions are not unchanging; (2) the purpose for which information is wanted sets what is looked for and how it should be classified; (3) use is never determined by existing conditions alone (unless those conditions are extremely severe) but is based on a combination of situation and purpose. Thus the Santa Clara campus in California can usefully be analyzed into areas of associated soil, climate, topography, and cover, but only because a general future type of development is foreseen. Even these "natural areas" will shift as development proceeds, however.

*"Permanent" data*

Useful long-term data are (a) relatively stable (geology or general climate); (b) organized in some neutral way that allows future modification (elevations from an arbitrary base, population per square mile); and (c) kept as disaggregated as is economically possible, so that they can be recombined later according to need. The data of most permanent value in site analysis turn out to be contour maps, soil and geological surveys, and climate records.

Nevertheless, the degree of permanence does not connote the degree of relevance. The crucial thing may be a shifting market or an ecology or an array of behavior settings. Emphasis will then lie on a framework that accepts and can correlate changing data (a situation map, a grid system, a computer) and on the use of such quasi-continuous sources as aerial photographs, social and economic accounts, and periodic censuses. It is all too tempting to gather too much information in order to be "comprehensive" or to put it in a specialized form that will not accept new data.

We have had little opportunity to practice continuous site analysis. The grounds of large institutions, or other agencies that control an area for long periods and for relatively stable purposes, could be exceptions. Here we would be justified in maintaining a continuing record of behavior settings, communications, ecology, microclimate, visual form, the repair equipment and capacity of structures, and the condition and use of roads and utilities. Periodic designs could be based on this ongoing bank of information. Continuous site analysis is a technique we should be developing now to prepare for the site planning of the future. It would be a spatial and local analogue to the standard economic and population data now continuously gathered at the national scale.

*Chapter 3*

# Organizing Place and Action

W<sub>e</sub> manipulate environment to make it easier for people to do the things they want to do or to give them new opportunities for action. Environment is an intimate part of human behavior. The setting, along with the institutions and the concepts of the actors, organizes the standing patterns of activity: playing baseball, enjoying a picnic, carrying packages, waiting for a bus, selling fruit, building a house, feeding a child. The setting instructs the action and supports it with space and equipment; the actor adapts to the setting or changes it in order to carry out what he means to do. Behavior and setting may be well fitted to each other or may be antagonistic, stable or fluid, demanding or permissive, repetitive or open-ended. The organization of behavior and its setting in time and space is the essential contribution of a site plan.

The plan begins with a diagram of the proposed location of activity and activity setting. The traditional language for such a diagram has been "land use," a term from agricultural economics, originally referring to a piece of ground and the economic use to which it was put: cropland, pasture, house site, or quarry. This was elaborated in planning to include the broad classes of human activity, customary in our culture, which could be located in space, coupled with the general physical forms usually associated with those activities, such as single-family residence, playground, retail shopping, or school. In architecture this type of diagram has

*Land use diagrams*

been expressed as clusters of activity normally occurring in certain types of rooms: living room, kitchen, laboratory, and office.

This traditional planning language is misleading. It focuses on the physical element rather than on the behavior to be supported. Many relationships of behavior and setting are simply taken for granted; the rich diversity of action that occurs within and between the customary spaces is often ignored. People struggle to carry out what they want to do, and the environment is thought to be timeless. We do not learn better ways of supporting behavior, nor do we discover how to open up new possibilities.

*Behavioral diagrams*    It is true that the activity diagram is an essential abstraction. It is not necessary to consider detailed form in order to relate stable clusters of action and setting. But these clusters must focus on what people really do and how they use their environment. The clusters must be coherent in that they must represent the recurrent behavior of people who are accomplishing a definite purpose in a definite locale. A single space may be occupied by diverse activity clusters that succeed one another in time or by overlapping sets at the same

FIGURE 6    *Older men enjoying the Paul Revere Mall in Boston, an outstanding example of a successful contemporary public open space in the United States.*

*Boston Redevelopment Authority*

FIGURE 7    *Street stairs in the squatter settlement of El Agustino, Lima, Peru. People of different ages are using the space for their diverse purposes.*

John F. C. Turner

time. Different people will be doing different things, and there may well be conflicts between them. There is rarely any one-to-one correspondence between activity and form, and yet the conventional "multipurpose" space is simply a perpetually inadequate setting for a cloud of vaguely imagined uses. The activity diagram must be precise and still show overlaps and organization in time — at the very least by showing the expected activity at the principal stages of the daily cycle. The units of the diagram will represent some standing pattern of behavior, accompanied by a broad specification of the characteristics of the setting rather than its particular form.

Observing what people actually do on the site, or on similar sites, and discovering what their purposes are give us the basis for determining what those units should be. Roger Barker's "behavior settings" are an example of this kind of analysis applied to a small midwestern town. His list of behavior settings for the town, with the man-hours that occupy

*Reference 10*

them, gives us a concrete sense of the quality of life there in a way that a traditional land-use map could never achieve. But for planning purposes Barker's behavior settings must be expanded to include a description of the behavior expected, the purposes of the actors, and the preferred nature of the setting.

*Programs*

If the behavior settings are quantified and costs are budgeted to them, this analysis becomes a *program*, the first step in creating a design. The program does not rely only on existing behavior but may encourage new patterns of behavior in new settings. Since qualities of the setting are now being determined, design has already begun when a program is made.

The traditional program is a dusty document stating a maximum total cost, listing the number of rooms or spaces or structures to be provided for that cost, and indicating the required access between the features. This schedule is most often furnished by the immediate client and considered to be something separate from the objectives, something to be "fitted into" the site, of which the design will be a three-dimensional elaboration.

*Reference 18*

Programming has a more central role to play. By describing the units in terms of behavior settings, it describes the intended outcome. It is linked to the restrictions and potentialities of the site, the requirements of the future actors, the general objectives, and the potentialities of future form. It is both a statement of detailed criteria and, inescapably, the essence of the design. It can also be the basis for collaboration between the behavioral scientist and designer because it is based on behavioral knowledge and exposes the hypotheses to be tested. Designer, client, and users should all be parties to preparing the program, which will necessarily be changed and refined as design proceeds, because design is a process of learning about needs and limits and possibilities.

The fully developed program will include a schedule of the quantity and timing of behavior settings, based on the understanding that settings will overlap or be extended in space or time. It will specify the desired character, the intensity of use, the connections that are wanted between them, and the expected management and service support. Estimated costs will be budgeted to each. The chronological order in which these settings should be completed, or their priority order, will also be given. The program may be broken into stages, each of which is a relatively self-sufficient working whole, so that the completion of one stage can be separated from another by a gap of time and each successive stage grows logically out of its predecessor.

The program will necessarily be rich and detailed, always expressing environment, management, and behavior together, but never confounding one with the other — never using "kitchen" as a description of an activity or "cooking" as a description of a setting. A program element might be described as "the cooking of small meals by one or two persons twice a day in a well-lighted, self-maintained, and heavily equipped space of 100 square feet costing $3000." "Cooking place" could be the code word for the element, as long as one realized that other units of behavior may successively occupy the same physical space, and that budgets must allow for this overlap.

A program may be generated by the intuitive recapitulation of expected activity, based on past personal experience, but it is better grounded in detailed observation made on the spot or from systematic past analyses. The requirements of settings may be stated as required thresholds ("at least 60 footcandles of light on all work surfaces" or "no streets to be crossed at grade by footpaths between any dwelling unit and its associated nursery school"), or as desired increments or qualities ("to reduce the journey to work by 20 percent" or "to communicate a sense of relaxation and privacy"). Since different groups of people will be taking different actions for different purposes in any place, program requirements specify for whom the settings are intended and how predicted conflicts are to be handled ("residents in the immediate vicinity of their dwellings should be unaware of passing motor vehicles, as long as police are able to overlook all public areas from their patrol cars"). Programs of this kind not only link objectives to specifications but allow proposed designs to be evaluated by the way they fulfill explicit requirements. Once built, the environment can be monitored to see if it is performing as predicted. In simple cases programs may be quite sketchy as to behavior, qualities, management, and costs, but in all cases these factors should, at least intuitively, be considered together.

The technique may be applied to a metropolitan region or to the layout of a backyard. The units of activity will be correspondingly general or detailed — "residing and its associated daily activities" or "hanging out clothes." Classification is treacherously simple. One looks for groups of activities that are interrelated through the purposes of their actors, that are located together in time and space, and that have coherent requirements of setting. The groupings are divided as finely as can be handled in the time available for observation and design. What is once assembled in a single category is

*Classification is treacherous*

rarely separated later. Having chosen "industry" as a class, one will rarely realize that different kinds of production may have different locational requirements, nor will one be aware of the rich diversity of behavior that actually goes on in most factory areas. Moreover, there will be a natural tendency to separate "industry" from other activities, excluding the possibility that residing and working might desirably happen in the same structure. Types of behavior should not be classed together because they are conventional groups or are legally wedded in the zoning ordinance or have similar names. Much of the sterile formalism of our plans arises from the habit patterns of our activity language.

On the other hand, classification of some kind must be used if a problem is to be manageable. In a site plan, it may simplify the problem if "delivery and removal of bulk goods and wastes" is a single class, but to put laundry drying in the same group so that it can be labeled "utility functions" will result in the selection of a poor place for hanging out clothes. Past classifications can be a guide, but each new problem requires one to think out once more the strategic clusters of activity that are appropriate for programming the new solution.

The diversity of the behavior settings, their stability and internal coherence, the efficient use of space and energy, and their openness to users are partial measures of the goodness of a site — in rough analogy with an analysis of the ecology of species. But the basic measure of value is the degree to which the behavior settings allow people to feel competent in doing what they want to do and the degree to which they favor personal development of competence and purpose.

*Activity and setting*

The setting should be of adequate size and appropriate shape for a given activity, have the proper climate (guaranteed by enclosure or other means), adequate access, and a floor of suitable slope and texture. The definition of those vague words *adequate, proper,* and *suitable* may seem to require specialized research. But actually we often do rather well in specifying them from experience, for any given activity, once our attention has focused in that direction. We watch what people do and talk to them about their expectations.

*Maintenance of setting*

Suitability for use includes suitability for maintenance of that use, given the form and the system of maintenance. Parkland that is scattered in many different areas or isolated from the road system will be difficult to maintain and to control. Intricate landscaping may require continuous, expensive care. The quantity of open space in a plan may be beyond the power of a community to protect from encroachment. It is often desirable to assign open space to some activity that will itself help to preserve and maintain that space, such as making it a productive forest or farm, a golf course, or a cemetery. Alternatively, it may be preferable to keep the space far away from access and potential invasion. In any case, suitability cannot be predicted until management and services are also specified, and these may be more critical than form.

After activity classifications have been determined, the linkages between them must be analyzed. The links may be movements of people, goods, and wastes or communication of information. They may be based upon amenity, such as the view afforded by a park, or they may be negative repulsions due to nuisance effects. The links connect units that are distributed in time as well as space. A theater may be next to a transit stop, but what if the transit ceases to run before the theater closes?

*Linkage*

The program analyzes existing links but also desired connections, which may be quite different. For example, there may at present be few contacts between black and white residents, between faculty members of different departments, or between shopping and enjoying a park, but the program may try to establish them. It will give quite a different weight to linkages that persist despite separation in space, such as the delivery of addressed mail, than to those which are sensitive to spatial location, such as spontaneous communication between people. And thought must be given as to how these links may change in the future.

It is not simply a question of how best to link a given set of activities. The planner considers whether additional activities should be introduced. In housing developments, when we trace behavior circuits and learn about expectations, we find that much of their quality consists in the nonresidential activities and facilities that are accessible to the dwellings: shopping, learning, religious worship, or recreation. Access is measured in time and cost rather than in distance. Directness of linkage is the result not only of spatial separation but also of cultural patterns and the means of communication.

In the diagram in the margin, the behavior settings of a small community are connected by lines whose thickness is proportional to the presumed importance of the linkages between them. There are six classes. The dwelling places of type 1 are to be extremely accessible to the shopping and

*Linkage diagrams*

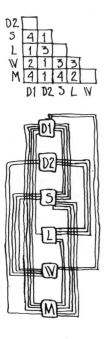

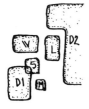

meeting places, fairly convenient to workplaces, and distantly related to the learning place. Type 2 dwellings have quite different requirements: good access to the learning place and a distant relation to the shopping, working, and meeting places. The shopping area should have extremely close access to the meeting place and a good connection to the working location. The learning place should have a good access to the workplace and a moderate connection to the meeting place. We are indifferent to the linkage between dwelling types or between working and meeting areas or shopping and learning places. These ideas concerning desired linkages are based not only on the probable interactions between activities, which are themselves based on the estimated actions and values of users, but on general ideas as to circulation, visual form, and site character as well.

This diagram can be rearranged to minimize the length and intersection of major connections. The rearrangement gives us a first clue to a preferred activity pattern. These are topological diagrams, that is, they are not drawn to scale, and they express nothing but the classes of use and their preferred connections. While the linkages shown are symmetrical, they could also be differentiated according to direction. It might be important for learning activities to be near working areas, but not vice versa.

If the areas required for the behavior units are drawn roughly to scale, the diagram can then be applied to an actual site. Each area of the diagram now indicates not only an abstract location but also a portion of space that is appropriate for the use intended or will be modified to be so. The diagram implies both activity and the general physical provision for that activity. If we were dealing with overlapping behavior settings, the analysis would be carried out on a series of overlays, which might lead us to quite new conclusions about densities or the juxtaposition of areas. In the design of complex building systems, optimum linkage diagrams are now regularly created with the aid of computers, although the diagrams still refer to a single point in time, and not to the temporal evolution of activities and their connections. The use of such computer techniques in site planning is imminent.

Pictorial neatness is seductive. It is easy to oversimplify the total pattern as well as the basic categories. All behavior of one type need not occur in one location, and it can be mixed with other activities. Distinctions or linkages between units are more indeterminate than we imagine. Mixtures in space or time may be desirable for reasons of contrast, for the contin-

uous use of a site, or to allow for linkages that cannot be foreseen. It is safer to put the burden of proof on proposals to separate activities than on proposals to intertwine them. An arrangement in which unit types cluster in a relatively pure state around focal points but grade outward into mixtures with other types is often a natural solution.

The site planner cultivates the habit of looking beyond the boundaries of his site to study the pattern of the surrounding community. Preferred arrangement on the site may depend heavily on outside links, such as the movement to work, the convenience to shopping or other facilities, and surrounding negative influences. A hospital may decide to provide cooperative housing in the community at large rather than in on-site institutional dormitories, or a housing development may be able to add a swimming pool to be supported by a larger area. The site planner will as a matter of course refuse to accept the boundary lines he is given, whether they are lot lines, political boundaries, areas of study, or just the edges of a convenient map. He is not compelled to harmonize with those surroundings if they are undesirable or of doubtful longevity, but he must take them into account.

*Context*

Space requirements involve the concept of density, or the intensity of activity occurring per unit area. Density has a far-reaching effect on the site plan and the quality of life within it. In the case of residential development it is usually measured in terms of the number of families per unit of ground area, since the family in our culture is a rather stable and independent small unit with many standardized requirements. Elsewhere, densities may be expressed in individuals, species, man-hours, energy, goods, or dollars of income. Physical density, as opposed to activity density, is often expressed as a floor area ratio, or the ratio of gross floor area of a building to its ground area. Another common physical measure is rooms per acre. All density measures in use today are some variant of an area density. In the future, as activity increases, and as technology weakens the connection of structures to ground or makes possible three-dimensional circulation systems, we may turn to measures of cubic density: intensities per unit of volume. Since we are also dealing with time distributions, the density may be a *rate*, a familiar idea in traffic flow but less familiar when applied to other types of behavior. But persons per square foot per hour can be an appropriate unit for measuring activity in a store, a classroom, or a public plaza.

*Density*

*Types of density measures*

The unit area upon which an area density is based may

be a room, an immediate activity area or building site (giving a net density), or the activity area or building site plus surrounding streets and other immediately adjacent and necessary lands (giving a gross density). Or it may be the area of a much larger region, which contains not only the buildings, activities, and their immediate circulation but all the necessary services and facilities at a community scale, including local shopping, schools, churches, and playfields (giving a neighborhood density). Many tricks can be played with density standards by shifting from base to base and from definition to definition. For his own protection, the site planner must be aware of these differences and be familiar with the concrete results of the various abstract numbers.

With lower-density building types, which have land or lots directly assignable to the building, the net density is a fairly precise measure. But when dealing with tall apartments set in open space, one finds it difficult to decide where the "immediately adjacent" land stops. Gross density gives a fairer picture of land requirements because it includes streets and nearby open spaces. But it can be quite vague unless what is to be included is clearly specified. Neighborhood density is a fairly stable measure (as long as local facilities can be separated from nonlocal). It reflects the demand for land which occurs as a result of higher net densities. It is useful for large-scale studies but less so for small site plans.

Despite their difficulties, these quantities must be employed to give scale to a plan. Like other important variables, if they are not used consciously, they will appear as thoughtless assumptions. Some sense of the meaning of residential densities in current practice is given in Chapter 14. Types of development and their normal densities are worth memorizing, primarily for use as starting points rather than as standards.

*Density ranges and thresholds*

There is no ideal density. For any given activity, there is a range of densities outside of which conditions are likely to be substandard and within which there are a number of thresholds marking a shift from one character with its particular advantages to another with other advantages. Thus in nonfarm housing, acceptable net densities may range from one-half family per acre to 120 families per acre, with lower densities becoming very costly in terms of services and social equipment and higher densities substandard in terms of light, air, and open space (given present technology).

Within this total allowable range there are thresholds defining smaller ranges in which a certain type of structure is most suitable. These thresholds are also likely to indicate some basic changes in visual or functional character, such as the density below which dwellings appear to be widely separated, or those above which families cannot have direct access to the land. Since density affects cost, we can say that in most parts of America today, given land of low value, the least expensive housing can be provided at net densities of about 15 to 20 families per acre. This depends, of course, not only on land cost but on technology, standards, and regulations (the fire rules of several generations ago made 40 families per acre the cheapest density).

The suitability of a density varies with the situation, the allowable cost, the group to be served, and the character of surrounding development. The site planner is not committed to a perfect number but is sufficiently familiar with the implications of density to suggest a wise choice in a given situation or to avoid a building type or an activity inappropriate to a density fixed by some other consideration. Density has other implications that belong to the sphere of city planning. Here one considers economy, function, social organization, and amenity of the city as a whole. While beyond the scope of this book, such considerations will often set densities at points somewhat in conflict with what might be suggested by the site alone.

There are two approaches to applying these activity diagrams, scaled by density, to the given site. The first is the placement of activity according to the accidents of site or according to detailed requirements of use or form or client. Such a plan locates tall buildings where there is a fine distant view, a hangout where it has traditionally occurred, row houses on a sunny slope, play lots at neighborhood focal points, and a park on some picturesque piece of terrain. The plan has a rich, if disorganized, content.

Alternatively, the pattern may be developed as a logical total organization of the activities and their linkages, usually with some general visual form in mind. This will look clear on paper and be orderly and perhaps efficient in function. But it will smother the site and disregard many small and sensitive connections.

Both patterns are developed, and then by a long process of trial and criticism they are reshaped until a new pattern is discovered that has the values of both: one that responds to the details of site and activity and still provides an efficient linkage system and a comprehensible general form. This is likely to be a difficult process since no law of nature requires

Site Arrangement by Local Pattern

*Site arrangement by general pattern*

36

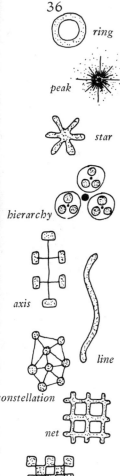

*ring*

*peak*

*star*

*hierarchy*

*axis*

*line*

*onstellation*

*net*

*checker*

*Formal
prototypes*

that a general form be inherent in any given situation, and human ingenuity is required to develop one. One must also be certain that a general form is really desirable — for reasons of cost or function or legibility — and is not simply valuable for its appearance on paper.

The detailed approach requires careful reconnaissance and meditation over the potentialities of each activity and of each piece of ground. The design of a picturesque, demanding site or a traditional way of life is easier to make than one dealing with flat or characterless ground, where limits, potentialities, and differentiations must be developed by the designer himself. The test is an item-by-item check to see that all functions are housed with adequate quantity and quality of space and that each advantage of site and time has been utilized with no waste. (Of course, what is commonly called "waste space" or "waste time" may have its own function, as will be seen.)

The general pattern approach is more difficult because it is more abstract. Very often, a basic arrangement is only unconsciously assumed. Unconscious assumption produces conventional organization. But when a general pattern is explicitly drawn, it often is equally conventional, a symmetrical hierarchy or the balanced axis, for example. These pattern habits are extremely difficult to break. Conventional forms may indeed be best in a given situation, but this assumption cannot be made until they are tested against other kinds of grouping.

Therefore the planner develops his capacity to imagine alternative general forms, being alert to see new forms in the world about him and to think of them as settings for various behaviors. A set of archetypal forms and a sense of their nature is part of his professional stock-in-trade. Some examples of these general forms are the ring, the concentric peak, the radial star, the symmetric hierarchy, the axis, the line, the constellation of clusters, the network, and the checkerboard. The form of each of these patterns has certain intrinsic functional implications, such as rigidity or flexibility, dispersed or concentrated communication, the relative accessibility between units, specialization or repetition of parts, the sense of identity and structure conveyed from various vantage points. Other characteristics appear only when applied to a particular situation.

General forms may be differentiated according to characteristics of district pattern (the shape of the boundary between development and nondevelopment or the way the internal parts are arranged in sectors, checkers, stripes, or rings), focal pattern (arrangements of the intensive focal points of activity or form), and network pattern (grid, radio-concentric, linear, capillary, and so on). We may discuss the density of development, or we may consider its "grain": that is, the extent to which activities or forms are differentiated, how finely these differing classes are mixed, and how sharp the transition is between them. For example, when we are putting two different kinds of houses together, the grain of that mixture may be fine or coarse, and the transition between groups may be sharp or blurred. Time distributions also have grain, as well as characteristics of rate, cycle, and synchrony (the parallel or sequential meshing of behavior). A solemn religious celebration may be very different from other events and extend over a long interval (a sharp, coarse grain), proceed at a majestic pace, recur only at long intervals, and be highly synchronized, both internally and with regard to other activities.

The pattern of site development affects many values, both quantifiable and nonquantifiable. The purposes of any plan are never standard, but several general types tend to recur and are worth a few comments. In addition to the specific aims of particular groups, these are the more general items that one would expect to find in any comprehensive cost-benefit analysis:

*Behavioral support*: The basic test is the way in which a plan supports purposeful behavior in detail: Is there space and time to do what people want to do? Is the site equipped and managed for that purpose? Is there a place to play baseball? Room to pile snow? Enough light? Does the setting reinforce the mood and structure of the action? The designer must know the people who will use his site; he must understand their wants and manner of life or how they hope to modify that manner of life. He puts himself in their place and in his imagination goes through the actions that will fill their lives there. What will it be like to mail a letter, talk to a neighbor, display wealth, dispose of trash, seek adventure? One needs to know both what people *do* and also what they experience and plan. That knowledge will be intimate knowledge when the designer is actually a member of the group for whom he is working. More often, in view of the volume of building that must be done, his clients will be diverse and their life strange to him. Sympathy is still the beginning of understanding, but he must now rely on the findings of formal social and psychological studies, or he must find ways to bring the clients themselves into the decision process.

*Communication*: Most plans are effective to the degree

References 13,
14, 16

See pages 131–132

that goods, persons, and information can circulate easily within them. We may wish to encourage additional communication or may only be concerned to permit it, while allowing an individual to have full control. Occasionally, we may want to decrease communication for the sake of privacy or to prevent conflict. A high level of social interaction on a local scale may mean less interplay on some larger scale. There can be too much interaction or too little. Given a homogeneous group, the desire to meet, and other social dimensions favorable to intercourse, a site can support and encourage communication by common entrances, by increased visual contacts, by focal points such as mailboxes, play yards, laundries, schools, and churches. Sharp boundaries, dangerous crossings, large open spaces, and the lack of connections tend to divide people. Putting site management into local hands generates increased local communication as its by-product. A fine grain of residential type may encourage communications between different types of people, but a coarse grain, with larger areas of homogeneity, will most likely permit a greater total volume of communication since interaction between similar people requires less effort. If we want residents to be able to control the rate of communication, then each dwelling can front on an intensely used common access and back onto a secluded area. The features of the movement system are critical to all these questions and will be developed in Chapter 6.

*Health and stress*: It would seem obvious that any environment should contribute to the health of its inhabitants and reduce the stresses upon them; noise, climate, pollution, glare, dust, accidents, and disease. We know something about the effect of environment on physical health and are learning more. During the last century we made great gains in elementary sanitation. But nominal clients may not be concerned with anything more than minimum standards of sanitation or structural safety. The dangers of a major accident or criminal attack are dramatic, but they may be ignored until they occur and then bring on an overreaction. Site form is not always as relevent to these visible evils as it may appear. Security from attack, for example, is less a matter of locks and walls than it is of dealing with root social causes or increasing effective social controls. Site form enters in primarily as it supports control, increases the scope of visual surveillance, or helps to define territories of responsibility.

The discomforts of minor accidents, a poor microclimate, noise, and pollution are more often disregarded; yet they are more closely tied to the site plan. People will suffer these conditions in silence, adapting to them as they can, sometimes even unaware of them. Indeed, our knowledge is most deficient in assessing the long-term hidden costs of environmental stress of the kind that men are able, at least on the surface, to adapt to so easily. The important relationship of environment to mental health is as yet largely obscure. Thus the site designer often finds himself responsible not simply for recommending patterns to reduce stress but also for pleading the importance of these objectives to his client.

Reference 11

*Adaptability*: Activity at a site will always change in the future, and so will the natural processes occurring there. Estimates of that future are uncertain. Furthermore, most people need some "give" or plasticity in their environment; they wish to mold it themselves. At the same time, they will be disturbed by sudden and sweeping changes. Clients are naturally obsessed with present needs, but the designer is responsible for testing his plan to see how well it will accommodate to future change without sharp ecological, technical, or psychological breaks, as well as for estimating the scope it gives for incremental individual adaptations. Adaptability seems to be facilitated by such general devices as low density or other kinds of excess capacity, by a good communications system, by separating the customary decision units from each other, and by sorting out the more permanent uses or those more resistant to change from the more temporary or easier-to-change activities. It is enhanced by conserving fundamental environmental resources and by establishing a self-maintaining, resilient, and healthy biological community. It can also be accomplished by "growth forms": patterns that leave room for activity settings to expand without disturbing other areas. Plasticity is encouraged by the presence of small territories that can be claimed by groups or individuals. The "waste areas" that come from a certain looseness in plan are the places in which people can operate directly on their surroundings and in which special ecological communities may survive. Here children make their own worlds out of imagination and discarded material; adults take the car apart, erect a shed, or plant a garden. Adaptability is as much a result of site management as it is of spatial form.

Reference 3

Figure 38, page 227

*Cost*: Development should be achieved and maintained at the lowest cost in labor, material resources, social or ecological disruption, and organizational effort, given the functions to be served and the standards to be met. The analysis must identify who will be paying the various costs, since costs are widely and unequally distributed. It is surprising that while costs are usually uppermost in the minds of those who make development decisions, these costs are of a restricted kind, and many decisions about them are heavily larded with irrationality. Last-minute budget savings are made by cutting out "luxuries," future maintenance costs are neglected, and isolated economies in the speed of decision or in regard to quantifiable factors cause heavy burdens elsewhere. It is rare to see a critical examination of the continuing general costs and benefits of basic alternatives.

Site construction costs are typically minimized by a regularity of form, by compact arrangements, by reducing expensive features such as roads, by using the highest density desirable for the given use and structural type, or, of course, by lowering standards. But lower standards may mean increased maintenance costs. In site planning, discounted maintenance costs are typically greater than initial construction costs, though rarely calculated. Likewise, site maintenance costs are minimized by simplicity of form but also by a self-maintaining ecological system, durable materials, and institutional arrangements that reduce vandalism. Allowable maintenance cost, as well as first cost, should always be part of a program. The cost differential between good and bad may sometimes simply be the additional design time required to discover a better solution. Design costs are small in proportion to total cost and project life, but these immediate outlays and delays loom large to the hard-pressed client.

*Financial feasibility*    Economic issues are in front while making site development decisions. Cost data are given in Chapter 13 along with a description of how those costs are likely to vary and some methods for making crude cost estimates. But simple cost data are only part of the economic calculation, which must deal with income, timing, and the incidence of cost as well.

In the United States most site development is now done by two kinds of relatively large-scale private developers: those who are building for sale to others, whether those others are homeowners or real estate investment firms, and those who will retain ownership and management, either as lessors or as actual occupiers. In both cases the key economic calculations focus on the costs and benefits for the developer, subject to the constraints of market demand and public regulation. Costs incurred by others are peripheral considerations. The principal difference between the two kinds of developers lies in whether or not future management costs are considered important.

In its simplest form the calculation first requires an estimate of the total construction and maintenance costs (inclusive of some margin for uncertainty) of a given development over the period of time thought to be necessary to achieve an acceptable return. Next, such additional time-contingent costs as interest charges, taxes, and depreciation are added. Then these costs are compared with cash returns (rents and sales) over the same period. The net surplus of returns over cost is divided by the equity capital invested by the developer to give the percent return. If this rate is equal to or more than what that equity capital can earn elsewhere, the development is judged worth doing. If not, adjustments are made until the return is adequate, or the project is abandoned. Adjustments may be made by changing the quality of the development in ways that will not decrease sales or rentals or by changing the developmental program, that is, the density or the mix of uses or clients, or by changing the timing of the development. These studies of financial feasibility come very early in the development process and are usually the principal determinant in initiating detailed planning and for setting the general program.

Such a calculation is sensitive to many different factors: the market demand for various kinds of facilities, fluctuations in construction and maintenance costs, prevailing interest rates and profit opportunities, land prices, public regulations affecting development—fire laws, building codes, subdivision regulations, or the standards and procedures for gaining special public subsidies. Income tax rules and the supply of available investment capital have strong effects. For example, large investors may be willing to supply money at moderate rates in order to gain the advantages of a rapid depreciation for tax purposes. Timing is essential: a seemingly favorable long-term investment may supply returns so much later than it incurs costs that large amounts of capital are tied up and interest charges wipe out the apparent profits. Developments are therefore evaluated by an economic model that itemizes the outlays and incomes by year, from the initiation of planning to the point of disposal or some conventional point of total depreciation. From these figures the model calculates the cumulative capital requirements, interest charges, and profit returns. In such situations there is pressure for rapid decisions, rapid design, immediate occupation, and quick return, with consequent effects on quality.

While the calculation is complex and subject to many exterior fluctuations, it is also stabilized and simplified by current conventionalities or uniformities, that is, prevailing land prices or construction costs or interest rates, fixed public regulations and tax rules, accepted types of uses and structures (single-family houses on quarter-acre lots, or regional shopping centers based on two department stores, for example), and accepted rules for the degree of uncertainty or the time period of calculation. These uniformities result in such rules of thumb as the ranges of land cost per square foot which are allowable for different kinds of development, ratios of land cost to development cost, appropriate overhead costs, and prevailing costs per square foot for different kinds of facilities (which, of course, depend ultimately on what is thought to be "adequate"). Using such uniformities, we can calculate rapidly the profitability of alternative mixes of use and density at given locations. Such calculations, now being computerized, are the keys to investment decision. But they are rational only to the extent that their underlying assumptions are so.

Site designers must be familiar with these calculations. They will prepare them if their task includes feasibility studies as well as design. At the very least, they must be able to read and evaluate them since financial gain is in a ruling position. Considerations quite remote from the actual performance of a plan — income tax rules are one example — may often dictate the form. An analysis of costs and benefits must indeed lie at the base of any rational site decision, and most site designers do not know how to make that analysis. However, an adequate analysis weighs costs and benefits of all kinds, nonmonetary — even nonquantifiable — as well as monetary, and considers who pays and who receives. By bringing incommensurate items as well as diverse parties into the transaction, we are forced again, despite all the refinements of decision theory, to make delicate subjective or political judgments, although it is possible to make those judgments more explicitly than we are accustomed to do.

*Failures of the market system*    The narrower calculations of profit return to a single developer, while also explicit, realistic, and conducive to economic efficiency of a restricted kind, have certain typical antisocial effects. Land prices, for example, may seem to force a use of residential densities that are too high in terms of current preference and need, even when additional land may actually be available elsewhere. High future maintenance costs may be incurred in order to achieve low first costs. Nonmonetary costs and benefits will be ignored. Need will not be served, either because the demand cannot muster the required price or simply because the market is not organized or vocal. Offices, banks, luxury housing, and shopping centers, on the other hand, will appear in abundance. Because of external fluctuations, development proceeds in jerky fits that do not correspond to the growth of demand and are wasteful of construction resources. Speed of design and decision is achieved but to the detriment of environmental quality. Investment is irrationally directed by such motives as tax shelter, prestige, or surplus funds. Owing to the delays of public regulation and the drive for security of investment, site development solutions become highly standardized. Market sales are kept up by an annual addition of "innovative" features, which may have little relation to long-term quality. And so on. Costs not incurred by the developer are naturally glossed over unless he is forced to attend to them by controls or by devices — such as user fees or special assessments — which add those costs to his own budget. Long-term effects on the ecology of a site and its environs are a frequently neglected external cost of this kind, as are the overloads put on the adjacent public service systems: streets, schools, transit lines, and utilities.

The imperfections of the market economy are a familiar theme and are not correctable by site designers, although these imperfections may affect their choice of clients. Some of these faults are remediable by adjustments in public actions and controls, which set the framework for market decisions. Some are ameliorated by a reliance on developers who have a long-term interest. Most of them await more fundamental changes in the rules of the game. We can expect more rational actions only when we use more inclusive cost-benefit analyses, within institutional structures motivated to take those more inclusive factors into account. Meanwhile, a knowledge of current methods for analyzing financial feasibility is essential for a designer's survival or for any attempts at counteraction.

General goals of the kind just listed must be reinterpreted for each specific case, but they appear again and again. Their very obviousness often allows them to be overridden in the site-planning process. When we have units and standards for behavioral support or access or stress or adaptability as we have units (but very partial ones!) for cost, then we are likely to achieve these qualities to a higher degree.

Thinking of these criteria makes it apparent why the management and support of a setting must be specified along with its form. Decentralization of decision, accurate information, and rapid management response enhance

Management

adaptability. Participation in environmental decision increases social communication. The timing of events causes overloads and underloads on physical facilities. Events have their proper time as well as their proper space. Group territories can be achieved by partitioning the time pattern, as well as by marking out physical boundaries.

*A graphic language for activity*

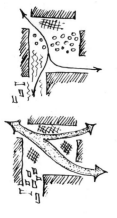

If the activity diagram, based on the behavioral program and budget, is to be one of the principal tools for design, it must become a flexible and expressive graphic language that can convey behavior and form quality, exhibit linkages, and appear either as a rapid topological sketch or an elaborate scaled diagram. Cyclical time patterns should be apparent, as well as the long-range strategy of development: the way one stage succeeds another, how areas are to be held in transitional use pending more permanent commitment, how the strategy itself will shift according to outside events. This might be done most aptly in some improbable medium, like a many-branched, animated film, but also by simple graphic sketches, drawn in successive stages or using time symbols. The technique must become as familiar and reliable as an architectural drawing if we mean to manage the real essence of a site plan. It should be as possible to denote and create new forms of activity settings as it is to do so with new forms of buildings.

Like any design, the synthesis of this pattern is not a logical, single-track process, proceeding inexorably from a knowledge of linkages to a final arrangement. Judgment and creative decision must be employed, and many alternatives must be developed. Chapter 11 will give a better sense of the total site-planning process. The activity plan is not a separate entity to be determined by itself. It is the Siamese twin of the circulation pattern, which will be discussed in Chapter 6. Its implications for the physical visual form must always be held in mind, however tempting it may be to leave this question to a final period of architectural adornment. Will the site organization allow a clear expression of the principal functions? Will the arrangement of activities bring about a desirable visual effect? The most serious danger of the method lies in the tendency to think in terms of areal designations on paper and to forget that what is being conceived is a form in three dimensions. Rough sketches showing the concrete implications of activity proposals, concurrent development of the general visual form, and manipulation of the activity pattern on a model rather than on a map may all help to overcome this danger.

*Activity diagrams and three-dimensional form*

*Chapter* 4

*Technique:*
# Site Form and Site Ecology

A n ecological system is a community of plants and animals cooperating and competing with each other in the same habitat, recycling nutrients, and exploiting the energy of the sun. Since man is a part of nature, urban areas are also ecological systems. Normally, and in the absence of external changes, these systems move toward a mature steady state in which the diversity of species and the standing crop, or biomass, are at a maximum, the structure of interrelations is complex, and the net production of organic matter, or surplus food, drops to zero. Characteristic associations are formed — rain forest, grassland, salt marsh, tundra — whose form depends largely on the levels of light, temperature, and moisture. The diversity of species seems to be connected to the stability of the system, and a drop in that diversity is an early warning of a disturbance. Stable communities regulate their habitat, as well as vice versa: for example, soil and climate are influenced by plants. Violent oscillations occur when some exotic factor affects the system — a new species, a shift in climate, a fire, an eruption, a new disease, a new chemical, or human action. Otherwise, the highly interlinked system regulates itself. Populations are kept at stable numbers and in specific locations by competition, predation, natural limits, and self-regulating processes such as territoriality. But changes occurring in one species will have far-reaching and unexpected ef-

*Reference 26*

*Ecology*

fects all along the food chain. Thus a change in one species may often be brought about by changing the general conditions or by operating on some other species, as well as by working directly on the species itself.

While the maximum gross production of organic matter occurs in such mature and intricate communities as coral reefs or marine estuaries, where net production is close to zero, the maximum net production for human consumption occurs in communities that are continuously upset so as to keep them "young" and biologically relatively poor: the cleared forest, the plowed grassland, the periodically drained pond. Moreover, there is a prevalent human habitat preference for a mix of forest and grassland — the savanna, or forest edge. Trees are planted on the plains and clearings made in the woods. Our preferences for food and habitat, as well as the density of human occupation, force us toward a constant management of the environment. Our means for management are now so powerful that mistakes can be far-reaching. Habitats can be so changed that they never return to their previous state, or only after a long period — a thousand years perhaps. New species are introduced that react violently with the ecosystem. Wastes are generated that overload the natural processes of decomposition or, worse, are of such a new kind that there is no natural process adapted to decomposing them.

Thus there is a typical conflict between human actions, directed toward human purposes, and the tendency for undisturbed habitats to reach stable mature states. Nevertheless, even man-free ecosystems are not completely stable — certainly not while undergoing succession but also not even at their climax. Evolution occurs, various external catastrophes impinge, and there are some evidences of processes of community "aging." With good management, men can maintain stable intermediate states that are appropriate to their purposes. Species diversity and a mix of habitats, as well as such basic resources as soil, air, and water, can be preserved. The recycling of scarce nutrients and the efficiency of energy utilization may even be improved. All this can be done while ensuring environments that fit human biological and cultural preferences. But it will require far more careful management both of environment and of the human population than we have so far exhibited.

Ecology describes the limits and conditions of human intervention without telling us what we *should* do, except insofar as it points to the value of diversity, partial stability, and the conservation of the whole system of living things. Conservation of a site as an ongoing system does *not* mean leaving it unchanged, but it will nevertheless often conflict with some of the human purposes to be applied to the site. We have little to guide us in resolving such conflicts and must usually end by favoring the human purpose — remembering that human purpose also excludes making the world uninhabitable. Ecology teaches us to be aware of the conflict, to allow the existing site system and the proposed human system to coexist wherever possible, and to be wary of the unexpected and often disagreeable side effects of human intervention. We also learn that we must re-create a system that is in itself reasonably diverse and stable. From ecological studies we have derived techniques both for changing and for stabilizing — for example, how to import parasites to reduce a pest or how to seed land, reduce grazing, and impound water to prevent erosion. Finally, a knowledge of ecology is helpful in many ways in the analysis of existing sites — for example, how plants are climate or soil indicators or how to spot the early signs of massive erosion. Much of the following discussion of specific site factors will emphasize their interrelations as an ecological system.

The form of the ground surface is of obvious interest to the site planner. It is most often represented on drawings by *contours*, or sets of imaginary lines that connect all points of some arbitrary equal elevation on the ground. The sets of ground points to be connected by these lines are separated vertically by some regular interval: 1, 2, 5, or 10 feet typically, if not in the metric system. Contour lines are always continuous within the space of any one map and do not merge or cross except at vertical or overhanging surfaces. The closer they are together, the steeper the ground. The more nearly parallel they are, the smoother and more regular the ground surface. In rolling land they take on flowing curves; in broken land they wiggle; over plane surfaces they run in straight lines. In any region, if a small portion of contour lines is looked at "downhill" (that is, with the lower contours away from the observer), the shape of the line is a (usually exaggerated) representation of the form of that small piece of land as seen in section.

One quickly learns the contour patterns of typical topographic features: stream valley, ridge, bowl, mesa, depression, flat grade, escarpment, barrow, pass, peak. But one must keep clear which contour lines are lower and which are higher, or the terrain will be read in reverse. The con-

Representing
Ground Form

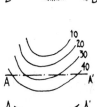

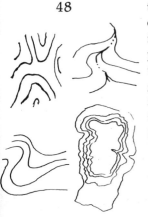

tour interval must also be related to the scale of the map in order to grasp the relative steepness of the different spacings. One can both read the exact elevations of particular places and also get a synoptic view of extensive terrain. Contours are easily sketched or adjusted to describe some new ground form. The swirling patterns, so incomprehensible at first, are soon eloquent. An easy familiarity with these patterns and the ability to relate them to what is seen in the field are essential for a site planner. Contour maps of almost all the United States at a scale of 1 inch equals 2000 feet and a contour interval of 10 or 20 feet are available from the U.S. Geological Survey. But more detailed contour maps must usually be prepared for anything except preliminary reconnaissance.

While contour maps are the standard way of representing ground form, there are other methods. One is to record the spot elevations of key points on the ground: the crests, valley bottoms, breaks in grade, floor levels of structures. This record may be systematized by giving the elevation of every intersection point of some imaginary grid, a method often used for precise calculations in small areas. The old method of hachures is still sometimes seen, in which short lines, perpendicular rather than parallel to the slope, are drawn side by side in curving rows. Their direction points directly up- or downhill, their length indicates the length of the slope, and their closeness together shows the steepness. They demand skillful drafting but cannot express exact elevation or precise form. If well done, however, they give a vivid picture of the general terrain.

*Models*      For reading the general form of the terrain, though not for precision, the best representation is the three-dimensional model. Simple cardboard contour models are the best tool for planning, as they are relatively easy to make, can be cut and patched, and relate directly to the contour drawing. Damp sand or Plasticine models are also used, because they can be molded easily and, if no material is added or taken away, will result in the facsimile of a new ground form that can be achieved with a rough balance of cut and fill. Much more elaborate models can be made, of course, for exhibition or for "selling" a proposal.

Indeed, the chief danger of models lies in their diminutive charm, which makes almost any condition or plan seem attractive. Rough models are preferable for this reason, as well as for their manipulability and speed of construction. Not only are observers seduced by miniaturization, but most of them (and many experienced designers as well) fail to read the model scale. Distances are understood to be smaller than they actually would be, and slopes seem less steep despite the apparent reality of the simulation. It is a common error to look endearingly at some model, as upon a toy world, without actually projecting oneself into it as a tiny being at its same scale. Despite these dangers it is usually advisable to study any plan for terrain in the model form, as well as on a contour drawing.

The form of a site is critical to how it may be used. *Topography* Ground slope is one of the more important aspects of the topography, since use and maintenance are dependent on it. This relationship will vary according to the pattern of activity, but there is a general classification worth remembering. Slopes under 4 percent (rising 4 feet in 100 feet of horizontal distance) seem flat and are usable for all kinds of intense activity. Slopes between 4 and 10 percent appear as easy grades, suitable for informal movement and activity. Slopes over 10 percent seem steep and can be actively used only for hill sports or free play. Gradients over 10 percent require noticeable effort to climb or to descend. Furthermore, it is more expensive to erect buildings on them, as a more complicated form and foundation and more difficult utility connections are required. In addition, slope has a bearing on drainage, erosion, and maintenance. Slopes under 1 percent do not drain well unless they are paved and carefully finished. Slopes over 50 or 60 percent cannot be protected from erosion in a humid climate except by terracing or cribbing (reinforcement by embedded wooden or concrete beams). The slope of a mowed lawn must be kept under 25 percent. The steeper the land and the more impervious its soil, the more the rain will run off its surface instead of seeping into the ground. This means a liability to erosion and the flooding of surface channels. Since the slope of ground is so critical, it is very common to analyze a site by marking off the areas of different slope: steep, moderate, flat, well or ill drained, subject to erosion, suitable for building or for outdoor play, and so on.

Another critical aspect of ground form is the way in *Ground form* which it limits circulation by means of roads and gravity- *and circulation* powered utilities, such as sewers. Here we are concerned not only with local slopes but with the way in which the total system of slopes allows continuous lines of suitable grade to be connected. Grades under 1 percent are difficult to drain, and large sewers may tend to "ride up" out of the ground.

On steep ground sewer pipes will have to be specially designed to prevent rapid, scouring flows. Roads are preferably kept at a less than a 10 percent grade; a 15 percent slope approaches the limit that an ordinary loaded vehicle can climb for a sustained period. The grades of circulation lines can be modified by the degree to which they are drawn parallel or perpendicular to ground slopes; thus the experienced designer looks at ground with an eye to how it may be connected into a system of acceptable character. There may be "passes," or restricted localities that offer the only opportunity to cross some rough terrain, ideal lines of approach, key external points to which connection must be made. The designer has to decide whether to follow ridge lines and stream lines or whether to cross them — whether to work with the land or to oppose it — and what the principal alternatives for main entrances or connections may be. Thus it is usually possible to analyze a site for its circulation capability, even at an early stage.

*Visibility*

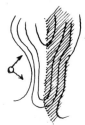

Another consideration is the visual form of the ground, which in its mechanical sense refers simply to visibility: what terrain can be seen from where. A contour map is often analyzed into visibility diagrams, which are shaded in every portion that is not visible from some given point (and therefore from which that point also cannot be seen). Such diagrams will be produced for several key locations in the terrain. The visual analysis of topography in this sense is similar to a military reconnaissance for fields of fire, which are like lines of sight. Concepts like the defile, an area shaded from view or fire from the outside, or the military crest are useful. The military crest, or the brow of a hill, is the point below the true crest where the grade steepens, and from which the entire downward slope is open to view. It is usually a more strategic — and harmonious — location at which to place a structure than at the very top. Conversely, the true crest may be the best place for locating low structures that are meant to be visually isolated from the bottom of the nearby valley, although anything on the skyline is always very prominent from a distance.

While visibility is a straightforward analysis of terrain, visual form also refers to many of the more subtle qualities that depend on the total context of land, cover, atmosphere, and activity. This is what we mean when we use the word *landscape*. These concepts will be discussed in some

*See pages 206–210* detail in Chapter 9.

Finally, the form of the ground affects the microcli-

mate, particularly in the way in which slopes face away
from or toward the sun or as they impede or channel the
winds. This aspect will be covered at greater length later in
this chapter.

See pages 68 and
74–75

Thus topography may be analyzed by the site planner
in a methodical way as a mosaic of slope areas, a potential
network of circulation, a set of fields of view, or a collection of
probable microclimates. It must also be judged as a total system, a unique landscape, a place of particular character.
The ability to make such judgments comes with experience
and depends on the analysis of many other site factors, as
well as a knowledge of development purposes and possibilities.

Topography is the result of geological and organic processes, and it is useful to understand how glaciation or ancient seas have had the results that we see on the surface.
Such a knowledge explains not only the genesis of terrain
but the present connection between surface and substrate.
We can thereby begin to predict conditions underground
from the appearance above. This subject — geomorphology — is unfortunately too complex to be covered here,
however useful it is for site-planning purposes, and readers
are referred to standard texts. If we link geomorphology
to ecology, we can then see the landscape as a complete
system, evolving over long periods of time.

*Geomorphology*

*Reference 23*

As we look beneath the surface, our first consideration
is the soil, the pulverized mantle of the earth, formed from
rock and plant remains by the action of both weather and
organisms. On the same parent rock, grassland and forest
produce very different soils. The soil is not static but is continually developing and wasting. Beneath the organic litter
of decomposing material, it is conventionally divided into:
the A level, or "topsoil," a mixture of mineral and organic
material, usually rather dark in color, with direct organic
functions, and with some of its minerals leached out to
lower levels; the B level, largely mineral in composition
and below most plant roots, but with some organic function, the level that has received the minerals washed down
from the A level above; and the C level, the fractured and
weathered parent material of the soil above, but with little
or no biological activity, and lying directly over the solid
bedrock.

Soil

The particles of soil are classified as being organic or
inorganic and by their grain size:

*Gravel*:    particles over 2 mm in diameter

*Sand:*  0.05 to 2 mm, gritty, the finest grains just visible to the eye

*Silt:*  0.002 to 0.05 mm, the grains invisible but can be felt; smooth, not gritty

*Clay:*  under 0.002 mm, smooth and floury or in stiff lumps when dry, plastic and sticky when wet

Soils are extremely variable mixtures of these particles, and these variable mixtures have equally diverse implications for site development. Soil mixtures are classified in two different ways: by soil scientists who began with an interest in the relation between soils and agriculture, and by engineers who were interested in the usefulness of soils for roads and foundations.

*Agricultural classification of soil*

In the first classification the whole mantle of soil in one place to depths of 6 feet or more is characterized as a unit, and there are generic types that refer to the basic climate, geology, and plant cover under whose influence the soil was formed. These great soil orders are further broken down into suborders, great groups, subgroups, families, and finally into series. Each series has an identifying place name and is further divided according to the texture of the surface soil, for example, "Merrimac sandy loam." The textural names refer to the relative percentages of sand, silt, and clay in the surface layers according to the three-dimensional graph shown in Figure 8 below:

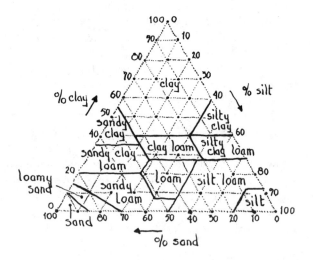

FIGURE 8 *A three-coordinate graph showing the percentages of sand, silt, and clay in the conventional soil textural classes, from the Soil Survey Manual of the U.S. Department of Agriculture.*

The series name groups soils of similar history, constituents, depth, and structure. Therefore they have roughly similar characteristics as to bearing capacity, drainage, and agricultural value.

Almost half of the United States has been mapped according to these soil classes, down to areas as small as a few acres. Over 70,000 soil classes have been identified. Some of this work is recent, while some was done a quarter century ago. Originally made for agricultural planning, these maps have value for site planning as well. By locating the soil types on a soil map and then referring to the description of those types, we can learn about potential water, sand, and gravel supply, about probable drainage, runoff, and erosion, and about suitability for earth moving and foundations, as well as for agriculture and forestry. Wherever such soil surveys have been done, they are of great service in early reconnaissance and general planning.

The engineering classification refers to the exact composition of a particular soil body, wherever it occurs, and is determined by laboratory tests on field specimens. It leads to accurate predictions of bearing capacity, for example, or the optimum mixture of that soil with some additive, to make it a better engineering material. Laboratory analysis is done by specialists and results in a quantitative description.

*Engineering classification of soil*

It is possible, however, to make a rough identification of soil in the field and from that to estimate its engineering implications. This rough estimate is of great utility in site reconnaissance and may be all that is needed for the siting of light structures. For this purpose soils are divided into ten classes, which can be identified in the field and have significantly different implications for siting:

1. *The clean gravels* (standard symbols GW/GP): in which the dominant constituent is gravel, and less than about 5 to 10 percent is silt or clay. (These gravels may be further subdivided as being "well graded" [GW] or "poorly graded" [GP], according to whether the particle sizes fill the whole range from fine to coarse or do not.)

2. *Silty and clayey gravels* (GM/GC): mostly gravel, but with more than 10 to 12 percent silt (GM) or clay (GC).

3. *Clean sands* (SW/SP): mostly sand, less than 5 to 10 percent silt or clay. (Also subdivided as well graded [SW] or poorly graded [SP]).

4. *Silty and clayey sands* (SM/SC): mostly sand, but with more than 10 to 12 percent silt (SM) or clay (SC).

5. *Nonplastic silts* (ML): inorganic silts or very fine sands, whose liquid limit is less than 50 (that is, which

begin to flow like a liquid when containing less than 50 percent of water).

6. *Plastic silts* (MH): inorganic silts with a liquid limit over 50.

7. *Organic silts* (OL): silts with substantial organic matter and a liquid limit under 50.

8. *Nonplastic clays* (CL): inorganic clays with a liquid limit under 50.

9. *Plastic and organic clays* (CH/OH): having a liquid limit over 50, and being either predominantly inorganic clay (CH) or a silt or a clay with substantial organic matter (OH).

10. *Peat and muck* (Pt): predominantly organic material, whether plant remains are visible (peat) or invisible (muck).

*Field identification of soil*

These ten classes may be distinguished by the following field procedures:

Take a handful of soil as a sample, dry it, and spread it out on clean paper. If more than half the particles are visible to the naked eye, it is a sand or a gravel. If this is difficult to determine even when the visible particles have been hand separated from the fine dust, then do the following: pulverize a dry sample, weigh it, cover it with 5 inches of water in a transparent container, shake it thoroughly, let it settle for 30 seconds, and then pour off the water. Continue to do this until the water poured off is clean. The remaining residue is the sand and gravel, and its *dry* weight can be compared with the original dry weight of the sample.

In distinguishing a sand from a gravel, if more than half the coarse (visible) particles are over ¼ inch, it is a gravel; if not, it is a sand. If less than 10 percent of the total soil sample is fine particles (invisible to the eye or poured off in the sedimentation test), then it is a clean sand or a clean gravel. If not, it is a silty or clayey sand or gravel. (To distinguish a well-graded clean sand or gravel from a poorly graded one, simply look at the range of particle sizes to see if all sizes are represented, as opposed to there being significant gaps or to the particles being mostly uniform in size.)

We have now identified the soil if it belonged to one of the first four classes. But if, at the beginning, it proved *not* to be a sand or a gravel, then two further mutually supporting tests are required. Both begin by picking out and discarding all the soil particles over about 1/64 inch in size, that is, the coarser ones that would interfere with molding and working the soil, and by taking a sample that will make a pat of soil about 1½ by 1½ inches, and ½ inch thick.

*Dry-strength test*: Wet the soil, and mold it into a pat. Dry it thoroughly, take it between the thumbs and forefingers of both hands, and try to break it by pressure of the thumbs. If it cannot be broken or if it is broken only with great effort, snaps like a crisp cookie and cannot be powdered, then the soil is a plastic clay (CH). If it can be broken and powdered with some effort, it is an organic clay (OH) or a nonplastic clay (CL). If it is broken and powdered easily or crumbles even as it is picked up, it is a plastic silt (MH), an organic silt (OL), or a nonplastic silt (ML).

*Thread test*: Add just enough water to a pat of soil so that it can be molded without sticking to the hands. On a nonabsorptive surface (such as a piece of glass), roll it out into a thread about 1/8 inch in diameter, then remold it into a ball. If it can be so remolded and the ball deformed again without cracking, it is a plastic clay (CH). If it can be remolded but the ball cracks when deformed again, it is a nonplastic clay (CL). If it cannot be remolded into a ball, it is a plastic silt (MH), or a plastic, organic silt or clay (OH), or an organic silt (OL). If it cannot even be rolled into a thread, it is a nonplastic silt (ML). In the course of this test, the organic soils (OH/OL) will feel spongy to the fingers.

These two tests in part confirm each other and in part serve to separate the borderline cases of the other — to distinguish a nonplastic from an organic clay, a plastic silt from an organic one, or a plastic from a nonplastic silt. The organic silts and clays (OH/OL) not only feel spongy but tend to be darker in color and, in particular, to have a musty odor if heated when wet. If it is desired to distinguish a clayey sand or gravel from a silty one (GM/SM), the same thread test performed on the particles under 1/64 inch will separate a clay from a silt. Peat or muck (Pt) is easily identifiable on sight by its black or dark brown color, its visible plant remains, its very spongy feel, and by its immediate organic odor.

These four tests — the composition of visible particles by size, the dry strength, the behavior of a plastic thread, and the smell when heated — serve to distinguish the ten soil classes. In addition, there are some other field indications, such as the spongy feel of organic soils and the soapy feel of plastic clay, which does not wash off easily and tends to stain. Between the teeth, sandy soils are hard and gritty. Silty ones are not gritty but the grains can still be felt. Pulverized clay feels smooth and floury; a dry lump of it sticks when lightly touched by the tongue. The organic soils are dark, drab grays, browns, and blacks.

TABLE 1. ENGINEERING CHARACTERISTICS OF SOIL

| Soil class: | Stability when loaded | Stability when frozen | Drainage | As a bearing for foundations or a road | As a base course for permanent roads | As a material for light roads if stabilized | For adobe construction |
|---|---|---|---|---|---|---|---|
| GW/GP | Ex | Gd-Ex | Ex | GW:Ex GP:Gd-Ex | GW:Gd GP:Pr-Fr | Gd | Nx |
| GM/GC | Gd | Fr-Gd | Nx-Fr | Gd | GM:Pr-Gd GC:Pr | Gd | Gd |
| SW/SP | Ex | Gd-Ex | Ex | SW:Gd SP:Fr-Gd | SW:Pr SP:Nx-Pr | Gd | Nx |
| SM/SC | Fr-Gd | Pr-Gd | Nx-Fr | Fr-Gd | SM:Nx-Pr SC:Pr-Fr | Gd | Gd |
| ML | Fr-Gd | Nx-Fr | Pr-Fr | Pr-Fr | Nx | Fr | Gd |
| MH | Pr | Nx-Fr | Pr-Fr | Pr | Nx | Pr | Nx |
| OL | Pr-Fr | Pr-Fr | Pr | Pr | Nx | Nx | Nx |
| CL | Fr | Pr-Fr | Nx | Pr-Fr | Nx | Pr | Fr |
| CH/OH | Pr | Fr | Nx | Nx-Pr | Nx | Nx | Nx |
| Pt | Nx | Gd | Pr-Fr | Nx | Nx | Nx | Nx |

Ex = excellent; Gd = good; Fr = fair; Pr = poor; Nx = very poor or not suitable

Some of the implications of these soils for site planning are summarized in Table 1. In general, gravel is a well-drained, stable material and bears heavy loads if it is well graded. Sand is also well drained and makes a good foundation if well graded, but it must be confined at the sides. Loose sands and gravels may settle initially under a load. If they have appreciable fine material, they lose much of their good internal drainage. Fine sands or sand-silt mixtures may become "quick" when saturated and flow like a liquid.

Silt is stable when dry or damp, although it will compress under a load. It is treacherous and unstable when wet. Because it swells up and it heaves badly when frozen, the foundations of roads and buildings must go deep enough to prevent this from happening, or be strong or elastic enough to cope with it. The erosion of silt is likely to be severe. Loess, or wind-laid silt, is strong when dry and can maintain itself in a vertical face without slumping to a flatter angle.

Clay is plastic when wet, stiff and cohesive when dry. Its reaction to frost is less extreme than that of silt. It tends to be impervious and to slip, swell, or soften when wet. But it will often be a strong bearing soil when kept dry. Dull gray-blue clays or mottled yellow or gray ones have very poor internal drainage. Thick layers of permeable soil, lying over an impervious clay layer on slopes over 10 percent are liable to slippage.

Peat — and to a somewhat lesser extent the other organic soils — is a very poor engineering material. It is elastic, weak, and has little cohesion. Normally it must simply be removed from the site unless land is to be left in an undeveloped state.

For foundations of light roads and buildings in undisturbed ground, the various sands and gravels are most likely to be suitable. Some of the nonplastic silts and clays (ML/CL) are likely to be usable; the plastic and organic soils (MH/CH/OL/OH) must be suspected. Clays will swell, silts will heave with frost, and organic soils will compress under loads. Peat is unusable. Foundations on fill are to be avoided, but if they are well compacted, the sands and gravels are acceptable, the others much less so.

Clean sands and gravels are very well drained and thus probably usable for sewage drain fields. All other soil types must be checked for their absorptive capacity, but it is likely that other sands and gravels, as well as the inorganic silts (ML/MH), will be usable. The clays and the organic soils are not likely to be so. Drain fields in fill should be avoided, but clean sands and gravels may serve the purpose.

The sands and gravels perform in varying degrees as a base course for permanent roads under a concrete or asphalt wearing surface. No other natural soil will do. The sands and gravels show marked hardening if stabilized by an additive in order to make a light road surface. Nonplastic silts (ML) can also be stabilized, whereas plastic silts and nonplastic clays (MH/CL) perform less well. Cement is the best additive for the silts and for most gravels and sands (ML/MH/GW/GP/GM/SW/SP/SM), while lime is the best for the clays (CL) and for the clayey sands and gravels (GC/SC).

*Soil as a plant medium*

The organic topsoil is critical for the living community. Its most important aspects are its drainage, its content of humus, its relative acidity (pH), and the presence of available nutrients, particularly the major elements potassium, phosphorus, and nitrogen (KPN). Any one of the latter may be deficient owing to leaching down to the B level beyond the plant roots. Phosphorus may be in an insoluble form and thus be unavailable, or waterlogging may have discouraged the nitrifying bacteria that ordinarily replenish the nitrogen supply. Impervious subsurface layers may impede drainage. The pH value will determine which species will grow most easily. Excess acidity (high pH) is particularly difficult for most plants to cope with, since the available ions of potassium, calcium, and so on, have largely been replaced with hydrogen. An abundant supply of earthworms is a reliable index of fertile soil of low acidity.

To learn what plants are best suited to a locale, as well as to learn what measures should be taken to improve the soil, it is normal to make simple tests for acidity and for the presence of available potassium, phosphorus, and nitrogen. Chemical deficiencies can often be remedied, acidity can be modified to some degree and temporarily, and drainage can often be improved. A compacted subsoil can be broken up by plowing before respreading the topsoil. Sandy soil is easily improved by adding peat or compost and adjusting the pH with lime. Infertile soil can be fertilized, and chalky soil can be improved with acid fertilizers. A heavy clay is more difficult to improve, but sharp sand can be added to it, or perhaps it is easier simply to cover it with imported topsoil. Even slag heaps and similar derelict wastes can be brought back by pulverizing and fertilizing them and by planting special pioneer plant species. The limits to these procedures are more economic than technical.

For engineering purposes, however, the topsoil is disregarded, since it will be stripped off during construction and then respread. Soil samples are taken from small pits or by earth augers or boring tubes. But soils are irregularly deposited and have an internal structure. They may change within a short horizontal or vertical distance and must be checked at many points, particularly at the point of construction. Where different types are intimately mixed, it is safe to assume the characteristics of the worst. Soil structure, which refers to the layering or clustering of soil particles and the presence of slippage planes or holes, will also affect bearing strength and drainage.

*Soil structure*

The distribution of boulders and the depth to bedrock is an important feature. It is useful to drive a pointed rod, 5 feet long and 5/16 inch in diameter, into the ground to test soil density and depth and to check for boulders and ledges. If bedrock and ledges are encountered, the critical distinction is whether they are hard and must be blasted out or sufficiently soft and loose for excavation by power equipment. Some shales, weak conglomerates, and highly weathered rocks are of the latter kind. Numerous large boulders will also add appreciably to site costs.

If major structures are contemplated, or if the ground is questionable, it will be necessary to take regular borings and to have soil and rock samples tested. Borings are usually taken at 50-foot intervals to depths at least 20 feet below the bottom of the eventual foundations. Subsurface characteristics may also be gleaned from examining previous structures and excavations, from looking at the sides of cuts, or from studying old records, aerial photographs, and geological reports.

Perhaps the most important subsurface variant of all is the presence or absence of water: the moisture content of the soil, its internal and surface drainage, and the position of the water table.

*Subsurface water*

The water table is the underground surface below which all interstices between soil grains are filled with water. Normally this is a sloping, flowing surface, which roughly follows the ground levels above and slopes down to ponds, lakes, streams, seeps, or springs, where it intersects the ground surface. Its depth below ground can vary markedly, however, and can fluctuate seasonally or over longer periods. Impervious subsurface rock or soil layers can also modify the water table, trapping water above or below themselves or guiding it through seams.

The water table is important for water supply and for vegetation. A high table causes difficulties in excavation work, as well as flooded basements, flooded utilities, and unstable foundations. A high table is indicated by the water levels in existing wells and diggings, by seeps and springs, by a mottled soil, and by the presence of such water-loving plants as willows, poplars, and reeds. A 6-foot test pit in the wet season will reveal the presence of a table high enough to cause trouble in ordinary residential development. In a flood plain the soil is likely to be rather deep and uniform, perhaps with alternating thin layers of coarse and fine material. Banks, stones, and tree trunks often show the marks of previous flood crests. The presence of underground water courses is particularly critical, and structures should not be sited over them. It is also important to avoid filling over and blocking existing surface drainage courses: culverts must be put in to allow continued flow.

*Subsurface problems*

In general, the most critical subsurface problems, the danger flags calling for closer investigation, may be summarized as follows: a high water table; the presence of peat and other organic soils or of soft plastic clay, loose silt, or fine water-bearing sand; rock lying close to the surface; lands previously used as dumps or containing new and unconsolidated fill; or any evidence of slides, floods, or subsidence. Total site improvement costs may increase 25 percent in rocky land and 85 percent in peat or muck. The latter may also substantially increase foundation costs. In areas of permafrost the erection of heated buildings on the frozen ground may bring on all the problems of a saturated soil.

Climate

We live in an ocean of air, constantly subject to its variations of temperature, humidity, and purity and to the light and sound transmitted through it. Within this ocean we have strong preferences for certain ranges or rhythms of light and noise intensity, air purity, and effective temperature. Natural climates can be erratic and violent; there are man-made intrusions of noise and airborne impurities. Men defend themselves by physiological adaptations and by clothing and shelter. But it is also possible to manipulate climate by the arrangement and choice of site.

The general climate of a region sets the stage. It is expressed in data on temperature, humidity, precipitation, cloudiness, wind speed and direction, and sun path. These are the outside constraints within which the site planner operates, and he must have them before him in some concise form. Although simplified data are desirable, average conditions will not suffice. It is the extremes that are uncomfortable. Ranges and average maximums and minimums are likely to be most useful. Such data are commonly available but must be evaluated for site-planning purposes: What is the duration and intensity of the precipitation that must be warded off and drained away? What are the favorable and the unfavorable winds? At what time of day or during what season should sun radiation be avoided or invited and from what direction? When does the effective temperature move outside the comfort zone?

The effective temperature is a sensation produced by the combined effect of radiation and ambient temperature, relative humidity, and air movement. Outdoor cold can be mitigated by clothing, shelter, and heating devices. Outdoor heat is more trying. The average adult must dissipate 400 Btu per hour while at rest, and 2000 at work. If his body temperature varies even slightly, he will be uncomfortable. If it rises 10 degrees, he will die or suffer serious damage. Thus one limit of human tolerance is the maximum temperature at which he can do extended work without raising his body temperature significantly: about 150°F in completely dry air and near 90°F in completely humid air.

Comfort, however, is a more frequent issue than extreme tolerance. The comfort zone may be roughly defined as follows: most people in the temperate zone, sitting indoors in the shade in light clothing, will feel tolerably comfortable at temperature ranges between 70° and 80°F, as long as the relative humidity lies between 20 percent and 50 percent. As humidity increases, these same people will begin to be uncomfortable at lower and lower temperatures, until the relative humidity reaches about 75 percent, when general discomfort at any temperature sets in. But if they are sitting in a draft, the range of tolerable temperature shifts upward, so that temperatures of 85° may be quite comfortable in the 20 to 50 percent humidity range if local air is moving at 200 feet per minute. Indoor air moving more slowly than 50 feet per minute is generally unnoticed, while flows of 50 to 100 feet per minute are pleasant and hardly noticed. Breezes from 100 to 200 feet per minute are pleasant, but one is constantly aware of them; those from 200 to 300 feet per minute are first slightly and then annoyingly drafty. Sensations of comfort are affected by previous experience, by cultural background, and by the degree of activity. In the United

*Climatic comfort*

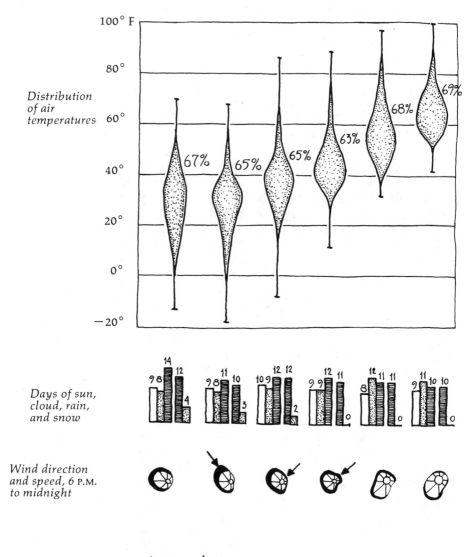

Jan. Feb. March April May June

Distribution of air temperatures

Days of sun, cloud, rain, and snow

Wind direction and speed, 6 P.M. to midnight

Maximum rate of rainfall

minutes hours

inches of rain

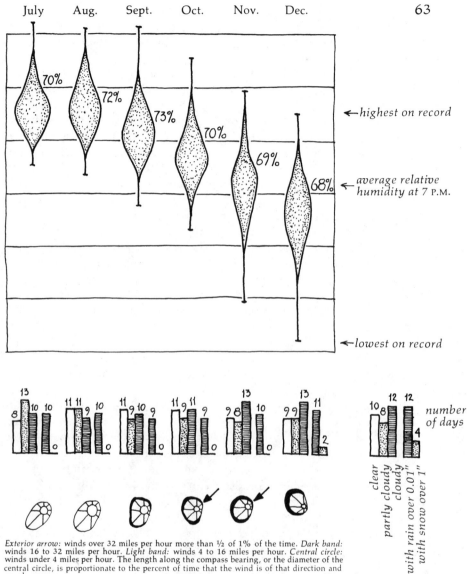

July   Aug.   Sept.   Oct.   Nov.   Dec.

70%
72%
73%
70%
69%
68%

←highest on record

←average relative
   humidity at 7 P.M.

←lowest on record

number
of days

*clear*
*partly cloudy*
*cloudy*
*with rain over 0.01"*
*with snow over 1"*

Exterior arrow: winds over 32 miles per hour more than ½ of 1% of the time. *Dark band:* winds 16 to 32 miles per hour. *Light band:* winds 4 to 16 miles per hour. *Central circle:* winds under 4 miles per hour. The length along the compass bearing, or the diameter of the central circle, is proportionate to the percent of time that the wind is of that direction and speed.

FIGURE 9   *The climate of the Boston region by months: temperature, humidity, precipitation, sun, and wind (Sources:* House Beautiful Climate Control Guide, *Hearst Corporation, and Climates of the States, Massachusetts, U.S. Weather Bureau).*

States 72°F is considered an "ideal" indoor temperature; in Great Britain 65°F is preferred. Active persons will be comfortable at cooler temperatures than those sitting still.

The designer will do what he can to see that indoor and even outdoor effective temperatures lie within this comfort zone. According to the general climate, he will induce or check the flow of air, let in or block the sun, humidify or dry the air, raise or lower the temperature. Outdoors the site planner is somewhat more concerned with summer climates, since in the wintertime clothing can be used for protection and less time is spent outdoors. Yet in the cold seasons a great deal can be done to moderate the severity of climate or to prolong the season of outdoor activity by the use of wind shields, radiation traps, or even outdoor heating.

Any climate is complex and usually variable. The distributions of air temperature, of relative humidity, and of wind direction and force, broken down by month and season, are the fundamental data for determining effective temperature and its relation to the comfort zone. In addition, the hours of precipitation and the maximum intensities of rain indicate the need for overhead shelter and the requirements for adequate drainage. Finally, the hours of sunshine (as a percentage of total possible hours) and the sun direction and elevation will dictate the measures that must be taken to invite or ward off solar radiation.

*Local climate data*

Other than sun direction and elevation, the climatic factors vary irregularly from place to place. They are given in Figure 9 for the Boston region to illustrate what is likely to be most significant. The chart shows that outdoor temperatures are frequently above the comfort zone in July and August, when the most useful cooling winds are from the southwest. Temperatures are almost always below the comfort zone from October through May, but in those two transition months the effective temperatures are often high enough to be modified successfully by using moderately warm clothing and by changing the microclimate. In the eight cold months the prevailing winds are stronger and come especially from the west and northwest. Sunless slopes, cold air floods, and exposure to winter winds are thus all to be avoided. In the humid Boston area precipitation occurs throughout the year but is heaviest from December through March. Cloudiness is rather evenly distributed, but sunny days are somewhat more frequent from August to October. Strangely enough, this is also the period of highest humidity, often very uncomfortable. Cloudy days, fog, rain, snow, and dampness must all be reckoned with.

Such a general analysis furnishes the first clues for the choice and arrangement of the site. When the designer works in a region new to him, a study of the traditional building of the locality and of its climatic advantages and defects will be of special value. But he is particularly interested in studying the microclimate, the local modification of the general climate that is imposed by the special shape of a small area: its topography, cover, ground surface, and man-made forms. The microclimatic effects give him clues for changing the general climate in a favorable way.

*Microclimate*

These effects are typically very local ones, since the microclimate often changes within distances of a few feet or less. As a significant phenomenon, it is confined to a shallow zone close to the skin of the earth, no more than a few stories high. It is a product of the movement and interchange of heat, water vapor, air impurities, and light and sound energy, as this interchange is influenced by the different surfaces and media it encounters. The fundamental phenomenon is the heat balance: the constant interchange between sun, earth, and atmosphere, producing small climates that fluctuate markedly on a daily or seasonal cycle, particularly at the interface between earth and air.

*Reference 37*

Heat is exchanged by radiation, conduction, and convection. There are three corresponding characteristics of the media to be considered: albedo, conductivity, and the nature of air movement. Albedo is a characteristic of surfaces, being the fraction of the total radiant energy of a given wavelength incident on a surface which is reflected back by that surface instead of being absorbed. A surface with an albedo of 1.0 is a perfect mirror, reflecting back everything that shines on it, without darkening the reflected image or receiving any heat itself. A surface whose albedo is zero is a perfect black matte surface, reflecting nothing and soaking up all the heat radiated upon it. These same properties also appear when the flow of radiation reverses: a hot surface of low albedo radiates quickly, as well as receiving quickly. Albedo may therefore be imagined as the relative permeability of a surface to radiant energy flowing in either direction: high albedo surfaces are resistant to this flow, and low albedo surfaces are permissive. In the same way surfaces may also be relatively absorbent or relatively reflective to the sound waves falling on them, although the albedo of a surface with respect to radiant energy bears no relation to its "albedo" with respect to sound.

*Albedo*

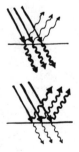

Albedos of natural surfaces vary markedly for radiation within the visible spectrum:

| | |
|---|---|
| Fresh snow | 0.80–0.85 |
| Cloud surfaces | 0.60–0.90 |
| Old snow | 0.42–0.70 |
| Fields, meadow, tillage | 0.15–0.30 |
| Sand and heath | 0.10–0.25 |
| Forest | 0.05–0.18 |
| Surface of the sea | 0.08–0.10 |

For the visible spectrum, the albedos of wet or dark-colored surfaces tend to be lower than those of dry or light-colored surfaces. But the albedo of a surface may be quite different for different wavelengths: for infrared radiation the albedo of most natural materials is rather low.

*Conductivity*

Conductivity refers to the speed with which heat or sound passes through a given material, once having penetrated its surface. Heat flows rapidly through substances of high conductivity, and slowly through those of low conductivity. Variation in conductivity is the basis of insulation and also controls the rate with which reservoirs of heat in the earth or the sea can be built up or released. Commercial insulation, for example, is a material of very low conductivity, thermal or acoustic. A piece of warm metal feels much hotter than wood of the same temperature simply because the metal, with its high conductivity, releases its heat more rapidly. In general, the conductivity of natural materials decreases as these materials are drier, less dense, and more porous. For example, the thermal conductivity of some natural materials decreases in the following order: solid granite, ice, wet sand, humus, wet marshy soil, still water, old snow, dry sand, fresh snow, peat, still air.

*Convection*

Heat and sound are also distributed by fluid movement, or convection. The significant factors here are speed and turbulence, or the degree to which movement occurs as random eddies rather than as a steady directed flow. Turbulence disperses heat or sound waves or impurities, while steady flow may contain them and thus preserve contrasts. Air turbulence may increase with height, at the microclimatic scale, and then decrease again in the upper levels of the air. Wind direction can be strikingly different at different levels, while wind speed tends to increase with height because of the surface friction of the ground: the wind speed 3 inches off the ground may be only 30 percent of the speed 6 feet above the ground. The speed 6 inches up may be 50 percent of that figure, and that 3 feet up 80 percent. Wind speed, by its rate of transport of heat, has a marked effect on cooling. A 30-mile-per-hour wind with air at 30°F has six times the cooling effect of still air at 10°F. Any frostbitten nose will testify to this. As another example, when a 12-mile-per-hour wind at 32°F is reduced in speed to 3 miles per hour before it strikes a house, fuel consumption in that house may be halved.

Finally, we must consider the ability of an object to store the heat it receives, an ability that results from its total mass and its specific heat, or the amount of heat energy absorbed by a unit mass for each unit rise in temperature. A cool object of high specific heat and large mass whose interior is accessible to heat flow via conduction or convection will absorb large amounts of heat over long periods. When exterior temperatures drop, it can also return that energy over a long interval. A house with thick masonry walls will be cooler in the heat of day and warmer at night than a flimsier structure. Large water bodies, with their internal convections and low surface albedo, act like climatic flywheels to even out the daily or seasonal swings of temperature.

*Specific heat*

Of first importance is the nature of surface materials. If the ground has a low albedo and a high conductivity, then the resulting microclimate is mild and stable, since excess heat is quickly absorbed and stored and as quickly released when temperatures drop. Surface materials of high albedo and low conductivity, on the other hand, make for a microclimate of extremes, since they do not help to balance the swings of the weather. Thus the sea or grass or wet ground tends to even out the climate, while the weather over sand or snow or pavement is more violent: hot in the sun and cold at night. The monthly range of temperature in June in one locality when the air temperature varied by only 45°F was 106° on a bituminous pavement and 52° in the grass. On a day when the standard temperature was 77°, the surface of a concrete walk was at 95° and that of a dark slate roof at 110°.

*The role of surface material*

Drainage of wet land increases the albedo and decreases conductivity and so makes the local climate more unstable. At the same time humidity will fall, and the cooling effect of evaporation from damp ground will be lost. A water surface usually has a low albedo, but not for light striking it at a low angle of incidence. Here the albedo increases rapidly, and the water acts as a mirror. Heat and light are directed at waterside objects both from the air and from the water surface. This effect may be unpleasant in a summer house facing the late afternoon sun across a lake, but it may be desirable for the growth of crops on steep slopes overlooking water to the east or west.

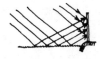

A high density of man-made structures or a substantial area of paving increases the albedo significantly and thus results in higher summer temperatures. Moreover, since the land drains more quickly and is more impervious to water vapor, the general humidity tends to fall. A deep fall of fresh snow will raise daytime temperatures by reflection, while insulating the surfaces it covers.

*Slope and orientation*

The slope of ground surfaces has an effect as important as that of surface material. The word *climate* is in fact derived from the Greek for "slope." The principal factors involved are the orientation of ground with respect to the sun and the general form of topography as it affects air movement.

Orientation is most critical in the middle latitudes, since in the far north much of the radiation is diffuse, coming from a cloudy sky and illuminating north slopes as much as south slopes. In the tropics the high angle of the sun tends to minimize the differences between the orientation of slope. Maximum direct radiation is received by the surface that is perpendicular to the direction of the sun, and this depends on latitude, season, and hour of the day. Thus a south slope will receive more sun than flat land, and in midsummer a northwest wall may even be warmer than a south wall. A 10 percent slope to the south will receive as much direct radiation (and to that extent have the same climate) as flat land 6 degrees closer to the equator, or the difference in latitude between Portland, Maine, and Richmond, Virginia. On a cloudless day at 40 degrees north latitude, the total direct and diffuse radiation on a 10-degree (17½ percent) slope attains the following approximate percentages of the possible maximum, depending on season and the orientation of the slope:

| Slope Direction | Midsummer | Equinox | Midwinter |
|---|---|---|---|
| North | 95% | 55% | 15% |
| East or west | 100 | 60 | 25 |
| South | 100 | 70 | 35 |

The same data for a perpendicular wall (where the possible maximum is about one-half of the maximum above) are:

| Wall Faces | Midsummer | Equinox | Midwinter |
|---|---|---|---|
| North | 40% | 15% | 5% |
| East or west | 90 | 70 | 25 |
| South | 50 | 95 | 100 |

Structures will receive substantially different amounts of radiation depending on their orientation. In the higher latitudes most of the rooms of a dwelling should get some sun on a winter day, and all of them should receive adequate daylight. Rooms with large glass areas should not face toward the low western sun of summer, which is difficult to shield off. Except for such simple rules, however, it is useless to set down any general precepts for building orientation. There are many techniques of sun shielding, but much radiation is diffuse and directionless, and a variety of outlook is also desirable. Windows to the north will look upon a landscape flooded with sun. Particularly when dealing with tall structures, we may be just as concerned with how their orientation and placement affect the radiation falling on the ground about their base. Artificial warming and cooling is far more difficult to achieve outdoors than in. Instead of relying on standard orientations, a whole system of measures must be taken to produce an optimum local climate.

Structures and trees modify the climate in their shadow by blocking direct sun radiation. In many cases the designer wants to arrange these shadows to avoid radiation when it is hot and to receive it when it is cold. Deciduous trees are ideal for this purpose since they cut off the summer sun and let the winter sun shine through. In other cases the site planner wishes to provide a variety of sun and shade at any moment so that the inhabitants may choose their own preferred climate. To study the whole system of moving shadows, the planner must understand the geometry of the sun path in the heavens and how it varies with hour, date, and latitude.

*Shading*

At the vernal and autumnal equinox, the sun appears to rise due east at 6 A.M., rising and falling in an arc that at local noon is at its highest point. At this time, in the northern hemisphere, the sun appears due south of the observer, and its angular height above the southern horizon equals 90 degrees less the latitude of the place. In midwinter the day is shorter; the sun rises and sets well to the south of the equinoctial points, and its noon position is 23½ degrees below equinoctial noon. In midsummer the day is longer, rising and setting are well to north of east or west, and the sun at noon is 23½ degrees above equinoctial noon. In 40-degree latitudes, for example, the midwinter rising is about 30 degrees south of east and an hour and a half later, and the setting 30 degrees south of west and an hour and a half earlier, than they are at the equinox, whereas at midsummer just the opposite occurs.

*Sun angle*

This rough description will give some sense of the

FIGURE 10 *Microclimate: the shade defines the crowd on a hot summer day (Via Calzaiuoli, Florence).*

shadow patterns arising from a given plan. But the designer usually wants more exact studies, and for this purpose there are tables available giving sun direction and altitude for different hours and seasons at various latitudes. Or he may construct such a table for himself (the method is described below). Using these statistics, he may draw shadow contours that show all the ground shaded during one given day or even during an entire year. Or, using sun direction and altitude at turning points in the year, he may make an analysis in section of the relation between a significant building or outdoor area and the objects that will shade it: trees, eaves, screens, and structures.

One of the most comprehensive and graphic methods is to place a model of all the potential shadow-casting objects on a device that will simulate the sun direction for various times and seasons at that latitude. A simple way of doing this is to construct a cardboard dial with a central pointer, marking it with the sun's shadow path at different seasons for the latitude, in other words, a crude sundial for the given place. Attach this sundial to a three-dimensional model of the proposed site plan, with the meridian of the dial oriented to model north, and then, out in the sunlight, tip and tilt the base of the model until the pointer on the little sundial indicates the right hour and season. The sunlight is now falling on the model in the same way it would fall on the real object at that time and place. Bright artificial light may also be used if the source is over 10 feet away. Shadow patterns are given directly, and even the interior lighting of rooms may be studied if window openings are to scale.

The seasonal variation of sun angle depends solely on the latitude of a site. Given the latitude and the season of year, the direction and altitude of the sun may be calculated for any hour (local sun time) by these two formulas:

$$\sin Al = \cos D \cos L \cos H + \sin D \sin L,$$

$$\sin Az = \frac{\cos D \sin H}{\cos Al}.$$

where
$Al$ = altitude of the sun above the horizon.
$Az$ = azimuth of the sun, measured east or west from south
(or from the north if the site is south of the equator).
$L$ = latitude of the place.
$D$ = declination of the sun for the given season above or below the celestial equator (which is also the apparent

*How to make a*
*sundial*

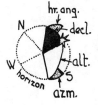

path traveled by the sun on that moment in spring and fall when day and night are of equal length), a northerly declination being positive and a southerly being negative (which is reversed in the southern hemisphere).

$H =$ local hour angle of the sun, east or west of the noon meridian. Each hour equals 15°, and thus H = 0 at noon, H = 15° at 11 A.M. or 1 P.M., H = 30° at 10 A.M. or 2 P.M., and so on. This is local sun time, and not standard time or daylight savings time.

Since the movement of the sun is symmetrical, it is necessary to make these calculations for only half the day, the altitude being the same for the same hour angles in the morning or afternoon, and the azimuth also having the same values, except that it is east of south in the morning and west of south in the afternoon.

Since the seasonal change is indicated by the change in sun declination, $D$, and this changes with rough regularity, it is usually necessary to calculate sun angles only for midwinter, midsummer, and the two equinoxes, spring and fall. These indicate the range and midpoint of sun positions, and the other times of year can be estimated between them. At the equinox, $D = 0$. At the winter solstice, $D = -23°22\frac{1}{2}'$; at the summer solstice, $D = 23°22\frac{1}{2}'$. However, if the exact declination of the sun is needed for any particular day of the year, it may be read from a solar ephemeris. In using negative angles in the formula, keep in mind that, for any angle $\alpha$, $\sin(\alpha) = -\sin\alpha$ but $\cos(-\alpha) = \cos\alpha$.

These formulas may be used for any place, any fractional time, and any particular date. It is not difficult to construct a table for a particular place, showing the altitude and azimuth of the sun to the nearest degree for each hour of the day at the solstices and the equinoxes. This is well worth the time for important work and for later reference in designs located in the same area. Such a table may be used to plot the shadows in plan or section for any critical time or date or to make a simple sundial to be used in orienting the shadow-casting model described earlier. Once azimuth and altitude are known for a given latitude, such a sundial is constructed as follows:

On a card, locate a point O, and draw a line NOS, which will represent the north-south line, while at O will be erected a vertical pin of any convenient height, $P$. For

any given hour and season, the shadow of the top of the pin is
located by drawing a line from O whose angle from north
equals the azimuth of the sun from south (since the direction
of the shadow opposes that of the light source) and which lies
west of north in the morning and east of it in the afternoon.
Lay off a distance X along this line out from O where

$$X = \frac{P}{\tan Al},$$

P being the pin's height and Al the altitude of the sun. The
point so obtained is the shadow tip at that hour and season.

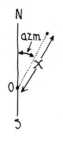

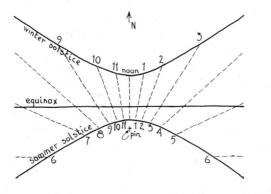

FIGURE 11 *A typ-
ical sundial dia-
gram resulting
from the proce-
dure described in
the text. It can be
used to orient a
model to a light
source and thus
to simulate the
angle of sunlight
at a certain hour,
season, and lati-
tude.*

This construction may be repeated, to give a diagram of
the form shown in Figure 11. The seasonal lines (the path of
the shadow tip at that season throughout the day) and the
hour lines (the location of the shadow tip at that hour
throughout the seasons) have been drawn by connecting the
separate points for particular hours and seasons. Since the
hour lines are always straight and converge on a common
point on NS below O, since the seasonal line at the equinoxes is also straight and is at right angles to NS, and since
the solstice lines are smooth parabolas, it is possible to sketch
this diagram without actually computing all 21 hour and
season points.

Having made the diagram, put a vertical pin of the
correct height P at O. Place the dial flat on a model, with the
line NO parallel to the north direction on the model. If the
model is now put in the sun and tilted so that the shadow of
the pin's tip falls at the correct intersection of hour and season lines, then the sunlight is falling on the model as it
would do in reality at that hour, season, and latitude.

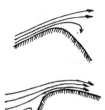

The topography affects air movement as well as orientation to the sun. Wind speeds on the crest of a ridge may be 20 percent greater than those on flat ground, and wind is generally quieter on the lee side than on the weather side of a hill. But the latter condition may be reversed if the lee slope is gentle and the weather side is steep.

Cold air floods are a nocturnal phenomenon on open slopes. A layer of air near the ground is cooled by the ground beneath it, which loses its heat by radiation outward to the night sky. This film of cold air flows downhill as a shallow sheet, gathering into a stream in open valleys or a still pool where it is blocked by some "dam" of topography or cover. Positions at the foot of long open slopes are notoriously cold and damp, and hollows become frost pockets. Such floods can be diverted by barriers uphill or prevented from pooling by breaching the downhill dam.

Cold air pockets may persist during the next day if they are large enough and especially if fog or haze has formed to prevent the sun from warming the ground surface. In this case the air is coldest close to the ground and warmer higher up, a situation called an "inversion" because it is the reverse of the normal daytime condition. The formation is stable because cold air is heavier than warm, and there is none of the customary upward movement of warm, light surface air. If the day should also be windless, then fog and smoke will not be dissipated, and thus smog will collect over urban areas.

Other local air movements, such as the shore breeze, may be set up by topography. At the shore of seas or very large lakes on an otherwise windless day there will typically be an afternoon breeze blowing from the sea and a night breeze off the land. This is due to the warm air rising sometimes from the land and sometimes from the water, depending on the relative warmth of each. The resulting inflow of surface air at the bottom of the rising column creates the surface breeze.

In brief, in the temperate zone the best local climates tend to be on south or southeast slopes, near water, and on upper or middle slopes rather than at their foot or crest.

*Climatic effect*
*of plants*

All these effects are in their turn modified by the plant cover or the structures that occur on the land. Plants alter the form of the surface, increasing the area for radiation and transpiration, shading the ground, braking air movement, and trapping air within the stand. The net result is a cooler, more humid, more stable microclimate. Plants will also trap a certain amount of smoke and dust, but this is more likely to

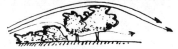

affect their own health than it is to purify the air in any substantial way. Thick belts of shrubs or trees are effective windbreaks. They reduce wind velocities by more than 50 percent for a distance downwind of ten times their height and by 35 percent even for twice that distance. If one is planting trees or shrubs for this purpose, the belt should be deep (50 to 150 feet), should rise gradually in height on the windward side, and should be somewhat open, to reduce air turbulence in its lee.

Structures, as well as plants, affect air movement. They block and divert winds or channel them through narrow openings. This may be desirable along a street in summer or may be quite disagreeable underneath a large slab building on stilts in a winter storm. Summer breezes can be invited and winter winds diverted if the prevailing wind direction shifts with the seasons, as it often does. However, we need not make the mistake of Vitruvius: winds do not always blow from standard directions!

*Buildings and airflow*

The course of winds affects the rate of cooling, the removal of impurities, the transmission of sound, and even such details as the play of fountains. Turbulent air disperses sound waves, and steady winds affect their audible reach. Airflows that are more than 6 feet off the surface on which people stand are of little avail in lowering the effective temperature. Local cover and structure has most effect when general winds are light and steady. With strong wind and much turbulence, their influence is more erratic. Under such conditions, for example, smoke contamination will disperse rapidly, even downwind from the source and regardless of local cover.

Unfortunately, we still have a great deal to learn about wind movements within groups of buildings. In general, the taller and the longer a building or other barrier to the wind is, the more extensive is the eddy on the downwind side, a zone of low pressure where air is relatively quiet and is moving erratically or even in a contrary direction to prevailing flow. But the thicker such a building is in the direction of airflow, the smaller the area of wind eddy, at least up to a point. Thus a thin, tall, long wall is the most effective windbreak. Surprisingly enough, it may be more effective if it is not completely impenetrable to the wind, so that pressure is not lowered so far that it causes strong air turbulence.

Air movement between groups of buildings is so complex that it may be desirable, for example, to bring a low building close up behind a tall building to improve the ventilation of the lower structure! Therefore it is useful to study air movements through the site on a scale model. Such studies are best made with technical apparatus, by trained personnel, in a low-speed wind tunnel; this is the only way to obtain quantitative data on probable wind speed and pressure. Without such apparatus, however, it is still possible to predict the general pattern of wind movement, including wind direction, the rough relative intensities of flow, and the regions of calm or of gustiness, by a simple device in which the general pattern of wind movement around a building group is deduced from an architectural model.

*A crude wind tunnel*

Make a rectangular box, open at both ends and large enough to contain the model. The larger the model scale, the better. Over one open end of the box place a fine screen, and attach a funnel-shaped intake, both of which will help to smooth the flow of incoming air. To the other end attach a large fan that will draw air through the tunnel. Luckily, the relationship of various physical constants operating at the scale of real buildings and at that of architectural models is such that the air speed through the tunnel need not move at the correct model scale as long as only the general wind pattern is under observation.

The tunnel may be made of glass or transparent plastic, or it may be provided with viewing ports. If background surfaces are made matte black and a strong cross light is directed into the tunnel, the effects are more visible. The model may now be inserted, the fan turned on, and smoke introduced at the intake end. Smoke can be generated by a cigar, a piece of punk, a beekeeper's smoker, or similar devices. The streamlines of smoke will make the general wind patterns clearly visible, and they may be photographed. The model may be turned about in order to study various wind directions.

The airflows may be studied in greater detail by means of a short piece of fine white thread tied to the end of a long thin rod. As this tiny "pennant" is moved about in the model space, it will make the local airflow visible by the way it streams out, droops, flutters, flies at an angle, or even turns backward.

No conclusions as to wind speed or force can be made by this method, but the general pattern is approximated. Strictly speaking, it is necessary to include in the model the environment some distance upwind, as well as the ground detail that acts as a brake on airflow. The effect of ground detail may be approximated by a low picket fence, 5 or 6 feet high to the model scale, placed at the intake end. To the extent that these two precautions are neglected, the device will falsify air movements at the upwind side of the model or immediately along the ground surface.

Man has modified the microclimate over much of the earth. He has simplified it by reducing contrasts by his drainage, forest clearance, plowing, and planting of standard crops. He has also invented a new microclimate, that of the city, which is the result of the extensive paving, the dense structures, and the emission of heat, noise, and impurities. Heat is emitted at such a rate that it is estimated that by the year 2000 the average man-engendered heat output per unit area from the Boston-Washington urban strip will be 50 percent of the incoming solar radiation in wintertime. Thus a "heat island" is formed over the city, and the upward convection within this "island" generates clouds overhead and draws land breezes in from the surrounding countryside. Rainfall increases; clouds and haze cut down solar radiation. This pall will blanket a far larger region than just the built-up area. Happily, this effect is reversible. For example, in London, where open heating fires have been banned, winter sunshine has increased 70 percent in the last decade, and ground visibility has improved three times.

*The city climate*

*Reference 41*

The extensive paved surfaces cause rapid runoff, with a loss of local humidity and cooling, and more frequent and more disastrous floods downstream. The multitude of structures check the wind, so that street level winds may be decreased by 25 percent, relative to rural areas. Thus urban areas are warmer, dustier, drier, and yet have more rain, cloud, and fog than their rural counterparts. The noise level is higher, there are high levels of air pollution, and there is more glare but less sunlight. Wind velocities are lower, while floods are more frequent and more sharply peaked.

All of these factors make the "city climate," which is one of the chief popular criticisms of city life. Contrary to belief, these defects are due not to the crowding of people but to the nature of city structures and to mechanical emissions. Healthy bodies give off no poisons to the air. The atmospheric ill effects of collecting people in confined spaces are mostly due to the resultant heat and humidity and to the psychological effect of odors. Only when a space is airtight must we worry about the oxygen level.

Once we understand the nature of microclimatic effects, it should be possible to make the urban climate more comfortable than the rural one, rather than the reverse. Manipulation of surfaces and structures and the use of direct artificial devices (refrigerated or heated panels, fans, water sprays) may produce climates more desirable than any "natural" alternative. By the end of the nineteenth century, equipment for indoor environmental control amounted to 10 percent of total building cost. Now it is 40 percent. Shall we see a similar trend in the out-of-doors?

When the site planner becomes aware of the variations in microclimate, he will use many sources beside his own judgment to evaluate a locality: the weathering of older construction, the knowledge of old residents, and the evidence furnished by existing plants. The types of plants and particularly their health, rate of development, and budding time are sensitive indexes of fine variations in climate. The designer tends to avoid certain situations or to make special provision for them: steep north slopes, west slopes facing water, hilltops, frost pockets, or positions at the foot of long open slopes, bare dry ground, nearby sources of noise or air pollution. There will be other situations that will attract him, such as middle slopes facing southeast to southwest, locations near water, well-planted areas, and so on. Even more important, however, he will use his knowledge of climate to change the local weather. Having evaluated his site in relation to the general climate, he will orient his structures to take maximum advantage of sun, shade, and prevailing winds. He will produce shade at the right spots by means of trees or artificial structures and channel or divert the wind or cold air floods with buildings and planting. He will select surface materials for their albedo. Neglect of these factors is bound to produce a worsening of climate in the act of building. Attention to them, even with our present incomplete knowledge, can improve it substantially.

It remains true, however, that we have much to learn about climate, particularly about its application to the art of site planning. The original studies of the microclimate were concerned with agricultural problems. The outdoor effects of man-made structures and materials are not yet well understood, and there is not much quantitative data that a designer can use in a precise way. Nor is there any large-scale systematic recording of the microclimate in urban and suburban areas. Because of its importance for comfort and health, should not a planner have microclimatic data, just as he has topographic, subsoil, and utility information as a matter of routine?

The control of noise outdoors is a special subject in itself. Little work has been done on it since attention has been concentrated on interior acoustics. Although an environment with too little noise is conceivable, the usual problem is to reduce either the noise level or the information content of the noise. Sound sources are increasingly powerful and ubiquitous.

Noise levels are measured in decibels, a logarithmic scale that is 1 at the threshold of hearing and 140 at the threshold of pain. Each interval of 10 decibels indicates a level of sound energy ten times greater than before, an increase that the human ear may distinguish as being roughly twice as loud. A noise 20 decibels higher than another has one hundred times the energy of the latter, and so on. For example, various sources scale roughly as follows:

| Decibels | Typical Source |
| --- | --- |
| 10 | Quiet rustle of leaves |
| 20–30 | Soft whisper |
| 40 | Hum of a small electric clock |
| 50 | Ambient noise, house kitchen |
| 60 | Normal conversation |
| 70–80 | Busy street |
| 90–100 | Subway close at hand (or a piano!) |
| 110–120 | Auto horn or pneumatic hammer |
| 160 | Jet airplane |

In most areas we like to keep noise levels down to 50 or 60 decibels, and down to 30 decibels just outside rooms devoted to study or sleep, if they are to be allowed the luxury of open windows. But noises are annoying or noticeable as much because of their frequency, that is, their pitch, as because of their level of loudness. High-pitched noises, or ones that interfere with the frequencies of human speech, will be particularly obnoxious. Sounds whose pitch contrasts sharply with the background noise will be picked up even if they are relatively soft. The frequency of noises audible to the human ear usually ranges between 20 and 20,000 cycles per second or 50 and 10,000 cycles at low noise levels. Ordinary street noises range in frequency from about 40 to 8000 cycles per second, while most human speech is transmitted in the 100 to 3000 cycle range.

Outdoor sounds are attenuated in many ways before reaching us. The most useful means available to a site planner is simply the "thinning out" of sound as it travels from

*Sound transmission*

the source. Each doubling of the distance between source and receiver causes sound levels to drop by 6 decibels. That is, noise decreases as the square of the distance from a point source. But from a linear source such as a highway, it decreases only directly as the distance, and thus sound levels may drop only about 3 decibels for each doubling of distance. To prevent the transmission of speech, windows that can be opened and that communicate with separate rooms should not be closer than 30 to 40 feet apart if face to face and no closer than 6 to 10 feet if on the same wall plane.

Sound is dispersed by turbulence and gusty winds. Barriers of planting or structure will also reduce sound transmission. Belts of trees are only partly useful, being most efficient against the noises of high frequency, whose wavelengths are not much greater than the average size of leaves and other obstacles they meet, that is, noises of over 10,000 cycles per second. Tests have indicated that 1000 feet of woods, thick enough to limit visibility to 70 feet, will decrease noise in the 200–1000 cycles per second range by only about 20 decibels more than would the open distance alone.

Solid barriers — earth, walls, and buildings — are more effective in cutting down noise. If the barrier is relatively impenetrable to sound, the noise reaching the receiver is what has passed around the barrier. The effectiveness of the barrier, relative to none at all, increases as barrier height increases, as it is moved closer to either source or receiver and as the frequency of the emitted sound increases. Thus a high wall close to the source will reduce high-frequency noise markedly, whereas a low wall, halfway between source and receiver, has little effect on low-frequency sound.

More precisely, a solid barrier reduces noise levels (in addition to reduction by distance) by the number of decibels

$$D = 10 \left[ \frac{30h^2 (a + b)}{\lambda \, ab} \right]^{1/6}$$

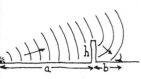

In this formula, $h$ is the height of the barrier in feet above the line between source and receiver, $a$ is the distance in feet from source to barrier, $b$ is the distance from receiver to barrier, and $\lambda$ is the wavelength of the sound in feet ($\lambda$ equals 1130 divided by the frequency of the sound in cycles per second). This calculation is valid where the source and receiver are on the ground and approximately level.

Finally, outdoor noise is absorbed to some extent by

ground and wall surfaces; thus the use of nonreflective textures will have an effect in reducing sound levels. But it is
difficult to make artificial surfaces that are both weather-
proof and also sufficiently fine textured to be efficient sound
absorbers. Snow and fine-grained natural vegetative covers
are somewhat effective. If noise levels cannot be brought
down to an acceptable point, it is often possible to mask the
unwanted sound by adding desirable or random sound: the
play of water, music, the rustle of leaves, even "static" or
"white noise."

Thus the site planner puts his first reliance on the
suppression of noise sources or on separating activities from
them by substantial distances. His next defense is to use
buildings or other solid objects as partial barriers to sound
transmission or to increase the background noise to mask annoying intrusions or to reduce their information content. As
his last stand, he completely seals his buildings and aban-
dons the outdoors.

The plant cover is a most sensitive index of soil and
weather conditions. To take only a few common trees as examples: red maple, alder, tupelo, hemlock, and willow mark
wet ground that is poorly drained. The oak and hickory association grows on warm, dry land, spruce and fir in cold,
moist places. Pitch pine and scrub oak are signs of very dry
land and of perfect drainage. Red cedars indicate poor soil.
The list can easily be extended in any locality. It is a list
worth learning and using as a predictor of site constraints.
The well-adapted local flora will be best for new plantings,
or at least it is a good guide to selecting new species of similar habit. The suitability of plants for any position depends
very much on drainage, acidity, and humus, as well as on
temperature, sunlight, moisture, and winds. Watching for
the order in which similar plants bud out in the spring is a
delicate index of small variations in microclimate. Some
sites are particularly difficult for plants. The inner city is
especially hard because of the lack of water, light, and
humus, and because of the air pollution, the heat reflected
from the pavements, and the poisonous chemicals used. But
there are also special difficulties to be met in flood plains and
wetlands, at seashores where plants are exposed to salty
winds, on dry barren ground, and so on. Any new planting
must respect these special limitations.

*Plants as Site
Indicators*

The plant cover is very likely undergoing succession
and so will not endure in its present form. Certainly it will
change as human use puts new pressures on it. The passage

*Plant
succession*

of feet and wheels·will destroy the native ground cover and compact the earth above the feeding roots of trees, if nothing else. The water table is likely to fall; pollution will appear; the climate will change. Thus it is rarely possible to retain the native flora intact. It must, at least in part, be replaced or modified.

Even if the plant association will be stable, the individual specimens will grow and die. It is a mistake to preserve large but ancient or decayed trees, while cutting out the young plants that would normally have replaced them. New plantations seem skimpy at first but are often later desperately overcrowded. They must then be ruthlessly thinned out. The advantage lies with plantings of mixed age, which are constantly growing their own replacements. Quick-growing trees can be planted for the immediate effect — beech or white oak may be put in for the future. New plants and changes in existing plant associations are therefore settled on with two criteria in mind: (1) their ecological harmony with the site and its intended use and (2) their fitness for a planned program of continuous management. Plants that have similar requirements of water, soil, and climate are grouped together. Those that require special care are usually avoided.

In any undisturbed wood the plants occupy a whole range of levels, from the dominant trees of the canopy down through the smaller trees of the understory, the shrubs, the large herbs, and the prostrate ground covers. True to their preference for the savanna, men tend to simplify this system to its extremes: the canopy and the ground cover — the tall forest tree and the grass. So the site planner is most often concerned with the ground covers and the ornamental trees and tends to produce his spatial effects with them. This is a mistaken simplification. In many localities, a closer parallel to the natural association is a more apt choice. Nevertheless, since these are the two plant types so often called for in practice, they are worth some further comment.

*Ground covers*    Mowed grass is not the only available managed ground cover. There are a number of others, each suitable for a particular situation: bearberry, bugleweed, clover, English ivy, ground ivy, prostrate juniper, creeping lilyturf, pachysandra, periwinkle, wichura rose, goldmoss stonecrop. Grass is too often used where it is deeply shaded or on too steep a slope. But it remains a good choice where the ground is to be a walking surface. Exhaustive plant lists may be found in other sources, and designers will do well to consult the local plantsmen. Even with regard to grass, there are dozens of useful varieties, and seed mixes are chosen depending on whether a fine or rough turf is wanted and whether the lawn is to be cut high or low, to have heavy or light traffic, to be in the sun or in the shade, on soil that is wet or dry, acid or alkaline, polluted or clean. Grass is usually directly seeded on a prepared and fertilized 6-inch topsoil layer but is occasionally established directly by transplanting turf. It can also be seeded hydraulically, along with a liquid fertilizer on difficult ground or when the rapid cover of an extensive area is required.

Trees are chosen for their ecological preferences and their maintenance, as well as for their texture, form, and color. It is preferable to use native trees and local sources, although nursery-grown trees are less likely to fail than those collected in the woods. Trees that have grown in a wood must be preserved in a clump since they have shallow roots, while trees that were originally isolated or in open fence lines should be kept so. Even if left in place, mature trees will not survive a violent change of habitat. They can lose some of their roots (even up to one-half of them if they have been carefully managed and pruned), but there must be no lowering of the ground level within their root space. The ground can be raised somewhat, but only if a large well is built around the trunk and the ground over the feeding roots is brought up to the new level with coarse stone fill. A change in groundwater or in the microclimate is likely to be fatal. Trees must be protected against damage to their bark during construction. Young trees can be transplanted rather easily, and so can large mature specimens — even 30 feet high — although this is expensive and requires special equipment.

*Trees*

*References 31, 32*

Although local plant lists and knowledge must always be consulted, it is nevertheless useful to list and describe here those most common trees which are so often used in site development in the United States. In other areas, of course, entirely different materials will be used. Even if plants are suitable, they may simply not be obtainable in many parts of the world where commercial nurseries are not developed.

The list to follow is an extremely restricted one. It includes only those particularly handsome or useful cultivated trees, over 40 feet high in maturity, which can be grown in most parts of the United States — that is, which can withstand winter temperatures of at least $-20°F$. Furthermore, these trees are not to be short-lived or disease-prone or to re-

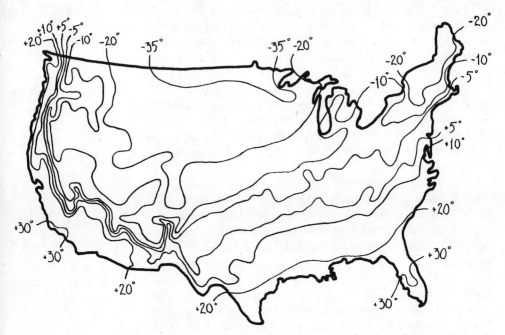

FIGURE 12    *Average annual minimum temperatures for the United States (Source:* The Yearbook of Agriculture, *1949, U.S. Department of Agriculture).*

quire any special maintenance. They must also survive urban or suburban growing conditions. If a listed tree should be doubtful on any one of these grounds, it is marked with an asterisk (*). These conditions are strict enough to shorten the list of trees to about thirty species, and many familiar trees are thereby excluded. It is not proposed that all tree plantings should be limited to this list. Smaller trees and trees native to a locality or adaptable to some special condition or favored for some special quality will often be preferred.

The list gives the height and spread of the mature tree, its rate of growth, its climatic and soil requirements, its texture, color, and form, whether it is an evergreen, can be transplanted easily, is disease-free, or requires some special maintenance. If it is particularly suited to some special habitat (inner city, seashore, dry ground), this fact is also noted. A simple line silhouette is drawn in the margin for each species, to a common scale. The accompanying map of the United States (Figure 12) shows the average annual minimum temperatures to be expected in various localities, which can be compared with the indicated hardiness of these or other species.

e               An evergreen tree

125 × 30        Height and spread of mature specimens in
                favorable conditions

r,m,s           Rate of growth:rapid (over 2 ft/yr); medium
                (1–2 ft/yr); or slow (less than 1 ft/yr).

− 30°           Hardy where the average minimum tem-
                perature is above this level

c               Hardy in severe inner city conditions

p               Particularly free of pests, diseases, and
                other maintenance problems

s               Tolerant of poor soil

t               Large specimens transplant easily

*               Not strictly within the criteria of the list for
                some special reason explained

*Abies concolor* (White Fir), e 120 × 60 m − 20°.
Pyramidal, almost columnar, dense. Foliage to ground persists to maturity. Bluish green needles in thick planes on
horizontal or down-sloping branches. Heavy, shadowed
texture. Needs moist soil, tolerates shade. Withstands heat.

*Acer platanoides* (Norway Maple), 50 × 40 m − 40° ct.
Broad, roundheaded, regular outline. Large broad leaves,
medium green, smooth. Coarse texture of light and shade;
deep shade under tree; difficult to grow anything under
it. Clear yellow in autumn, leaves persistent. Yellow flowers in April. Good street tree. Will tolerate seashore conditions.

*Acer rubrum* (Swamp, Red, or Water Maple) 60 × 40 r
− 40° t.
Round or oval, dense, ascending branches. A multitude of
tiny red flowers in early spring; brilliant scarlet, orange,
yellow leaves in early fall. Smooth light gray bark on
young wood. Prefers wet ground but adapts. Sun or shade.
Tolerates seashore.

*Acer saccharum* (Sugar or Hard Maple), 75 × 40 m − 30° t.
Short trunk and upright branches form dense, compact,
oval crown. Large deep-cut leaves, smooth dark green,
whitish beneath, brilliant yellow, orange, and scarlet in
autumn. Lacy yellow flowers in spring. Sweet sap. Needs
moist, well-drained soil, pure air, full sun. Finest of the
maples.

*Aesculus hippocastanum* (Horse Chestnut), 60 × 30 m − 35° ct.

Roundheaded, pyramidal, visible stout stem and branch structure, bold silhouette. Large leathery leaves in horizontal clusters, medium green. Open, coarse, feathery texture. Large creamy upright flower spikes at twig ends in late spring, like candles. Makes litter of leaves and nuts. Large varnished buds in winter, leaves open suddenly in spring. Needs rich moist soil, sun. Brittle; subject to leaf scorch in late summer. Tolerates seashore conditions.

*\*Ailanthus altissima* (Tree of Heaven), 50 × 30 r − 20° cps.

Open form, coarsely branched, spreading, stark winter silhouette. Large compound bright green leaves, malodorous when crushed. Staminate flowers also malodorous, but soon gone; pistillate flowers turn to coppery red fruit. Self-seeding, very vigorous, grows anywhere. Coarse "tropical" texture, striped and dotted shade. Smoke-, dust-, disease-resistant, roots penetrating. Tolerates salt spray, wet or dry or poor soils. Brittle. Short-lived: only 25–30 years.

*Catalpa speciosa* (Northern Catalpa), 60 × 40 s, − 20° cs.

Generally pyramidal, but an irregular outline. The thick, irregular, but generally horizontal branches are clearly visible. Large long-stalked light green leaves in bursts on ridged branchlets. Heavy, plastic texture, many holes. Showy spotted white flowers in June and July. Long, slender curving pods, persistent in winter, rattling in wind. Withstands heat and drought.

*Cercidiphyllum japonicum* (Katsura Tree), 60 × 30 r − 25° p.

Spreading or ascendant; loose, willowy outline; branches close to ground; leaves close to branches. Fine texture. Can be made columnar in habit. Foliage rosy in spring, blue-green in summer, yellow and scarlet in autumn. Rich moist soil and full sun.

*Fagus sylvatica* (European Beech), 100 × 70s − 20° t.

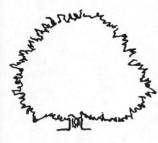

A great solid, spreading, oval tree. Needs growing room. Branches sweep ground, forming hollow within. Dense, dark green, small, thin, shining leaves: bronze and persistent in autumn. Gray smooth bark like muscled skin, heavy trunk and branches. Dark full texture, a massive sculptural tree. Rich, moist, well-drained soil, sun. Long-lived. Can be trimmed for hedges. There are fastigiate, weeping, and copper- or purple-leaved varieties. Long-lived: over 300 years. Cannot tolerate fill or compaction around roots.

*Fraxinus americana* (White Ash), 80 × 50 m − 35° cs.

Tall stem, compact, long oval head with regular outline, stout ascending branches, fairly high off ground. Large pinnate leaves, a dense rich texture striped with light and shade. Grass grows well beneath it. A stately tree. Deep purple or yellow in autumn. Seeds self vigorously. Must be sprayed for oyster scale.

*Gingko biloba* (Gingko), 80 × 40 s − 25° cpt.

Tall, spiky, ungainly outline becoming open and spreading; side branches diagonally erect. Fan-shaped leaves on short twigs, leathery light green, pale yellow in autumn. Fruit on pistillate tree malodorous, but pit is edible. An ancient and picturesque tree, perhaps the oldest surviving tree species.

*Gleditsia triacanthos inermis moraine* (Moraine Locust) 70 × 30 m − 25° cpst.

Roundheaded, loose branching, lacy compound foliage, feathery outline, open underneath, light shade. No thorns or pods on this variety. Leaves appear late in spring and drop off early in fall. Long-lived.

*Juniperus virginiana* (Eastern Red Cedar), e 60 × 20 s − 50° ps.

Narrow, upright compact. Can vary from a tall tree to a bush, depending on soil and climate. Tiny, scalelike or pointed, dark green leaves, aromatic, persistent for several years, gradually turning brown, giving a rusty overtone. A dark, fine, but rather open texture. Bark thin, red, stringy. Dark blue berries attract birds. Tolerates seashore and any soil but a swamp.

*Liriodendron tulipifera* (Tulip Tree), 150 × 70 r − 20° p.

Tall, straight stem, short branches high from ground. Oblong but irregular outline. Broad shining leaves, pale beneath, turning clear yellow in autumn. An open, spotted, trembling texture. Tuliplike flowers in June, greenish yellow with orange markings. Rich moist soil. Long-lived.

*Nyssa sylvatica* (Tupelo, Sour or Black Gum, Pepperidge, Beetlebung), 80 × 40 m − 20° p.

Erect, cylindrical or pyramidal, rounded crown, but variable. Short, rigid, crooked, horizontal, twiggy branches; bold winter outline. Rough, dark bark. Leaves leathery, dark green, dense, shining, turning flaming red in autumn. Fruit attracts birds. Shallow roots; wind may uproot tree if exposed. Needs rich, acid, wet soil. Tolerates seashore. Difficult to transplant except when small.

*Phellodendron amurense* (Amur Cork Tree), 40 × 40 r
−35° cst.

Low rounded outline, open interior. Low trunk; spreading, picturesque, corky, climbable branches, highly visible. Compound leaves, medium green, aromatic, at ends of branches, appearing late. Planes of light and dark. Abundant, persistent black fruit on female trees. Light shade.

*Pinus nigra* (Austrian Pine), e 80 × 40 m −30° s.

Pyramidal when young, later flat-topped with spreading branches. Horizontal branches in whorls, from close to ground; regular outline, dense foliage on exterior, open within; yellow-brown scaly bark. Long, stiff, thick needles, dull dark green. A heavy, dark, somber, rugged tree. Good windscreen; tolerates seashore, sand, acid or lime soil. Needs full sun. Transplant with care.

*Pinus resinosa* (Red or Norway Pine), e 75 × 40 m −50° ps.

Tall straight pyramidal tree, branched to ground, becoming wide-spreading when older. Stiff drooping branches, reddish scaly bark. Rather open outline and interior. Long, soft, coarse needles, shining dark green. An open, needly, gnarled texture. Long-lived, fairly disease-resistant, hardy, will tolerate rocky sandy soil. Needs full sun.

*\*Pinus strobus* (White Pine), e 100 × 40 m −35° t.

First a symmetrical pyramid; then tall and rather cylindrical; finally of picturesque wide-spreading outline in old age. Horizontal, open branches in regular whorls from tall dark gray stem. Long fragrant soft green needles in massive horizontal planes of a softly shaded, sculptural texture. Ground beneath carpeted with brown needles, intersected with twisting roots. Any moist but well-drained soil, needs sun. Long-lived, may grow very tall, but can be pruned. Subject to weevil and to white pine blister rust. But a majestic tree.

*Pinus sylvestris* (Scotch Pine), e 75 × 40 m −50°.

Open, pyramidal, when young; roundtopped, irregular, and picturesque when old. Stiff bluish green needles, red bark in older wood. Unique form and color. Seashore hardy.

*Pinus thunbergi* (Japanese Black Pine) e 60 × 30 s −5° t.

Dense and spreading, with crooked trunk and asymmetric head. Characteristic form achieved early, in old age rugged and picturesque. Retains lower branches into middle age; good for screening and mass planting. Very tolerant of seashore.

*Platanus acerifolia* (Sycamore, Buttonwood, Plane Tree),
90 × 60 r — 15° ct.
  Roundheaded, upright stem, spreading branches, deep
  shade beneath. Mottled gray and creamy trunk. Dense
  foliage, large maplelike leaves, light green, easily
  clipped, a cheerful spotted play of light and shade. Best
  in rich moist soil but adjusts. Tolerant of seashore. Subject
  to anthracnose and canker.

*Pseudotsuga taxifolia* (Douglas Fir), e 200 × 20 r — 20°.
  A regular pyramid with branches to ground when young;
  in age a towering stem with relatively small branches at
  top, and clear of them for one-third of height to ground.
  Very long-lived: 400–750 years. Soft blue-green needles
  on pendant branchlets; a dense fine texture. Cones in
  clusters. Can be pruned. Prefers a light, moist, rather
  acid soil, full sun. Rapid growth when young. Only the
  mountain variety hardy to — 20°. Subject to wind damage.

*Quercus alba* (White Oak), 80 × 60 s — 30°.
  A rounded, ragged outline; large, crooked, wide-spreading branches. Trunk and branch structure visually dominant. Broadens with age, requires growing room. Long-
  lived. Rough, light gray bark; deeply cut, dark green
  leaves, turning russet, wine-red in autumn. Leaves in
  clusters on the branches, persistent in winter. Best in
  dry, gravelly, sandy soil, but adaptable. Tolerates seashore. Difficult to transplant except when young.

*Quercus borealis* (Northern Red Oak), 70 × 40 r — 20° c.
  An irregular, roundheaded tree. Short massive ridged
  trunk divides into several stout branches, fairly high off
  ground. Finely cut leaves, medium green, turning dark
  red in autumn. A coarse, branchy texture.

*Quercus palustris* (Pin Oak), 75 × 40 m — 20° t.
  Stately, erect, cylindrical. Numerous slender horizontal
  branches downsweeping near ground. Lower branches
  drop off with age. Dense, deep-cut, shining green leaves,
  red in autumn. Best in moist, not alkaline, soil.

*Salix babylonica* (Weeping Willow) 40 × 40 r — 20° t.
  Roundtopped and full, with long pendulous branches,
  graceful, billowy and picturesque. The foliage is fine and
  narrow, set on fine branches, and moves in any breeze.
  Leaves appear early in spring and fall in a drought.
  Weak-wooded, cracks easily, subject to storm damage.
  Requires moist ground; roots penetrate and clog sewers
  and drains within 50 feet. Subject to diseases and pests;
  requires much maintenance. Use only in special situations, for the graceful and symbolic habit.

*Sophora japonica* (Pagoda or Scholar Tree), 70 × 50 r −30° cst.

A compact, low, round head of graceful, lacy outline, becoming like *Fraxinus* in habit with age. Decorative, bright green pinnate leaves. Trembling delicate texture, takes pruning well. Large clusters fragrant yellowish white flowers in August. Yellow pods through winter. Poor, dry soil. Tolerant of heat.

*\*Tilia cordata* (Little Leaf Linden), 70 × 40 s −30° ct.

Tall, rounded, broad-based, dense and regular. Branches often sweeping to ground, forming a "cave" beneath. Dark shade. Takes pruning well. Smallish bright green leaves, forming a dense, fine texture. Abundant fragrant yellow flowers in early summer, attracting bees. Needs moist soil. A solid, handsome shade tree. Needs spraying for aphids and leaf-eating insects.

*Tsuga canadensis* (Canadian or Eastern Hemlock), e 90 × 30 m −40°.

Pyramidal but rather open, feathery outline; scattered horizontal branches on tall stem, persistent to ground, many small drooping branchlets. Fine short needles, shiny dark green above, light green below. A fine feathery texture, open at the edge, dark at the stem. Ridged red-brown bark. Dark shade beneath. Long-lived, shade tolerant; deep moist soil, cool north slopes. Takes pruning and then grows dense; much used for hedges and mass plantings. Intolerant of city air.

*\*Ulmus americana* (American Elm) 100 × 80.

Stately, vase-shaped, high-branching, symbolic of old New England towns. It has no equal as an urban tree. Now disappearing, owing to two fatal diseases. In the hope that they may be conquered, specimens of the elm should regularly be replanted, lest it become extinct simply through disuse.

Aerial
Photographs

Vertical aerial photographs are an excellent source of detailed, renewable site data. Most designers see only woods, water, buildings, or roads in these photographs. They are put off by the ambiguous shadings, the doubtful scale, the way the photographs come in little pieces, no one of which ever covers the area of interest. Thus the clear, stable map is preferred. The map has exact boundaries, a fixed scale, and well-selected detail. But the designer misses a great deal and may even begin to think that the world is like a map. He is ignorant of the numerous compromises and generalizations that map making entails.

With a little practice, aerial photographs can be read

for soil type, plant cover, building type and repair, minor paths, traces of occasional activity, numbers of persons or cars present, drainage, erosion, or flooding, even for some underground or underwater features, or for the otherwise invisible traces of ancient occupation. These seemingly hidden things are evidenced by slight variations in soil color, ground level, or the vigor of plants, which can be read as a pattern when seen from the air. Pairs of photographs can be read for general or detailed topography or for lines of sight or the exact elevation of given points. Moreover, successive photographs indicate the changes in the landscape, whether caused by human or extrahuman agency. Because of this wealth of available data, any site planner should know how to interpret aerial photographs. In addition, sets of aerial photographs can be converted by specialists into contoured maps of great accuracy and detail. Supplemented by ground survey controls, they have become the preferred means for mapping extensive areas.

Photo interpretation includes the ability to recognize all kinds of features, how to orient and match the separate prints, how to determine scale and to correct for distortion, and how to use stereopairs for reading the landscape in three dimensions. Pairs of prints can be read with a very simple pocket instrument or even with the naked eye after a little practice. The result is a vision of what seems to be a marvelously detailed miniature three-dimensional model of the ground. Photo interpretation is covered in various manuals, *References 33, 43* too lengthy to summarize here. It is an easily acquired skill, based more on practice than on the theoretical study, and one well worth acquiring.

Finally, it is useful to set forth a checklist of site data of **A** Checklist of the kind that would be acquired in some rather normal example of site planning. Such a list would be drawn up after an initial analysis of the problem to guide the first sweep for information. Information would be gathered continuously as the problem developed, however. Its nature would change as the problem shifted. Too much data should not be gathered in the first stages, not only to save energy for later investigations but also to prevent being drowned in partly irrelevant material. Many of the topics listed here would at first be handled quite sketchily. The following list is appended simply as an example of its kind. The reasons for disdaining model lists have already been covered in Chapter 2. *See page 21*

1. Initial personal reconnaissance — notes, sketches, photos — apparent character, problems, and possibilities
2. Collation of existing data: base and contour maps, aerial

photos, geological soil and water surveys, climate records, ecological studies, engineering reports, borings, census material, histories, social studies, market reports, traffic studies, legal and public control documents, official proposals, records of current controversies

3. Summary description of the off-site context and its changes: geographic location, surrounding populations, social and political structure, general economy, ecological and hydrographic system, land-use patterns, access system, principal off-site destinations and facilities

4. Data on the site and its immediate context:

   A. *Physical data*

      (1) Geology and soil:
         a. Underlying geology, rock character and depth
         b. Soil type and depth, value as an engineering material and as a plant medium
         c. Fill, ledge, slides, subsidence

      (2) Water:
         a. Existing water bodies — variation and purity
         b. Natural and man-made drainage channels — flow, capacity, purity
         c. Surface drainage pattern, amount, blockages, undrained depressions
         d. Water table — elevation and fluctuation, springs
         e. Water supply — quantity and quality

      (3) Topography:
         a. Pattern of landforms
         b. Contours
         c. Slope analysis
         d. Visibility analysis
         e. Circulation analysis
         f. Unique features

      (4) Climate:
         a. Regional data on variation of temperature, precipitation, humidity, solar angle, cloudiness, wind direction and force
         b. Local microclimates: warm and cool slopes, air drainage, wind deflection and local breeze, shade, heat reflection and storage, plant indicators
         c. Sound levels, smell, atmospheric quality

      (5) Ecology:

      a. Dominant plant/animal communities — location and relative stability

      b. Their dependence on existing factors, self-regulation, and sensitivity to change

      c. Mapping of general plant cover, including wooded areas

      d. Specimen trees to be retained: their location, spread, species, and elevation at base

  (6) Man-made structures:

      a. Existing buildings: outline, location, floor elevations, type, condition, use

      b. Circulation facilities (roads, paths, rails, transit, etc.): location, capacity, and condition

      c. Utilities (storm and sanitary sewers, water, gas, electricity, telephone, steam, etc.): location, elevation, capacity

  (7) Sensuous qualities:

      a. Character and relation of visual spaces

      b. Viewpoints, vistas, visual focal points

      c. Character and rhythm of visual sequences

      d. Quality and variation of light, sound, smell, feel

B. *Cultural data*

  (1) Resident and using population:

      a. Number and composition

      b. Social structure and institutions

      c. Economic structure

      d. Political structure

      e. Current changes and problems

  (2) On-site and adjacent behavior settings: nature, location, rhythm, stability, participants, conflicts

  (3) Site values, rights, and restraints:

      a. Ownerships, easements, and other rights

      b. Legal controls: zoning and other regulations

      c. Economic values

      d. Accepted "territories"

      e. Political jurisdictions

  (4) Past and future:

      a. Site history and its traces

      b. Public and private intentions for future use of site, conflicts

(5) Images:
   a. Group and individual identification and organization of the site
   b. Meanings attached to site, symbolic expression
   c. Hopes, fears, wishes, preferences.

C. *Data correlation*

   (1) Classification of site by areas of similar structure, quality, and problems
   (2) Identification of key points, lines, and areas
   (3) Analysis of current and likely future changes — the dynamic aspect of the site
   (4) Identification of significant problems and possibilities

*Chapter* 5

# *Technique:*
# Social and Psychological
# Analyses

Understanding how people use and value the spatial environment is the key to planning sites that fit human purposes. Environmental behavior has only recently received any systematic attention, and the literature is still composed largely of proposals for research. There are pockets of data, which most often relate to obvious and well-financed practical issues or to the research interests and techniques of established fields. For example, there are data on traffic behavior as affected by road networks, on shopping behavior and the layout of stores, and on the interaction of men and machines, particularly in regard to the reading of instrument panels. There is information on the relation of temperature and light to work efficiency, on human perception under laboratory conditions, on the performance of rats in mazes, colonies, and while pressing levers, and on the fit between values and environment in primitive societies. But site designers have most often had to fall back on their own personal feelings, modified by random observation.

There are things that we are unlikely to learn from systematic study, such as how to evoke the very personal, inner essence of environmental experience or how to determine new possibilities from a study of existing images and actions. There are things that we should not like to know, such as how to force people to act in some predetermined way by manipulating their spatial enclosures. But there is knowledge that would be useful, such as how environment blocks or facilitates purposeful behavior or how it opens up possibilities for changing behavior or how it facilitates or enriches personal images. And some of this information may be amenable to systematic study.

This chapter will not be a summary of present knowledge. It will focus instead on the methods of analysis that may be used in site planning, since, at least for the time being, most useful data will have to be generated during each particular design task. Even in the long run, the findings in one particular situation are less likely to apply to another situation than are the study methods themselves. I shall discuss those methods that are now useful in applied work, rather than the many techniques that may later become useful or that may be important in basic research. Since I am constructing a list of possibilities, I do not mean to imply that any site analysis should use any, or even most, of these techniques. The situation will indicate which will be most useful within the limitations of resources. Rapidly constructed small-scale designs may use only the crudest techniques, while large-scale prototypes can justify extended and sophisticated studies. But *some* analysis of the requirements of those who will experience the environment is essential even in the simplest task.

*Types of social analyses*    Analyses may be done in the laboratory or in the uncontrollable and complicated real world. Despite its technical disadvantages I prefer the latter. Studies may investigate the actual user of a place or, when necessary, some surrogate for him, such as a person of similar class or age. Investigations may take the passive stance of simple observation or a more active one of experiment and intervention in order to learn the effects of controlled change. The latter is more effective but technically more difficult. Sometimes it is ethically questionable, since the analyst is interfering in the conduct of human life. He may justify this approach on the grounds that a new site plan will change living patterns in any event. Or he may wait for someone else to do the interfering, as by analyzing the result of building a new highway or of a natural disaster. But the ethical issue must be faced. Analysis is not neutral science: any observation changes something. Ethics and technics are bound up together.

Analysis may be done by an observer who is outside the system observed and has little effect on it. This situation never occurs in absolute form in reality, although it may be approximated by someone counting traffic on a busy street. But even then, his findings may eventually affect that traffic. The neutrality and objectivity of this kind of observation is balanced by the difficulty of getting "inside" the environmental experience of those being observed, and of sorting out irrelevant from relevant observations. Most studies to date have been of this kind.

One may use the methods of anthropology, in which the observer temporarily becomes a participant in the system being studied: a celebration or a culture or a school for the blind. These techniques have produced what is perhaps our most valuable material. But they are difficult; they require years of preparation; and they raise touchy ethical problems as well.

Finally, one might employ self-study methods, where the user of the environment consciously studies his own actions and feelings toward it. This is a little-developed technique, technically promising and ethically rather straightforward, which has the quality (both disruptive and hopeful) that the subject of analysis is likely to change himself in the course of study.

Data are most often sought for making predictions: "What will residents do, and how will they feel, if each one gets a private garden?" More properly, in most situations, research would be directed toward learning what people are trying to do and how those purposes may be facilitated: "Do residents want to plant flowers, and how can the site help them to satisfy that desire?" But analysis may also be used to uncover problems or possibilities of which the users are quite unaware. Or — and this is a rare event — analysis may be used to help people to understand themselves or even to transform themselves: "Now that I have tried gardening, I see the world differently."

All these methods focus on the persons and groups of persons who will live in and use the environment. Thus the first step is to determine who these people are and how to observe them or communicate with them. This may be obvious enough in a place already in use. But if a site is yet to be developed, a complicated prediction of the future residents may be required. Ways of categorizing people, as by class, ethnicity, personality, or role, then unfortunately become important. Useful as these abstractions are, they must not blind us to the fact that we are dealing with whole persons.

One of the strategic ways of classifying site-planning situations is on the basis of what we know about the client or

*The nature of
the client*

user. In the most straightforward situation, the client is the user, and he is present, vocal, and homogeneous: if there are plural users, they have common values and common environmental purposes. Since the client is present and vocal, these values and purposes are relatively easy to discover. This might be true in the design of a private garden to be attached to an existing house. Site designers can perform rather well in such a case.

The problem becomes more difficult if the clients or users are no longer homogeneous but complex, holding different values and purposes. This is almost inevitable in large site plans or those for public areas. Now each type of client must be identified, and ways must be found of satisfying their diverse requirements without mutual interference, often by arranging for separate spatial or temporal territories. To the extent that this cannot be done, the diverse requirements must be compromised, inevitably a political process. The designer may now play a role of mediator or catalyst, but not of authority.

Very often, in addition to the users being complex, some of them have no direct voice in the proceedings. Students do not generally help to design schools, nor children homes, nor patients hospitals, nor prisoners jails, nor employees offices. In some cases while the user has no direct voice, he may exert considerable indirect influence, as shoppers affect store layout by their propensity to buy. But wherever an effective market mechanism is not present, the designer faces a particular and familiar difficulty: there may be important clients of whom he is unaware or with whom he cannot easily communicate because it is not customary for them to enter into the decision. Even if he can communicate with them, he may not be able to influence the design in their favor, except secretly or in areas of low priority. A political change is thus required.

If the clients are not present on the site, then the problem is more difficult still, since they will not have that concrete experience with the place that is a firm basis for design, nor will they be able to modify the form of the site as it takes shape. They may already be assembled, however, or otherwise be so well identified that it is easy to communicate with them. Thus they may be members of a housing cooperative or the truck drivers for a warehouse that will move onto the site.

A still more difficult case occurs when clients are neither assembled nor reachable, even though the *type* of client may be well known. They will assemble after the site is organized: they may be suburban house buyers or shoppers or laborers in a new industry. Even though not assembled, these clients may have a way of asserting themselves through the market, but very often they are silent and powerless. Analysis now falls back on surrogate clients, similar to the expected users in class, or other dimensions or on findings made in previous developments. This is the case unless some way can be found to convert absent clients into present ones, unassembled to assembled. This may be done by organizing future buyers before planning begins or by leaving some site-planning decisions open, to be made after clients have arrived on the site.

Worst of all, the client may be not only unreachable but unknown, either because he is unpredictable or not yet alive. Any site plan sets limitations for users yet to be born, and even the near-future use of some areas is very doubtful. The designer then guesses at future requirements as best he can, using all the devices of adaptability and resource conservation. The designer's responsibility is heaviest in providing for the voiceless or the future client.

These conditions can be summarized in a diagram:

The client or user is:

$$\left.\begin{array}{l}\text{present}\\\text{absent but reachable}\\\text{not reachable but known}\end{array}\right\} \text{and is} \left(\begin{array}{c}\text{homoge-}\\\text{neous or}\\\text{complex,}\end{array}\right)\left(\begin{array}{c}\text{vocal}\\\text{or}\\\text{silent,}\end{array}\right)$$

or he is:

    unknown

The great majority of site plans actually fall into three or four main categories, each of which has a typical client condition and therefore requires a particular set of analyses. In the most common case a new or cleared site is being organized, and the client is somewhere else. Sometimes clients are organized and vocal, but more often they are not yet assembled or are represented only by their indirect effects on the nominal client who is making the decisions — a housebuilder or a college administration or an industrial firm. If the clients are assembled but voiceless — the students of a college about to relocate or the employees of an industrial firm — the designer will communicate with them if he can. If they are not assembled, he will turn to indirect analyses, unless he can find some other way to bring them together, as by helping to organize a cooperative or a user's association. Since more and more site planning is done in

*Types of
site-planning
problems*

this remote fashion, we shall continue to get inhumane environments unless we not only improve our basic knowledge of environmental behavior but also find better means of assembling future clients.

Where site planning is being done for an already occupied site, then usually all or most of the clients are already present and on intimate, familiar terms with it. While the site modifications may now be technically more difficult, relations with the client are much easier to solve, at least in theory. Most of the types of direct analyses can be used, and all segments of the client group are there to be heard. If we so often fail to let them be heard, it is certainly a political failure but also a technical one. It is here that participant observation, especially self-analysis, is so logical a tack to take.

Finally, some site plans are not for complete, particular places but have to do with systems of things — systems that may be repeated in various localities, usually where the total spatial environment will not be controlled by that one system design. This type of plan may be for a prototypical trailer park, a major road system, or a standard bus stop and its furniture. Site planners are less accustomed to work in this way, but it is an efficient way of using scarce design talent and is fitted to the way in which many components of our landscape are produced and installed. Clearly, the client is complex and not directly reachable in this case. He may also be partly unknown. On the other hand, he is usually engaged in some rather specific role, which simplifies the analysis. Moreover, the large number of settings that will be controlled by the design make it economical to use sophisticated analyses and to learn from carefully monitored experiments. It is also often possible to leave room for particular client adaptations and for ways of modifying the system as experience is gained.

*A glossary of psychosocial analyses*

What follows is simply a rough glossary of social and psychological analyses, relevant to environmental behavior and currently useful to the site planner. This means that I am excluding many techniques of interest primarily to research, as well as those which may be of great practical importance but which do not bear directly on man-environment interaction. In the latter class there are many required analyses, which must precede the preparation of a program. Their relevance is obvious, and their methods are well established. I refer to demographic studies of the size and composition of the present and future population: age, sex, ethnicity, class, income, education, employment, mobility, and so on. I also include analyses of the economic, social, and political structure and indexes of function, such as health, welfare, crime, and the like. They will be the necessary background upon which the man-environment interaction can be understood. Passing over them here is not a negative comment on their usefulness but a result of the relatively high degree to which their methods and their relevance are clear. They are well covered in many other text sources.

I have classified the following techniques by the means used for evoking information, while at the end I list some of the methods that are not yet immediately useful to the planner but show promise in research. The first group are the most indirect, or "passive," where reliance is placed on indirect evidence of past spatial behavior. While these techniques provide rich fare and may be done with the least interference to the existing population, the design implications and causative links of the data are often difficult to extract.

*Past spatial behavior*: One can analyze what locales have been used for what particular behavior when some choice was available: Where do people move? What housing do they buy? Where do they go for recreation? The information is objective and reasonably reliable in the sense that it reveals what people actually do rather than what they say they will do, which is often quite a different thing. Wherever past behavioral choices can be related to site-planning choices, this is almost always useful information, and many plans are wholly based on it. The method has three difficulties: First, it is usually hard to tell whether past behavior depended on the site plan characteristics in which we are interested or on other factors, such as social or economic pressures. Second, even when these factors can be distinguished, the implications for future behavior are only empirical. Without a theory of man and environment, we are always unsure about how people will act next time. And third, the technique deals only with existing choices. Although everyone may be leaving center city for the suburbs, it does not follow that the movement cannot be reversed, given a new center city. Only to the extent that we can penetrate into *why* the exodus occurs can we hope to see whether a reversal might work.

*Existing environment*: One can analyze the form of stable and accepted existing environments, or of the environment of origin of a group, with the thought that such environments must have some fit with existing values and activity and that new environments like them will appear "right" to displaced people. This is a slippery area of investigation. The environment of origin should always be investigated, if for no other reason than to learn the point of departure and to be able to sense what will be novel and what will be familiar. It is also clear that some continuity of form is desirable, particularly in traumatic moves. Where such continuity is not provided, residents themselves will often produce it. But it can rarely be told from simple observation what elements of the existing environment are working well, and no one can be sure how they will operate in a new context.

*Data on dysfunction*: One can go to evidences of dysfunction which are directly related to locality: rates of disease, accident, crime, social disorganization, environmental destruction, abandonment, and so on. These data are objective and surely related to the purposes of a site plan. But one cannot easily determine if tuberculosis is caused by bad housing, poor diet, despair, random infection, or some combination of these factors. Many arguments for environmental reform are based on these shifting sands.

*Content analysis*: One can search various media — newspapers, radio, television, guidebooks, novels, paintings, political speeches, and so on — for references to the environment that will establish the widely held opinions and images about the subject. One can analyze typical views of what urban areas and their problems are or the common stereotypes for various types of areas, or one can uncover the archetypal ideal environments (such as our single-family house in the open, rural countryside). More concretely, one can study past conflicts over environment — battles over highways, parks, or clean streets — as an index of what is felt to be important. The latter method is particularly useful since it reveals things that people cared about enough to fight for. But all of these methods tend to be scrappy and inconclusive. Only by chance will they light on some question of site planning that is at issue.

*Literature search*: Finally, one always consults previous experience: What analyses of the kind wanted were previously done? What developments of this type have been built and with what luck? This should be a major source of information and in the future may become so. At the present time the existing studies are distressingly thin, and previous projects have rarely been analyzed for performance. Most reporting stops at that magic moment when a new project is just completed but not yet occupied. This is idiocy since most site planning solves the same problems again and again. Any regular analysis of actual performance would soon build an impressive body of evidence.

The second group of methods is based on direct, on-the-spot observation of behavior as it occurs in the real world. This is a rich but largely unused source of objective data. It is the sort of information on which science is founded, and every setting — every room and street and park — is a relevant place for such observations. Every completed site plan should be subjected to them, so that the planner can learn from past mistakes. The behavior being observed is usually visible behavior, but other sense data, such as sound, can be recorded. Although sophisticated instruments can be used, the basic observations can be made by any alert observer with a notebook, supplemented by a camera and perhaps a tape recorder. We can watch all the behavior in a single area over a continuous period, or we can sample it by tracking selected people or by focusing on parts of the area in turn or by checking the whole area at given moments. Successive photographs from a high vantage point (a rooftop, a helicopter) can provide useful information.

Behaviorists would say that direct observations are the only proper data — nothing else is reliable. Unfortunately, exclusive reliance on it engenders two difficulties. First, watching people presents us with a bewildering mass of observations. Since we have no adequate theory to direct our attention, it is tedious work. Much of the action has little to do with the spatial setting. Worse, we cannot tell whether it does or not. The moments of clear relevance may be infrequent. Second, even were we able to extract the relevant action, we have learned nothing about the *inner* experience: the feelings, images, attitudes, and values that accompany the action and give it its character. If people are deflected by a wall, how can we evaluate that wall unless we know where people want to go and how they feel about being deflected? We may insert our own intuitions, but they can be treacherous.

*Movement patterns*: The classical type of observation is the recording of movement patterns: the flow of traffic in particular but more recently the detailed tracking of the movement of individual persons in space. Movement patterns have an obvious relation to provisions for circulation,

**D**irect
Observation

*Reference 15*

and they may indicate preferences and repulsions as well, although this relation is harder to define. Simple counts are the easiest to conduct: we count the number, and perhaps the type, of vehicles or persons passing a point in both directions or making certain turns per unit period of time. This count may be limited to average and peak rates of flow and turnings, which are critical for channel capacities, particularly those of streets but also of intensively used sidewalks. A coordinated series of such counts can determine flows in an entire network or, by manning all possible crossings of some cordon line, determine the total buildup or decline of persons or vehicles in a given area. Sample persons or vehicles may be stopped to find out the origin and destination of their trip. In smaller areas we may go beyond flow counts to track individuals, with the aim of understanding how the environment affects their motion. Motions may be recorded by hand on a map if movement is light, or the scene may be recorded by cameras at predetermined intervals so that sample individuals can be identified and traced. In at least one installation, movements in a public room have been tracked by pressure-sensitive switches in the floor. While the information gained is abundant and objective, its usefulness will vary with the designer's concern with circulation or with his ability to make specific hypotheses as to the effect of environment on motion. Tracking or counting is easier and more useful when motion is purposeful rather than exploratory and when confined to channels rather than free ranging.

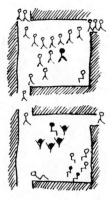

*Localized behavior*: Rather than concerning itself with flow, observation may be directed toward the total set of visible human behaviors in a place to see how they interact with the spatial setting as a whole. In its most comprehensive form, such a record would indicate where each individual was and what he was doing throughout the entire period. This procedure is simply exhausting, and it requires a large staff of observers who have mastered a graphic notation similar to that used in the dance. Analysis of the results is tedious and may produce less than would justify the effort. It is therefore advisable to simplify the observation by classing individuals into groups, lumping activity into classes, and recording the presence and number of persons by group, activity, and by arbitrary subareas, at sample intervals of time. Automatic cameras viewing the scene are useful. The data will bear on questions of capacity and perhaps of area or facility preference or on latent environmental problems such as unused places or danger spots. Observation becomes even more selective when one simply becomes immersed in the scene and looks for something interesting or revealing. Regardless of its doubtful objectivity, the latter type of observation often produces new clues. Experienced designers do it habitually.

A more systematic kind of observation can be made if the planner confines himself to a "behavior setting," in which some standing pattern of behavior repeats itself at regular periods in a definite locality. Thus he may watch the buying of newspapers at a corner stand, an evening ball game, or a regular meeting. Since the behavior and the overt purposes of the actors are regularized, it is easier to record and understand their significance. Recording the territorial and temporal limits of behavior settings, their relative stability, and the nature of their participants furnishes us with the basic elements for which sites are organized.

References 10, 18, 20

Alternatively, we may watch a "behavior circuit," or the actions of an individual or small group as they carry out some coherent purpose in space: obtaining food, going out for an evening's entertainment, doing a day's work. This observation has the same organizing value that a behavior setting does, although it is more difficult to track. Both still suffer from their inherently descriptive nature.

*Specialized behavior*: To make observation more efficient, we may concentrate on certain items of behavior that are more likely to illuminate the interaction with environment. For example, we may watch and record only the visible and material interactions: pushing open doors, walking up steps, sitting on seats, digging, or climbing. Or we may focus solely on evidences of difficulty in the interaction: stumblings, falls, hesitations, collisions, the retracing of steps and other evidence of being lost, apparent anger or frustration, destruction, and so on. While not frequently overt except in very unpleasant environments, the more subtle signs of frustration are often there, and they are quite revealing if detected.

We can also look for occasions on which users have changed or adapted their environment to their own purposes. Nothing is more revealing than the shades drawn over the picture window, the furniture set out on the public lawn, or the dirt path worn in the grass. These are particular kinds of behavioral observation, rich in useful information and available to any alert observer but unfortunately limited and partial.

Leon Lewandowski

FIGURE 13 *It is revealing to watch how people must use the street detail in ways for which it was never designed.*

Walker Evans

*Response to intervention*: The experimenter may gain more accurate information and information better suited to his purpose if he is able to make modifications in the environment and then observes any resulting change in behavior. If the modification is planned for the purpose — a new wall or door, new benches or a new color scheme — he can fit his experiment to just what he wants to know. But such experiments may be costly and are generally confined to minor changes. More important, such changes are an intrusion into the lives of residents. They may be justly resented and must be kept well below the critical level. Certainly no one would remove a pedestrian crossing in order to see if traffic fatalities would rise. Sometimes an observer can take advantage of a "natural" experiment, in which a bridge is closed for other reasons or construction disrupts a site. The observer must have the luck to foresee and be able to use such an event, which happens to fit his desire to learn something. But planned disruptions can have planned experiments built into them. Experiments of this kind have a more solid theoretical and ethical basis if they are being carried out voluntarily by the users themselves. Self-experimentation may be one of the most fruitful ways of advancing our knowledge, as will be discussed later. Perhaps the most hopeful source of data of this kind will come from programming. If the program for a new development is properly made, it will contain a specification of the behavioral results desired. The spatial design is then a hypothesis that such a form will induce such a behavior. By building according to the design, we set up the opportunity for an experiment from which we can learn directly. Postconstruction comparisons of actual results with the original program should be routine.

*Reference 18*

One can go beyond observable external behavior by communicating directly with people about their images, feelings, experiences, and values in regard to the real world about them. This is one of the most valuable areas of environmental research now opening up, and it is a necessary complement to behavioral observation. Yet externalizing the interior experience of people is a difficult task, whose vagaries are familiar to psychology and psychiatry. Analyzing environmental attitudes is luckily somewhat less difficult than understanding interpersonal feelings, since the former are not quite so highly charged with emotion. But questions can be raised about each of the various methods, and they must be used in combination to ensure any sort of reliability in the data. Most of the techniques are new and evolving.

Direct
Communication

*References 11,
12, 20*

*Free descriptions*: Persons may be asked to give a free and open-ended description of a place in order to evoke their perceptions, feelings, and knowledge about it. They may be asked to do so while at the place itself or while moving through it, or they may be asked to describe it in retrospect. Answers may be noted in coded form, or the entire proceedings may be recorded and transcribed to preserve vocal inflections and a great mass of detail. It is even possible to photograph the gestures and expressions of the respondent in the process. The interview may be entirely open-ended, or it may be guided by various leading questions, for example, "What first comes to your mind?" or "What is the most outstanding feature here?" or "What does this remind you of?" "How do you feel here?" "What kind of people live here?" People may be asked to respond graphically, rather than verbally, as by asking them to make a sketch of the place. They may even be asked to construct a model of it from a store of parts.

All these methods produce a rich and chaotic set of

data, difficult to compare or quantify but often extremely suggestive. Thus they can be most useful in an exploratory stage or if one wants to get a rapid impression of the impact of a place. The circumstances of the interview, the set of questions, and the relations between interviewer and interviewed, all affect the material received. The respondent often repeats what he believes the interviewer most wants to hear or what he thinks it is proper to say under the circumstances. The interviewer will therefore try to take as neutral a stance as possible, attempting to show uniform interest and encouragement to whatever is said. Or, having a theory as to the hidden factors he wishes to uncover, he may use probing questions, at the serious risk of answering them himself in the process of probing. He may give the respondent some difficult task, such as making a sketch under the pressure of time, so that the respondent loses some conscious control over his output. But he cannot then be sure whether or not the difficulties of the medium have sharply distorted the output. The answers to such an open-ended approach are comparable only with difficulty and are very much subject to the interpretation of the analyst. Nevertheless, they are almost indispensable as an entering technique, and they correspond to natural ways in which we communicate to each other about our environments.

*Spatial images*: In somewhat the same vein, but in a narrower and therefore more precise sense, we may attempt to evoke the image of a place, the mental concept of it which allows us to recognize it, to organize its parts, and to operate within it. Thus we get, not the whole meaning of a place, but the cognitive structure to which these meanings are attached. A number of techniques have been developed for this purpose, including requests for maps to be drawn, for descriptions of a route to some destination with its associated decisions, for the recognition of places in photographs or in reality, for directions to a place from passersby in the streets, or for an analysis of remembered direction-finding behavior. While subject to the same criticism that each medium imposes its own distortions, it seems to be possible, by using these combined techniques, to construct a fairly stable and objective representation of the image held by some person. The techniques are reasonably well developed and have been used in many different situations. For the purposes of site planning, problems of orientation and cognitive grasp, as well as feelings of territory, can be deduced, but the values to be placed on these features arise only in part from the data. The techniques are also useful for many kinds of sociological and psychological purposes that are not directly related to design.

*Temporal images*: This same type of investigation may be applied to a person's sense of time, as embodied in the environment. Specifically, he may be asked to describe his view of past, present, and expected future environmental changes, or the way his surroundings evoke past or future events. While less well developed as a set of methods, the questions about the perception of past and future change and who is accomplishing that change and what it means are almost always relevant to a designer who is engaged in shifting the scenery. The general relevance of the setting to our crucial image of time has yet to be explored, however.

*Current spatial behavior*: Respondents may be asked a more direct set of questions: How do they now act in the environment? Where do they go, what do they do there, why, when do they do it, what do they use, with whom do they interact? These relatively objective data, built out of current memory, can give us a solid and yet wide-ranging picture of how people in fact use their world and relate to each other. At the same time, that picture will be organized in terms of purpose, as a solely visual observation of behavior cannot easily be. Memory, especially long-range memory, can be faulty, but current memory is less likely to be so, while it still serves as a useful filter to the mass of data. Memory may be supplemented by current diaries, if respondents can be motivated to keep them, or by outside observation. Through these descriptions of daily life, we may learn a good deal about its problems and pleasures.

*Problem identification*: We may ask respondents to identify their problems directly, as well as to outline their satisfactions in the environment. The answers are of direct interest to the planner. Problems are usually easier to perceive than satisfactions, and the former will be emphasized. Problems and satisfactions may also be stereotyped expressions, put in ways learned from the mass media, rather than arising directly from experience. People may simply be unconscious of some of their real problems and satisfactions, particularly since they are unaware of other kinds of environment that are possible. Or they may hide them consciously because they do not seem proper. We may therefore ask the respondent his opinions about problems that *other* people have. The results will also be more precise if we ask what specific frustrations have been encountered today.

*Past memories*: A rich source of information, about which many respondents are pleased to speak, comes from their own personal memories as they are associated with their surroundings. Childhood memories, in particular, will evoke a flood of strong feelings. Distorted and filtered as these are by the passage of time, they are a convenient means of exploring many strongly held values and associations. Like free descriptions, they are difficult to compare and quantify, but they are often quite moving. Since they refer to stages of life now passed by, they must be used with caution in analyzing present desires. But since they are present idealizations, they must be used with equal caution in analyzing the requirements of children.

*Predictions and preferences*: The material of most interest to the site planner, but unfortunately the most unreliable, is the respondent's sense of what he is likely to do in the future and of what he would prefer to do. Predictions and preferences are notoriously unlike actual future choices, yet they point to strong current motivations and hence must be taken into account. The inability to foresee the future actions of others, plus an imperfect knowledge of possible environmental choices, plus an equally imperfect knowledge of self, all make the answers dubious. The question "What kind of environment would you like to live in?" will usually produce a banal answer. Moreover the respondent might not choose it in the real event. Intended or preferred future behavior is less misleading than general environmental preference. One gets a more accurate answer to "How would you prefer to eat your meals?" than to "What kind of dining room would you like to have?" But a systematic series of environmental experiments is the best guide of all. Nevertheless, expressed preferences may be useful indicators of present dissatisfactions and also indicate points of takeoff for future proposals.

The Use of
simulation

So far we have been considering ways of learning about the personal impact of the real, existing world. Often enough it is not convenient to bring that world before the respondent, or the available world does not have the features about which we want to learn. The site planner, since he is dealing in futures, typically wants to know how people will feel about, or act in, some possible but still nonexistent world. Thus there have been attempts to present respondents with simulated evironments — photographs, drawings, models, films, or verbal sketches — in the hope that their responses to the simulation will predict their response to their reality. The transition is shaky, and we have rather little information on how well that transition can be made. Yet since we do it recurrently in the process of environmental design and decision anyway, we are forced to go on experimenting with it. The simulations may attempt to be as true to reality as possible, within the limits of the medium, or they may be abstracted or altered in various ways, whether for economy or to test the effect of certain changes.

Many of the techniques listed in the preceding section may also be applied to simulations: one may be asked for free descriptions, for the associations evoked, or for the spatial or temporal image or an evaluation of an environment presented in photographs. Simulations may be presented on one occasion and their description from memory requested in another. Meanings and affects may be explored, preferences expressed, or the imputed consequences of the simulated environment for self and others discussed. But some additional kinds of tests are also possible, as noted in the following paragraphs.

*Attention analysis*: Perhaps the simplest type of special study is to record what the respondent attends to — in particular, what he looks at, for how long, and in what order. This may be done crudely by simple observation or more precisely by an eye-movement camera, which superimposes the location of the point of visual fixation on a movie of the total scene. Even more sophisticated equipment may soon permit us (via measurements of pupil dilation) to record the degree of attentiveness, as well as the locus of fixation. All this equipment is extremely bulky and complex and useful only in rather refined studies. It has occasionally been used outdoors.

*Puzzles*: The respondent may be given tasks, problems, or puzzles so designed that in the course of accomplishing or solving them he reveals something about his mental structure of the world. He may be asked to do a freehand map of a large city or to make a model or sketch of a place or to describe the route between two obscure locations. While concentrating on the problem, the respondent uses and reveals his cognitive map. The investigator may also encourage free play, asking someone, for example, to create a "city" or a "village" out of available model parts or even to sketch or describe an ideal city or building or utopia. While these last techniques have been used only tentatively and raise many problems of standardization, they look promising.

*Stereotypes*: People may be asked to sort representations — photographs, for example — either into groups according to labels supplied by the interviewer or into classes that the illustrations themselves evoke in the observer's mind. These may be descriptive of physical qualities (new, old, dense) or of the social implications (slum, nice residential area) or evaluative of the environment itself (beautiful, uncomfortable). Both preferences and cognitive structuring are revealed and associated with environment features. The representations may be systematically altered, as by adding or subtracting features in photographs or drawings, to trace the linkages between association and the features of the setting. While the correspondence of simulation to reality still remains a question, this method is otherwise a relatively accurate way of probing for environmental meanings. It is also rather easy to carry out. The association evoked thereby may be put in quantifiable form by using semantic differentials: carefully chosen pairs of polar adjectives among which the respondent is asked to indicate the ones most appropriate to what he sees, as well as the degree of appropriateness.

*Gaming*: In order to avoid evoking wishes that may have no relevance to real choices, the respondent may be asked to play some game that is a simplification of reality but whose rules, penalties, and benefits parallel the situation one is trying to simulate. Most people will enter such a game easily and play it with conviction. Thus a person may be given a sum of imaginary dollars and be asked to spend them on a combination of housing and services, each possible choice having its particular price and its particular benefits. One can then learn, for example, how various people might trade off the time distance to work against the size of their house lot.

Games become particularly absorbing when they include diverse groups who have different objectives and who compete or cooperate with each other for the use of resources. Such games, which require complex rules of governance, substantial data, and carefully designed responses to the actions of the various actors, can simulate systems of behavior as large as the development of a metropolitan region. While they cannot accurately predict the evolution of such real systems, they do illuminate how people make choices under realistic conditions of uncertainty and competition. They are particularly useful for teaching the nature of some complex process to a set of players.

Games are so absorbing and attractive that they raise special problems. In a game one does not question the rules; one accepts the given role and its objectives. This situation has many parallels in real life, but fortunately not in all its aspects — it is not a model of ideal behavior. In its intensity and temporal compression, the game favors competition, shallowness and rigidity of purpose, and a view of the world that sees it to be rapidly changing but ever the same. Thus the game has its dangers as a teaching device while being quite useful for more limited purposes of uncovering how people might react in bounded, stereotyped situations of choice.

*Empathy*: Gaming is a kind of role playing, under set conditions. Role playing, or projection of oneself "inside" another person or situation, is a powerful and very human road to understanding. If empathy is difficult to standardize, it is nevertheless the basis for any nonroutine communication between persons. It is thus a means for intimate relations, for ethics, and for literature. Actors are trained to gain such insights into how other people feel and behave. Serious designers also habitually put themselves into the place of those who will occupy their structures, but with indifferent success because the designer is rarely trained to "forget himself."

Role playing, systematically pursued, can nevertheless be a rich source of insights and is particularly useful as the preliminary step before a more standardized study is begun, since it can generate testable hypotheses about behavior. One can ask a designer, or even the member of a school board, to imagine that he is a child walking to school, although most adults must be harried before they will actually do so. Asking the child to imagine that he is member of the school board is much easier and will be just as informative.

Actually acting as one of the persons for whom an environment is being designed is even more useful for the designer. Thus someone planning housing for the blind should spend a week living blindfolded; a school architect should go to school, and a mental hospital designer should become a certified patient. The experience is sometimes shocking.

Respondents may also be asked to project themselves into some situation rather than into some other person. In the standard thematic apperception test, a respondent is shown a picture of some situation, which is evocative in form but also open to different interpretations. He is then asked to complete some sentence about that picture (which may be something being said by one of the characters represented there) or to tell a brief story about it. For example, a picture of a child alone in a forest or of two people talking on an apartment balcony high in the air may be shown. Stories invented for those situations can then be analyzed for the emotional feelings that the respondent holds toward those environments.

## Neutral Observation

These techniques have been described as they would most often be used: by some outside "neutral" observer who is studying the environmental responses of present or future residents of a place. But since an external observer has difficulty in penetrating into another person's inner feelings, since observation inevitably disturbs the thing observed, and particularly since information once collected can be used for or against the interests of the person observed, this mode of observation raises a number of ethical and scientific problems. They may be small when we are studying gross visible behavior that is relevant to widely shared purposes, such as the analysis of traffic for the purpose of reducing accidents. But these problems are more troubling, for example, if we are analyzing residential preferences as a prelude to relocation.

## Participant observation

One way of overcoming some of these obstacles has been the device of participant observation which developed in anthropology. The investigator lives with the group he is studying, joins in their pursuits, and makes himself as much a part of their world as he can manage. By gaining their confidence and the right to share in their intimate and informal communications, as well as by the partial transformation of himself into a member of the group, he gains a much more profound insight into their feelings and images. He begins to understand underlying but inarticulate systems of belief, latent functions, and hidden agendas. Indeed, the most useful background material for environmental design has often proved to be an anthropologist's view of society rather than the more precise but remote data of sociology.

The participant observer is in an ambiguous position, however. He is both an insider and a stranger, sharing intimacies but also telling tales. By collecting information to be used by others, he may be violating an unspoken trust. Keeping enough objectivity for accurate reporting while also being a participant may be a tightrope exercise. The method was first used by "advanced" scientists studying "primitive" societies, where there was no fear of the scientist becoming a primitive and no conscious doubt that the scientist really knew better than they did what was good for them. As the method is applied to people more and more like ourselves, the underlying ambiguity of the position becomes more obvious. Moreover, it requires careful training and years of observation before it can begin to generate useful information. Thus while it offers valuable background material if already available, it is of doubtful use to the site planner as a survey method.

A new mode of observation is currently developing. For this method the present or future residents of an environment are trained to employ the survey techniques themselves and to analyze their own use and conception of their own surroundings. Most of the methods already described can be so used: indirect analysis, direct observation, direct communication, evoked response. But the nature of the method changes with the changed roles. Observing the response to environmental change, for example, becomes self-experiment, in which both the potentialities of the setting and one's own nature are being explored in parallel.

In this case the ambiguity of the observer's role disappears. The expert becomes a teacher of analytical technique and a creator of environmental possibilities. The information generated remains in the hands of those who produce it and to whom it is relevant. It is possible to explore inward feelings as well as outward signs. The very act of survey establishes the design and control of the setting by those who will use it.

The act of observation continues to disturb the thing observed, however. In fact, the disturbance is likely to be radical, since the feedback is rapid, internal, and self-conscious. Participants can be expected to change their perceptions of environment and some of their values about it, and the process may move in unexpected directions. These analytic techniques of environmental assessment may, in fact, prove to have a use well beyond that of professional design. They may turn out to be strategic ways by which people can begin to understand themselves and their world, and to learn how to organize themselves to be effective in it. Survey becomes self-transformation.

While the latter possibility remains speculative, it appears that self-analysis is a powerful way of studying the impact of environment. At the same time it is politically and ethically far less ambiguous, and it is a step toward laying a solid base for participatory design. It develops clients who are aware of their proper interests in the environment and are able to speak forcefully for them. Since it is educative and self-transforming, self-analysis may lead in unexpected directions, however. The technique is only now being tested and may have unforeseen latent difficulties. It may raise hopes that can only be frustrated. It is certainly more time-consuming than a standard analysis by outside professionals.

The theoretical and ethical problems that have led to its development make it clear, however, that we cannot continue to conduct surveys in the old impersonal manner. Even when observation is done by professionals, it must be done with the knowledge and consent of those observed, and the information generated must be available to them as well as to the observing agency. Sometimes it must be made available to the latter only with the consent of the former. This principle has technical consequences. It favors those simpler survey techniques that are more suited to decentralized control and that return their information more rapidly to their investigators. Designers are not yet accustomed to think of inquiries about behavior and requirements and wishes as being politically sensitive. Information is power, and surveys, even environmental ones, are easily used for further concentrating the control of information and thus solidifying the structure of power.

We have attempted an inventory of social and psychological analyses relevant to site planning which are presently of proved value in some typical situation. Many other techniques are being invented and experimented with. Many of them will in time be added to the useful repertory. We shall mention some of them here in passing.

It may soon be possible to record detailed expressive actions as well as gross behavior. Thus we may be able to photograph, record, or diagram such things as facial expression, the tone of voice or the fragmentary vocalizations, hand gestures, body positions and movement, dilation of the pupils, galvanic skin reactions, brain rhythms, internal chemistry, and so on. Most of these techniques are routinely used in other kinds of analysis, and a few have been toyed with in studying external settings. They would provide us with richer data on the way human beings respond to the world about them. For the time being, they require elaborate equipment, and, more serious, they would bury us with information that we are not equipped to use.

In the laboratories, respondents can be subjected to artificially distorted stimuli: people may be blinded, deaf-

Evolving
Techniques

ened, blinkered, isolated from sensation or overloaded, or be subjected to very brief exposures or to reversals in time or space. Special situations of this kind have been of great value in laboratory investigations directed toward understanding the perceptual or cognitive process. They are only recently emerging into the real world, and their value there is as yet uncertain.

Preferences may be evoked in much freer ways than those we discussed earlier. People may be asked to create utopias, or even kakotopias, or to compare very unlike places in ladder rankings. These methods can sometimes be useful for evoking latent feelings, but unfortunately most people are ill trained for letting their preferences wander. If people are so trained, however, some of these methods may produce important results.

Respondents may play roles not only as other people but also as things. They can be asked to imagine that they are the Empire State Building and required to comment about the people inside them or about the streets at their feet. Someone may imagine himself as a bathtub as a prelude to designing a tub or a bathroom. The method seems odd, but it occasionally produces new insights or design possibilities. It has not been applied in site planning.

Analyses of environmental preference may be carried out in depth by methods usually associated with psychiatry: depth analysis, hypnosis, dream interpretation, and so on. The scanty published material of this kind which refers to environment has been interesting. Although the techniques are difficult and possibly dangerous in unskilled hands, such studies are of great theoretical interest but are less likely to become useful tools for the designer.

Many other techniques will undoubtedly be developing in the near future. The problem for the designer will be to choose the ones most apt for his particular problem. It is evident, however, that he must cease to rely on his simple intuitions for predicting the effect of what he designs and cease to think of data as so much neutral lumber, the raw material he will shape into a design. Getting to know something is a political as well as an intellectual act, and the process of doing it intimately affects the eventual quality of behavior and setting.

*Chapter* 6

# Movement Systems

$\mathbf{A}$ccess is a prerequisite to the usefulness of any block of space. Without the ability to enter, leave, and move within it, to receive and transmit information or goods, space is of no value, however vast or rich in resources. In one sense a city is a communication net, made up of roads, paths, rails, pipes, and wires. This system of flow is intimately related to the pattern of localized activities, or land use. The economic and cultural level of a city is roughly in proportion to the capacity of its circulation system, and the cost of that system is usually the most significant element in total site cost.

*Flow types*     Flows are of many different types: the movement of people, of goods, of wastes, and of information, carried in wheeled vehicles, on foot, on rails, in the air, in pipes or wires, and on endless belts, under, on, and above the surface. Even on the scale of a site plan it is important to think of these flows as a total system within which one element can often be substituted for another. Telephone calls or televised communications may substitute for personal trips, and the flow of gas in a pipe for the haulage of solid fuel. Bus routes replace car trips. The layout of streets affects the pattern of underground utilities, and the location of telephone cables depends on the method being used to transmit power. It is in this domain that the site plan is the most sensitive to technological change.

*Channel types*     The channel types in most common use today are the graded and surfaced rights-of-way for pedestrians or wheeled vehicles, the rail systems, the wires conveying power and information, the gravity flow sewers carrying off surface drainage and waterborne wastes, and the pressure pipes supplying such fluids as water, gas, steam, and even bulk materials in water suspension. Vehicular paths are normally laid on the surface and the pipes beneath it. Wires are placed underground or strung overhead.

Of all these channels the vehicular rights-of-way are likely to be the most critical. They convey persons as well as a variety of objects, they are demanding of space and sensitive to alignment, and they are fundamental to the usefulness and quality of the locations that they border on. The other channels tend to be patterned in conformity with this dominant system. All too often, indeed, even the walkways are thought of only as insignificant adjuncts to the streets. As a first approximation in design, it is possible to consider the layout of roads and walks before that of the rest of the circulation system and then to refine this layout by study of the other components.

Among the utilities (the pipe and wire channels) it is the water supply that is likely to be most critical at the community scale. The quantity, potability, and pressure of water available may exercise a serious check on development or even prevent it. The disposal of sanitary sewage will also influence growth at the larger scale, especially when topography prohibits gravity flow to a good disposal point. But sewage disposal is becoming less of a determinant as the technique of small disposal plants improves.

*Critical utilities*

At the local site-planning scale neither water supply nor sewage disposal is likely to have a significant influence on the plan, whereas the management of surface drainage through the storm sewers may impose important modifications because of the size and cost of the storm sewer system and the need to tie it into the natural drainage pattern of the area. Therefore it is likely to be the first utility network to be analyzed. It involves the flow of rain and meltwater over the entire site, moving in sheets over the open ground, concentrating in ditches and swales, then running into the street gutters, entering the underground pipe system, and finally reaching the natural drainage lines of river, lake, or sea. The designer is concerned not only with the sewer system itself but with the drainage of the ground surface and its flooding and erosion, as well as with the downstream burden he imposes on rivers, lakes, and oceans. The technique of underground circulation is rather backward in comparison with that of surface systems. Subsurface structures are expensive and inelegant, their design highly empirical and traditional, the hidden layout chaotic to an extreme. This is painfully visible when a street is opened up.

In general, circulation systems may be integrated or dispersed. That is, water may come through great aqueducts from a single metropolitan reservoir, or each house may have its own well; sewage may go to a central disposal plant or be disposed of in individual septic tanks; lanes may lead only from village to fields or be connected in a nationwide system; storm water may be diverted into local brooks and ponds or be carried in great collecting lines; electricity may be distributed on a regional grid or be furnished by individual generators; and so on. The choice between extremes, or the stations between, is dictated by density, topography, function, custom, and available facilities. But it is more usual to use integrated road systems, centralized sources of electricity for economy and reliability, and a central water supply for reasons of public health. Storm drainage systems, on the other hand, are usually as dispersed as possible.

Distribution lines may also be differentiated in other ways. There are the systems in which materials, energy, or information is conveyed under "pressure," some external applied force that is confined to the channel. These systems include the water, gas, electricity, and telephone lines. Here the channels are small in cross section, continuous, flexible, flowing full, typically fitted with valves and subject to frequent breaks. Their pattern will usually appear as a large interconnected network or web. Then there are systems in which materials flow by gravity, the storm and sanitary sewers in particular. These must be laid carefully to consistent slopes; they are rigid, jointed, relatively large, typically flowing only partially full, and have a branching pattern in plan. Finally, there are the channels along which objects move by self-propulsion: the walks, roads, rails, and air lanes.

Along some lines, materials move out from a central source, such as a well or a generator; along others, they go to a single terminus, such as an outfall or a giant factory. Elsewhere, both origin and destination are multiple. These differences have clear consequences for the circulation pattern. Then there are systems in which the moving elements are not interchangeable — as they are in pumping water or electric charges — but must go from a particular origin to a particular destination. Complex switching is then required, or the moving unit must be allowed to find its own way. There is interference at the joints, and capacities fall. Most complex of all, finally, are those movements in which persons are directly involved, where we must therefore consider the moving experience itself, as well as the fact of arrival. If drivers were unconscious and would be content to arrive at any address, how simple highway design would be!

Circulation systems must be considered not only for the way in which they handle their assigned flows but for their influence on surrounding activities. This may be negligible for some underground utilities, but usually it is a significant concern, and at times a dominant one, as in designing residential streets. Therein lies a persistent, if often neglected, conflict. Skilled design can sometimes turn this antagonism into mutual support.

Despite the variety of type and constant innovation, physical circulation has certain consistent general characteristics. When the quantity of flow is more than insignificant, it must be organized in defined channels with terminals and interchanges. These channels are then organized into networks, which distribute the flows over large areas. This is true not only of roads or pipes but of footways, wires, and air lanes as well. The greater the flow, the greater the necessary definition, control, and specialization of the channel, with more elaborate terminals and interchanges, and with the route from origin to destination becoming more indirect, though not necessarily more inefficient. The network is more clearly separated from the region served and more difficult to live with. Superhighways are an example. Rail transit moves on special structures, carrying large numbers and making infrequent stops. It corresponds to heavy, concentrated demands. Since one kind of communication can substitute for another, a circulation plan seeks an optimum present balance, without blind reliance on a single mode. Design of a path system requires a decision as to the desirable allocation of trips to cars, buses, trains, and bicycles. It is unwise to depend solely on the car, because of the diversity of present need and the unpredictability of the future.

These networks of channels may take one of several general forms. Very often they occur as a uniform, rectangular or triangular grid. The seldom encountered triangular grid produces more difficult intersections but allows straight travel in three instead of two directions and so comes closer to

*Consistent characteristics of flow systems*

*Grid patterns*

providing uniform access. A hexagonal or triangular grid may be used for a street system but at a small scale tends to produce awkward sites for development.

Grids in general are useful where flows are shifting and broadly distributed. Although generalized, they are clear and easy to follow. They are well suited to networks serving complex areas at large scales. The rectangular grid is still the system more commonly used for patterns of streets. For such use, it has been criticized for its visual monotony, for its disregard of topography, for its vulnerability to through traffic, and for its lack of differentiation between heavily traveled and lightly traveled ways, which prevents specialized design and the economical use of space and paving.

These criticisms are not inherent in the pattern itself. Heavy or through traffic can be directed onto particular lines of the grid, and monotony can be avoided by the variation of the building and landscape pattern. The grid can be curved to fit topography or to discourage through movement. The essence of a grid system is its regularity of interconnection. It need not be composed of geometrically straight lines, nor must it enclose blocks of equal size and shape.

The grid may be modified by controlling the traffic flow through it. For example, all flows may be made one-way, alternating in direction between one line and the next parallel one. Capacities will increase, and intersections will be simplified, with most of the conflicting maneuvers eliminated. But travel requires more forethought and a lengthier journey. An extreme example of this type is the so-called "steady-flow system," in which movement is directed clockwise and counterclockwise around adjacent blocks, so that flow in any one channel is one-way but reverses its direction between each intersection. There are no direct crossings, only weaving movements, as in a rotary. The system may work for small-scale access networks where flows are heavy, but it makes any continuous trip exceedingly indirect. Blocked grids are a further refinement. In order to direct through traffic and to allow the differentiation of paths, occasional interruptions are made in the grid, while leaving the whole pattern intact. This system will often take a swastika form.

None of these modifications are needed where the moving units are not self-directed, of course. A grid of water or electric power lines is a very simple and effective solution. The grid pattern has definite advantages of simplicity, convenient access, good orientation, and suitability for complex distributed flow. On level or moderately rolling land it may be a very good solution. Its familiar faults are primarily due to poor application.

*Radial patterns*

Another general form is the radial system, in which channels spread out from a center. This system is appropriate where flows have a common origin, interchange, or destination, such as single water source or sewage disposal point, a central telephone exchange, a common workplace toward which commuters are destined, or even a symbolic center such as a royal palace. The radial system gives the most direct line of travel for such centrally directed flows, although at high levels of traffic the central terminus becomes difficult to handle. It is a relatively rigid system in comparison with the grid and does not respond easily to shifts in the central activity, nor does it work well if some flows have neither origin nor destination in the center. Rings may be added to the system to make a radioconcentric net, which still favors central flow but allows bypassing movements as well. This system may work well where the central flow is still predominant. In its outer reaches and at a large scale this net acts like a rectangular grid. A radial system of local streets was once highly regarded, but it is now rarely used since it causes problems in local flow and creates difficult building sites.

A further modification of the radial system is to allow branchings at other points than the center itself. This is the classic pattern, in nature as well as in design, of central distribution or collection. It is commonly seen in water, power, and sewage systems. It allows the most direct line of travel, favors the specialization of major versus minor arteries, and makes the intersection problem manageable by distributing intersections instead of concentrating them at the center. Otherwise, the branching system has the general difficulties of the radial type, being especially frustrating to noncentral flow. Thus the use of dead-end streets in residential layouts permits lightly built, safe, minor streets but creates difficulties for emergency or delivery vehicles. Any branching system is also very sensitive to interruptions at single points on the main lines, whether it is a broken water main or an arterial occlusion in the human body.

There is a third general circulatory pattern: the linear system. It may consist of a single line or a parallel series, to which all origins and destinations are directly attached. This is particularly useful where major flows run between

*Linear patterns*

two points rather than to or from a single point. In addition, since all activities are grouped along the line, all subsidiary flows also have direct lines of travel. It is an economical form when the first cost of the channel is high but terminal cost is low and when there is little saving to be gained by building branches for lower capacities. Since there are no intersections, frontage along the channel is used to its maximum. Thus the linear system is typically seen in developments along freight railroads, canals, or trolley car lines, in pioneer agricultural areas where road cost is relatively high, and in strip development along highways. Its disadvantages are its lack of focus and the overloading of the channel that may easily occur because of the innumerable on-and-off movements along its length.

At the site-planning scale the system may appear as a linear settlement or "roadtown," or it may be used in conformity with the limitations of some linear site along a topographic edge. The linear pattern may be modified by directing it into specialized channels, with some that take through movements and others that take the local flows: a spinal main street bordered or intersected by minor ways. Another system connects minor loops on alternate sides of a major way, providing two continuous paths, one major and direct, the other local and sinuous.

Closing the line upon itself to form a loop improves the characteristics of flow by giving two choices of direction to each destination. With one or two inlets added, this becomes a loop distribution system, which is generally preferable to the branching radial system for the distribution of electricity or water. Similarly, a minor residential street that comes off the main artery as a loop rather than a dead end is the more efficient unless the cul-de-sac is very short. Here the loop allows alternate exits as well as continuous progressive movement for service circulation.

Sometimes a deliberate disorder of local streets may be created to discourage through movement, to adjust to intricate topography, or to create interest in the street picture. This disorder need not cause waste of land or excessive street frontage. It can be justified on difficult terrain, where the ground form, rather than the streets, will give a sense of pattern. It can also be used in small areas, enclosed within a more rational layout, to give a sense of intimacy, mystery, or special character. But if continued over areas of any size, such a scheme becomes confusing and exasperating.

General circulation forms are worth understanding as

*Disorder*

alternatives. They need not be geometrically pure and are of course modified by the external influences of land use or topography. Whatever system is chosen must fit into the general pattern of the region of which the development is a part.

Defined channels usually have a characteristic and fairly consistent cross section located along a continuous center line. This center line must have a definite location in three-dimensional space, an *alignment*, which is usually analyzed for design convenience into a horizontal and a vertical component. Each type of channel has its own requirements for these two alignments, depending on the expected speed, volume, and nature of flow. Standards tend to shift from time to time and from place to place, as technology, climate, or culture changes. The size and rigidity of these alignment standards are in conflict with the fluidity and irregularity of the landscape. Thus it requires considerable skill to make a major road seem to "flow" with the land, to arrange a harmonious joint between a tree and a telephone wire, or to grade the land smoothly between a driveway and a sloping garden. While alignments are detailed and formalized only toward the end of the planning process, the designer is thinking in terms of their requirements as he sketches the circulation system in his preliminary layout.

*Alignment*

*Grain*

A recurring issue in the design of circulation systems is that of grain: the degree of specialization of flow and the fineness with which these specialized types are mixed. Greater flows can be accommodated with safety if pedestrians and cars travel on their own systems. Efficiency will also increase when one sorts out trucks, bicycles, children, idle strollers, and so on. It is similarly advantageous to put fast long-distance traffic in special channels of its own, separate from slow local flow. The advantage lies both in the efficiency of homogeneous flow and in the savings that can be realized in being able to build channels designed for a more restricted purpose, such as allowing light pavements on minor streets.

On the other hand, each gain in specialization is a loss in flexibility; it becomes more difficult to change from one mode of transportation to another, and paths are more indirect. The system is likely to be more complex and more difficult to change as need arises. If, for example, trucks, cars, and pedestrians are all completely separated in a residential area, then trips will be longer, the system will include frequent grade separations, and each dwelling will require three entrances. Our expensive superhighway systems,

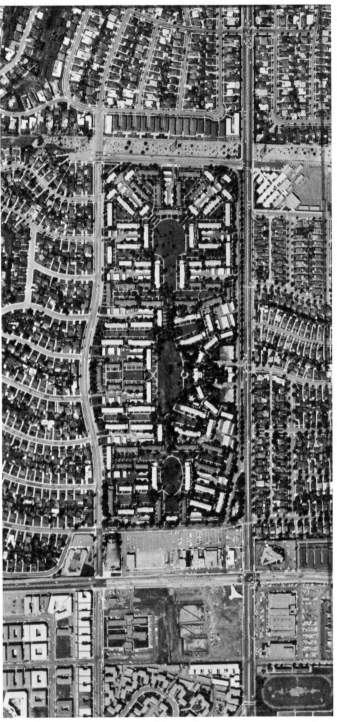

Fairchild Aerial Surveys

FIGURE 14 *Air view of Baldwin Hills, Los Angeles, classic example of the superblock. Designed by Henry Wright and Clarence Stein, the interior is devoted to a common park. Note the variation in pattern of the surrounding residential development.*

demanding their own special rights-of-way and requiring massive engineering structures, have markedly increased capacity and speed for a particular type of flow. Should this type of circulation lose its dominant importance, this specialized system may become a serious obstacle to a readaptation of the environment. As another example of specialization, a one-way traffic system speeds flow but makes it more difficult to reach a given destination.

*Superblocks*

Large superblocks, which increase the grain between the circulatory and noncirculatory zones, improve the amenity of the living areas at the price of frustrating through traffic. The superblock is a large piece of developable land surrounded by a continuous street. As a result of its size, the surrounding street system is more indirect. The block is often curved to fit the topography. The size of the block may be further increased by the use of culs-de-sac or minor loops, which penetrate inward without dividing the block. Superblocks as large as 50 acres within the bounding rights-of-way are not impossible. By eliminating street intersections, this technique minimizes expensive street frontage per unit. It tends to concentrate through traffic, keeping loads light on the minor streets. Large and relatively inexpensive interior parks can be provided. If interior footways are included, pedestrians can cover substantial distances without crossing a street.

Originally it was thought that pedestrian and motor access could be completely separated within these blocks, but experience has shown that the loop or cul-de-sac street, the point of motor access, is also used as the principal foot entrance to the units about it. It attracts most of the pedestrian flow, much of the close-to-home play activity of the children, and becomes the social focus. Therefore it is important to provide a link between it and the main walkway system within the superblock, while branch walks, giving access to the rear of the individual units, can often be dispensed with.

At the normal residential scale at least, complete dissociation of foot and vehicular travel now seems neither necessary nor desirable, except for the traditional separation of street and bordering sidewalks. But major walkways that cut across long blocks or pass through their landscaped interiors at some distance from the streets and carry a substantial number of pedestrians are very desirable as additions to the normal channels. Of course, these separate walkways must be adequately maintained, policed, and lighted. Even the sidewalks along the streets need not follow the road alignment slavishly but can merge and diverge in response to minor accidents of terrain, in consonance with the nature of pedestrian movement. Sidewalks, as well as being footpaths, are places for meeting and play and are an essential element.

Superblocks impose a more and more circuitous path on local vehicular traffic as their size increases. Moreover, if no internal walks are provided, movement on foot becomes very difficult. For this reason there are certain commonly accepted maximums for the lengths of blocks, culs-de-sac, and *See page 143* loop streets, which are quoted in Chapter 7. Some of the disadvantages of long culs-de-sac may be mitigated by interconnecting their ends by footpaths, waterline easements, or emergency service roads, in other words, by converting them into loops for special purposes. To facilitate circulation and social intercourse, there are distinct advantages in keeping block lengths short, particularly where flows are less intensive and disruptive.

*Hierarchies of channels*

Thus there are always pressures both to increase and to decrease the grain of circulation, and the proper balance depends on the particular situation. Most likely, the best solution will provide high specialization of traffic at centers where flow is intense, grading to low specialization where flow is small, for example, by using freeways at one end of the system and walking-driving-parking-play areas at the other. In a total system some hierarchy of channels is likely to be needed. The conventional hierarchy of urban streets begins with the loop, cul-de-sac, or minor streets that give access to the low-intensity uses fronting on them. The minor streets lead to the collector street, on which front local centers, special small-scale activities, and moderate-density housing. The collector empties into the major arterial, built for heavy flows, with intersections at longer intervals, intensive fronting uses, and access controlled but not excluded. Any moderate-intensity use on an arterial will front onto an intervening service road. From the arterial one enters the freeway, with widely spaced grade-separated intersections and no fronting access.

*Interchange*

The problem of interchanges and terminals appears when the elements of flow are individually oriented, that is, when a given car or telephone message must reach a particular destination. It becomes acute where flows are intense, channels are specialized, and trips are multimodal. Here the stopping and shifting that occurs throughout a nonspecial-

ized line is concentrated at the point of interchange. The delays and conflicts at these points tend to become the chief losses in the system, as evidenced by the notorious terminal time of the airlines. The growth of these difficulties may call a halt to further specialization, or force the distribution and reduction of termini.

A typical contemporary puzzle of this kind is how best to enter a building when arriving by car. There are functional problems of deceleration and of entry and storage capacity. There are esthetic problems of a change of scale and a danger of isolating the entrance behind a forecourt of parked cars. There must be clear orientation and a visual transition between velocity and repose. It may be desirable for the car to pass close to the entrance before parking, after which its passengers approach the same entrance a second time on foot. Parking may be dispersed, placed in separate levels, or threaded with lines of activity or landscaping that afford an inviting pedestrian access.

The maximum capacity of a channel, in vehicles, persons, messages, or volume of material per hour, is a measure of its ability to perform its function. Estimations of capacity require knowledge of the distribution of flow between the various modes of movement. Eventually we shall be able to analyze simultaneously the capacity of a total system of roads, as we now can do for a water supply network or an electrical power system. For the time being, however, we calculate the capacities of elements of a system and assign probable loads to those elements by sequentially applying assumptions about driver behavior. In the road system it is usually the intersections and intakes that are the bottlenecks, and their capacity is the limiting factor. Road systems also produce serious problems of terminal storage or parking, since if the automobile is predominant the carriers are large in comparison with the object carried, and they are individually operated and idle much of the time. Parking occasionally becomes a problem insoluble by site-planning means alone.

The circulation system is the most expensive feature of site development, and its layout has significant cost implications. Rationally, future operating costs would be considered together with first cost, but this is rarely done at the site-planning scale. A few general rules may be stated for reducing initial cost, at least. The first is simply to minimize the length of channel per dwelling or other unit of activity. This implies a minimal number of intersections, each of which entails special costs and requires length that can-

*Capacity of channels*

*Reference 38*

*Cost of circulation system*

not be developed as frontage. It also implies continuous development on both sides of the line, with minimum frontage per unit. A heavily developed, endless, single line is the cheapest layout from this point of view, and increasing the size of blocks approximates it. An exception to this rule occurs when roads on very steep land run parallel to the contours; in this case, it may be so difficult to connect development on the lower side with the road and its utilities that it is cheaper to develop only one side of the path. Second, it is usually cheaper to specialize short of the point where elaborate interchanges are needed. Thus a plan with arteries and minor streets will be less expensive than an undifferentiated grid. Third, it is usually cheaper to lay out channels so that they have gentle gradients and no more than gentle curves. Sharp curves, steep grades, and very flat grades all increase costs because of earthwork, drainage, and other special features.

The road layout also has a decisive effect on the development potential of the land not only because of the way the roads confer access but also because of the shape of the plots that remain: the holes in the net. Other things being equal, the larger and more regular these plots are and the more nearly their corners approximate right angles, the easier they are to develop.

*Relation to slope*

A road that runs parallel to the contours of a slope permits level foundations for buildings fronting on it, but if the cross slope is sharp, then access to these buildings may be labored, sewers difficult to reach, and the visual space lopsided. In this case it may be necessary to widen the right-of-way to take up the cross slope and to disassociate the facing buildings visually, or it may be necessary to use separate utilities for the lower structures or one-sided frontage or special building types on the lower side of the street, which are entered at an upper story. For these reasons, contour-following roads should normally be kept back from the brow of a hill if double frontage is intended.

Roads perpendicular to the contours avoid these problems, although foundations must now be stepped (a somewhat more expensive process), and street and utility gradients may become too steep. Rear lots may have awkward cross slopes requiring substantial terracing, but it will be possible to use special step-down building types in a dramatic way. Roads diagonal to the contours produce plots that are the most difficult to use, and should be avoided except

Ogden Tanner, Architectural Forum

FIGURE 15 *Neighborly talk along a common walkway in Chatham Village, Pittsburgh, one of the most skillfully designed row house developments in the United States (Henry Wright and Clarence Stein, again).*

where slopes are gentle or where they are so steep that neither parallel nor perpendicular roads will serve.

For the channels along which people move, there are social and esthetic effects to be considered. These effects occur wherever people go and not only when they happen to be on foot. In reaction to the horrors of American traffic, we think of persons as being unrelated to cars, which are mechanical monsters to be kept in tunnels and underground garages. But cars have drivers who are as human as the rest of us.

The path system affects communication between people. One prime way to encourage contacts between neighbors is to let their dwellings open on a common pathway. Friendships are made along the street rather than across the park. Conversely, the designer can foster privacy, division, or isolation by providing separate routes or masked routes such as apartment hallways or doors that are not mutually visible.

As the scale of flow increases, however, and the path becomes more difficult to cross and entrances no longer open directly upon it, it suddenly reverses its role and becomes a barrier. Thus even a crowded but slow-moving downtown

Paths and
Social Contact

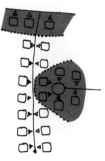

street can be a central place, while an expressway is a divisive wall. A cul-de-sac will focus a neighborhood group, while a broad planted parkway may delimit it. These effects can usually be inferred by going through routine movements in the imagination and noting what casual contacts would thereby arise.

The pattern of streets or paths may provide or destroy the sense of focus or center in the plan, since persons in motion are oriented to the forward direction and a focusing of paths automatically gives the feeling of a strategic common point. Surprising effects of apparent association or disassociation with neighboring areas can be produced by connecting or disconnecting one local street system with another. Real estate developers are well aware of this effect and usually seek to attach their roads to those of the "best" districts in their vicinity.

*Multiple use of rights-of-way*

The traditional street served many functions beyond that of passage. It was market, workroom, and meeting hall. We have shouldered these functions out of the right-of-way, to the advantage of traffic and to society's loss. Now we improve streets still further by widening the auto lanes at the expense of pedestrians, trees, and other marginal nuisances. Sidewalks are still playgrounds, however, and street corners hangouts. Aqueducts make fine linear parks. Thus pathways should be designed with an eye to supporting other functions — by paying attention to the form and furniture of the sidewalks or to their relation to bordering uses, for example. Road pavements themselves can on special occasions be dedicated to other activities. Shoulders and medians are unexploited wastelands. Seeing the road and its associated uses as an opportunity for integrated development is a fairly new appoach in site planning.

*Visual sequence*

Pathways are the locus of points from which the development will be seen. They therefore have a profound effect on the visual character of the whole. They should have a clear order of their own and build up a basic image that is expressive of the function and nature of the site. Along them the traveler should experience a pleasant sequence of space and form, a subject to be treated more fully in Chapter 9. The path system is a powerful means of expressing the underlying topography, whether it runs submissively along the contours or aggressively opposes them. To the man in motion, roads and paths are seen as sharply foreshortened objects in perspective, and not as patterns from the air. Minor deviations will appear significant, pronounced curves will seem startlingly abrupt, and complex patterns will be incomprehensible. The pathways should seem to go to their destination, and changes in direction should appear reasonable. To do this, it may at times be necessary for the planner to introduce artificial obstacles of terrain or structure or to mask possible shortcuts.

There is some conflict, particularly in residential areas, between the functional desirability of a continuous network and the visual pleasures of bounded spaces. The long straight street will seem to go nowhere, and even the curving layout, though blocking the "infinite" view, becomes wearying as the endless curves pass by. For this reason, designers resort to T junctions on minor streets, with an important structure on the axis. But this method is unworkable for an arterial and may bring on chaos if used for too many minor streets. Other techniques include the opening and closing of building or planting lines to make visual compartments along a continuous road and the use of more definite direction changes, with important objects at the break to act as visual termini.

*Path character*

The character of the line depends on the speed with which it is traversed. A footpath responds nervously to minor changes in terrain and has intimate spaces, whereas a highway will take a sweeping line and pass through expansive spaces. Pedestrian motion, like a flow of water, has an apparent fluid momentum. It follows lines of least resistance, shortening distance by cutoffs. It sweeps wide on curves, eddies about obstacles, forms pools above and below restricted channels, such as stairs or corridors. The flow may be smooth or turbulent, purposeful or meandering. It can be deflected or encouraged by visual attractions, by levels, openings, or the character of the floor. A walk may be arcaded, heated, cooled, or its floor warmed to melt the snow. It can be provided with benches, plants, kiosks, cafés, display cases, or information devices. As a fine highway expresses the nature of vehicular movement, so an adequate walk system reflects the pleasures and characteristics of motion on foot.

*Why hide utilities?*

Because of the prevalent ugliness of much of our circulation equipment, we consider roads and utilities as regretfully necessary things that must be supplied but should be hidden. Electric lines and transit lines are put underground, parking areas planted out, and roads decked over. Yet since the flow system is one of the two basic attributes of a developed site and has much to do with its usefulness, in-

FIGURE 16 *A portion of the Central Artery in Boston. The rigidly specialized expressway, with its demanding alignment, slashes through the old city fabric.*

terest, and meaning, we should demand an even clearer expression of the essential elements of this system, instead of camouflaging them. Power lines and highways can be an expressive component of the landscape; exposed pipes can be handsome.

*Environmental impact of circulation*

At the same time, the possible negative effect of circulation on the surrounding areas must regularly be taken into account. Just as we have standards for technical road function, so we should have corresponding standards for its environmental impact. These criteria would govern such nuisances as noise, pollution, the danger of accident, actual or apparent difficulty in crossing, ecological damage such as the blocking of drainage, or the taking of valued space or structures. The standards would be keyed to the nature of the site traversed: the character of activity, the density of

*Reference 45*

pedestrian movements, the ecological quality. Buchanan, for example, suggests a standard for residential streets which sets the maximum time delay that may be experienced in crossing a street by a prudent adult. The delay then depends on street width, traffic volume, and the system of crossing. Other quantitative standards for noise level or carbon dioxide emission could as easily be constructed.

The detailed technical standards for layout of walks, roads, and utilities are dealt with in Chapters 7 and 8. It is usual to begin with the walks and streets, since they have the most critical effect, and to check the other utilities later. The system is designed together with the visual form and the activity pattern, and its influence on these two factors is reviewed constantly. Studies devoted solely to circulation may be made, especially at an early stage, but these will be done only to develop a sense of the situation. No design decisions can be reached without making sketches or models that show use, flow, and form as an operating whole. All these features are usually brought up through many alternatives to a detailed sketch stage, and then the engineering of the flow system is investigated to see what modifications may be required.

In the analysis of site plans the circulation system should be tested in every dimension. Does the system acquit its proper function; that is, can the necessary movements be accomplished along it at acceptable standards of time, cost, and safety? A plan of streets and walks should always be checked by mentally making the routine trips and noting their nature. While automobile movements may be provided for, there is a tendency to neglect movement on foot, or by bus or bicycle. How does one get from car to house, and what is this approach like? How do children walk to school, or adults to a bus or to the shops? How does one get access to a building or a site for repair and maintenance? Can one ride a bicycle safely? Can an efficient set of bus routes be laid out? The check should be quantitative as well: Can the particular channels carry the amount of flow desired, given the predicted distribution by modes? As our knowledge develops, we shall proceed from the checking of single channels to the quantitative analysis of entire networks.

*Testing the system*

The plan for the circulation system should also be criticized to see if the right balance of modes and of channel specialization has been struck, and if the interchanges and terminals are workable. It must be tested for cost, particularly for the length of road or utility per using activity and for the presence of special features. The likelihood of imposing nuisance, danger, or other damage on its surroundings must be analyzed as well as the potentials for using the right-of-way for other functions than pure movement. The design should be checked to see that the parcels remaining for development are good ones, suited to the use proposed and capable of adjustment to other use. The social consequences of the path system as well as its visual impact — both the views of and from the road — can be analyzed.

The circulation system will finally be judged as a totality. Is the general pattern one that is suitable for the basic task? Will it seem orderly and well oriented to someone on

the ground? Can it be abstracted as a differentiated system into a basic structure of main lines on which are dependent a set of subsidiary lines? Does it provide for a balance and a diversity of modes of movement? Do its regions of high capacity coincide with the focuses of activity? Is its structure coherent with the structure of use? Is it in balance with the intensity of activity, neither overwhelming nor being overwhelmed? As a total system, will it help to express site and function? Does it connect smoothly with the surrounding systems?

The circulation system is the one most prone to technological development, and therefore it must be most adaptable to future change. If a self-contained water and sewage purification cycle for the individual unit becomes economical, as it is now technically feasible, then it may become unnecessary to tie a building to an underground water and sewage system. If future land vehicles will hover over the ground on compressed air, rather than rolling on wheels, then road characteristics will be revised. If urban areas are roofed with vast light spans, then surface drainage loses its significance. If we can develop an acceptable dispersed transit system, we could shake off our dependence on the individual automobile. If we learn how to move large numbers of people in three-dimensional conveyor systems, then central districts will be transformed. Videophones may change commuting habits. Certainly there will be many less radical innovations that will at least modify the design of circulation systems. It is for this reason that such general considerations as pattern, balance, diversity, the degree of specialization, and the social and visual impact should have more weight than precise technical standards.

*Chapter* 7

*Technique:*
Streets and Ways

Vehicular ways are laid out with a cross section that
most often remains fixed for substantial distances. This
cross section is normally located by the center line of the
pavement. The principal features of the most common cross
section, not drawn to scale, are these:

*Cross sections*

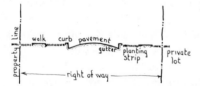

Many cross sections are possible, each with distinct technical and visual implications. The minimum dimensions of
the elements of the cross section are controlled by the varying regulations of local governments, most often with unnecessary rigidity.

The pavement itself is usually crowned at the center
for drainage, the cross-sectional slope being ¼ inch per foot
from crown to edge for concrete and bituminous pavements,
and ½ to ¾ inch per foot for earth and gravel roads. Pavements sloping to one side are used when a height differential between opposing curbs is allowable, as with a median
strip. Where heavy rain or freezing is not likely to occur, the
pavement may be sloped to its center line, using the street
itself as the drainage channel and so saving on the length of

storm drains. A 6-inch vertical curb and gutter is used on major streets, while a 4-inch roll curb may be used in rural areas or on minor streets where residential densities are low. A simple turf or gravel shoulder, flanked by a shallow ditch about 3 feet wide and probably sodded, may be employed at very low densities. In residential work, the use of a ditch requires a culvert under every driveway and at each intersection, but it does allow surface water to seep back into the ground. This may be more expensive than a roll curb or other device that uses the street as the drainage channel. The curb also prevents the breakdown of the pavement edge.

*Pavements*

Depending on traffic, the pavement may be concrete, bituminous macadam, gravel, stabilized soil, or simply a graded and drained earth surface. We seem to have forgotten the technique of building an earth or gravel road, surfaces that are quite suitable for light traffic if the crown and ditches are maintained. An earth road may be stabilized by spreading and mixing portland cement into the upper 6 inches, 3 to 5 percent by dry weight if the soil is a gravel or

*See page 58*

a sand or 4 to 10 percent if it is a silt or a nonplastic clay. For clayey soils and clayey sands or gravels, it is advisable to use hydrated lime, in similar proportions. Temporary, expedient roads may be built of corduroy (logs and brush), of planks, or even of wire mesh and burlap.

*Dimensions*

Road width is computed by summing up the number of traffic and parking lanes required. Curbside parking lanes, if provided, should be 8 feet wide. Each of the traffic lanes

*Reference 34*

should be 9 to 10 feet wide on minor roads, and up to 12 feet wide on highways. The minimum vertical clearance is now 14 feet, to allow for the passage of trucks with high loads. A practical minimum pavement width for minor residential streets with light parking is one parking lane plus two traffic lanes, or 26 feet. If parking will never occur, or at very low densities where parking will be very sporadic, this minimum may drop to 20 feet for a two-way minor road. On a one-way street with parking on only one side, the pavement may be 18 feet. Such a street might be used as a short loop, or as a marginal access road alongside a major thoroughfare.

The purpose of the planting strip is to separate the walk from the street for convenience and safety, to allow room for utilities and street fixtures above and below ground, to provide for piling of snow, and to permit the planting of street trees, although this usually places them too close to the moving traffic. It should be at least 7 feet wide if it contains trees or 4 feet wide for grass alone. If paved and used only for utilities, it may be reduced to 2 feet. In commercial areas it is sometimes eliminated, and poles and hydrants are placed in the widened sidewalk. In any case, street poles should be set in 2 feet from the curb for safety. On important roads the opposing traffic lanes may be separated by another planting strip, or median, for reasons of safety, the channelizing of intersection maneuvers, the management of steep cross slopes, or visual amenity.

Sidewalks should have a minimum width of 4 feet, which allows three persons to pass or walk abreast, although where they lead directly to single-dwelling entrances they may be only 2½ feet wide, with a widening at the door. Collector walks handling numbers of pedestrians must at least be 6 to 8 feet wide. In central areas, where large pedestrian flows are expected, sidewalks must be sized to demand just as roads are. Walks, like street pavements, should be crowned, or have a ¼ inch per foot cross slope. Walkways are normally and rather monotonously made of concrete or asphalt, but gravel, brick, or stone may also be used, or the concrete may be textured, colored, or laid in patterns. Walks may occur on only one side of the street in low-density residential areas. While the major walk system may be designed to be independent of the road system, there must be a walk on at least one side of all streets, except very short local streets, service drives, or roads in rural or semirural areas with no substantial fronting development. People persist in walking along the street. Walks are useful for children's play and quite necessary where snow is frequent. In high-density areas they cannot be skimped but must be wide enough to accommodate all the movement and social activity that will take place upon them. Occasionally, additional levels of walkway may be used, where pedestrians are numerous and easily motivated to use that additional level, as by elevated shops, a fall in grade, or an underground transit terminal. Elevated walks are usually feasible where floor area ratios are near 15, and perhaps mandatory at 25.

Travel by bicycle has the advantages of quietness, economy, no pollution, good exercise, easy parking, and safety for others. At the same time, the accident rate for cyclists is very high when they are mixed with automobile traffic. Separate cycleways will encourage cycling for recreation and for regular journeys, and such separate ways are considered necessary wherever the flow of cyclists is likely to exceed 1500 per day or where heavy peaks are ex-

*Sidewalks*

*See pages 149–151*

*Cycleways*

pected, as at industrial plants or schools. Cycleways are normally built of light pavements 12 feet wide, with gently curving alignments and easy grades. Crossings should be offset, and T junctions are preferred. They should be grade separated from motor traffic, or their crossings should be controlled at intersections with signals, since to merge cycleways back into heavy traffic may actually cause a heavier accident rate than to have no cycleways at all. These ways may safely be combined with major pedestrian routes, or even allow the use of electric carts and low-powered motorbikes of very restricted speed.

The private property line is set only a nominal distance beyond the edge of the walk unless there is public planting there. Street trees are perhaps best planted at this point, or in private front lots, rather than in the planting strip. This prevents branches from interfering with overhead poles, lights, and wires, keeps roots from disrupting the pipes and cables underground, and protects the tree from all the chemical poisons used in road maintenance.

*Variable cross sections*

Although standard cross sections are commonly used for roads of similar type and simply applied to the changing ground surface as if a rigid template had been trundled along the center line, it makes much more sense to adapt the cross section to the context. Walks may move toward and away from the curb; road lanes may separate to save some landscape feature, or change elevation with a dividing strip between them; cut-and-fill slopes may match the flow of the terrain; trees may be planted in irregular groves. The adaptations mean added design and supervision but add far more to appearance and usefulness and often decrease construction costs as well.

The right-of-way is the total public strip of land within which there is public control and common right of passage and within which all pavements and utility lines are located if possible. Its width depends on the features included within it. The minimum is commonly given as 50 feet, but this width can actually be reduced on minor streets to as little as 30 feet. This makes for a more economical and flexible plan, particularly in rough ground, and improves the visual scale. Where the future traffic load is uncertain, it may be necessary to use a wider right-of-way, while beginning with a relatively narrow pavement. At the other extreme, a major freeway may use a right-of-way that is 600 feet wide.

*Horizontal alignment*

Horizontal alignment of the road is based on the pavement center line, which is marked off in 100-foot "stations" for reference, beginning at some arbitrary end of the system. A separate numbering system is used for each single continuous line. All significant points, such as the intersections of one center line with another, or the beginning and ending of horizontal and vertical curves, are located by reference to this numbering system.

Center lines are made up of two kinds of elements used alternately: straight lines, called "tangents," and portions of circular curves, to which the connecting straight lines are tangent. If two curves are directly joined without such an intervening straight line, both curves are made tangent to the same imaginary line at their junction. Tangents and circular curves are used for ease of layout and so that curves, once entered, can be negotiated with one setting of the steering wheel. On major roads, the joint between tangent and circular curve may be softened by a "spiral" curve, which is one whose radius begins by being infinitely long (that is, it is a straight line) and then progressively decreases until it reaches the radius of the circular curve that it is introducing. These spiral curves of transition are rarely used on minor roads and will not be treated further here.

The circular curve has the elements shown in Figure 17.

*Horizontal curves*

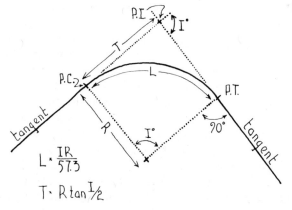

FIGURE 17    *Elements of the circular curve used in horizontal alignment.*

The curvature of a road is sometimes given in degrees, a 1-degree curve being one whose length is 100 feet for each 1 degree of internal angle that it moves through, while a 2-degree curve has the same length for 2 degrees of angle, and so on. Conversion may be made by the formula

$$R = \frac{5730}{D}$$

where $R$ is the radius in feet and $D$ is the degree of the curve. The sharper the curve, the shorter is its radius and the higher its degree. I shall use the curve radius in the following discussion. The rules and standards are based on the characteristics of today's automobile and will change with it.

*Curve*
*combinations*

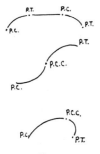

*See page 156*

It is preferable to avoid two curves in the same direction, separated by a tangent of less than 200 feet (a "broken-back" curve). It looks awkward and is hard to drive through. Similarly, it is best to avoid two sharp curves in opposite directions, separated by a tangent of less than 100 feet. Gentle reverse curves may be directly joined without a tangent, however. Two curves of the same direction, but of different radius, which are directly joined together ("compound" curves) should be avoided where possible but are occasionally necessary. The minimum allowable radius of a curve depends on design speed, that is, the maximum safe speed that can be maintained continuously on that piece of road.

On residential streets, tangents may be joined without an intervening horizontal curve where the angle of intersection is less than 15 degrees. This may also be done at much sharper turns, where it is obvious to the driver that he must slow or stop before negotiating the turn, as at a street corner.

*Intersections*

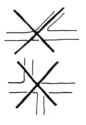

Street intersections should be within 20 degrees of the perpendicular for 100 feet each way from the intersection. Intersections of acute angle are difficult to negotiate and limit the approach visibility. Direct crossings, or crossings that are offset by at least 150 feet, are preferable to slight offsets, which frustrate the cross traffic and disturb flow on the line that is being crossed. On minor roads, where the complications to cross flow are not of importance, the T intersection, sufficiently offset from the next junction, may be preferable to the straight cross for reasons of safety or for closure of the visual space. Intersections with an arterial road, or major street, should be no closer than 800 feet apart to prevent disruption to the major flow. On freeways, intersections will be limited to 1-mile or ½-mile intervals. The curb at corners should have a radius of 12 feet for minor streets, or

50 feet at intersections with major streets, to allow easy
turns.

Minimum forward sight distance must be maintained
at all points on the line to give drivers ample time to react to
dangers appearing in the road. It can be scaled from the
plans and should take account of buildings, hills, landscaping, and other blocks to vision. The minimum value depends
on the design speed. A driver 75 feet from an intersection
should see the entire intersection plus 75 feet of the intersecting street on each side.

*See page 156*

The maximum depth of a loop drive is usually given as
700 feet and that of a cul-de-sac as 400 feet. The maximum
allowable block length is 1600 feet. All of these standards
are based on the same reasoning: as block, loop, and cul-
de-sac length increase, general circulation becomes more indirect, service deliveries longer, and emergency access more
liable to misdirection. These rules are commonly held standards of "reasonableness." Not all site planners agree to
them, however. Obviously, the rules would not apply where
through circulation is already blocked for other reasons, as on
a narrow peninsula, ridge, or pocket of land.

*Limiting
dimensions*

A minimum turnaround at the end of a cul-de-sac
should have a 40-foot outside radius free of parking, so that
vehicles such a fire engines can negotiate it. This requires a
large circular right-of-way and may defeat the economic
and visual purposes of small culs-de-sac. A T-shaped terminus or shunt is an alternative way of providing for backing
turns on very short dead ends. The wings of the shunt
should be at least a car's length deep on each side, exclusive
of the width of the street, and at least 12 feet wide if no
parking is allowed. The inside curb should have a 20-foot
radius. As long as these turning requirements are provided
for, free of obstacles, a small short residential cul-de-sac
need not adhere rigidly to these shapes. In fact, a freely
formed parking and arrival court may be quite desirable.

*Dead ends*

Individual driveways should be 8 feet wide, the curb
at the entrance being rounded off with a radius of 3 to 5 feet.
Driveway entrances should be at least 50 feet from any
street intersection to prevent confusion with the turning
movements there. Separate driveways and entrance walks
should be provided for each dwelling unit unless they are
made common to large numbers of units. Walks and drives
that jointly serve two or three units are potential sources of
friction in regard to maintenance.

*Driveways and
walking
distances*

The maximum distance from the street to the door of a dwelling unit is often given as 150 feet for carrying convenience, but perhaps it should be 100 feet. For similar reasons there should not be a steep grade between house door and street. This street-to-door distance standard is also in dispute: some would restrict it to 50 feet; others would relax it to 300. It has an important effect on cost and on design freedom. It depends on the way of life: in America, both by preference and by necessity, this maximum distance is shrinking. In countries where much walking is customary, the distance could be substantially longer.

Houses should be located so that car headlights will not shine into ground floor windows and so that there will be no danger of the house being struck by cars out of control. This argues against axial positions at sharp curves or T intersections, especially at the foot of slopes.

*Parking lots*

Parking may be provided in various ways: on the street (which is convenient but expensive and disturbing to moving traffic), in small parking bays, in large parking lots (which is the cheapest method but may be inconvenient or unsightly), underground, or in ramp structures or garages (the most expensive ways of all).

Parking lots can be laid out if the following dimensions for the modern juggernaut are kept in mind: each stall should be 19 feet long and 8 feet wide if attendants park cars, and 8½ by 20 feet if drivers park their own cars, or even 9 feet wide to give a sense of ample room. If front bumpers cannot overhang the curb, then stall lengths may have to be increased by several feet. Stalls may be parallel, perpendicular, or at 30-, 45-, or 60-degree angles to the moving lane. Angled parking requires one-way traffic flow, which may be confusing. Aisle widths range from 12 feet for one-way lanes serving 30-degree and 45-degree parking to 22 feet for two-way lanes serving perpendicular parking. For efficiency, there should be stalls on each side of each moving lane. Herringbone dividers placed between the inner ends of angle stalls will save some further space. Dividers and curbs may hamper snow removal and the future rearrangements of the lot, however. The perpendicular layout is the most efficient, and 30-degree angle parking the least. As a rough guide, overall space requirements of large and efficient lots run from 250 square feet per car for attendant-parked lots in which cars are stored three or four deep to 400 square feet per car for generous self-parking.

The maximum allowable slope in any direction is 5 percent, and the minimum 1 percent.

The circulation within large lots should be continuous, with dispersed exits and a minimum of turns. Lot entrances should be at least 12 to 14 feet wide if one-way. Thought should be given to the movement of pedestrians to and from the cars. One solution is to provide a raised and planted strip between the ranks of vehicles. Tree planting will improve the climate and look of a parking lot, but trees require substantial space for root feeding. Lots may be screened with walls or planting or sunken a few feet to allow vision over them. For convenience, visual scale, and individual control over the car, it is preferable in residential areas not to allow parking in groups of over six to ten cars. Even in large lots serving commercial areas, it is desirable to keep the cars within 600 feet of their destinations, unless special transportation is provided.

*Loading areas*

Large tractor-trailer trucks are about 50 feet by 8 feet. They require a minimum outside turning radius of 60 feet and a vertical clearance of 14 feet. Curb radii at corners must be 30 to 40 feet where such trucks are common. Loading docks for trucks should be 10 to 12 feet wide per truck, set at truck-bed height — about 4 feet off the pavement — and arranged so that, when backing, the trailer swings clear of the driver's line of vision. A 50-foot parking and maneuvering apron is needed in front of the dock. A general rule is that the floor of a loading dock should be about twice the floor area of the beds of all the trucks that could be brought up to the dock at one time: this allows room for unloading and temporary stacking.

*Road capacity*

The capacity of a road depends on the characteristics of the road — width, surface, alignment, conditions at the edge — and the characteristics of the traffic — vehicle type, speed, control, driver skill. The theoretical capacity of one lane of traffic is 2000 cars per hour where this flow is completely steady, uninterrupted, and at optimum speed and spacing. It might be approximated by an organized convoy moving on an ideal pavement. In practice, a multilane freeway may carry up to 1500 or even 1800 cars per hour per lane, while a congested street with frequent side friction due to cars parking and entering may carry only 200 to 300 cars per hour on the outside lane. A local residential street will carry about 400 to 500 cars per hour per lane. Four lanes in each direction seem to be the widest road that one can

*Reference 38*

drive on without loss of sanity. Expected local street volumes in suburban areas may be roughly estimated by assuming that each dwelling will generate about seven one-way vehicular trips per day, or one or two per peak hour. Larger, denser, or more complex areas require more careful traffic assignment studies.

When traffic flow is heavy, the critical limit to capacity is the intersection. Even where total volume through an intersection is as low as 500 cars per hour in all directions, up to 50 percent of the approaching cars may have to stop before going through or turning. Such an intersection, or any one handling higher loads, will require some treatment. The simplest is a stop sign on the secondary street. From there, the designer may go to traffic signals, channelization, or grade separation. The design and analysis of high-capacity roads and intersections is a matter for traffic engineers, but some mention of it must be made to give the site planner a sense of the problems involved.

Intersections are designed to avoid conflicting maneuvers, to moderate their difficulty, or to separate them in time or space. These conflicting maneuvers include merging, diverging, and crossing, and their danger is proportional to the relative speed of the approaching vehicles. For example, the relative speed of two cars in a head-on collision is the sum of their individual speeds, while that of two vehicles going equally fast but merging into the same traffic stream from two slightly different directions is almost zero.

*Traffic signals*

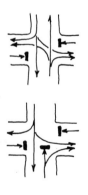

Traffic signals, by alternately stopping some entering movements, reduce the number of conflicts. Signals may be warranted when intersection volumes rise above 750 vehicles per hour, with at least one-quarter of the flow on the minor street. They may have a simple two-phase cycle, which alternately passes the traffic of one street and then the other, with a yellow warning interval between each change from green to red. Or they may be more elaborate, with three, four, or even more phases, to allow unhindered left turns. Total cycles are usually from 35 to 50 seconds long, and each intervening yellow interval is about 3 seconds. The capacity of such a controlled intersection can be computed by assuming that as many as 1000 vehicles can move through each lane during each hour of total green time, that is, excluding for each movement all its red and yellow (stop and warning) periods. This is a high figure attainable under optimum conditions and does not allow for the effects of heavy trucks, left-turn or pedestrian conflicts, or any stopping or parking at the crossing. Actual figures are closer to 300 to 600 vehicles per lane per hour of green.

Channelization, which is the separation of lanes by the use of islands and medians, does not reduce the number of conflicts but separates them in space and time so that only one conflict need be dealt with at one moment by the driver. It allows drivers to wait for a favorable chance to conduct one maneuver without preventing other drivers from conducting other maneuvers. It also makes all maneuvers either merging-diverging at low relative speeds or direct right-angled crossings, where the driver has better visibility and the conflict is of shorter duration than in angled crossings. Channelization is often used in conjunction with traffic signals at major intersections. Even on minor intersections, islands may be used to improve safety, to provide room for planting, or to allow an easier adjustment to steep cross slopes.

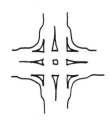

The rotary is a device to convert all crossings into merging and diverging sequences, that is, into weaving operations, which are safer because of their low relative speeds. Since only one lane can weave at a time, the total capacity of a rotary is never more than can be gained with one lane of crossing flow around the circle. The width of the rotary pavement, however, should at least equal the number of entering lanes on the largest incoming street, plus one lane. Rotaries are useful where total intersection flow is approximately 500 to 3000 vehicles per hour, depending on the predominance of through and left-turn movements. At this volume of flow, they are particularly useful where more than four roads converge. The length allowed for weaving is critical for capacity. At 25 miles per hour, a 100-foot weaving section may carry only half the normal single-lane capacity, and 400 feet may be required to give full single-lane flow. At higher speeds, 800 feet may be required for full capacity, and 300 feet for half capacity. Minimum weaving lengths are usually set at about 200 or 250 feet. The rotary keeps traffic moving smoothly where flows do not exceed these single-lane levels and where the circle can be made large enough to give adequate weaving length. But where rotaries are small or flows exceed the capacity of the single weaving lane, traffic is liable to "freeze." Thus rotaries have only a restricted usefulness and tend to consume tremendous areas of ground. The enclosed circle is normally barren. Rotaries are also dif-

ficult for pedestrians to cross, except by bridges or tunnels.

Grade separations are expensive, space-demanding, confusing to the driver, and inflexible with regard to future change. They should be used only where necessary, that is, when a channelized intersection with signals cannot carry the load. A grade separation is often considered necessary when the flow on the major channel is over 3000 vehicles per hour.

One of the most common types of grade-separated interchange is the cloverleaf, with its indirect left turns. Cloverleafs may be full or partial, depending on whether all possible turns are allowed. They take much space and are confusing in form, but the public is by now somewhat adjusted to them. Capacity is high, except with regard to the left turn, where no more than a single lane can diverge and speed is slow around the tight reverse turn.

If left-turn volumes are high, as for example where two urban freeways intersect, then a direct left-turn interchange will have to be used, which requires a complex and expensive structure. More than one lane can be pulled off, and in a direction that makes sense to the driver. Left-turning ramps may be provided for all left turns or only for particular ones.

Where only one channel is of major importance, it is common to use either a bridged rotary or a diamond intersection, in which conflicts are allowed on the secondary road but not on the major one. The diamond type, in particular, is saving of space in tight urban situations.

Many special types of grade separation are in use or can be developed. However complicated, they can be analyzed by tracing out each possible through or turning movement and by checking the capacity of each part of the intersection with expected flows in that direction. Special types for particular problems can best be developed by the use of movement diagrams, beginning with the expected pattern of heavy flows. Such diagrams explain the conflicts resulting from alternate patterns. Colors can be used to separate levels diagrammatically and to indicate the bridging required, which is indicative of the total cost.

Rough scale drawings can then be used to check whether the intersection would be workable and to indicate the space required. The requirements that are most critical for the size and feasibility of a separated intersection are the maximum ramp grades, the minimum ramp radii, and the minimum lengths of acceleration and deceleration lanes.

Maximum ramp grades are usually given as follows:

| | |
|---|---|
| Up ramps | 4–6% |
| Up ramps, high volume | 3–4% |
| Down ramps | 8% |

Minimum ramp radii are the same as those for any traffic
pavement and depend on design speed. Design speeds of 20
to 30 miles per hour are usually employed on such ramps. *See page 156*
The required length of acceleration and deceleration lanes,
including the entering taper, depends on the relative speed
of traffic on the main road and on the ramp being entered or
left. Given a ramp designed for 20 miles per hour, the required total lengths are:

| Design speed of highway (miles per hour) | 40 | 50 | 60 |
|---|---|---|---|
| Length of deceleration lane and taper (ft) | 250 | 350 | 400 |
| Length of acceleration lane and taper (ft) | 250 | 450 | 700 |

The capacity of such complex intersections must be analyzed part by part: the through lanes, the turning lanes,
and so on. Limits to capacity are likely to be met at the acceleration lanes, where turning traffic is merging back into
through traffic. Here, if the maneuver is smoothly designed
with an adequately long acceleration lane, total flow in the
merging line may come up to 80 percent of full single-lane
capacity. Where major flows are coming together, it may be
possible to bring in two lanes instead of one, although merging cannot be effected for a long distance. In the extreme
case, it is also possible to allow two, three, or even more separate lanes to merge or diverge simultaneously into or from
an equal number of through lanes by using separate on or off
ramps for each set of lanes. Obviously, this is a complex, expensive solution.

Pedestrian spaces may also be analyzed for their ca- *Standing room*
pacity. Space for standing is unimpeded when there is an *only*
area of more than 13 square feet per person, and it is easy to
move about. This is a desirable standard for crowd spaces.
Below this point, circulation is somewhat impeded, and people must resort to polite warnings or touches to move through
the crowd. Below 7 square feet per person, standing becomes
constrained: only limited internal circulation is possible,
and people move as a group rather than as individuals. This
is the tolerable minimum for crowd spaces. At 3 square feet
per person, there is no internal circulation, and people are
forced into physical contact with each other, an unpleasant
situation in this culture and dangerous if panic movements

should occur. It is, however, physically possible to pack people into spaces of even less than 1½ square feet per person.

The capacity of walkways is summarized in Table 2. Since average speeds vary from over 300 feet per minute

| TABLE 2. CAPACITY OF WALKWAYS | Rate of flow (persons per minute per foot of walk- |
|---|---|
| Quality of flow | way width) |
| Completely open | under ½ |
| Unimpeded: free movement; walking groups are maintained easily | ½–2 |
| Impeded: groups must shift and re-form; much maneuvering but few conflicts | 2–6 |
| Constrained: groups cannot be maintained; cross flows cause conflicts | 6–10 |
| Moderately congested: touching necessary; frequent conflicts throughout the stream | 10–14 |
| Heavily congested: even slowest walkers are obstructed | 14–18 |
| Jammed: enforced mass movement or a stand-still | 0–25 |

(brisk walk) in open flow to less than 150 feet per minute (shuffle) at maximum rates of flow, the total walkway space occupied by a single pedestrian in the examples given can vary from over 600 square feet in open flow to less than 6 square feet in a jam (that is, the condition of "constrained standing"). Six persons per minute per foot of walk width may be taken as the desirable maximum rate and 10 as the tolerable maximum in the ordinary case.

Pedestrian flow usually comes in pulses, or "platoons," as crowds are intermittently released or interrupted, and as slower walkers impede more rapid ones. This effect is more noticeable where flows are moderate rather than where they are heavy or very light. The instantaneous rate of flow while a platoon is passing may be 1½ to 2½ times the flow averaged over a 15-minute period. Rates of flow will also vary throughout the day, when employees pour in and out of an area at the rush hours or when shoppers and lunchers frequent the stores and restaurants at midday. Average flows during peak periods of this kind may be 2 to 4 times the average flow for a normal 15-minute period. Flows must be calculated from direct observation or from assumed relations between the quantity of residents, employees, or shoppers and the quantity of floor space provided. In midtown Manhattan, for example, 1000 square feet of residential floor space attracts 6 in-and-out trips per day, while a similar amount of office space attracts 14 trips, and this amount of department store space, 300 trips.

Two-directional flow on a sidewalk is not much less efficient than one-way flow, since pedestrians adjust themselves into nonconflicting streams. This is not true, however, when there is a small reverse flow opposing a major stream. When the reverse flow is only 10 percent of total flow, for example, total walkway capacity may be reduced by 15 percent.

*Stairs and crossings*

Public stairways, under normal and easy conditions, do not average more than 2 persons per minute per foot of width. This rate may rise to a maximum of 16 persons, when a crowded stair is fed by a permanent queue and when there is no passing or any reverse flow. Escalators do not increase the rate of flow moving up stairs; they simply reduce the effort of mounting. Wherever flows of more than 2 persons per minute per foot are expected, bunching at the head or foot of stairs and escalators will occur, and reservoir space must be provided for this.

Similarly, reservoir space should be provided where pedestrians must wait at street crossings, especially when the flow of the feeding sidewalks is more than 2 persons per minute per foot. Crosswalks should be *wider* than the incoming sidewalks, since two pedestrian streams will meet head on. And when adjacent walk flows rise to 6 or 10 persons per minute per foot, grade intersections will be chaotic, with people waiting in the street or crossing against the lights.

Vertical Alignment

The vertical alignment of the center line of a road is also made up of straight tangents — constant upgrades or downgrades — with vertical curves at the junctions. These vertical curves are parabolic rather than circular. Parabolic curves are used because they are easy to set out in the field and they make a smooth transition between the intersecting grades. The grades of the tangents are expressed in percentages, or the feet of rise or fall per 100 feet of horizontal run. By convention, grades are given as positive percentages when uphill in the direction of increasing numbers in the stationing and negative when downhill. This vertical alignment is conventionally shown on a series of *profiles*, or contin-

Gradients

See page 172

See page 156

uous sections of the center line of a stretch of road, drawn to an exaggerated vertical scale.

The minimum grade of tangents so that water will drain off the road surface is 0.5 percent. In special cases, the pavement may be laid dead flat. But if possible, the street profile has positive drainage throughout: there are no sag curves or downhill dead-end streets occurring at points that will be difficult to drain on the plan.

The maximum grade of streets depends on design speed. Maximum grades should not be long sustained. A passenger car cannot stay in high gear if the grade is continuously above 7 percent, while a large truck must shift down on sustained grades of over 3 percent. Maximum grades are somewhat flexible, depending on winter conditions and on local habits due to prevailing terrain. Where icing is severe, anything over 10 percent may be too steep, while in San Francisco regulations may allow grades up to 15 percent on minor streets. A 17 percent sustained grade is the most that a large truck can climb in lowest gear.

The maximum grade of sidewalks should be 10 percent, or less if icing is frequent. Short ramps at breaks in grade may go up to 15 percent, however. If steps are used, there must be at least three risers, so that they will be noticed, and accidental falls avoided. The steps should be designed to prevent bypassing. In the stepped ramp, there is a single riser to each long, gently sloping tread (5 to 8 percent). The tread is long enough to require an odd number of paces to traverse it. Since a normal pace is about 2½ feet, preferable tread depths are therefore 2'6", 7'6", and 12'6". The size of the normal pace should also be remembered in placing stepping-stones. A useful rule for proportioning conventional exterior steps is that the height of two risers added to the depth of the tread should equal 27 inches. Riser height may vary between 6½ inches as a maximum and 3 inches as a minimum. Stairs in heavy public use should never rise above a gradient of 50 percent.

Vertical curves

The symmetrical parabolic vertical curve has the elements shown in Figure 18. This parabolic curve drops below the original tangent line in proportion to the square of its distance from the point of curvature, but it can easily be laid out graphically with sufficient accuracy for residential work. Choose the length L, locate the PC and PT so that they are equidistant horizontally from the PI, and draw the chord. Then locate the intermediate point of the parabolic curve, which is halfway, vertically, between the chord and the PI. The PC, the intermediate point, and the PT are three points on the required parabola, which can then be drawn with a French curve.

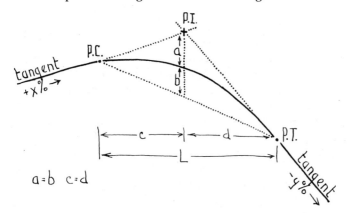

Where the algebraic difference between tangents is more than 9 percent, the long low modern cars will strike the road surface in passing the break in grade. (In Figure 18, for example, the algebraic difference between the intersecting tangents would be $x\% - (-y\%)$, or $x + y\%$). Therefore, vertical curves must be inserted in any driveway where such a break occurs, using a curve that is 1 foot long for each 1 percent of algebraic difference in grade.

FIGURE 18  *Elements of the parabolic curve used in vertical alignment.*

The required length of a vertical curve in an ordinary street, however, is controlled by "roadability" — the avoidance of an unpleasant jolt in the vehicle making the grade transition, a jolt which is caused by an excessive acceleration or deceleration of vertical velocity — and by the need to maintain adequate sight distance. For roadability, a vertical curve is required wherever the algebraic difference in grade is 2 percent or more. The minimum length of the curve depends on design speed and the difference in grade. If, for example, the gradients in the diagram were $+5$ percent and $-8$ percent and the design speed was 30 miles per hour, then the required curve length would be: $20 (5 + 8) = 260$ ft.

*See page 156*

Minimum forward sight distance must be maintained throughout the vertical as well as the horizontal alignment. This is computed as being vision from a point 4 feet above the road to a point 4 inches above the road and may be scaled

*Sight distance*

154

from the profiles. Sight distance may sometimes require longer vertical curves at summits than are needed for road-ability. In sag curves the resulting length of headlight beam must also be checked to see that it is equal to minimum sight distance.

Profiles should be flattened at street intersections so that halted vehicles need not hang on their brakes and can start easily. There should be a "platform" of not over 4 per-cent grade extending at least 40 feet each way from the in-tersection. This often causes difficulty where many cross streets intersect a street on a steep gradient and must some-times be sacrificed.

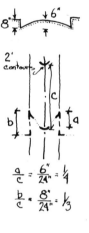

*From profiles to contours*

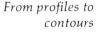

Once the profile has been constructed, it may at any time be converted to a contoured map as follows. First, the draftsman locates where each contour crosses the center line on the profile and transfers this to the map. Then, knowing the fall from crown of road to gutter, he can see that the con-tour will cross the gutter at a point proportionately as far uphill toward the next contour above as the fall from crown to gutter is in proportion to the contour interval. Thus, if the gutter is 6 inches below the crown and the contour interval is 2 feet, then any new contour will cross the gutter, in plan, one-quarter of the way uphill between the point that the same new contour crosses the center line in plan and the point that the next-higher contour crosses the center line. This can easily be approximated by eye. In the same way the new contour crosses the curb, in plan, as far downhill from the gutter crossing as the height of the curb itself is in pro-portion to the contour interval.

Once the draftsman has located where the contour crosses the center line, gutter, and top of curb with tick marks, he can draw freehand a smooth curve between them, a curve that has the exaggerated form of the road cross section itself. The degree of exaggeration is less on steep slopes and greater on flat ones. Like all local contour forms, it "points" downhill. Thus, a road that is first rather flat, then rises, then falls steeply into a sag, and rises again more gently would if contoured have the appearance that is shown here:

This is a general technique for drawing the contour pattern that represents a surface of known slope and elevation, and it can be used for any predetermined terrace, bank, ditch, parking lot, floor, or other form. It consists of locating all the points where even contour lines must cross lines of fixed profile, or where they must appear between points of known elevation. Then the contours can be drawn outward from these points so that their pattern exhibits the slope and characteristic form of that given surface. Difficult to follow in words, it is quite easy to do after brief practice.

The horizontal and vertical alignments must be considered together, since what is being planned is actually the locus of a single center line in three-dimensional space. The perspective view of that center line in space is an important visual feature of the landscape: it is markedly different from the road alignment as it appears in plan. Small unexplained dips and bumps look awkward, especially when they are clearly visible, as on a long flat curve or a long grade seen from the side. Some shapes give the sense of discontinuity or twisting: a dip just before a curve, a dip in the tangent within a broken-back curve, a horizontal curve that begins in a dip, or a bridge that is skewed to the road or whose deck does not fit smoothly into the vertical alignment. There are also handsome combinations, for example, when vertical and horizontal curves coincide or when the approach alignment is arranged to display a fine bridge from the side. It is a good rule to avoid the partial overlapping of horizontal and vertical curves or to make sure that no visual distortion results from the overlap. It is often useful to construct a simple string or cardboard model of the road center line and thus to analyze its appearance directly.

For reasons of safety, sharp horizontal curves should be avoided on high hills, in deep cuts, or at the foot of steep grades. The change in direction on a reverse curve should not occur when going over a summit. Where a horizontal curve occurs on a grade of over 5 percent, the maximum allowable percent of grade on the curve should be reduced by 0.5 percent for each 50 feet that the curve radius is less than 500 feet.

Table 3 indicates the variations in alignment standards according to design speed. An appropriate design speed for minor residential streets is 25 miles per hour. Major streets would be designed for 35 or 40 miles per hour,

*Alignment as a related whole*

*Numerical standards by design speed*

and highways for 50 or 60. Maximum grades at the slowest speeds may be increased somewhat where ice and snow are infrequent, but these grades should not be continuous for long stretches.

TABLE 3. ALIGNMENT STANDARDS IN RELATION
TO DESIGN SPEED

| Design speed (mph) | Minimum radius of horizontal curves (ft) | Maximum % of grade | Minimum forward sight distance (ft) | Minimum length of vertical curve for each 1% change of grade (ft) |
|---|---|---|---|---|
| 20 | 100 | 12 | 150 | 10 |
| 30 | 250 | 10 | 200 | 20 |
| 40 | 450 | 8 | 275 | 35 |
| 50 | 750 | 7 | 350 | 70 |
| 60 | 1100 | 5 | 475 | 150 |
| 70 | 1600 | 4 | 600 | 200 |

Chapter **8**

# *Technique:*
# Earthwork and Utilities

$A$ll site development requires a remodeling of the earth's surface, and sometimes it calls for a very large disturbance. The remodeling is specified by a grading plan, which comes to be the key technical document in site planning. Grading has a strong influence on cost, utility, and appearance of the completed project. Changes in earth-moving technology have been more striking than in any other aspect of site construction.

Grading operations begin by stripping off the topsoil, which is stored in heaps and will later be replaced over the new shape of the subsoil. There must be a place to put these temporary piles where they will not interfere with surface drainage or with building operations. Grade stakes showing the required new levels are then set at intervals in the subsoil — often, but not always, after most of the major structures have been erected. The grade stakes are put at critical points, such as peaks, changes in grade, outlets, culverts, roads, buildings, as well as at regular intervals in any featureless ground. Stakes also indicate the lines along which areas of cut and fill merge back into the existing grade or into each other. Machines then cut or fill the ground to the staked levels and shape it into a smooth curve between the stakes. Allowance is made for the depth of topsoil that will be replaced and for the expected settlement of the fill.

*Grading process*

*Reference 40*

Material cut out of the ground fluffs up to as much as 145 percent of its original volume as it is being handled in a loose state and then recompacts as it is replaced in fill. The final ratio between the volume of earth before it is cut out and after it is filled in elsewhere varies according to the material and the method of handling. This ratio must be known when earthwork volumes are calculated. If there is no machine compaction, the volume of fill may exceed the cut from which it came by 15 percent or even 25 percent. If it is compacted well, there may be 10 percent less fill than cut. In normal work, it is customary to make the preliminary assumption that the filled material will be 5 percent less in volume than it was before being cut. This is good only as a first guess, however.

The degree of compaction is partly controllable, and the ideal degree is one that produces a soil dense enough so that it will not settle after the occupation of the site, yet loose enough so that internal drainage is not destroyed. In areas in which settlement will not be critical, fill can be dumped as it comes, from whatever source. When settlement must be controlled, the composition of the fill will be selected, its moisture content will be set so there is just enough to allow the soil grains to slide into stable positions at the right density, and the fill will be pressed down by rollers or loaded vehicles that run over it a specified number of times. Where greater stability is required, the fill will be placed in thin layers, each of which is independently moistened and compacted. However, particularly in areas to be replanted, the subsoil may have inadvertently been compacted too much by the movement of heavy machinery over it, so that it will later form an impervious layer under a waterlogged topsoil. Thus breaking up the top layers of the regraded subsoil by plowing and harrowing is often specified before the topsoil can be respread. The stable balance of the original soil system is difficult to regain.

*Loss of soil*

Other disturbances appear during the grading process. Topsoil and subsoil may be mixed together, and valuable organic material is thereby lost. Even when topsoil is saved as it should be, the natural soil profile is a continuous gradation down to the bedrock, and the overturning and mixing of the subsoil usually means that the biological performance of the new surface will be impaired. Surface erosion will appear on newly graded ground stripped of vegetation, even on 2 percent slopes after a light rain. This results in a loss of topsoil and the pollution of downstream rivers and ponds. Heavy silting in a watershed is a common accompaniment to large-scale development. One remedy is to schedule grading so that it does not remain unfinished but is quickly followed by replanting and occupation. New techniques of grass seeding, as by spraying water, seed, and liquid fertilizer from a vehicle, will also help. All newly graded areas should be dammed at their lower edges by temporary berms (low banks) of earth sufficiently high to impound the local runoff for the time required for the soil particles to settle out. The impounded water seeps through the berm or runs out through small pipes, which act as weep holes. When site construction is complete and the groundcover established, then the berms are removed. Nevertheless, construction sites are notorious for their mud, dust, and polluted outwash.

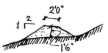

Despite all these difficulties, earth-moving technology offers many compensating potentialities. The power that can be applied to moving ground is now so large that hills can be regraded, solid rock cut out, large lenses of soil removed or imported, hard infertile soil pulverized and made productive. It becomes economical to terrace the Santa Monica mountains for small houses, to make smooth new land in Michigan for cherry orchards, or to throw up artificial hills in Detroit from highway cuttings. The results may be good or bad, but they are surely startling.

Earth is moved by a large variety of machines, and the designer should know something of their capabilities. The tracked bulldozer can push the earth ahead of it with a heavy blade that can be raised, lowered, or tilted. It is the most versatile of the earth machines, particularly good for banks, plateaus, and extensive irregular resurfacing, but it is used wherever a pushing or pulling force is needed — including the felling of trees, the removal of boulders, and the traction of other earth machinery. It can turn on circles of 12- to 20-foot radius and work on slopes up to 85 percent.

*Earth-moving machinery*

*Reference 44*

The huge wheeled scrapers, self-powered or drawn by tractors, take up earth from their undersides and then carry it along to be released at will. They are particularly useful for shallow cuts and long hauls over rough ground. They can turn in 30 feet and operate on slopes up to 60 percent longitudinal and 25 percent transverse. The high-wheeled graders, with a long, delicately adjustable blade suspended underneath, are used for the final shaping of the surface. The power shovels, which cut into material from below with their toothed scoops, load the dump trucks for long hauls over roads, handle weak or broken rock, and excavate hills, rock faces, and other volumes at their elevation or higher. They turn on 20- to 40-foot circles.

The buckets of the draglines hang from cables at the end of long booms, which in some monster mechanisms may be 300 feet long but are more normally 25 to 85 feet. The buckets are dragged toward the operator, through the material to be excavated. Draglines are useful for large cuts and channels below the level of the machine and for making valleys, mounds, slopes, and banks. They can turn on 40- to 80-foot radii.

Occasionally, soil may be moved hydraulically, being transported as a slurry of water and 20 percent soil, through pipes whose outlets are moved from point to point. After the water runs off, the soil is left at the outlet location as an alluvial fan, which may have a 75-foot radius with a 6 to 7 percent slope.

Finally, there are various kinds of rollers and scarifiers to break up or compact the ground. An economical grading plan will respect the limitations and capabilities of these machines in order to avoid expensive hand shoveling. The curves of new contours should not be sharper than the minimum radii of the expected equipment. Equipment cannot work on slopes that are too steep for it, nor can it work economically in confined places or on small scattered sites.

Normally, new grades are kept as close to preexisting grades as possible, since these usually represent an established equilibrium. Departures upset the drainage pattern, expose or bury the roots of plants, disturb old foundations, and may make visually awkward shapes. The agricultural value of the land must be conserved since it is a resource that only slowly renews itself. Topsoil is stripped, stockpiled, and replaced. Even then, the disturbance to the total soil profile can be serious, especially when the soil will be cut away. One therefore avoids unnecessary shallow cuts. But the site must be disturbed to some degree, and sometimes a dramatic disturbance is best — a hill sheared off, a river drained. One does not do this lightly but, on the other hand, never automatically excludes that possibility.

*Grading criteria*    The principal criteria for a new surface are its fitness for the purposes of its occupants and its ability to be maintained as part of a stable system. It is necessary to imagine acting and moving over it and to check it for its intended plant cover, for erosion, and for drainage. Grassy slopes should be kept below 25 percent, while special ground cov-

ers like ivy may hold stable cut slopes of up to 100 percent.  **161**
Beyond that, it is necessary to crib or terrace the ground.
The angle of repose (the limiting steepness beyond which
soil grains will slip downhill) is a further limitation if one is
making slopes of new fill. The limiting angles range from 30
percent for very wet clay and silt to 80 percent for wet sand.
Even here, a stepped slope, a terrace at the foot of the slope,
or drainage at its top will help to prevent slippage.

The ground should have positive drainage throughout, *Drainage*
without any isolated depressions, to prevent local flooding.
Drainage from sites upstream should not be blocked, nor
should the discharge upon downstream sites be increased.
Water should flow away from buildings and roads, and not
be concentrated in valleys and swales in which no provision
is made for the additional flow.

The new ground must have a pleasing visual form,
harmonious with its landscape context. In most instances, *See pages 206–209*
this will be a simple, smoothly curving, visually stable
form. The ground shape must be imagined from many viewpoints and approaches. Most likely, it will be studied in a
model.

For economy, the amounts of cut and fill (less allow- *Economy*
ances for compaction) should balance out over the site as a
whole or, preferably, within subareas of the site. This is true *See pages 163–168*
except in special situations such as where bedrock is close to
the surface or large volumes of peat are present, when it is
unavoidable that earth be brought in or taken out.

Earth machines demand broad simple forms. Fussy
shapes as well as shallow cuts and fills are to be avoided.
The machinery performs best when it runs along parallel
movement lines — for distances of less than 500 yards.
Undulating hill and valley forms are cheaper than terrac-
ings. So are repetitive land forms. All these cost rules refer
especially to larger areas, perhaps over 5 acres in size.

The most common difficulties that appear in a grading *Grading*
plan are excessive or unbalanced cut and fill; drainage *failures*
pockets in the land, on the roads, or against the sides of
buildings; steep grades that allow erosion or are dangerous or
make use, access, or maintenance difficult; a poor visual or
functional relation between a building or a road and its
immediate surroundings; a visually awkward transition between one section and another; the destruction of existing
trees by changes in the ground level; and the frequent use
of expensive and undesirable steps and retaining walls.

The new surface is usually represented by a drawing

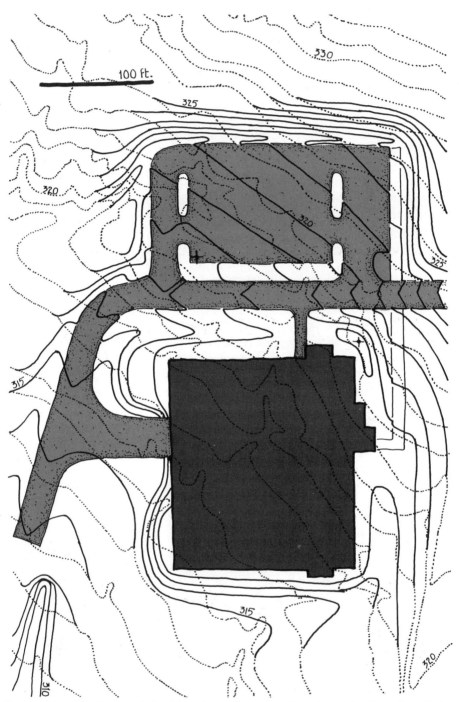

FIGURE 19 *Grading and paving plan for a small industrial plant, by Hideo Sasaki, landscape architect.*

that shows the new contour lines in relation to the old ones, supplemented by spot elevations at some key points. Occasionally, in small areas where there is little to be done, only the spot elevations may be shown. Or if a small area is to be graded to a very exact surface, the new elevations may be given at each corner of an arbitrary but close-meshed imaginary grid. In any case, it is best to sketch the contours first, or to use a model, in order to visualize and control the topographic form.

More often than not, the new form is simply the best transition that can be found between a set of fixed points — the roads, buildings, sewers, and special landscape features — and the existing land at the site boundaries or at the edge of construction. This sought-for transition respects all the criteria mentioned earlier: function, economy, drainage, appearance, and minimum ecological damage. Sometimes, however, the designer is not simply making a trouble-free transition but is handling the ground as a sculptural medium. In either case, contour sketches are his language, and he must be fluent in that language.

Balancing cut and fill or estimating site costs requires a calculation of the earth volume to be moved. Among the several methods of calculation are the contour-area method, the end-area method, and the use of elevation changes at grid corners. The first is best for general site-planning purposes since it is accurate enough for first estimates, fits directly into the process of developing a contoured grading plan, and gives an immediate graphic picture of the quantity and location of earthwork over an extended area. The use of end areas is common in highway work or any linear earth moving, where it is accurate and appropriate for determining the best strategy for hauling cut to fill. The last method, like the first, can be used in more extensive earth moving or for building excavations, but with greater precision and correspondingly less graphic control. All these methods can be supplemented by rough studies and calculations in model form. Therefore the first method will be discussed in some detail and the others in passing.

*Earthwork
calculations*

The first step in the contour-area calculation is to make an earthwork diagram on a copy of the grading plan. The new contours are brought out where they differ from the old and the boundary lines of no-cut, no-fill are drawn. These boundaries are drawn by interconnecting the points where new contours rejoin the old ones and represent the boundaries between disturbed and undisturbed land or between

*Contour-area
method*

areas of cut and of fill. Along these lines, the new surface corresponds to the old one. Next, one should shade the areas between old and new contours at each level, using one color or pattern for cut and another for fill. The result is shown in Figure 20.

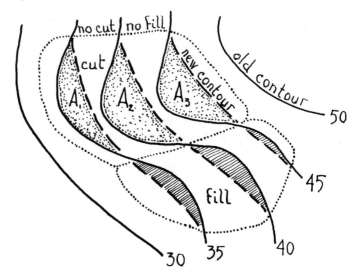

FIGURE 20    *An earthwork diagram, showing the extent of cut and fill.*

The diagram already gives a good visual image of the amount and balance of cut and fill, since the volumes of earth to be moved are proportional to the sums of the shaded areas. Using this visual image alone, one can quickly re-sketch the new contours to get a better approximation of balance. The diagram also conveys the depth of cut and fill, since where the shaded areas almost touch, the depth is almost one contour interval, where they overlap, it is more than one interval, and where they are widely spaced, the depths are shallow. Moreover, as in any contour drawing, small regions of the earthwork diagram, when looked at downhill, convey a somewhat exaggerated picture of how the ground would look in section, with the new grade line cutting through the old surface. When cuts or fills are several contour intervals deep, however, the shaded lenses overlap each other in multiple layers. For deep disturbances, then, this method can be confusing.

The diagram is valuable not only for visual inspection but also as a basis for a quantitative estimate, using an approximation to the volume of a prismoid, or solid figure with two parallel faces. In each continuous cut or fill figure (that is, the region bounded by one no-cut, no-fill line) measure the shaded areas with a planimeter or by some other approximation and sum them up. When this sum is multiplied by the contour interval, the product is the volume of cut or fill in that particular region. In Figure 20, if the contour interval is 5 feet, the total volume of cut, $V$, in the upper region, in cubic feet, would be approximately $V = 5(A_1 + A_2 + A_3)$, where the shaded shapes $A_1$, $A_2$, $A_3$ were measured in square feet, using a planimeter and the map scale. (A planimeter will read with less than 1 percent error if properly used.) This is an approximate formula, which assumes that the volumes between each contour are a regular prismoid, and that the top and bottom of a volume of cut or fill is a regular cone. By summing all the volumes in every region of cut, one can compare their total with a similar sum of sums for all regions of fill, to see how close one is to total balance. The percentage of loss or gain due to compaction must be applied to the sum of cut volumes at this step.

Moreover, if the site is large, various groups of cut and fill regions can be compared to see if there is local balance, which would avoid long hauls. Where balance is lacking and this imbalance is not acceptable, the grading plan is reworked by redrawing the new contours in those regions of cut or fill where local balance is most sharply out, and the volumes for those regions are then recomputed. A few approximations will usually suffice to achieve the necessary balance, and meanwhile the entire topographic form has been kept under visual control.

The end-area method uses the same mathematical approximation: that the volume of a prismoid with two parallel but irregular faces is equal to the average area of those faces times the perpendicular distance between them. But the parallel faces are now vertical rather than horizontal. Sections are drawn at regular intervals along a road center line, showing the new cross section as applied to the existing ground. This is a two-dimensional representation of the cut and fill perpendicular to the center line at that point. Counting cut as positive and fill as negative and allowing for compaction, sum the areas at each section, average that sum with the corresponding sum at the next section, and multiply by the horizontal distance between sections (conventionally, one station, or 100 feet). This gives a total volume of excess cut (positive) or excess fill (negative) between those

*End-area method*

sections. If those cuts and fills are progressively cumulated along the center line, a graph called a mass diagram can be drawn; this shows the surplus or deficit of soil that would be carried if one had begun at the very beginning of the road. Inflections (changes in direction) in this mass diagram correspond to points on the road where cut changes to fill, or vice versa, and the displacement of the line at the end of the graph is the total imbalance. More important, cut and fill are equal between any two locations defined by any horizontal line that cuts two points on the line of the mass diagram. The length of that horizontal line equals the maximum haul distance required to achieve that balance. Thus the mass diagram is useful for planning a strategy of earth moving in the field, as well as for adjusting the balance.

Calculations based on the elevations of grid corners are appropriate for the volume of a borrow pit or a building excavation, as well as for more extensive regrading. They are more accurate than the contour-area method and do not require the use of a planimeter. But they do not permit continuous visual control of the process of adjusting the grading surface, and the successive approximations needed to achieve a balance are more laborious. The method is based on the assumption that a volume of earth of irregular depth but within the four vertical faces of a prism based on a horizontal square is equal to the area of that square times the average depth of the volume at each of the four corners of the prism.

*Calculation by grid*

An imaginary horizontal square grid is applied to the site or the excavation. Existing and proposed new elevations are determined for each grid corner, and the difference computed — points of cut, where the new elevation is below the old, being positive, and points of fill negative. All the differences must then be adjusted for compaction. For example, if cut earth will eventually pack down to 95 percent of its original volume when replaced in fill, then all positive differences should be decreased by 5 percent. In the diagram, if all the elevation differences at salient corners (which are part of only one grid square) are labeled $c$, those at the sides (common to two squares) are labeled $s$, those at reentrant corners (common to three squares) are called $r$, and the internal corners (at the junctions of four squares) are called $i$, then the volume is calculated by the equation

$$V = \frac{x^2}{4} \left( \Sigma c + 2\,\Sigma s + 3\Sigma r + 4\Sigma i \right),$$

where $x$ is the horizontal dimension of the side of every square. This total volume is positive if there is a surplus of cut, negative if there is a surplus of fill, and zero if there is a balance. The total volumes of cut and fill, irrespective of balance, can be computed by separating the summation of positive and negative differences. Local balance can be identified by separating parts of the grid and treating them as if they were isolated figures. Balance is achieved by raising and lowering the various points and recomputing the whole, which may require three or four runs. This is laborious by hand but easily done on a computer. It is a problem, however, to keep in mind the form of the whole surface as discrete points are pushed up or dropped.

A simpler version of this method, used only for checking balance, neglects the differential effect of interior and exterior corners and is therefore appropriate to large areas or where there is neither cut nor fill at any exterior edge or corner. In this case, the sum total of all the existing elevations at grid corners is compared to the total of all new elevations. Equality indicates a balance, or balance may be achieved by adding or subtracting enough at the new elevations to make the total equal to the existing total.

Another method of approximating balance is to model the existing ground surface in damp sand or Plasticine. If the model surface is changed without adding or subtracting material, then it is a new topography that is achievable by balanced cut and fill (although the compaction factor has been neglected). Like the contour-area method, this is an excellent way of simultaneously controlling form and balance. But the new form must still be transferred to a contour drawing for field controls and adjustment to a precise balance. Making a contour drawing from a model is unfortunately more difficult than the reverse. It involves measurements down from a grid suspended over the model terrain or tracing out the new contours with an accurate cantilever arm set to successive contour levels or perhaps by submerging the model in a tank filled with successively higher water levels.

*Calculation by model*

Lengthy computations for earth volume and balance are now being done by computers, and it is unlikely that site planners will often have to make them in the future. It is more important that they understand the basis of those computations and be able to use simple methods where computers are unavailable or uneconomical or where they are giving the wrong answer. Most important, designers must be able to produce grading plans that approximate a balance, or in which they are aware of the degree of imbalance, and at the same time keep control of the ground surface as an important element in the design. It is for this reason that modeling and the contour-area earthwork diagram will probably retain their usefulness.

## Storm Drainage

The storm drainage system takes off the flow of surface water. It is a substitute for natural surface drainage, and it may be unnecessary in low-density development of less than 1 or 2 families per acre. It need not be a continuous system but can discharge into local streams, lakes, and gullies wherever this will not cause flooding or increase pollution. However, storm waters are not free of pollutants once they have run over disturbed land or through the debris and chemicals of the streets or have taken up the fertilizers and pesticides of the fields. Large storm discharges must often be controlled or treated, and every effort must be made to decrease pollution at the source both by modifying the use of chemicals and by stabilizing the new earth surfaces. If natural water bodies or drainage lines are not available, it is possible to discharge into settling pits or overflow basins. These are made in pervious soil and must be big enough to hold water from the worst storm. They can be used to economize on the length of main needed to reach a stream or public sewer, but they render useless a substantial piece of ground and are not very handsome.

Since the required pipe sizes are often large, the underground storm drainage system is expensive, and every effort is made to minimize or eliminate it. Where economic resources are scanty, underground drainage may be avoided by keeping development at low densities, decreasing paved surfaces and increasing planted ones, grading carefully to ensure gentle slopes and positive flow, and relying on ditches, check dams, short culverts, and continuous maintenance. The pipes of large diameter at the bottom of runs in the underground system may cause difficulties in the grading plan by tending to "ride up" out of the ground as they maintain sufficient elevation to reach their destination or as they flatten out to prevent scour inside the pipe. Nevertheless, since the roofs and paved surfaces of residential developments usually interfere with existing surface flow and sharply increase the runoff, some kind of artificial drainage structures, however simple, are usually required to prevent flooding during storms. The storm system is today kept separate from the sanitary drainage to minimize the volume that must be treated in sewage disposal and to prevent backing up of sanitary wastes.

The storm system is made up of a drainage surface, a set of open gutters and ditches, and probably a series of underground pipes, usually made of vitrified clay and laid straight to line and grade, connected by manholes and fed by inlets. Large sewers, over 42 inches in diameter, are made of concrete instead of clay. When the pipes are large enough for a man to enter for inspection or cleaning, they can be gently curved in horizontal alignment. It is now becoming accepted practice in some localities for all sizes of sewer lines to be laid in regular horizontal curves, as long as the radius is not less than 100 feet and the vertical grade is constant. Particularly where streets are curving, this technique minimizes sewer length and the number of manholes and allows the sewer to remain in a standard location with reference to the street and other utilities. The smaller lines cannot then be inspected visually, and flow is somewhat slower, but modern cleaning machinery can easily be sent through such curves. Small curved sewers may not be permitted by local ordinance, however.

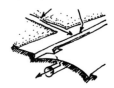

Manholes — man-sized circular pits — are used to enter the lines or to look down their length. They are placed at the upper end of lines and at every change in horizontal or vertical direction or curvature. They should also be placed no more than 300 to 500 feet apart to permit the use of cleaning apparatus. An economical design will minimize their number.

Surface water first flows in a film across the ground, and it is kept spread out as long as possible. The aim is to keep this surface water moving, but not so fast as to cause erosion. Allowable slopes therefore depend on the volume of water expected, the surface finish, and the amount of damage that can be done by local flooding. Planted areas and broad paved areas should have a minimum grade of 1 percent, although open land far from structures, where occasional ponding can be permitted, may slope as little as 0.5 percent. Streets and other paved surfaces that are laid to exact elevations may also have a minimum grade of 0.5 percent. Land should slope away from all buildings for 10 feet with a minimum grade of 2 percent. Drainage swales and ditches require a similar minimum of 2 percent and a maximum gradient of 10 percent, or of 5 percent if the area drained is over half an acre. Lawns and grass banks can have a maximum slope of 25 percent, while unmowed planted banks can slope up to 50 percent, or perhaps up to 60 percent in firm, undisturbed soil. Expensive cribbing or retaining walls are needed to hold steeper slopes.

The ground should be sloped so that there is positive drainage throughout, even if there is also an underground system, since that underground system may at times be clogged. Undrained sinks should be avoided. The designer must be aware of the quantity and velocity of flow entering his site from the outside and of how it may change in the future. On the other hand, if he wants to avoid claims for damages, he contrives to let surface water leave his own property only along the drainage courses previously existing and never in greater amounts than before.

*Gutters and ditches*

Surface flow over a uniform, moderate slope will often begin to cut small rivulets within 500 feet. Before it begins to concentrate naturally and to form these gullies, it is concentrated artificially and put under control in man-made channels. It is picked up by the walks or in grass ditches and delivered into the street gutters or ditches. Where swales or ditches drain more than one lot of land, they must be open to common maintenance, and easements are required. Natural creeks and gullies may now receive increased flows because of the hard-surface development. They will erode and be laden with silt, and bankside trees will be undermined. To prevent erosion, check dams must be installed to reduce velocities, or the channel may be paved, or drains may have to be installed. But if storm drains are laid, trees in a wooded swale may be lost in any case as a broad swathe is cleared for construction. The best solution may then be a bypass drain, leading water away from the draw.

In the street gutter the storm water can be allowed to flow for some distance before being taken up by the underground drains or discharged into streams or off the property. This gutter flow should not be allowed to run across a street or walk, and thus it must be picked up at least once on each block, at the lowest corner, or be carried under the crossroad in a culvert. Usually the gutter will have sufficient capacity to carry the flow from one block, although it is desirable not to allow water to run more than 800 to 1000 feet before reaching the sewers, and then only in fairly level ground with efficient inlet systems. If necessary, the capacity of a gutter to carry any given flow can be tested by the Manning formula. No substantial gutter flow should have to turn a sharp corner or meet a sudden obstacle, such as a protruding

*See page 177*

driveway apron. If it does, a heavy flow may jump out of the gutter and cause erosion and flooding.

The flow from gutters and ditches, if not previously turned into a natural drainage course, is finally caught by inlets placed in the gutter or face of the curb, usually at street intersections or at low points in streets or grounds. Inlets have a grating to hold back large debris and are connected by short branch lines to the main drain, preferably at a manhole. Catch basins (or "trapped inlets," as they are called in some localities) are sometimes inserted here to collect the grit and trash. But since these basins may become nuisances and require frequent cleaning, they are used only where much grit is likely, because of sandy soil or earth roads, and where slopes are flat and velocities low.

*Reference 42*

Sewer lines must be covered deeply enough to prevent breakage and freezing (4 feet in the latitude of New England, for example), while if they are buried more than 20 feet deep, the excavation work will be costly. Lines must have a minimum slope so that the velocity of flow allows self-cleaning. The slope required to achieve this velocity depends on pipe size and quantity of flow, but it may be taken as 0.3 percent minimum in preliminary trials before size and quantity have been determined. In later calculations, this minimum velocity is taken as 2 feet per second when flowing full, which will provide for sufficient speed when the sewer flows only partially full. On the other hand, the slope must not give velocities over 10 feet per second, which begins to cause scouring of the pipe. This may demand large pipes and flat slopes in the lower ends of lines as quantities build up.

*Sewer lines*

Changes in slope may be made only at manholes. Manholes may be of the drop type, where the upper line enters above the lower receiving one. Otherwise, the ends of two connecting lines are laid so that the tops or center lines (not the bottoms!) of the pipes are at the same level. However, the vertical position of pipes is traditionally specified by giving the elevation of the invert, or the lowest point on the internal surface. A pipe is never allowed to discharge into one smaller than itself since floating matter might jam at the smaller entrance.

The storm sewer system is initially laid out in plan, with the first inlets located as far down the slopes as possible, within the limit for flow in the open gutter. The pattern of converging sewers is then arranged so that there is a minimum length of line and a minimum number of manholes,

*Sewer layout*

which are nevertheless placed to be close to all necessary inlets and to allow straight runs (or perhaps regular circular curves) within the right-of-way between their locations. Since repair and cleaning are usually done at the manhole rather than in between, the manholes must be in the right-of-way, but the sewer lines themselves may occasionally run through easements separate from the right-of-way. Preliminary profiles of the top of the sewer pipe are then plotted on the street profiles, with the pipe as close to ground surface as possible within the limits stated for cover and minimum slope. Since the system must meet the outfall sewer, settling basin, or stream at the right elevation, it is easier to draw this preliminary profile upward from the discharge point. Finally, pipe size must be computed by the site planner or his engineer in order to estimate cost, check velocities in the pipe, and avoid excessive depth of cut. Technical problems of the storm drainage system will sometimes require modification of the general site plan. In laying out the system and computing pipe size, the designer must take account of other areas draining into the area under study and of the possibility that more intensive development may increase future drainage.

Occasionally a development has to be laid out on a completely flat or swampy site, which causes problems for all the utilities. Storm drainage can sometimes be handled by keeping the crown of the road dead level but letting the gutters alternately rise and fall so that they will discharge into a series of inlets along their length. Here the water falls into the underground system, or if there is no outlet for an underground system, the water runs off through ditches to overflow basins, where the water is ponded until it seeps into the ground. The land surface is graded so that house sites and paths are above the pond levels, and thus the critical parts of the site are protected from flooding. Such retention basins, or even the street itself, may be used for temporary ponding so that pipe sizes lower down can be more efficiently sized. But temporary ponds leave a muddy scar and must be sprayed against the breeding of insects.

*The runoff formula*     As a preliminary to finding required pipe size, flows are computed by the so-called "rational" formula $Q = CIA$, in which $Q$ is the quantity of runoff in cubic feet per second, $I$ is the intensity of rainfall in inches per hour, $A$ is the drainage area in acres, and $C$ is the coefficient of runoff. The quantity $Q$ is in cubic feet per second, even though $I$ is in inches per hour and $A$ in acres, simply because the unit "inch-acres per hour" happens by chance to be very closely

equivalent to cubic feet per second (1:1.008). A complete
exposition of the assumptions and techniques involved in the
use of this formula is unnecessary for general site-planning
work since an engineer experienced in these utility systems
would be required to detail them and there are other methods
of calculation in use, particularly for major hydraulic instal-
lations. It is worthwhile, however, to understand the basic
method, since the formula may be used in all minor drainage work and also because it is useful to be able to make a
rough check of quantities, sizes, and slopes in ditches, culverts, and in the lower ends of storm drainage lines. In any
case, the minimum diameter is 12 inches for a storm sewer
that drains a street and 10 inches for one that drains a yard
area. These minimums are set to prevent stoppage by trash.

The coefficient of runoff $C$, the fraction of total rainfall
that runs off on the surface, may vary from almost 1 on
waterproof surfaces — or even over 1 where warm rain falls
on ice or snow — to as low as 0.01 in dense old woods with
spongy soil. The coefficient for any area may be estimated
from the following approximate values:

*Runoff coefficients*

|  | $C$ |
|---|---|
| Roofs, asphalt and concrete pavements, other waterproof surfaces | 0.9 |
| Macadam, compacted earth and gravel, without plant growth | 0.7 |
| Impervious soil, with plant cover | 0.5 |
| Lawns and planted areas, with normal soil | 0.2 |
| Woods | 0.1 |

These values for $C$ are for flat slopes. They should be increased somewhat for slopes over 3 or 4 percent. Or they
may more quickly be estimated for composite areas from the
following:

|  | $C$ |
|---|---|
| Residential development at 10 families per acre | 0.3–0.5 |
| Residential development at 40 families per acre | 0.5–0.7 |
| Dense urban commercial areas | 0.7–0.9 |

Variations within the ranges depend on the perviousness of
the soil, its plant or artificial cover, and the steepness of
slopes.

The intensity of rainfall $I$ depends on the general climatic region in which the site is located and also on the cho-

*The year of storm*

sen "year of storm," or the frequency with which a storm of a certain intensity is likely to occur. Thus a "5-year storm" has an intensity which was equaled or exceeded as many times in all the years of record as if that had happened once every 5 years. It may happen any time, of course, but the probability of its happening in any future year is 1 in 5. A "20-year storm" is an unusually heavy one whose probability of occurrence in any year is 1 in 20, and so on. A low year of storm may be chosen as the basis of calculation for scattered, low-value development where an occasional overload of the system is not critical. A higher year of storm would be used for a dense, high-value area where even infrequent flooding might be serious; the resulting system will be an expensive one, rarely used to capacity. Thus, 10-year, or even 5-year, storm frequencies may be used for residential development, and 25-year, or even 50-year, frequencies for shopping centers, but local regulations vary.

*Rainfall rate*

The intensity of rainfall during a storm also varies from moment to moment. It is usually assumed from general experience that average intensity decreases as storm duration increases. Thus the average intensity of rainfall of any storm, up to any given moment, depends on the climatic region, the chosen storm frequency, and the elapsed time since the storm began. This rate is estimated from the past rainfall experience of the area, as summarized in local hydrologic or weather data. The simplest estimation formula is

$$I = \frac{K}{t + b}$$

where $I$ is the average intensity in inches per hour, $t$ is the time in minutes since the beginning of the storm, and $K$ and $b$ are constants that depend on the storm frequency and the climatic region. Table 4 and Figure 21 give these constants for regions of the United States.

*Time of concentration*

The value of $t$ used in a calculation for pipe size is the time required for the crest of maximum flow to reach the point in question. At the top of a sewer line, this time is the interval needed for the largest volume of water to reach the topmost inlet from its tributary area. Inlet times vary from 5 to 40 minutes and may be taken to be 10 minutes in suburban residential development. In general, inlet times vary directly with the distance to the farthest point of the drainage area, and inversely as the coefficient of runoff and the square root of average slope. Since peak flows fall off as time of concentration increases, it follows that flows (and

FIGURE 21 *Rainfall regions of the United States, to be used in Table 4.*

TABLE 4. INTENSITY OF RAINFALL BY REGIONS

| Fre-quency (years) | Coeffi-cients | Region (see Figure 21) | | | | | | |
|---|---|---|---|---|---|---|---|---|
| | | 1 | 2 | 3 | 4 | 5 | 6 | 7 |
| 2 | K | 206 | 140 | 106 | 70 | 70 | 68 | 32 |
| | b | 30 | 21 | 17 | 13 | 16 | 14 | 11 |
| 5 | K | 247 | 190 | 131 | 97 | 81 | 75 | 48 |
| | b | 29 | 25 | 19 | 16 | 13 | 12 | 12 |
| 10 | K | 300 | 230 | 170 | 111 | 111 | 122 | 60 |
| | b | 36 | 29 | 23 | 16 | 17 | 23 | 13 |
| 25 | K | 327 | 260 | 230 | 170 | 130 | 155 | 67 |
| | b | 33 | 32 | 30 | 27 | 17 | 26 | 10 |
| 50 | K | 315 | 350 | 250 | 187 | 187 | 160 | 65 |
| | b | 28 | 38 | 27 | 24 | 25 | 21 | 8 |
| 100 | K | 367 | 375 | 290 | 220 | 240 | 210 | 77 |
| | b | 33 | 36 | 31 | 28 | 29 | 26 | 10 |

therefore pipe sizes) may be decreased by increasing the inlet time, that is, by slowing down the rate at which rainwater flows across the land, whether by flattening slopes or by increasing the runoff coefficient C (as by planting), or even by temporarily impounding the flowing waters.

The time used for calculating intensity at any lower point in the sewer is the original inlet time plus the time required for the crest of flow to run down the line to that point. The crest is carried down from manhole to manhole, the time gradually lengthening and the average intensity therefore gradually slackening.

For many parts of the world, there are no detailed data that permit the estimation of average storm intensity by year of frequency and time of concentration. Much rougher calculations must be made. There may be a record of the heaviest one-hour storm that occurred in the last 20 years, which can then be used without correcting for time of concentration. Or the record may have been for only a shorter period, in which case one can convert from one year of storm frequency to another by a formula based on general experience:

$$\frac{I_x}{I_y} = \frac{1 + k \log x}{1 + k \log y},$$

where $I_x$ is the intensity for a storm of $x$ years of frequency, and $I_y$ of $y$ years, and $k$ is a constant that is 1.0 for areas of moderate rainfall and ranges from 0.65 for areas of high rainfall to 1.75 for areas of low rainfall. That is, in dry areas there is usually a greater difference between unusual and normal storms. The rainfall record in a place is even more likely to refer to maximum rainfall during a 24-hour day than to the maximum average intensity for one hour. The former can be converted to the latter by the rough guess that 40 percent of a day's rain fell in the peak hour. Obviously, one uses better data whenever available.

*Drainage areas*

The area $A$, expressed in acres, is simply the total area drained by each set of inlets. With the knowledge that surface water flows perpendicularly to the contours, the "divides" between inlet drainage areas can be drawn, and the size of each area can be computed by planimeter. Off-site as well as on-site drainage areas must be included in the analysis.

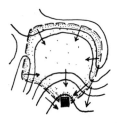

The total flow leaving any manhole to enter the next section of pipe is therefore the sum of the rate of flow of the crest arriving from any line above, plus the rate entering at that moment at the manhole's own inlets. The latter quantity is computed from $Q = CIA$, using the values of $C$, $I$, and $A$ proper to this set of inlets.

*Size of storm
drains*

If the rate of flow in any pipe and its slope from the preliminary profile are known, its required size may be computed from the formula

$$D = \left(\frac{Q}{10\pi s^{1/2}}\right)^{3/8}$$

where $Q$ is the rate in cubic feet per second, $S$ is the slope written as a decimal, and $D$ is the inside diameter of the required pipe in feet. Since $D$ will come out as a fractional number, the pipe chosen for use should be the next standard size larger. Standard sizes of sewer pipe increase by 2-inch intervals from 4 to 12 inches, and thence by 3-inch intervals to 36 inches. Pipe should never be much oversize, however, since resulting velocities at light loads may be too small.

This formula for pipe size is derived from the Manning formula for flow in open channels:

$$V = \frac{1.5}{n} R^{2/3} S^{1/2},$$

where $V$ is the velocity of flow in feet per second, $S$ is the slope written as a decimal, $R$ is the hydraulic radius, and $n$ is the coefficient of roughness of the inner surface of pipe or channel. This coefficient varies as follows:

|  | $n$ |
|---|---|
| Smooth, clean, metal pipe | 0.01 |
| Smooth concrete | 0.013 |
| Brick or vitrified clay | 0.015 |
| Smooth earth | 0.02–0.035 |
| Rough channel, overgrown | 0.03–0.05 |

The hydraulic radius $R$ is equal to the cross-sectional area of the flowing water, divided by the length of that part of the cross-sectional perimeter of the channel which is in contact with the flow.

This formula may be employed for pipes at atmospheric pressure, as well as for ditches, open channels, gutters, and streams. But it should not be used where velocity is over 10 feet per second, or where the hydraulic radius is greater than 10 feet. It is used to calculate velocity, given the slope, the hydraulic radius resulting from the depth of flow in the channel, and the coefficient of roughness due to the type of channel. The rate of flow is then the product of this velocity times the cross-sectional area of the flowing water.

The general formula for the size of sewer pipe, given earlier, has been derived from the Manning formula by assuming the use of vitrified clay pipe ($n = 0.015$), circular and flowing full, since the purpose is to find the smallest pipe that will carry the expected flow. In this case $R$ is equal to one-fourth the inside diameter of the pipe, and the cross section of flow equals $\pi D^2/4$.

After pipe size has been calculated, the velocity of flow

must be checked, by the Manning formula, for the occasions of maximum flow. By our simplification, the resulting velocity is

$$V = 40D^{2/3} S^{1/2},$$

$S$ being the slope as a decimal and $D$ the actual internal pipe diameter in feet. If the resulting velocity in the pipe is outside the preferred range of between 2 and 10 feet per second, then the slope of the pipe must be readjusted. Velocities below 2 may fail to keep the pipe clean, and those above 10 may scour its inner surface. Then the required pipe size and velocity must be recomputed and the process repeated until a satisfactory combination is found.

Normally, this system would be computed and designed by an engineer specialist, but it is useful for the site planner to understand the computation and its implications and to see how it can be applied to all kinds of drainage work and flow in open channels. With this knowledge a designer can always check a particular ditch or gutter or run of pipe that may be critical for size or slope. Since trouble often appears at the bottom of a run, the last pipe is worth a check.

*Approxima-
tions at critical
points*

The quantity of flow at the end or at any point in the line can be approximated by using the "rational" formula, $Q = CIA$, first extimating the overall $C$ and then computing an $A$ that covers the entire site drained by every inlet up to and including the last one upstream. Next, one takes an $I$ that is an average between the value expected at the top inlet ($t$ = inlet time) and the value of $I$ that would be expected at the last inlet just upstream if the crest had moved down from the longest branch at some reasonable constant rate, say 4 feet per second. The quantity $Q$ computed from these values of $C$, $I$, and $A$ can then be tried out at the slope tentatively given for the line in question.

*Culverts*

A short length of pipe that is inserted under a road or other barrier to carry storm water or a small brook is called a culvert. It is, in effect, a fragmentary storm drainage system. Normally, culverts are circular in cross section and are made of concrete or corrugated metal. They should be straight, should cross the road approximately at right angles, and should use the line of the old channel if possible. But in any case they should cross the road at the first opportunity, and should not allow water to course along the uphill side of the road, which causes erosion.

Where possible, culverts are laid at the slope of the old

channel, but with a maximum grade of 8 to 10 percent and a minimum grade of 0.5 percent. The gradient just below the outlet must be at least as steep as the slope just above the inlet to prevent silting. Inlets and outlets require wing walls and aprons to prevent erosion. To protect it from being crushed, the culvert should be covered with a depth of fill that is equal to one-half the pipe diameter but must be at least 1 foot.

The size of culverts is calculated in the same way as the size of sewer pipes, by computing the quantity of flow from the proper values of the acreage of the watershed and its average coefficient of runoff. The flow should be calculated for a 25-year storm, or even for a greater one, since the culvert cost is small and the consequences of an underestimate serious. As in the approximation given earlier for making a spot check in a sewer system, the rate would be based on an inlet time equal to the time that water might take to flow halfway to the culvert from the farthest point of the drainage area. The required culvert size then depends on the slope of the culvert itself and on the calculated quantity of flow, as shown in the foregoing computations.

Sometimes subsurface drains are installed to carry the water away from wet ground, to prevent seepage through foundations or at embankments, or to correct frost heaving or a high water table. Most often these are 4- to 6-inch tile pipes, perforated or with open joints, laid in a gravel fill. They lead into the storm system or into natural drainage courses. They are put 2½ to 5 feet below ground: deeper and more widely spaced in permeable soil and shallower and closer together in more impervious soil. *Subsurface drains*

Sanitary (a euphemism for insanitary) wastes, such as those from sinks and toilets, are generally kept out of the storm drains but are carried down in a system quite similar in form. This waste is usually carried to a disposal plant, which converts the sewage into an effluent that can safely be discharged into some body of natural water. It is no longer tolerable to allow raw sewage to flow into lakes or rivers. Moreover, we are learning that we have as much to fear from chemical and thermal pollution as from biological pollution and that elaborate treatment, or recycling, of wastes is now imperative. Indeed, if we cannot modify our habits of polluting the water, air, and land, we may soon be able to dispense with site planning and other problems of civilization. *"Sanitary" Drainage*

Sanitary drainage is typically a converging system of manholes and straight pipes, or pipes of gentle horizontal curvature, leading to a disposal plant. Unlike the storm system, it is likely to be continuous over large areas, and it sometimes must be pumped up over divides in order to reach a common point of discharge. Pumping is avoided if possible at the site-planning scale. Sanitary drains may be critical at the large scale, but the layout itself is rarely controlling at the site-planning scale.

Unlike storm sewers, sanitary sewers form a closed drainage system connected, not to open inlets, but directly to sink and toilet drains via traps that seal off the sewer odors. The branch lines leading to houses connect into the main all along its course rather than just at the manholes. If permitted by local regulations, manholes may be replaced by simple and relatively inexpensive cleanouts at the upper ends of lines and also at branchings or breaks in alignment either of house lines or of short laterals bearing the flow of not more than 10 to 12 houses to a main sewer. Where a cleanout is used at a change in direction, the change must be less than 90 degrees. Where two branches join at a cleanout, only one branch should change direction. Lines, particularly short laterals, need not always be entirely within the right-of-way as long as manholes and cleanouts are accessible: a properly designed system rarely needs repair or even cleaning. Otherwise, the layout technique is similar to the storm drainage system.

*Size of sanitary drains*

The minimum size of sanitary sewer pipe is set rather large in relation to rates of flow in order to prevent stoppage: 8-inch pipe for mains or laterals and 6-inch pipe for house branches. Only the main outfalls of extensive areas require a larger-size pipe. Because of the small quantities flowing in the upper ends of the system, where the pipes are much larger than capacity requires, there is a danger that slopes may not be sufficient to maintain the minimum self-cleaning velocity. Thus a standard of minimum slopes for pipes serving small numbers of houses must be set, a standard more restrictive than the storm drain minimum of 0.3 percent:

| *Number of houses served* | 1 | 2 | 3 | 4 | 5 | 10 | 20 |
|---|---|---|---|---|---|---|---|
| Minimum slope (percent) | 1.4 | 1.1 | 0.85 | 0.75 | 0.7 | 0.5 | 0.4 |

The street mains must be set low enough to receive the house laterals, dropping at these minimum gradients from the cellars of buildings. The mains are therefore likely to be set at least 6 feet down, and more where land slopes down from the street or where there are deep basements.

If a public disposal plant is not within reach, it is possible to construct an economical private disposal plant, although this will require operation and maintenance. A small private plant would consist of a septic or Imhoff tank, followed by one or more sand and trickling filters. This plant should be set several hundred feet from any house and could be economically designed to serve from 50 to 500 dwelling units.

Where soil is sufficiently pervious and groundwater low, it is possible to dispense with a common drainage system in low-density development and to give each unit a septic tank discharging into an underground drain field. Drain fields must be kept 100 feet from any surface water or well, and they should be neither heavily shaded nor crossed by any vehicles. Their required size will depend on the absorption capacity of the soil.

*Septic tanks*

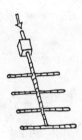

Absorption capacity may be checked by digging a test pit at the drain field site in the wet season to the depth that the field will lie. Then the pit is filled with 2 feet of water, which is allowed to fall to a 6-inch depth, and the drop is timed from 6 to 5 inches. This procedure should be repeated until it takes the same time to make this 1-inch drop for two tests running. The allowable absorption rate of the soil, in gallons per square foot of drain field area per day, is shown in Table 5. If the time of fall is much longer, it is doubtful

TABLE 5. ALLOWABLE ABSORPTION RATES OF SOIL

| Time for 1-inch fall (min) | Absorption rate (gal per sq ft per day) |
| --- | --- |
| 5 or less | 2.5 |
| 8 | 2.0 |
| 10 | 1.7 |
| 12 | 1.5 |
| 15 | 1.3 |
| 22 | 1.0 |

that a drain field is usable. Given the rate, the necessary total field area can be calculated in a housing development by assuming that total sewage flow will equal 100 gallons per person per day.

If properly installed, septic tanks should give no future trouble and are more economical than a sewage system complete with disposal plant. The small community disposal plant has the advantages that it can later be hooked into a future public system, with no loss on the investment in the sewers themselves. Either system, however, tends to make future extension of public sewers more difficult to justify economically.

*Pits and privies*

In the simplest case, sanitary disposal may be reduced to a system of soakage pits and privies, or earth closets. Short pipes take the drainage from sinks, showers, or washing sites to soakage pits or cesspools — pits filled with coarse gravel and covered over. Absorption capacity is computed as before, although the flow per person per day may be much less in a primitive situation. Pits, like septic tanks, are kept well away from structures and from wells. Water-flushed toilets do not discharge into these pits. They are eliminated in favor of privies, which are tightly built and also put at some distance from other buildings. Pits will require an occasional cleaning, and privies must be moved to a new site periodically. The system is inconvenient, requires low densities, and demands constant care to prevent insect-borne disease and unpleasant odors. But while it is officially frowned upon and illegal in most developed regions, the system is quite sanitary if properly made and maintained.

**W**ater Supply

The potability, quantity, and pressure of water supplied to residents of an area are vital to their health and convenience. Clean water is the most critical utility, a necessity even in the most primitive settlement. Yet, while the water supply may make the development of a given site either feasible, costly, or impossible, it rarely imposes controls on the pattern of the site plan itself. The pipes of a pressure system can be laid with bends and gentle curves and can easily be adapted to most layouts.

Waterlines leak or break rather frequently and therefore must always be located in the public right-of-way, preferably close to a traffic pavement that can carry repair vehicles. Furthermore, care must be taken to prevent contamination. The mains for potable water are directly connected to using fixtures, and there are no cross connections with other lines. Sewer lines are laid below water mains and where possible on the opposite side of the street or 10 feet distant horizontally. Water is usually brought into the buildings, but in low-cost development it may be conveyed only to a public tap or fountainhead, from which it is carried into dwellings.

*Layout of the water system*

As with any pressure system, there are two basic distribution layouts that may be used. One is a treelike pattern, with lines branching out from the point of entry. A second is a loop or interconnected network, which may have more than one point of entering supply. The treelike pattern is likely to minimize length of line and thus be cheapest, but the loop or network is much the preferable system since it avoids the drop in pressure at the ends of long branches and the difficulty of keeping dead-end pipes clear, while few or no units will be cut off from service when a main breaks. Where dead ends do occur, as at the ends of culs-de-sac, hydrants or blowoffs must be installed to allow occasional cleaning.

Since this utility is the one most seriously affected by frost, in New England it is normally laid under 5 feet of cover. The line may rise and fall with the slope of the surface, as long as positive pressures are maintained at the high points. Since water supply is paid for according to the quantity delivered, meters are installed in the line at individual dwellings, at groups of dwellings, or at the boundary of an entire development. Valves are placed in house branches where they leave the mains and in the mains at points necessary to cut off sections in the event of breaks. These valves must be no more than 1000 feet apart. Fire hydrants are put along vehicular ways at intersections and other points so that all parts of buildings may be reached by hose lines not over 500 feet long from one and preferably two hydrants. Yet to keep them usable in case of fire, no hydrant should be closer than 25, and preferably 50, feet from any structure. In high-value commercial districts, a special high-pressure system for fire fighting is sometimes installed separately from the potable supply.

The minimum diameter for water mains is 6 inches, or 8 inches in high-value areas. Computation of required pipe size is complex. In developments of up to moderate size, however, the 8-inch main is usually adequate. Pipe size is based on the requirement of delivering maximum instantaneous demand while maintaining minimum pressure. The latter is usually given as being 20 pounds per square inch at the hydrant or dwelling. Maximum instantaneous demand is the sum of the demand for fighting a fire and the maximum demand for domestic use, unless there is separate fire-fighting supply. On the basis of the probability of simultaneous demand, maximum domestic use declines from 40 gallons per minute for one house to 9 gallons per minute per dwelling unit for ten houses, to 2½ gallons per minute per unit for 100 houses, and to 1 gallon per minute per unit for 1000 houses. Fire demand, expressed in gallons per minute, may be estimated from the formula

*Size of water pipe*

$$G = 1020 \sqrt{P\left(1 - \sqrt{\frac{P}{100}}\right)}$$

where $P$ is the population in thousands of people.

Pipe size for any one piece of line is estimated by finding the diameter that will deliver the quantity wanted with no more than the allowable pressure loss in the line. The allowable pressure loss is the entering pressure minus the desired leaving pressure, minus pressure losses in meters and valves, and plus or minus the pressure gain or loss due to rise or fall of the pipe. Since each portion of pipe is interconnected with an overall grid, whose flows and characteristics also affect the terminal conditions, the problem is usually indeterminate in form. In site-planning work, where the sizing and detailing of the system are left to specialists, layout of the water system is usually confined to location of the lines, valves, meters, and hydrants in the public right-of-way. This rarely calls for changes in the design itself.

Calculations of capacity for the water supply, rather than for the distribution system, use average demand rates. These requirements depend on population, climate, industrialization, and the prevailing standard of living. In U.S. cities, for example, average demand varies from 120 to 250 gallons per capita per day. In rural or low-density developments, individual wells can take the place of a common water supply. Like privies but unlike septic tanks, they are not recommended except where unavoidable. They are generally unreliable, often expensive, and not easily supervised to maintain purity. A private group water supply is quite feasible, however, and its maintenance can be supported by water charges on the users. Such a system, consisting of a well, or group of wells, a pump, and pressure or gravity tanks, can serve developments of 50 to 500 houses. The wells must be at least 100 feet from the nearest sewer or drain field. There is a threshold in cost at about 200 dwelling units, where more than one well must usually be put in. But the principal cost is in the distribution system rather than the pump or well. A large and professionally operated public water system is still the preferable solution wherever possible.

**Electric Power**

Power is brought in on primary high-voltage lines and then is stepped down at transformers to enter secondary low-voltage lines going to points of use. Since low-voltage transmission is wasteful, secondary runs should be kept down to 400 feet, with transformers placed in the center of the load. As with the water system, the electric lines may follow either a branching pattern, fanning out from the point of entry to the points of use, or a loop distribution. The first pattern is cheaper, but the second is preferable. However, the difference is not as important as it is in the water system.

The conductors may be placed overhead on poles or underground in raceways. Underground distribution may be two to four times as expensive in the first cost, but it reduces breaks, does not interfere with trees, and eliminates the clutter of poles. Once breaks occur, however, they take longer to repair when underground and cause more disruption. When power poles are located on the street, they are also useful for mounting streetlights, telephone lines, signs, and call boxes. Nevertheless, consumers may often be willing to pay the premium for underground electric lines for visual reasons. Costs of underground installation are most favorable in light soil, and new techniques of laying cable are making them more favorable. Where there is rock or a high water table, the cost difference is likely to be prohibitive, and poles therefore become mandatory. Elsewhere the principal difficulty may be the transformers, which must be designed to disperse internal heat if put underground and which, if above ground, bulk large in a residential area.

If the overhead system is used, it is even possible to string the secondary lines on the buildings when siting permits it. But this entails a risk to building repairmen and adventurous children. Normally, all lines but those directly entering the structure are strung on poles, where they are guyed at changes in direction and at the ends of lines, and the poles are spaced 125 feet apart or less. Transformers are hung on poles or installed partially or wholly underground, with exterior venting. Where poles or raceways do not follow streets, an 8-foot easement is required. The choice of putting pole lines on the street or at rear lot lines is usually dictated by whatever minimizes the length of secondary runs. Placing poles at the rear to "beautify" the street is questionable where the dwellings are low, since the poles are even more prominent on the skyline than when directly overhead. Poles at the rear lot lines are also more difficult to service.

Exterior lighting is required on all streets other than rural roads or local ones in low-density development and on all pedestrian ways on which people may be expected to move at night. On local roads without streetlamps, individual dwellings may be required to maintain door or post

*Lighting*

lamps to illuminate their entrances and the adjacent walk. Light is especially needed at entrances, intersections, steps, dead ends, and remote walkways. Powerful lights high in the air give a strong even illumination and are therefore specified for roads, but they produce a general pallor that lights up houses unpleasantly. Walkways are safe with much lower and variable illumination as long as entrances and potential lurking places are well lit. Unfortunately, sodium and mercury vapor lamps are the most economical, hence the yellowish, greenish glow of our highways. The old incandescent lamp has the warmest color but is more expensive since much of its energy is dissipated in heat. Incandescents may be used on walkways, however, or highway lamps may be color corrected at some cost. In any case, the visual requirements of drivers and pedestrians are quite different, and their lighting environment should be different.

Standard mounting heights for lights are 30 feet over roadways at spacings of 150 to 200 feet. Lamps are designed to give average illuminations of 1 footcandle on arterial roads or large parking lots, or ½ footcandle on local roads. Areas of lowest illumination are not allowed to fall below 40 percent of average levels on arterials or below 10 percent on local streets. Tall lamps must be shrouded to prevent glare into windows, private sitting areas, or drivers' eyes. Their location must be correlated with adjacent buildings and plantings.

Lamps on walkways are normally 12 feet high. One can see physical obstacles at very low illuminations; the critical factors are the quality of the light and the psychological sense of safety. Thus shrubs and trees may be well lit, as well as doorways, steps, and intersections. Such spots may receive 5 footcandles, while the path itself is irregularly lit at average levels of a fraction of a footcandle.

Power and light poles are an obvious part of the daytime visual scene. The designer should insist that these poles be as handsome as the other features of his landscape; therefore, they must be carefully sited and designed. The pattern of the exterior lighting will obviously have a predominant effect on the night landscape, as noted in Chapter 9, and it should be studied from that viewpoint. Sketching how an area will look at night should be a routine part of its design. Night lighting can identify and structure a darkened landscape so that people can more easily find their way or recognize the familiar features of the daytime scene. Light will also convey a sense of warmth and activity. But flood-lighting the grounds or lighting empty buildings for "effect" may only underscore the absence of people. Ideally, unless they are symbolic landmarks, buildings should be lit from inside, in accordance with their real nighttime use. Outdoor light should be concentrated where the people are and where they want the light to see by. Darkness is a necessary foil for the play of light, as silence is for sound. Outdoor lighting has generally been guided by one simple rule: as even and as high a level of illumination as possible over every square inch. The result has been ghastly.

*Gas*

Gas is piped underground in a system similar to the water distribution network, in a branching or a loop pattern, with its own valves and meters. The pipes are of small diameter. The principal problem is the danger of leakage or explosion, and thus lines must not be laid under or close to buildings except when entering them, nor should they be in the same trench with electric cable.

*Telephones*

Telephone lines are strung overhead on the electric power poles, if the voltage characteristics of the power lines are suitable. Otherwise, telephone lines are rather easily laid in underground conduits or more simply as buried cable. In urban areas, connections to a master television antenna are now common. In the future, we may expect similar connections to central computers and to cable television.

*Heating and cooling*

Where central heating is provided, the heating medium, usually high-temperature steam, is distributed in insulated underground pressure mains, equipped with valves and set in raceways or running through the basements of structures. Space is required for a central plant in one of the structures or in a structure of its own. This heating plant will have a tall stack and provision for large fuel deliveries. Its location is preferably in the middle of the development on low ground to facilitate the return of condensate. In unusual situations, group cooling systems may be installed.

The choice between central or group heating plants, operated by management, and individual plants, operated by tenant or owner, as well as the choice of fuel to be used, is an economic problem. It depends on the type and number of dwelling units, the attitude of residents, maintenance costs, the relative efficiency of plants, and the relative cost of coal, gas, oil, and electricity. A central plant is worth investigating when one is dealing with from 100 to 200 families or more. The choice has an important effect on the site plan. When individual plants are used, provision must be made for the delivery and storage of fuel. If coal is burned, it should be possible to chute it directly from truck to bin over no more than 20 feet. Hoses on oil delivery trucks have a maximum reach of from 100 to 200 feet. Gas and electricity can be brought directly into the unit.

*Interrelation of utilities*

In general, the location of all utilities must be considered together, avoiding cross connections, minimizing trenching, and keeping required separations between incompatible systems. In particular, the layout must be checked in three dimensions to see that crossings in plan will not result in actual intersections below ground.

Where curves or grades permit, it is desirable to keep utilities in a uniform location relative to the street and also to put them underneath the planting strip in order to prevent periodic digging in the road. In intensive development, where utility systems are numerous and of large capacity, it may save installation and maintenance cost if groups of them are placed in a common conduit, big enough to allow men to enter and inspect the lines. Where the site plan consists of fairly continuous structures under single control, it is sometimes better to run utility lines, except for gas, in basements or crawl spaces. This saves excavation and simplifies repairs.

*Solid waste*

Large quantities of solid waste, including organic material and combustible and noncombustible rubbish, must be removed from inhabited areas. These may be picked up in varying combinations and at various times. Some of this material may be destroyed on the site in incinerators, but this method only puts the burden of waste disposal on the atmosphere — a practice now dangerous in large urban areas. If householders are willing to make the effort, a good portion of the organic waste can be converted to useful compost at the site. But the noncombustible material must in any case be hauled away unless, in a rural or low-resource situation, it is locally buried. Group collection stations may be used if they are screened and drained, but separate collection from each dwelling unit is preferable. For separate collection, a drained and protected area must be provided for the waste cans, convenient to the dwelling unit and as close to the curb as possible. The route from the waste cans to curb should not be too steep and preferably should be paved. If structures are close to the road, it is possible to put waste containers within the unit, so placed that they can be filled from inside and be picked up and emptied from outside.

# Chapter 9

# Sensuous Form

$A$ place affects us directly through our senses — by sight, hearing, touch, and smell. The sensuous quality of a place is a consequence of form and of how and by whom it is perceived. It is irrelevant in a sewer layout or in an automated warehouse. But wherever people are involved, it is as important as cost or shelter or circulation. Sensuous requirements may coincide or conflict with other demands but cannot be separated from them in designing or judging, nor are they "impractical" or merely decorative, or even nobler than other concerns. Sensing is indispensable to being alive. Perception includes the esthetic experience, where the dialogue between perceiver and object is immediate, intense, and profound, seemingly detached from other consequences. But it is also entangled with many other purposes: comfort, human interaction, orientation, and the communication of status, for example. All of these must be dealt with together.

Most people will understand this need when arranging a living room but may ignore it in the arrangement of a site plan. We attend to technical features, but often pass over their integration into a visual whole. It is as though we were concerned with the amount of furniture to be put in a room but let the movers put it down at will. What we require is a *landscape*, technically organized so that its parts work together but perceptually coherent as well, whose visual image is congruent with its life and action. This concept of landscape as a visual and functional whole is a relatively recent one in Western culture. A whole in nature represents a mature stage of development, shaped by the consistent impact of well-balanced forces. In art it is the result of comprehensive purpose skillfully applied.

*Perception of space*

In essence, the sensuous experience of a place is spatial, a perception of the volume of air that surrounds the observer, read through the eyes, the ears, the skin. While outdoor space, like architectural space, is made palpable by light and sound and defined by enclosure — overhead, alongside, and underfoot — it has peculiar characteristics of its own. These characteristics have fundamental implications for the art of site planning.

In contrast to architectural space, site space is much larger in extent and looser in form. The horizontal dimensions are normally much greater than the vertical ones. Structure is less geometric or demanding, connections are less precise, shapes more irregular. An irregularity in plan that would be unbearable in a room may in a city square be tolerable or even desirable.

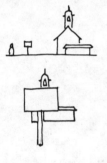

The site plan uses different materials, notably earth, rock, water, and plants, and is subject to constant change, whether it is the rhythm of human activity and of natural cycles or the cumulative effects of growth, decay, and alteration. The light that gives it form shifts constantly with weather, hour, and season. It is seen in sequence, over an extended period of time.

*Spatial illusions*

All these differences call for corresponding differences in design technique. The looseness of outdoor space — combined with the difficulty that all but trained eyes have in estimating distance, geometry of plan, level, or gradient — allows a certain freedom in layout. Formal flaws can be masked and optical illusions achieved: two bodies of water coalesce because their outlines seem to match, a large object "disappears" when blocked out by a small object nearby, an axis appears straight though in reality it is bent. Level areas may tilt by contrast with adjacent counter-slopes, or the relative elevations of objects may be reversed by the treatment of the grades surrounding them.

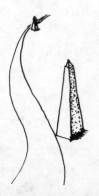

The freedom to deceive carries with it a responsibility to make a clear and connected whole. A simple, readable, well-proportioned space in the outdoors is a powerful event. Structure can be explained in a way that purely natural forces rarely accomplish; connections that defy time and distance can be established. Dimensions that are difficult to grasp are made legible by the use of roads, trees, or other measuring devices; the connection of part with the whole is intimated by symbolic echoes of shape or material.

The designer uses every resource to confirm the form he intends to establish. Except in the special cases where he wants an air of mystery and doubt, he makes sure that his spaces are well defined and clearly joined at marked transitions, whether the volumes themselves are crisp and geometric or irregular and flowing. Rhythm and direction will be supported by the form of all visible elements. Changes in plan will coordinate with changes in section.

Spatial dimensions are reinforced by light, color, texture, and detail. The eye judges distance by many optical features, and some of them can be manipulated to exaggerate or diminish apparent depth: the overlapping of more distant objects by closer ones, the parallactic movement of objects disposed in depth, the expectation that farther things will be higher above the horizontal base line, the smaller size and finer texture of things far away, the bluish color of distant surfaces, the convergence of parallel lines. Used with restraint, these manipulations add to the spatial effect. As with any illusion, there is a danger that from another viewpoint, or in another season, the trick will be exposed. Illusions of features indirectly perceived, such as geometric plan, distance, or level, are the easiest to achieve and maintain. Illusions of characteristics seen directly, such as the attempt to imitate the color and texture of one material in a substitute, are much more difficult.

*Vertical elements in outdoor perception*

Outdoor spaces are rarely created by complete enclosure. They are only partially bounded; their form is completed by the conformation of the floor and by smaller vertical elements that mark out imaginary aerial definitions. Since the out-of-doors is dominantly horizontal, vertical features or changes take on exaggerated importance. A great hill in fact occupies only a very small vertical angle in our visual field. This fact is illustrated when we photograph an awesome mountain landscape and find we have recorded only a minor disturbance of the horizon. Even a gentle gradient can dominate a scene. Level changes will define spaces; they can open views; and they can create effects of silhouette, truncation, or dynamic movement. Steep slopes or drops are difficult to handle within a regularly organized space: it is a safer rule to make up vertical differences in the approach to important openings or in the separations between them. The general shape of a site plan may have less

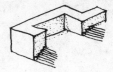

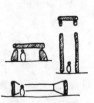

*Proportion and*
*scale*

bearing on its visual success than the small projections, levels, or focal objects that make up the real visual space on the ground.

Once a readable space is established, it has a strong emotional impact on the observer. The intimacy or constraint conveyed by a small enclosed space and the exhilaration or awe of a great opening are universal sensations. Even stronger is a transition between the two: the powerful sense of contraction or release.

Spaces differ in character according to their shape and their proportions. Proportion is an internal relation and may be studied in a model, but spaces are also judged by their scale with respect to objects outside themselves. Outdoor en-

FIGURE 22 *The vast space of Central Park, New York City.*

closures, for example, contend with the vast scale of the sky. They must connect their own size with that of the earth's atmosphere (by large openings or the use of verticals) or reduce it to a backdrop. A relation to the scale of the surrounding landscape must also be established. Fitting new functions into a mature and established landscape without disrupting the old scale is an exacting task. Finally, a space has a scale with respect to the observer himself and either appears measurable by him or takes on an awesome and superhuman size. In each case, the scale relationship should be decisively intended and decisively carried out.

A few tentative quantities can be assigned to the size and proportion of comfortable external spaces. Developed empirically, these rules seem to derive from the characteristics of the human eye and from the size of the objects that

FIGURE 23 The narrow, rich, intensely human space of a Florentine street (the Borgo Allegri).

are generally of greatest interest to it, that is, other human beings. We can detect a man about 4000 feet away, recognize him at 80 feet, see his face clearly at 45 feet, and feel him to be in direct relation to us, whether pleasant or intrusive, at 3 to 10 feet. Outdoor spaces of the latter dimension seem extremely or intolerably small. Dimensions of 40 feet appear intimate. Up to 80 feet is still an easy human scale. Most of the successful enclosed squares of the past have not exceeded 450 feet in the smaller dimension. There are few good urban vistas much over a mile in length, unless they are distant panoramas seen over a featureless foreground, such as views over water or from high places. The foregoing observations refer to the stationary observer or the man moving slowly. Space perception at high speed is quite another animal.

There are limits to the angle of clear vision and to the rapidity of scanning. An object whose major dimension equals its distance from the eye is difficult to see as a whole but easier to analyze in detail. When it is twice as far away, it appears clearly as a unit; when it is three times as far, it is still dominant in the visual field but tends to be seen in relation to other objects. As the distance increases beyond four times the major dimension, an object simply becomes one part of the general scene, unless it has other qualities to focus our attention. Thus it is often said that an external enclosure is most comfortable when its walls are one-half or one-third as high as the width of the space enclosed, while if the ratio falls below one-fourth, the space ceases to seem enclosed. If the height of walls is greater than the width, then one does not see the skyline or easily judge the wall's height. The space comes to resemble a pit or a trench. These rules assume viewing positions near the edge of the space and the intent to produce comfortable yet clearly bounded areas. Changes of light or level will also affect these impressions.

As another example of an esthetic standard based on the human anatomy, we find it unpleasant if the line of sight at eye level is ambiguous. Ambiguity may be caused by a narrow barrier at that level or by a vertical surface terminating there. Preferably, vision is either kept clear at this sensitive elevation or decisively blocked. Walls should be low or over 6 feet high, and railings at eye level are to be avoided.

*Enclosure*

Spaces may be enclosed by opaque barriers or by walls that are semitransparent or broken by gaps or windows. The space definers may be visual suggestions rather than visual

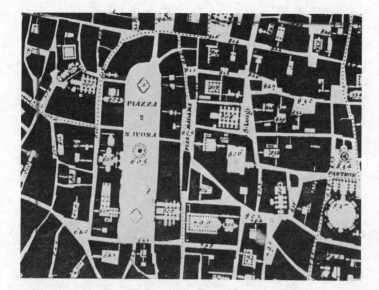

FIGURE 24 *A portion of Nolli's map of Rome, 1748, showing the interconnection of the interior and the exterior spaces.*

stops: colonnades, bollards, changes in ground pattern, imaginary extensions of objects. Buildings have been the traditional enclosers of urban space, but this function has become more difficult to accomplish as the demand for open areas around buildings has grown. To some extent these breaks in enclosure may be masked by such devices as staggered openings, overlaps, buildings that bridge a street, screen walls and colonnades, or even continuous lines of a low fence, as in a New England residential street. Enclosure may be achieved by planting. But we can also modify the intended spatial effect to fit the new conditions.

Spaces vary in effect by the way in which they are entered, passed through, and left behind, as well as by the related spaces that precede and follow them. Their appearance is modified by the activity that goes on within them, by the color and texture of walls and floor, by the way in which they are lighted, and by the objects and details with which they are furnished. Wall Street on a Sunday morning and Wall Street during the weekday lunch hour are quite different spaces; a familiar square can change mysteriously under artificial light. An empty room is notorious for appearing smaller than that same room with furniture; distances seem much shorter over open water. A scale relation between a man and a vast space can be established by the use of a few "man-sized" objects; a tall object may relate

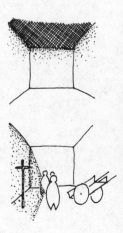

*Light*

a small space to the larger world. Blue or gray walls strengthen the atmospheric perspective and thus seem farther away. Surfaces of hot, strong color come closer. Downhill views appear to be long and uphill views foreshortened.

The direction and quality of the light that bathes a space is a determinant of its character. Light will sharpen or blur definitions, emphasize silhouette or texture, conceal or reveal a feature, contract or expand dimensions. Silhouetted objects are prominent visual features, and the designer is always careful of objects that will appear against the sky. He is also aware of the apparent outward radiation of bright surfaces, which makes light sources seem fat and silhouetted objects thin. Shadow patterns can be distinctive, whether they are large masses or delicate traceries, dark and opaque or scintillating with light. Shadows may be employed to focus attention or frame a view, or a long shadow may be directed to explain the modeling of a surface.

To some extent, the designer can manipulate outdoor light by casting shadows, using reflecting surfaces, or filtering light through screens. More often he is concerned with creating a form that will receive natural light gracefully, that will reveal itself equally well to the hazy sun of winter and the blaze of summer, and that seems coherent in the

FIGURE 25   *The night lighting sets the mood in the Tivoli gardens in Copenhagen.*

morning and the evening alike or under the bright moon. To do this, he must be aware of the geometry of sun and moon position, of the light effects of various kinds of weather, and in particular he must be sensitive to that quality of light which is special to his locale and climate.

The planner has another resource in artificial light. Most sites are used at night as well as in the daytime, and some may be inhabited even more intensively after dark. Artificial light, in all its variation of color, direction, motion, and intensity, can produce a new visual world. Spaces can be modified or even created with light alone, planes made to advance or recede, objects brought to the foreground, and textures transformed. Light can reinforce the familiar daytime setting or transform it. It can pick out the structure of paths and the locations of entrances, indicate the presence of activity, and confer a special character on a place. At important points there can be intriguing displays of changing light. It is pleasant to look from darkness into light or vice versa, to watch a rhythmical play of light patterns, or to see an object transformed by a steadily changing light source. This is a cheap and effective resource, now almost unused. Lighting today is ruled by crude utilitarian standards, mechanically applied.

*Artificial light*

Other senses besides vision convey the shape of a space. Most notable is the sense of hearing; nocturnal animals and blind human beings depend on echo location in moving through the world. The character of a space is given to us partly by the quality of the sound reflected to our ears; an absence of echo, for example, is interpreted as openness. Similarly, though to a lesser extent, we are affected by the feel of a surface (or by how it looks as if it should feel) and by the radiation of heat to or from our skin. Thus the visual impression of a wall may be reinforced if it is highly reflective to sound, looks rough to touch, or radiates heat. Places have particular smells that are part of their identity, even though it is undignified in our culture to refer to them. Site planners never consider this factor, except to worry about unpleasant odors. The microclimate is a marked feature of our perception of a place beyond any consideration of simple comfort: the site will be remembered as cool and moist, hot, bright, and windy, or warm and sheltered. All these sensations of light, sound, smell, and touch can be used by the designer, although he is not accustomed to doing so.

*Other senses than vision*

Space forms and their furnishings have symbolic connotations that seem to be common to our culture: the awe-

*Symbolic connotations*

FIGURES 26, 27, AND 28 *Three examples of traditional types of space: the Italian piazza (Venice), the French place (Nancy), and the English square (Bath).*

26

27

28

someness of great size and simple form or the pleased interest evoked by diminutive scale and intricacy; the aspiration
of tall, slender verticals and the passivity and permanence
of the horizontal line; the closed, static appearance of circular forms and the dynamism of projecting, jagged shapes;
the protection of the low cavelike space versus the freedom of
the prairie. Strong feelings are evoked by fundamental elements of human shelter, such as the roof or the door, or by
basic natural materials, such as earth, rock, water, and
plants.

There is a rich vocabulary of types of external space
that can be drawn upon: the vista, the court, the slot, the
maze, the tunnel, the avenue or axis, the canopy, the free
form, the hemicycle, the park, the bowl, the crest, the slope,
the valley, the honeycomb, and many others. Most of these
forms are part of the experience of everyone, but the designer has the habit of consciously examining them whenever he has the opportunity: checking real against apparent dimensions, making imaginary corrections, exploring
the particular impact of the type. Such a storehouse of remembered spatial effects is part of his working equipment.

*A vocabulary
of spaces*

The designer makes his acquaintance with typical
and harmonious natural landscapes, such as the prairie,
forest, meadow, dune, and marsh, and with those more complex spaces that are associated with particular human activities and particular historic periods: the English residential square, with its town houses set about a small fenced
park, or the urban Italian *piazza*, completely paved and in-

tensively used. Perhaps he remembers a succession of inter-linked college quadrangles or the formal French *place* or the cathedral close. Planted spaces may be managed as English parks, as formal gardens, or as groves. There are the winding, romantic suburban street, the broad avenue with its ranks of trees, the American parkway, the waterfront promenade, the arcade, the terrace. All of these are particular kinds of space, useful as solutions in particular situations. We hope that new types of space will develop in our culture, just as new building types are evolving. Their success will depend on the creative efforts of many site designers and site users.

**V**isible Activity

If visible space is the perceptual quality over which the designer traditionally exercises control, it is neverthe-less not the salient impression of most places for most ob-servers. People are most interested in other people. The sight and sound of human beings in action are usually the prominent features of the perceptual form of a place. This obvious statement surprises designers, who are accustomed to equating "design" with things and who categorize per-sons as the users and observers of things, but not as being themselves part of the visible environment. The lifeless pre-sentational photographs of architectural magazines are testi-monials of this limited point of view.

Places without people or other living things simply hor-rify us, and those that conceal the human trace, as many of our new buildings do, are cold, dull, and depressing. To see or hear active people is endlessly entertaining. We are al-ways interested in who are there, what they are like, what they intend toward us, what they are doing. Seeing and being seen, promenading on a busy street, and watching a construction crew are permanent pleasures.

Although we can imagine an outdoor place in which costumed actors perform in a prescribed way at prescribed times, the site planner rarely exercises any direct control over this aspect of the visible form of a place. This is surely fortunate. But a site plan can support or suppress the visible trace of activity; it can let people become aware of one an-other. This can be done in many ways: by concentrating and mixing the location of different activities so that they are intervisible; by providing places for meeting, celebra-tion, and mutual observation; by exposing to sight circula-tion flows or the basic public or productive activities; by pro-viding ways in which human action can leave its trace on the inorganic environment.

Spaces must be sized to the expected intensity of activ-ity. A square in a central location may seem oppressive be-

Paul Spreiregen

FIGURE 29 *Each event should anticipate the next: entrance to the Piazza Grande, Arezzo.*

cause of the crowds of people using it, while it would appear empty, vast, and lonely at the periphery, where pedestrians are few. A footpath along back lots may seem excessively long, while if it were bordered by varied activities and used by many people, it would appear exciting and relatively brief. Spaces should not merely support the activities that occur within them — they should *visibly* support them. Action can be clarified and expressed, its emotional mood and proper conduct visibly reinforced. I am speaking of behavior settings again, emphasizing how the look of a place and its action can stabilize and heighten that action. Outdoor distances and outdoor light will determine whether we can read faces. The sound level makes conversation easy or difficult. The shape of the space and the location of its detail will help or hinder us as we try to delimit behavioral territories. Part of the pleasure of an outdoor concert is the sense of being one of the audience, and some outdoor activities, such as the *paseo* or the hot-rod parade, are essentially concerned with mutual visibility.

Openness, transparency, and overlook can bring what is happening into view. The obvious danger is an intrusion on privacy, the exposure of activities that someone would prefer to keep hidden. Therefore we expose only those functions about which both viewer and viewed wish to communicate or in which the exposed function is an impersonal trace of human action: the movements of cars and ships, the hollowed step, or handworn rail. By these means a place seems warm and alive.

**Viewpoint**

A landscape is usually seen from a rather limited set of viewpoints. These are the paths along which the observer moves — and along which the forward look is distinct from the backward one — and certain key stationary views, as from windows and principal entrances. The lines of sight from these critical fixed or moving points should be carefully analyzed. This may be done by quick perspective studies or by traces of the cone of vision on plan and section. Computer programs are now available to produce outline perspectives, given a plan, sections, and the location of the observer. The design may be studied in model form by placing the eye close to the ground level of the model. Various devices increase the sense of reality in a model: pinhole viewers, mirrors, or periscopes that project the observer into any part of the model and allow him to see it as though he were walking through it.

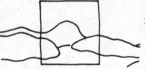

Sight lines may be manipulated by slight shifts in ground level or the position of opaque elements. The eye may be directed by framing the view or drawn along a rank of repeated forms. It may be attracted to some focal object, thus in effect blotting out surrounding detail. A distant view can be enhanced by some foreground object to which it is contrasted. Often it is improved when subdivided by a nearby structure so that attention is concentrated. Thus the total view may be organized into parts, or perhaps only a hint of its full sweep is given.

Since the landscape is usually experienced by a moving observer, it is not the single view that is important so much as the cumulative effect of a sequence of views. The sensation of release when the observer comes out from a narrow slot into a broad expanse is a powerful effect. Lack of formal balance at any one moment is of less consequence than compensations and balances over time. This is the radical difference between landscape and pictorial composition and explains why it is impossible to take good photographs of some fine environments.

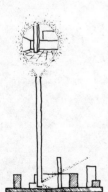

The sequence of views or spaces is crucial in a site design. For example, a major view may be hinted at, be succeeded by a more intimate view of something else, be repeated with a dominant foreground, disappear in a confined

Photo Edwin Smith, from: The English Garden, Hyams and Smith

FIGURE 30 *The great English garden of Stourhead is a rich succession of space and incident along a path that circles an irregular lake. Here we look from the Temple of Flora to the Temple of the Sun.*

space, and finally reappear in its full sweep. The expected direction and speed of the observer are critical since sight becomes restricted to a narrower forward quadrant as speed increases and since spatial effects that are pleasant at a walking pace may be imperceptible at 60 miles an hour, and vice versa. Attention is focused at the points of decision. Each type of motion has its appropriate scale of spatial treatment.

Questions of orientation become significant: the apparent direction toward a goal, the marking of the distance traversed, the clarity of entrance and exit, the explanation of the basic structure and the observer's place in it. A succession of arrivals, like the series of runs and landings on a stair, will be more interesting than a single protracted approach. Each event should prepare for the next one without completely foretelling it so that the observer receives each

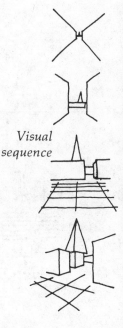

*Visual sequence*

1

2

3

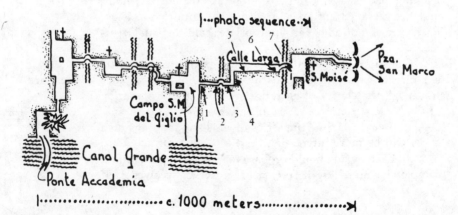

FIGURE 31    *An episode in the walk from the Accademia Bridge to the Piazza San Marco, Venice: a dramatic sequence of space, activity, and texture.*

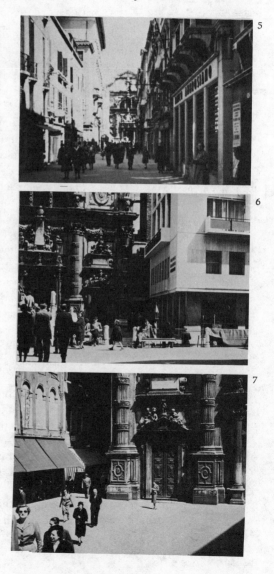

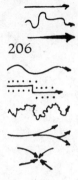

*Reference 28*

G round Form

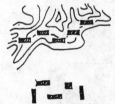

as an ever-fresh but coherent development. The environment should have a form that is readily apparent to the distant glance and yet reveals new features and organizations when inspected more closely. The form of the motion itself had esthetic meaning: it may be direct or indirect, fluid or formal, smooth or erratic, delicate or brutal, divergent or convergent, purposeful or whimsical. Furthermore, objects can be disposed to clarify or heighten the visual sense of motion of self. The dancing of the landscape as one moves by it can itself be a pleasure. Potential motion takes on importance: a road suggests direction, and the eye follows it as a connecting thread. Broad, flat steps will seem easy and inviting. Those that are narrow, steep, and curving appear dramatic and exciting, seeming to lead to some hidden promise.

A site should be a coherent succession of spaces or textures or objects, in which each part relates to the next but in which there is a constant play of variation on the basic theme. A chain of spaces should seem to be part of one extended whole, even while alternating from open to closed, from simple to intricate, from brilliant to subdued. An early step in site planning is to analyze the visual consequences of the spatial form when seen as a sequence. It is often useful to outline the space lying between opaque objects, emphasizing this primary visual sensation. The spaces should not be seen flatwise but as a progression through which one moves.

In an urban area, space may be defined by man-made structures, in less dense development by the basic natural materials: earth, rock, water, and plant cover. In either case, the surface underfoot is the only continuous one, and it plays a dominant role. The configuration of the floor is determined by the preexisting topography, whose modeling must be thoroughly understood before work begins. Inspection will reveal certain key points in the shape of the land, such as the place where gradients change abruptly or from which commanding views may be enjoyed. The land may be divisible into small regions, each of homogeneous character and with certain strategic linkages one to the other. Most sites will have a decided character or pivotal features to which the plan can respond. These aspects pose problems for the designer and at the same time present him with special opportunities. Sites of strong topographic character will tend to dictate the basic organization of a plan and to call for a simple, regular arrangement that will clarify the terrain. Flat ground or sites of more neutral character will allow a much freer, more intricate patterning.

There is an easy visual relation between a man-made structure and topography when the long dimension of the structure, whether it is a road or a building, lies along the contour line. The building or road can be set low to the ground, and the natural contours left as undisturbed as possible. This often proves to be the cheapest solution, as well. At other times, the best solution may be just the opposite: let the road or the axis of the building plunge directly across the contours. This will dramatize the topographic structure. When the structural axes are diagonal to the contours, a most difficult relation occurs, occasionally successful in skillful hands but liable to be awkward.

The designer arranges views and approaches so that the basic structure of the land can be appreciated. Sometimes he uses "unnatural" designs, planting the hills and clearing the valley bottoms to emphasize the drainage and exaggerate the heights, or making a deep cut through a crest to expose the earth and make a dramatic entrance. San Francisco, whose streets seem to ignore the contours, is in fact very expressive of its site. The "natural" landscape pattern, with tall trees on the rich bottom land, and dwarf plants on the hills, actually tends to blur our sense of the underlying ground.

Buildings of uniform height, with their differentiated planes of roof and facade, may be arranged in step fashion on a hill, to give the sense of "piling up." Tall buildings may be placed on the heights, and low structures in the valleys. Long slabs may set back in echelon as they climb, or they may be stepped in vertical section. Special views may be opened up from the lowest to the highest points, and vice versa.

Inevitably, a new development changes the contours. These new ground shapes should fit harmoniously into the older landscape or else be obvious artificial intrusions. If a harmonious fit is desired, transitions must be smoothly made; new land forms must be of the same family as the existing land forms both in shape and scale; the whole should make a consistent pattern. In humid temperate climates, for example, slopes are usually continuous and flowing, curve running into curve without intervening breaks, slopes meeting flat land with a concave profile. Every landscape will have its own consistent family of landforms caused by the base material and its stratifications and angle of repose, the history of vulcanism or glaciation, the erosion cycle, the climate, and the vegetative cover.

At times, the ground form may be willfully shaped to

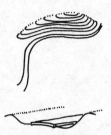

add interest, to mask unwanted features, to gain privacy, to increase apparent size, or to make the flow of roads and paths seem pleasant and easy. Slopes and level can be managed to give a calculated succession of views, allowing sequences of revealing and concealing, or affording a sudden visual surprise. Paths and ground can be manipulated so that the movement of a road is psychologically explained and affords a fine experience of movement in three dimensions. An obtrusive road may be made to disappear by dropping it in a shallow steep-sided cut.

Where the topography is monotonously level or shapeless, as it occasionally is, or where it must be radically disturbed for other reasons, then the designer will resort to a new and totally artificial topography. The whole problem of surface modeling shifts from the expression or modification of preexisting structure to that of abstract sculpture on a vast scale, a sculpture that will unfold as the observer passes through it. This has rarely been done for esthetic motives, but it is now technically possible. Residential terracing in the Los Angeles mountains has been roundly condemned, for visual reasons as well as for fear of landslides. But until the pip-squeak houses are added, these vast terraces are awesome, handsome forms — indeed more "mountainous" than the original. The creation of large-scale topography in imitation of natural form is quite difficult, however simple it may seem, and totally new topography is perhaps more safely confined to obviously man-made shapes.

Problems of topographic form are best studied in a model, even though decisions are more accurately conveyed to the contractor by a contour map. The work is sculptural; thus there is no substitute for pursuing it in a sculptural medium. Simple cardboard contour layer models may be used, which are cut and patched to show new dispositions. In a more complex modification of the ground, it may be best to use a plastic material. The model will begin with the existing ground surface, and reshaping it without addition or subtraction of modeling material indicates a solution in which cut and fill will roughly balance. Decisions will later be transposed from the model to more accurate drawings, or even directly to the field.

*Ground texture*      The textural finish of the ground can be a source of delight in itself. It can also set a general visual character and scale. It may be a harmonious background that unifies and sets off the whole scene, or it may be a dominant surface that communicates the principal patterns and directions of the plan. The texture of the floor imparts sensations of touch as well as sight. The pattern of surface activity can be expressed in the textural pattern, and such differentiations then play a role in guiding or controlling the activity: distinguishing roads and footpaths, bicycle and car stalls, drainage runnels, play areas, or spots for standing and sitting.

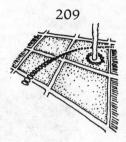

Fine ground textures — moss, monolithic pavement, or close-cropped grass — tend to emphasize the shape and mass of the underlying ground and to increase its apparent size. They act as a background for the objects that rise from them. Coarse textures — rough grass, cobble, bricks, or blocks — work in the opposite way, calling attention to the surface itself, rather than to the underlying mass or the objects above it. A centrally dished floor gives us a static sensation; a valley guides our vision along its course. Changes of level act as space definers, or they can be used to vary the point of view or to separate activity areas, as when raised beds protect planting from intensive traffic. The surface may be left rough or in natural growth, as a region for imaginative play.

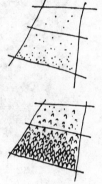

Since the ground has such visual importance, we should consider its enrichment, and not leave it to the casual attentions of the pavement or landscaping contractor. We use a very scanty palette: little more than mowed grass, bituminous macadam, or monolithic concrete. Their antecedents are the gentleman's park and the drill ground. Reliance on these materials results in ground that is monotonous, sometimes ugly, and often quite unsuitable. Concrete is poor for running games; grass cannot bear intensive traffic. Ground is usually either skinned clean or put under trees and buildings. But the range of surfacing available is in fact far wider. It includes cultivated or stabilized earth; low shrubs and ground covers; overhead planting and natural thickets; tanbark; macadam; sand or gravel; asphalt or concrete with fillers, jointings, or surface aggregates; wood block or decking; terrazzos or mosaics; and pavements of bricks, tiles, cobbles, stone blocks or slabs. These materials may be used in many combinations. It is wise to remember how they will be maintained, whether mowed or swept or washed or weeded. Small curbs and gutters at the edges of beds or pavements, or between steps and a wall, will be very useful.

*Rock and earth*

Rock and earth are the primary site materials, our environmental base. Cuts and fills, pits and outcrops, cliffs, caves, and hills communicate a sense of mass, a feeling of

FIGURE 32 *Stone walls and natural rock at Machu Picchu: expressive strength and rich texture.*

*Chinese stones from the Stone Catalogue of the Plain Garden (17th century)*

space, an intuition of the planet whose surface we inhabit. Rock is an especially handsome material. We keep it hidden with topsoil or prettify it in rock gardens. But it expresses strength and permanence, the working of powerful forces over long spans of time. It is highly varied in form, color, grain, and surface texture, expecially when weathered. Though often expensive, it may be used to great effect in walls, paving, and steps, or as outcrops and isolated objects. Here again, in a scene intended to be continuous with some natural landscape, the manner in which local rock is exposed must be observed and imitated: as ledge, as talus, or as scattered boulders.

*Water*    Water is equally elemental — simple in nature but extremely varied in effect. The very number of descriptive terms in the common language indicates its potential richness in design: ocean, pool, sheet, jet, torrent, rill, drop, spray, cascade, film (plus an equal number of words for liquid motion: trickle, splash, foam, flood, pour, spurt, ripple, surge, run). The range of form, the changeableness and yet the unity, the intricate repetitive fluid movement, and suggestion of coolness and delight, the play of light and sound, as well as the intimate connection with life ( and its attraction for birds and animals), all make water a superb

material for outdoor use. It can evoke moods of gaiety, serenity, sorrow, mystery, majesty, contentment, or sheer volup-
tuousness. It is as attractive for play as it is for contemplation; it affects sound, smell, and touch as well as sight. Unfortunately, it also entails problems of maintenance and
safety as well: it may get dirty, breed insects or weeds,
flood, or erode its banks. If the water will lie in a pool, then it
must either be organically balanced, with a mud bottom and
a complete system of plants, insects, fish, amphibians, and
microorganisms, or be sterilized, emptied, and cleaned
regularly.

Moving water gives a sense of life. Still water conveys
unity and rest and may be used to clarify a plan. Usually it
is wise to place still water at the lowest point in its immediate surroundings. It must appear to lie naturally within the
land, for if the land should slope in any way but down into
the water surface, that surface may itself appear tilted and
unstable.

Water plays with light and acts as a mirror. It can reflect the changing sky, in which case it should lie still and
brimful in its container, with open borders. If the water is in
shade, it will catch the images of sunlit objects near or above
it. It may be made to reflect ground objects if the optics of reflection are kept in mind (the angle of reflection equals the
angle of incidence) and if the water surface is not disturbed
with plants or movement. If the pool is shallow, a dark bottom surface will improve its reflectivity.

FIGURE 33   *A water pavement in the Miyajima Temple, Japan.*

Philip Thiel

Paul Ryan

FIGURE 34 *Lawrence Halprin's magnificent fountain in Portland, Oregon, allows people to sense and use the water directly.*

The sound and movement of running water is enhanced by the form of its container. Channels may be designed to throw water in the air, to strike it against obstacles, or to increase its turbulence. A tiny drip will strike a musical note. If the lip of a fall is undercut, all the volume will be visible; otherwise, much of the water will flow invisibly and noiselessly down the face of the fall.

The edge of a water body is a focus of attention. A water edge of simple shape conveys clarity and stability; if it is complex and partly hidden, as along a wooded and irregular shore, it can evoke a sense of expectancy and extended space. A few large stones set just below the water surface will convey a sense of depth. The edge may be made abrupt and definite or low, shelving, and obscure. But if there are many people about, it will not take heavy wear, and it is often wise to pave it. In nature, the water edges take on very characteristic forms due to waves, currents, and the underlying geology. The alteration of undercut bank and gravel bar, for example, and the streamlined shape of islands and projections are characteristics of the meandering stream.

Water is a center of interest in a landscape, near or distant. It is not just to be seen and heard but to be felt directly on the skin. Perhaps we might reconsider our abandonment of the public fountain, our rush to fill small ponds, and to put streams into culverts.

Next in importance is the living plant material — trees, shrubs, and herbs — the material popularly associated with landscape work. Site planning is thought to be the spotting of trees on a plan after houses and roads have been located there. But in our terms it is the organization of outdoor space, in which the plant cover is only one element. Many great landscapes are treeless; there are handsome squares that do not include a plant of any description. To cover everything with trees, grass, and vines is not an eternal principle of design. The outdoor world is not divisible into woods, parks, and farmers' fields. Even the best traditional use of grass, forest trees, and flower borders is ludicrous when imported into unsuitable climates. Nevertheless, plants are one of the fundamental landscape materials, and if in public we worship the tree, in private we often destroy it. Planting is considered the "extra" in site development, the first item to be cut when the budget pinches.

Dimitra Katochianos

FIGURE 35 *A sparing use of vegetation may enhance its visual power. A street in the Cyclades, Greece.*

*References 22, 24, 27, 28*

*See pages 84–90*

At the site-planning scale, one thinks of groups of plants and the general character of planted areas rather than individual specimens. Trees, shrubs, and ground covers are the basic materials; their growth habits, form, and texture are their most interesting features. Species are first screened for those which are hardy for the given climate, microclimate, and soil condition. They must stand up to the wear of expected traffic and demand no more care than can be furnished at the expected level of maintenance. These characteristics were detailed in Chapter 4, especially for some of the tree species that are especially useful for urban development in the United States climate.

Even after screening, there is a great range of effects available; colors, textures, and outlines can be played one against the other. The visible surface of the plant may have a texture that is fine or coarse, dull or shiny, closed or open, stiff or trembling, clustered or even, smooth or modeled in depth. Its habit of growth may be prostrate or upright, its shape rounded or angular, pyramidal or fastigiate, vasiform or cylindrical, or one of many other types. Of course, forms will vary with the season and between youth and maturity. Each species has its own pattern, its own peculiar way in which leaves, buds, and stems arrange themselves, a pattern distorted in the individual only by the accidents of age and exposure. Some forms, like the linden, are regular and symmetrical and can be counted upon, barring some strong environmental pressure. Other plants react unpredictably to more subtle influences.

*Plant arrangement*

Species can be sited to create a general effect or to contrast with one another. Plants of similar form but dramatically different texture may be juxtaposed, or shapes may be contrasted: an angular, dynamic tree beside a rounded, static shrub, or an arrangement of upright, recumbent, and prostrate forms. A delicate fern may bring out the character of a massive rock. Since it is easier to predict the texture of a plant than its particular form and since that texture does not vary from different points of view as much as does the individual shape, it is advisable to dispose plants principally according to their textures and according to the masses that will be produced by large numbers of plants. A number of specimens of one species are often concentrated to give the effect of that type. Even in mixed groups, only two or three species are used, and these are not intermixed evenly but located in clusters that thin out into clusters of another type. The plant list is consciously limited to a few dominant and subordinate species, all related in their ecology and texture. However, it is unwise to plant only a single species, since a fatal disease may snuff it out, as has happened to the chestnut and the elm.

The choice of plants is influenced by their fit with the setting: the relation of their shapes to the shapes of buildings and ground, their apparent harmony with climate and native vegetation. Many landscape designers feel that plants exotic to an area should never be used except in gardens that are obviously artificial. This is certainly a safe principle since it guarantees material that is hardy to an area and also customarily associated with it. Intellectually, the principle is more difficult to defend since many self-maintaining "natural" species are in truth fairly recent exotics, and the apparent visual harmonies that depend on familiar associations may be superseded by new experiences. Objective requirements for hardiness and maintenance, plus the subjective requirements of visual fit, are better guiding principles. Traditional regional species are a tested source for these qualities, but even these may jar one's sensibilities. Excluding exotics may be a useful rule in special cases where one is preserving the historic or ecological features of a given landscape. Certainly we should attend to the way in which an existing landscape maintains itself or is changing: the nature of the forest climax, the condition at the wood edge, succession in an old meadow or a weedy vacant lot. Many kinds of designed arrangements, while perfectly feasible and hardy, will later exact a toll of maintenance, or restriction of use, that we are not prepared to pay. Conversely, new methods of weed control or of cutting, fencing, and seeding may create stable plant systems that were previously thought to be completely "unnatural."

*Use of exotics*

The appearance of a planting arrangement must be imagined at its beginning as well as its maturity, in winter as well as in summer. At planting, trees should be set far enough apart from each other and from structures to prevent interference unless a distorted shape or a solid mass is desired. Large forest trees, for example, if meant to come to full size, must be 50 to 60 feet apart and 20 feet from buildings. Trees take time to mature: "final" effects may not be seen for 30 or even 50 years, and what seems to be pleasant in the beginning may later be desperate overcrowding.

*Evolution of the planted setting*

This problem of maturity is a perennial one in landscaping. New sites are typically barren, and old ones overgrown. To some extent barrenness can be avoided by the pres-

ervation of existing trees, but in dense development this is usually possible only for avenues or clumps in strategic locations or for occasional fine specimens. The ground surface is disturbed too much for any general retention of existing cover. Mature trees will not survive a violent change of habitat. Saving large ancient trees, past the prime for that species, is questionable, since their removal after development is complete will be more difficult.

For immediate effect, mature specimens may be put in. This is an expensive practice, to be reserved for key places. If large trees are used, they should be placed carefully: turned and shifted on the site while still balled, just as the final position of a piece of sculpture might be arranged. Another solution is to use succession planting, in which quick-growing and slow-growing species are planted together, the quick plants being cut out as the others mature. Or plants may initially be put in at close spacings, to be thinned out later. Both of these techniques require stern maintenance — stern enough to cut despite the protests of tree lovers. Landscaping is not done once and then forgotten. An area should be growing successive generations of trees, according to a regular program.

*Planting frameworks*

If land can be held in reserve, it might be possible to preplant lines and masses of trees in a pattern suitable for future development. The initial investment would be small, and when development occurred, it would benefit from a mature planted setting. Where this has happened accidentally, as in the resumption of development in an abandoned subdivision, the effect has often been quite handsome.

In any case, planting is not a frill to be left to the future. The main framework should be completed before occupancy. Nor is landscaping a green stuffing to be packed between buildings, nor a series of small settings for individual structures. It must be conceived as a total pattern, continuous throughout the site. Lines of tall trees, visible from a distance, may mark major axes in the plan, masses may define major spaces, and special textures may be used for important areas.

It has been customary, in housing developments, to plant only the public areas, leaving private lots to be landscaped by the tenant. Along the streets, we use a single solution with monotonous regularity: the double line of street trees. While the planted avenue can be handsome, particularly when it is broad, set with high arching trees, and when it leads to some important destination, it is not our only available style. The avenue may be all the more dramatic if its use is confined to the major ways. Minor streets can be planted as spatial compartments or with occasional tree masses or specimens, or only on one side, or in other ways. Small trees may often be in better scale with narrow streets or low structures. The designer need not confine himself to the street or to a single solution on that street.

A site includes many man-made details. Their number becomes apparent when we try to catalog the furniture of some existing area: fences, seats, signal boxes, signs, utility poles, light poles, meters, trash cans, fireplugs, manholes, wires, lights, and so on. It is curious that the mere list conveys a sense of clutter and disharmony, a feeling quite opposite from that evoked by mentioning houses, trees, water. The near world of detail affects the appearance of the whole, particularly for the habitual user of an area. The texture of the floor, the shape of the curbs or the steps, and the design of a bench are things close to the person and his purposes. They present themselves directly to his eye. At the same time, if not directly used by him, they will often escape his conscious attention. Designers put much stress on harmonizing all the street furniture, yet most observers will hardly be aware of their effects. Details require a substantial investment of design and supervision if they are to be finely shaped. Does the real visual effect justify that investment? The form of a light pole or a fireplug may be of little consequence to a user, while he is sharply aware of a bench or trash container.

Design and placement of detail are normally left to hazard, which may be successful where a design tradition is in control but dangerous when technology is evolving rapidly. Therefore the designer must consider the critical details, thinking not simply of their harmony but of how they are used. This brings him to placing telephones, alarms, and mailboxes where they can be quickly found; it makes him think about the route over which the trash can must be moved; it reminds him to provide public seats and public toilets.

Instead of paying to hide the power lines, we might do better to make them handsome, as high-voltage lines already are. It could be confusing if all the technical apparatus of a site were apparent to the eye, but there also could be ways of expressing them as a group or of emphasizing the legibility of selected elements.

Fences and walls are of particular importance in the

Detail

*Fencing*

site — functionally, as they limit territories and confer privacy, and visually, as they form spaces and provide vertical texture. Fencing should be provided from the beginning to accomplish these objectives. Too often, fencing is added later in a haphazard way, or the alternatives converge on that unique solution, the chain-link fence. Link fence has the emotional meaning of barbed wire. Along with asphalt paving, it is one of our less than happy contributions to the beauty of the world. Unfortunately, it is a cheap and effective barrier. To reduce its visibility, if it must be used, it should be dark in color, buried in a hedge, or kept from being seen in silhouette.

There are, however, many other fencing materials. Wooden rails, pickets, stakes or lattice, wooden boards or sheets, woven saplings or reeds, stretched or woven wire, iron rails, plastics, canvas, woody plants, brick, stone, earth, poured concrete, and concrete block are all amenable to inventive use. Numerous patterns are part of our own historical tradition — picket fences, rail fences, serpentine brick, fieldstones, wrought iron, and high hedges — and their symbolic connotations are strong. Throughout the world, gardens — Japanese gardens in particular — are rich sources of fence patterns, and many new forms are being invented today by American landscape designers.

The height of a fence in relation to the eye defines its meaning. It can be solid or perforated, but even a perforated fence will seem opaque if it is light in color. To make a fence seem transparent, keep its members thin and black. A fence can be lost in a hedge or under a vine, or it may carry planting containers. It is invisible if set at the bottom of a swale; the traditional English "ha-ha." As fences are subject to severe exposure, they must be well made. Indeed, the traces of time and weather on an old fence are its greatest charm.

*Signs*
Another site detail merits a separate discussion: the signs that have become such a dominant, and generally such an ugly and chaotic, part of our landscape. Designers try to suppress them as something intrinsically bad. Yet they are necessary to explain and direct activity, and they can add to the interest of the scene. A landscape must communicate to its users, whether by conventional signs or by the observer's knowledge of the meaning of visible shapes and motions. In an increasingly complex world the messages carried by a landscape must increasingly be embodied symbolically. Signs are ugly and chaotic, not by their na-

ture, but because they are thoughtlessly used, ambiguous, redundant, and fiercely competitive. Above all, they are ugly when they are intended to deceive or exploit the viewer. The designer's task is not to suppress but to clarify and regulate the flow of information so that priority signs cannot be missed and also so that more accurate information is transmitted more easily and expressively.

Signs and symbols expand what a man can learn not only about goods and services but also about history, ecology, the presence of people and their activities, the flow of traffic or information, weather, time, politics, events to come. In some locations a spectacular sign can be a piece of dazzling and joyous scenery; in others signs should be subtle and muted. The elements of any landscape should be expressive of their function, as well as the human values attached to them. Meaningfulness arises automatically in a settled landscape, long occupied by the same group, who are engaged in the same activities and hold the same values and aspirations. In a newer, more mobile situation the consciously devised sign is more important. Our objectives should be to enhance the beneficial power of signs and to remove those that are extraneous to the scene, as for example the advertisements of products produced and consumed elsewhere.

Perceiving an environment is creating a visual hypothesis, building an organized mental image that is based on the experience and purposes of the observer as well as on the stimuli reaching his eye. In building his organization he will seize on congenial physical characteristics: continuity and closure; differentiation, dominance, or contrast of a figure on a ground; symmetry, order, repetition, or simplicity of form. Structure and relatedness can be facilitated even in areas too extensive to be seen at one glance. Rhythmic repetitions may be used, such as the appearance of open spaces or dominant masses at regular intervals. Parts may be related by maintaining a common scale of space or mass or simply by similarities of form, material, color, or detail, such as common building materials, a homogeneous ground surface, or uniform planting. The parts may reveal a common purpose or the impact of a dominant force like a powerful climate or a highly organized culture. In a more subtle way, features of one part may recall those of another without directly imitating them, as when fountains recall the sea.

Paradoxically, sharp variations are also a way of re-

**Visual Structure**

lating parts if there is some continuity of access, form, or character between them. A dark and narrow street is related to the broad avenue into which it emerges, and a quiet park is tied to the intensive shopping area fronting on it. Related contrasts, seen in sequence or at one glance, bring out the essence of a feature and put us in touch with a wide range of experience. Near may be contrasted with far, fluid with fixed, familiar with strange, light with dark, solid with empty, ancient with new.

Continuity depends on the important transitions — the joints between house and ground and between house and house, corners, gateways between spaces, decision points on a pathway, or the upper edge of objects at the skyline. Transitions are often the most noticeable features at the outdoor scale. They must be articulate if the spaces are to be readable and coherently joined. The classic architectural emphasis on cornices, base courses, and door moldings can be shifted to the silhouettes, steps, and entrances of the site plan.

As a consequence of the great number of objects in the exterior scene, grouping and contrast must be used to bring the complex under perceptual control. Clusters of structures may be set off by open space, or a large space may be surrounded by dense occupancy. Houses of a similar kind are grouped in visual units, or trees of one species planted together, to give the sense of "street" and "birchwood" rather than "house" and "birch tree." Parts may be interrelated by referring them all to the same dominant feature, such as a church steeple or a central space.

The sought-for effect is usually broad and simple rather than precise and intricate. Richness is inherent in the material, and an intricate plan may end in confusion. Not only is the material complex, but it is in motion, seen in different lights and at different stages. The scene must be able to accept all this variation without losing its form. This does not require the use of formal geometry but only that breadth of treatment which is in consonance with the scale of the work being done. A good site plan is straightforward. While it may be highly refined at critical points, it is often almost coarse overall.

*Hierarchy and other models of structure*

The main structure of a site design is most often some sort of hierarchy, dominance, or centrality. Thus there may be a central space to which all other spaces are subordinate and related or a dominant path linking many minor paths together. Similarly, in sequences, it is customary to organize a principal approach that has a gateway or point of beginning and is developed to a climactic point of arrival, where there is a strong sense of place and of being at the heart of things. Such arrangements are tested structural methods, which underlie most of the successful site designs of the past.

The pattern just described is, of course, not the only possible structural plan, especially in large, complex changing landscapes. The designer may use many-centered forms, interlinking networks of paths, continuously varying characteristics of activity and space, or multiple sequences that have no determinate beginning or end. Such forms are complex and more difficult to employ without a lapse into disorder. Moreover, they still rely on variations sequentially organized, on emphasis, and on grouping.

Spatial structure is an obvious aim in site planning. Temporal structure is rarely considered but equally important, since time and space are the great dimensions within which we act. The landscape can strengthen our sense of the passage and organization of time. The cycles of the sun and of human activity can be celebrated, and our orientation to the past can be maintained. Even some features of the possible future can be made visible. Moreover, current transitions can be explained and eased. We scarcely think of such things, but we like to imagine that a site design is isolated in time, appearing suddenly, itself changeless and enduring. True enough, we do save a few historic scraps but never try to express the stream of time that a place has endured or show how it will respond to the recurrent rhythms of light and activity. Yet it is this very rootedness in time that attaches us emotionally to a place.

*Temporal order*

A good design saves evidence of the previous occupation of a place, especially that which conveys a sense of intimate human use or of profound symbolism. By contrasting new with old, we feel the depth of time. Room is left for coming inhabitants to make their own mark or to express what they wish for the future of the place. Materials are chosen because they will weather handsomely. Structures are planned to be destroyed and replaced. How a planting will grow, mature, and decay is part of the scheme. Places are planned for evocative contrasts in different lights and seasons: day and night, winter and summer, holiday and workaday. The planner provides for the celebration of present time — the

Martin Hürlimann

FIGURES 36 AND 37    *The expression of site: the towering Potiala at Lhasa and Frank Lloyd Wright's magical Taliesin East in Wisconsin.*

John Amarantides

great anniversaries and events. He also arranges stable, permanent features to give continuity to the environmental flux.

*Congruence*        Perceptual structure must also be congruent with actual use and ecology. Visual climaxes must correspond to the most intensive or meaningful activity locations; the principal sequences should be along the important lines of circulation. Perceptual territories should fit social territories, and visible traces of time should recall critical histories. The basic aspects of site organization — activity location, circulation, and sensuous form — should function together in detail and also have a similar formal structure.

*Building and site*

Interrelation is further complicated by the necessity of coordinating the design of individual structures with that of the site plan as a whole. These structures have a pattern of use, circulation, and visual form that should mesh with the corresponding patterns of the site plan. The internal circulation of the building is an extension of the external site circulation. Interior architectural space is part of the total site space. Visual sequences begin in the hallways of houses; views from windows are significant; building shapes are fundamental elements of the external spatial form. Inside form should fit outside form, but all walls need not be glass, nor must rocks and trees invade every room. The relation of floor level to ground level and the character of the openings in the building envelope are of special importance. For this reason, architectural and site design are ideally done simultaneously, either by a single individual or by a cooperating team. The cases where site design must be separated from structure design, along with the special problems that this entails, are discussed in Chapter 10.

*See pages 229–237*

The designer uses a strategy of concentration. In achieving his effects, he is always confronted by a shortage of resources, whether of money, of public open spaces, of structure, of movement, or of activity. So he concentrates his resources: conserves his views and displays them at their best, brings things together at focal points and along main lines, economizes here to afford some luxury there, avoids open spaces or pedestrian ways that are beyond his power to equip or maintain. One of his crucial decisions is how much area or activity or visual experience he is able to organize. Can he control a large landscape by means of axes and dispersed elements, or must he be content to structure one strategic point?

*Design strategy*

In some cases, the designer will not be in complete control of the sensuous form of a site, or he may be making only a long-range skeleton plan. He may then specify only a sensuous framework: the character of the major paths and the rhythm of views from them, the landmarks, the concentrations of visible activity, the districts of consistent visual character, dominant spaces, the land and building masses. These major elements can be located, and for each of them a sensuous *program* can be specified, which specifies their character without fixing their exact form. Thus in setting

*Sensuous programs*

the location of a major landmark, he will require that certain aspects of its activity be visible from a particular place, that it communicate the nature of the former building on its site, that it be easily identifiable and distinct from its surroundings, that it be seen from a mile off on any approach, and that its form serve to distinguish each approach from any other. Many particular solutions could satisfy these visual performance characteristics.

*The representation of sensuous form*

The accepted languages of site planning — plans, sections, details, written specifications, illustrative perspectives — are ways of communicating many of the sensuous elements of a site, but not all of them. They fail to convey the quality of the visible activity, for example, nor do they communicate much about the ambience (light, sound, climate, smell), the sequential experience, the cyclical changes, or the predicted development. Additional drawings, such as sequential illustrations of the stages of development or of cycles or of the moving view, can be made, while activity can sometimes be symbolized abstractly. New notations for visual sequences are being developed, and there are movie or computer capabilities for the same purpose. It remains true, however, that we have no effective graphic way of representing some of these important sensuous dimensions.

Sensuous Criteria

The preceding discussion takes it for granted that we know why we are manipulating the sensuous form. Our recommendations imply the reasons, and most designers are content to leave them implicit. But if we wish to advance our skill, to evaluate alternative site possibilities, or to argue the importance of sensuous form, and particularly if we want to deal rationally with the varying needs of the great diversity of site users, it is necessary to make our reasons explicit — to bring them into the light of day, where they can be used, tested, rejected, or modified. While specific criteria will always depend on client and situation, it may be useful to conclude with a list of typical sensuous criteria for planning the environment. More precise statements of these criteria will depend on our purposes, and especially on the nature of the site user, as revealed in the kinds of analyses described in Chapter 5.

*Comfort*

1. Sensations should be within the range of comfort: not too hot, too noisy, too bright, too cold, too silent, too loaded or empty of information, too steep, too dirty, too clean. Climate, noise, pollution, and visual input are perhaps the most critical factors. The acceptable range has a partly biological, partly cultural basis, and will vary for

different people engaged in different tasks. But in any one group there will be large areas of agreement as to what is unpleasant or intolerable.

2. An adequate diversity of sensations and environments should be available. This is a prerequisite for giving the inhabitant a choice of the environment he prefers at any time, and corresponds to a widely felt pleasure in variety and change. It is an important support for human cognitive development and, indeed, for the very maintenance of the perceptual and cognitive system. It is much more difficult to define what is an "adequate" diversity, as well as what are the critical elements that should be diversified. They will depend very heavily on the interests and past experience of the client. We look to market behavior, and the expression of preference, to find the kinds of diversity people are presently seeking. But present choices are constrained by past experience and perceived possibility, and a good designer also seeks to open up new choices. Diversity is not a matter of mixing together a large number of varied sensations but rather of constructing consistent, accessible subenvironments of distinct and contrasting character.

*Diversity*

3. The sensuous environment should support the action that people want to engage in there. This is part of the larger functional criterion, seemingly obvious but too often neglected. Sound and light levels must permit communication. How to move, how to act, and how to find something should be clear. Territories must be visible. It should be possible to sense and enjoy the active presence of other people. Behavioral conflicts may be moderated by visual and aural and spatial separations. One checks for the criterion by mentally enacting the behavior that will occur in a place. The principal difficulty is to realize how many varieties of persons use most outdoor spaces and how diverse their needs and wishes are.

*Behavioral support*

4. Places should have a clear perceptual identity: recognizable, memorable, vivid, engaging of attention, differentiated from other locations. The "sense of place" is the cornerstone of a handsome and meaningful environment. Without it, an observer cannot make sense of his world, since he cannot distinguish or remember its parts. Identity depends on the knowledge of the observer and can be transmitted indirectly by verbal symbols. But a unique set of perceptual characteristics is a powerful, concrete reinforcement of it.

*Identity*

5. These identifiable parts should be so arranged that

a normal observer can relate them to each other and can understand their pattern in time and space. This is not a universal rule, since there are occasions when it is desirable that parts of the environment be hidden, mysterious, or ambiguous. But at least the general framework of a living space, as well as the linkage of its public places, must be legible — not only in the street but also in memory. Legible structure has an obvious value in facilitating the practical tasks of way-finding and cognition. It can be a source of emotional security and a basis for a sense of self-identity and of relation to society. It can support social cohesion and be a means of extending one's knowledge of the world. It confers the esthetic pleasure of sensing the relatedness of a complex thing. It must be flexible enough to facilitate the several different preferences for environmental organization (map organization, sequence organization, and schematic organization, in particular). It must work for the anxious tourist, the old inhabitant intent on his practical task, and the relaxed and casual stroller. Yet certain elements will be crucial to all: the main system of circulation, the basic functional and social areas, the principal centers of activity and of symbolic value, the historic points, the natural site, the major open spaces. Spatial legibility is the more obvious aspect, but temporal legibility is equally important. The sensuous environment may be used to orient its inhabitants to the past, to the present with its cyclical rhythms, and even to the future, with its hopes and dangers.

*Meaning*
    6. The environment should be perceived as meaningful, its visible parts not only related to each other in time and space but related to other aspects of life: functional activity, social structure, economic and political patterns, human values and aspirations, even individual idiosyncrasies and character. The environment is an enormous communications device — people read it, they seek practical information, they are curious, they are moved by what they see. Congruence of the visible and the social world will facilitate action and make both those worlds more comprehensible. Signs and symbols can speak to us, and basic economic and social processes can be left open to view. Unfortunately, the symbolic role of the landscape is little understood, and to deal with meaning at the larger community scale is difficult since significant meanings and values differ widely among various groups in our society. Formal legibility is at least the common visible base on which all groups can erect their own meaningful structures.

7. Finally, the environment has a part to play in the intellectual, emotional, and physical development of the individual, particularly in childhood, but perhaps also in later years. The negative effects of highly impoverished environments can be shown. We can speculate on the sensuous characteristics of cities that might facilitate human development. Some of the characteristics just noted are valuable for development: surely perceptual diversity, as well as legibility and meaning — particularly if the latter are not immediately obvious but communicate a simple meaning that becomes more complex and subtle as the object is observed more closely. An educative environment would visibly encourage attention and exploration, particularly when the observer is not task-oriented — when he is at play, traveling, or just waiting. It would provide opportunities for children to manipulate the environment directly, whether by building, reshaping, or even destroying. An individual should be able to alternate between high stimulus and quiet privacy. Such a world might even present visual shocks, puzzles, and ambiguities — challenging the observer to find a satisfactory organization for himself.

There is more to a fine visual environment than the criteria just listed, but it becomes progressively more diffi-

FIGURE 38  *Children make their own worlds.*

cult to define. Moreover, if we could achieve a comfortable, diverse, supportive, legible, meaningful, developmental landscape, then we have the basis, and indeed much of the essence, of a beautiful landscape.

For any particular application, these general criteria must be turned into specific statements or questions. The nature of these questions and their importance will vary from place to place, in relation to the environment itself, the needs and values of the people served, and the purposes of the planning. The sensuous criteria will interlock with other criteria at many points and must be made consistent with them. Visual legibility may be emphasized, for example, in order to increase circulation efficiency or to develop a sense of civic cohesion.

*Chapter* **10**

# Problems of Control

Sometimes a site planner will exercise only partial control over an environment. This occurs in the layout of subdivisions, in the preparation of long-range site plans, or in "urban design" situations where there are many developers. Although these three activities are quite distinct, they share the same qualities of incompleteness and indeterminacy, and are worth discussing and comparing.

Subdivision is the process whereby vacant land is divided into lots and public rights-of-way, providing sites for future individual buildings that will occupy those lots when they have been transferred to other developers. This process may or may not be accompanied by the actual provision of roads, paths, utilities, and landscaping. Subdivision is a common method of putting land to use for low-density residential development; it is used occasionally for other purposes, such as industry, agriculture, or even commerce. It is a technique with a long history, which has been the basis of urban development throughout the world.

In planning a subdivision, the designer controls the position of roads, paths, and utilities, the location of public facilities and public open space, the shape and position of lots, and perhaps also such features as landscaping, grading, and detail. But he can influence the siting and planning of buildings only indirectly. His plan must be made without simultaneous consideration of the architecture.

*Subdivision*

Since in an urban setting the buildings are crucial, the subdivider can only speculate about how site and structure will fit into each other. The division of responsibility may be compared to asking one man to set canvas size, the frame, and abstract shapes of a painting, while asking another to paint the picture. The results would likely be undistinguished and perhaps disastrous.

Subdivision may operate fairly well where the character and siting of buildings is prescribed by custom, but it is much more dangerous when design traditions are weak and technical possibilities numerous. The result is that circulation and property boundaries are emphasized, spatial effect is neglected, and internal and external design is not coordinated. In reviewing subdivision plans, it is possible to pick out those that will result in disorder or poor living conditions, but it is quite difficult to separate the distinguished from the indifferent.

Nevertheless, there are reasons why development by subdivision continues to be employed. First, and most important, subdivision does not require a large concentration of capital. The subdivider need only invest in the land, its survey, and its legal division. He may also put in roads and utilities and perform the grading and landscaping. In either case, subdivision is typically the device of a modest economy. Second, subdivision decentralizes decision, relieving the developer of architectural design and allowing later owners to exercise some choice about their structures. Third, it is well suited to a slow tempo, allowing land to be put to use piecemeal as demand develops and permitting governmental agencies to exercise control over general development without being asked to make similar deliberations each time a building is proposed.

For all these reasons subdivision has social advantages despite its adverse effect on site-planning quality. Therefore it is important to know what can be done in such situations. It is often a strategic juncture at which a site designer can easily achieve permanent effect.

*Subdivision layout*

Good subdivision design can prevent the worst. It can ensure good circulation, adequate facilities, sufficient open space, and basic order. Since the circulation system at least is concretely provided for, it may be designed and tested by all the criteria discussed in Chapters 6 and 7: principles of flow, social communication, and visual effect, plus technical standards for horizontal and vertical alignment and for in-

*Reference 36*

tersections, turnarounds, block length, rights-of-way pavement widths, and so on. The road pattern should conform to the general circulation plan for the area and provide for future roads and connections. The first basic test for any subdivision plan is to move in imagination through its streets, checking their technical, social, and esthetic quality.

The second fundamental test is to arrange a typical building on each lot, making sure that each lot has at least one good location for a structure. Rules about the widths, depths, or proportions of lots are often given, but the placement of a building is the test. If sufficient access, outdoor space, good views, privacy, and ease of maintenance can be achieved with a normal building, then the shape and size of a lot are up to standard. The minimum lot frontages commonly used in contemporary subdivision regulations impose uneconomic and monotonous designs. The use of performance standards referring to access, space, privacy, maintenance, and view would permit us to abandon those rules without risking substandard arrangements.

Lots nearly rectangular in shape that avoid acute-angled corners are easiest to develop. A common rule prescribes that side-lot lines should be perpendicular to the street lines, to avoid the waste of land that a sawtooth arrangement of facades would create along the block. Yet such rules also depend on the building arrangement and may be superfluous. Special lot shapes, such as circles, hexagons, or interlocking L's or T's, may have advantages in some situations. No reasonable rule will require all lots to be of uniform size.

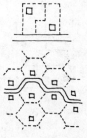

Building lines, or limits within the lot lines beyond which a structure may not protrude, are often made part of a subdivision plan. These may be private contractual restrictions, or they may reflect controls prescribed by law. They further restrict the site and must be taken into account in checking the "buildability" of a lot. Their primary purpose is to ensure privacy, access, and sufficient light and air. Once more, they need not be uniform, nor need they be used at all. Squeezing lots with a mechanical set of front, side, and rear setback lines wastes land and results in a uniform building location on each lot. This uniformity gives a monotonous "dentelated" effect as it is repeated down the street.

The final test that may be applied to the design of a subdivision is to see that adequate reservation has been made for such community areas and facilities as schools, parks, playgrounds, churches, and shopping. These areas should be accessible, adequate in size, and located on ground suited to their purpose.

By giving thought to the street pattern, to the usefulness of lots, and to the provision of sites for community use, the designer of a subdivision can ensure basic functional adequacy. He can also do a little to give the area a positive visual character. His strongest resource is the street and path system, since it is while people move along these ways that they will see his development. Thus the sequence and dynamic shape of the roads, their fit to the ground, the way they point or lead to the more intensive uses, and their relation to the building lines along their course can have a visual impact on the observer.

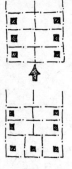

The disposition of intensive uses and public lands can create focal points and open reaches, as well as emphasizing the basic structure of the land. Lot and building lines may within limits be employed to vary setbacks and to create building clusters. Lot location and shape may be used to encourage buildings at desired points, such as at the head of a cul-de-sac for visual closure or on the end of a narrow block to prevent the view down backyard fences. The landscaping may convey a general character or even, by going beyond the customary obsession with street trees, create a general visual structure.

It remains true, however, that the subdivision method is an unnatural disruption of the design process and that lack of coordination between site and architectural design inevitably blurs and coarsens the final product. To avoid this division, it might be possible for a subdivision plan to deal only with major streets, general use locations, and principal landscaping, leaving minor paths, lots, and details to be planned in small areas as actual buildings are demanded and designed in accordance with stated performance standards. This is the procedure generally followed in industrial land subdivision, where lots are rarely fixed before a buyer and his building requirements are known.

Long-range
Site Planning

Somewhat similar to the problem of subdivision is the process of long-range site planning: the preparation of plans for growth twenty years or even further into the future. Such planning is possible for a large and stable organization, occupying a permanent site, subjected to protracted growth, and able to exercise long-term control and direction. A university, a hospital, and a large manufacturing plant are examples of this type of client.

The problem of long-range site planning is like subdivision in that the future uses and the shape of the volumes they will occupy are not precisely known, although a general plan for land improvement, circulation, and use location is required. It differs from subdivision in that the agency for whom the plan is being made will also eventually control the building design. The agency can therefore develop long-range policy and will be able to revise its general plan in the future. However abstract it may be, long-range site planning is a legitimate exercise. It occupies a natural division in the design scale of increasing area and time and is not, like subdivision, an artificial separation of what should be a unitary design process.

Nevertheless, the difficulty of long-range site planning cannot be denied. Not only is building shape unknown but so is anything more than generalized future use. Such a design must normally be preceded by planning studies of future growth and function and future trends in the environs, which lie beyond the scope of this text. Long-range site planning is, indeed, a halfway house between site and city planning.

Once future growth and function have been predicted and preferred density and land requirements determined, a generalized site plan is prepared. This will consist at least of a land-use and major circulation pattern. Since some guide to future physical form is also desirable, it has been customary to prepare a site plan showing building shapes fixed for the ensuing twenty years. Masses are simplified, and precise designations are left off the structures. Detailed adjustment is relied upon to meet future needs.

*Future building shapes*

Long-range site plans showing future building shapes have been universal failures. Sometimes they are abandoned quickly; at other times they are maintained for a while, gradually slurred over, and finally forgotten in the course of time. Occasionally they have been stoutly defended until the strain of misplaced function becomes intolerable and the plan is abruptly if regretfully discarded. In most large institutions the pace of functional change is too rapid to allow fixing the form of the buildings far into the future.

What can be projected, beyond general use, density, and the circulation pattern? While these elements ensure orderly functional development, they have only a secondary effort on the quality of the future complex. Skillful designers of individual buildings will at best produce interesting structures in harmony with their immediate neighbors. Only by chance or tradition will a form or character develop which is apparent at the scale of the whole. Form at this larger scale, created in advance of a specific program, has rarely been successful.

*Future circulation*

As in subdivision design, the character of the path system may be set in advance. The sequence of views as the observer enters and passes through may be considered, the paths and their directions made identifiable by landscaping and detail, and the whole network shaped into a clearly visible structure. It is possible at times to make the path system the dominant impression, with individual structures strung along it as incidents.

*Future spatial form and character*

It is also possible to determine the major spatial form in advance of construction. This is most simply and commonly done by the reservation of open areas, such as plazas and parks. Street spaces or edges of development may also be defined by setting building and height lines that will have visual effect regardless of detailed design. Large plants or plant masses may create spaces independent of the buildings. Spaces so created may then be linked to the path structure.

Instead of defining the exact spatial form, it may be possible to prescribe spatial character, such as recommending a continuous network of small courts linked by short tun-

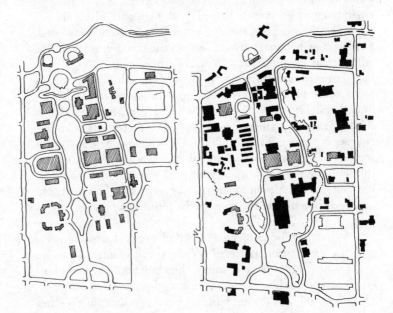

FIGURE 39 *Plan for the University of California campus at Berkeley, officially adopted in 1914, and the actual development in 1956 (Source: Long-Range Development Plan for the Berkeley Campus, University of California, August 1956).*

FIGURE 40 *Coherent spatial character in an extended district: an aerial view of Trinity College, Cambridge.*

nels, having certain characteristics of use and performance. Instead of precisely mapping the location of these future courts and tunnels, new construction would simply be tested for conformity to this general but explicit pattern. Harmonious spatial continuities of this kind, which give a strong character to the whole, are illustrated in many old towns where tradition, rather than explicit plan, was the guide.

The structure and character of spaces and paths is probably the principal tool by which the long-range site planner can shape future form. But there are others: he can lay out the major landscaping, using dominant plant types

*Other long-range controls*

to give areas particular character or using large specimens or concentrations to mark out the key paths and nodal points. Trees may be set out long before an area is to be used, so that users can enjoy them in their mature form. The planner can specify the mix of outdoor use and equipment, or design systems of objects (such as signs, lights, or vehicles) that will later be employed and located according to need. He may prescribe the skyline profile or the points at which major architectural accents will be allowed. In addition, he may suggest materials, colors, textures, the character of fenestration, or even the nature of massing or detail. He will use just that level of control which will confer character and continuity while imposing a minimum of restriction on the shape and function of future structures.

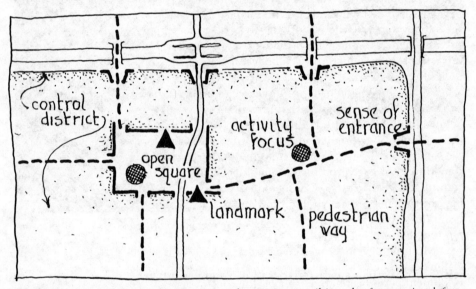

FIGURE 41 *Fragment of an imaginary diagram prescribing the future visual form of a place, which will develop over a period of time. Like a land-use plan, this diagram sets general character but not exact form, although the degree of regulation varies at different points. In the control district, for example, buildings would be regulated by their height, coverage, wall texture, and the general character of their open spaces, while around the square the building lines, cornice heights, and facades would be exactly defined. A typical cross section would be prescribed for the pedestrian ways, as well as their landscaping, lighting, signing, and furnishing. Landmarks are required to be tall, visually distinctive structures, and activity focuses are meant to indicate the location of visible, interesting public activity at ground level. Such a diagram would be supported by a series of rules, specifications, sketches, and illustrative views and details.*

His plan, therefore, instead of being an abstract site drawing, will consist of a diagram of land use, circulation, and major spaces, supplemented by diagrams, statements, and illustrative details to guide the character of future growth. Like any large-scale, long-range plan, this will not be fixed for all time but be subject to constant revision and development.

"Urban design" is a vague term usually applied to that kind of relatively dense site development which is a single, continuous, and reasonably short-term transaction but which is carried through by many independent agents, temporarily bound together by contract. This pattern of development occurs in urban renewal, in the development of many commercial areas, in world's fairs, and in some "new towns" or other large residential projects. The client for whom the site planner is working may be either public or private, a client who in function is a superdeveloper or packager, assembling the land, the financing, the market, and the subdevelopers (who may themselves be either public or private agencies), and who provides a general plan and an infrastructure by which those subdevelopers can coordinate their efforts.

As in subdivision or long-range site planning, a framework site plan is required without firm knowledge of use or detailed building design. Unlike planning for a stable institution, long-range predictions may not be necessary, but at the same time the site planner is not in direct control of, and sometimes not even in direct communication with, the design of actual structures. Conflicts between parties regarding the scheme are inevitable, and purposes, clients, and programs typically shift rapidly as the package is gradually put together.

Multiple-developer design is fractionated, like subdivision design, but not necessarily so hopelessly, since the development period is relatively short, the contractual relation is close, and good communication is possible, though less often achieved. Indeed, rapid and accurate intercommunication — of constraints, criteria, and possible solutions — is essential to a satisfactory product. The site designer must be able to respond continually and to prepare a whole sequence of possible layouts, which gradually serve to explore and define the problem and the actors, and to develop and fix a coordinated action. This coordinating site plan is similar to the long-range site plan but more fluid, serving as an object of bargaining, richer in illustrative detail and alternative possibilities. Contractual controls will eventually be developed from the coordinating scheme.

The superdeveloper must anticipate the subdeveloper's capabilities and devise controls that will carry out its own intent and yet allow for the latter's motives and for the unforeseen. The subdeveloper must make a detailed plan in the spirit of the general one and yet know when to break out, to reexamine the general plan because of a new idea or a new situation. Ideally, both try to penetrate each other's function, the subdeveloper helping to shape the general program, and the superdeveloper making detailed illustrative plans to convey or test his general principles. Analyses of site, market, and social need and the preparation of concrete performance criteria and illustrative solutions give substance to this intercommunication. In situations where communication is blocked, as in many cases of urban renewal, or where there are time lags, financial and human disasters are commonplace.

*Loss of contact with the ultimate user*

Contact with the ultimate user is especially difficult. The shifts and conflicts among potential builders absorb all the administrative energy. Many ultimate users are transient or voiceless, and even the more permanent ones are only very indirectly represented. Were subdevelopers controlled by, and therefore directly representative of, the needs of users (residents, transit riders, shoppers, students), the built result would serve felt need directly. As it is, the site designer near the top of the pyramid may be unaware of his remoteness, or if he is aware, his attempts to communicate with the ultimate clients are abortive. He may obtain useful information from formal studies of the behavior and attitudes of potential users. But his best strategy is the communication of information and criteria to those clients in a form that can be understood and that may provoke a reaction upward from the bottom of the pyramid.

Site Controls

Subdivision, long-range plans, and multiple-developer situations all involve the question of control: the achievement of continuity and the prevention of inferior work by means of regulation rather than design. Controls, imposed either by ordinance or by covenant, are clearly necessary in order to avoid very poor performance.

Controls are widely accepted if they are limitations on use, density, and the layout of circulation — even if they should not be. They are viewed with greater suspicion when applied to visual form. Controls are negative and passive measures, as opposed to the positive technique of design. They stifle innovation and restrict individual freedom; in a world of skill and goodwill they would be unnecessary. If not used with restraint, they produce an environment of competent mediocrity.

The trick is to use controls as sparingly as will achieve the end in view and to prevent unwanted side effects (such as the exclusion of low-cost housing or the imposition of new monotonies). Certain proved kinds of control leave many dimensions of freedom to the individual. Density controls, for example, have a fundamental technical, social, economic, and even visual impact and yet when fixed still allow a great variety of building forms. Control over the street system is another useful regulation. Limitation on land use is also widely practiced and makes sense if the exclusions are based on real, and not imaginary, conflicts. But the imposition of precise use controls and the strict avoidance of use mixtures overshoot the mark. Wherever possible, it is preferable to control use by setting up performance standards for nuisance effects and by prescribing the intensity of use rather than the type.

Building lines are often applied both vertically and horizontally. If the objective is to control density or to ensure light and air, then there are other more flexible ways of attaining the same ends. The principal value of the building line is either to achieve a visual effect or to reserve a certain access or area of ground. It is not necessary to set uniform lines; they may be flexibly drawn to produce spatial coherence and variegated character. Occasionally, in key locations it may be desirable to set minimum as well as maximum lines.

*Building lines*

Performance criteria are the preferred means of control where they can be capably administered. They may set requirements for normal or emergency access, for visual or acoustic privacy, for the emission of light, noise, or pollutants, for views, for the conservation of land, water, or vegetation, for the maintenance and usability of outdoor spaces, and for lighting, visual communications, and textures. Thus one may require that all structures be reachable by fire apparatus and be no farther than some given distance from parking and another given distance from transit. Prohibited noise levels can be specified by decibels; unacceptable levels by lighting can be specified by lumens and the visibility of the source, coupled with minimum lighting requirements for public ways. The blocking of certain views, as

*Performance standards*

well as windows that closely overlook other windows or private open spaces, can be prevented. The cutting of trees may be restricted, new plantings encouraged, the filling of wetlands or stripping of topsoil outlawed. But if the provisions are complex or difficult to monitor in the field, their implementation will defeat itself.

Other controls may refer to the detailed quality and design of components, such as specifications for roads or utilities. Sometimes controls deal with building materials or with signs, planting, and fences. Occasionally, and even more dangerously, they will refer to design or style. All of these restrictions may have unforeseen results. There must be some mechanism for future modification of the controls whether by action of a central agency, such as a board of trustees or a government, or by provision that the controls will lapse at a specified time and must then be renewed, or by their devolution into local hands.

*Costs and side effects of controls*

Controls have often been designed for their secondary effects, a practice that is always devious and usually wasteful and hazardous. Developers are required to install expensive improvements, for example, in order to block or slow down their operations, or minimum house sizes are set to exclude people with lower income levels. Direct exclusion of race or class has fortunately been declared illegal, but many seemingly innocent devices continue to carry out that aim. By enforcing standards, limiting options, and imposing delays, controls also inevitably add to the cost of development. These costs must be balanced against the ends to be achieved. In particular, the delaying effects of complex controls do not usually confer corresponding benefits.

Special powers of exception allow control bodies to release developers from restrictions in return for some desirable space, density, or design excellence. Designers may be able to exceed density maximums at certain spots while keeping gross density low, or they may mix building types or uses while maintaining the general objectives of zoning categories.

*The power of review*

One useful technique of flexible control is the establishment of a board of review, to which all designs must be submitted but which has only persuasive power. If it is not to be arbitrary, such a board requires some guidelines. Performance criteria can furnish them. It may also be appropriate to set up a local association of owners to exercise and modify some of the controls as well as to maintain and operate common facilities such as parks, pools, planting, walkways, streets, sewage disposal or water supply plants. But municipal agencies may be jealous of such local power or be concerned that associations may not have the permanence necessary to carry out their functions over a long period of time.

Controls are based on standards — formal statements about the stable characteristics of environmental features that are presumed to make them universally desirable or acceptable. Thus we have national standards for pavement widths, pipe sizes, street lighting, fire egress, building spacing, ground slope, playground size, the separation of uses, the required drawings for subdivision approval, and many more. Some refer to form, some to the process of creating it, some to its subsequent performance. Some are legal minimums; others are desirable optimums used as guides in design; some refer to established ways of doing things ("current good practice"); some are predictions (that is, if so many square feet of retail space are provided, then a store will have sufficient business); others are simply arbitrary standardizations that limit unwanted variation in form (screw threads, for example). Planning manuals, reports, and ordinances are full of such standards. This book is no exception, although every opportunity has been taken to caution the reader.

Standards are a necessity in order to simplify the large and shifting body of information about site performance so that decisions are not lost in detail and uncertainty. Moreover, subsidiary questions can be handled summarily, and inexperienced participants are enabled to avoid major errors. Standards provide an equitable basis for legal control and a way of regularizing production. In conflict or doubt, it is comforting to have an established way of separating right from wrong.

The danger lies in this very way of sharply distinguishing good and evil, since the context of a decision will be ignored and side effects neglected. Requiring two means of fire egress from apartment buildings not only raises costs (which was foreseen) but makes it difficult for police to patrol interior hallways (which was not foreseen). Setting a 50-foot minimum for the right-of-way of minor roads is expensive and gives many subdivisions a barren look. Both rules, reasonable enough in their intent, are now nationwide and have had an immense effect on the form of the world we live in.

Standards are often set arbitrarily. They may be the

*Standards*

*Reference 46*

expressed opinion of some professional, repeated by some others, accepted as the best readily available statement for some legal requirement, and eventually codified across the nation. The connection to original purpose is often glossed over, even forgotten. The relation of standard building set-backs or standard lot frontages to health and welfare is quite obscure. Skilled site planners will often violate accepted standards and produce better environments while doing so.

*Performance*
*standards*

Unfortunately, we cannot jettison the whole structure of standards. They are dangerous necessities, to be treated with suspicion or avoided where that will not cast too heavy a load on decision makers. They are best stated as a desired performance rather than the means to attain that perform-ance: desired daylighting rather than desired building en-velops or spacings. In the same spirit, I have recom-mended programs that specify the behavior setting rather than the physical form itself.

Unfortunately, performance standards have their own difficulties. They may force the repeated testing out of a long chain of consequences from proposed form to predicted per-formance. It may also be difficult to specify desired perform-ance in any clear way. Saying that many new trees should be planted in residential areas is much easier than specify-ing the visual or climatic values to be gained thereby, even if there is no doubt that such a gain will occur. Finally, the performance to be tested for may occur only later, after occu-pation, while the likely point of control is earlier, during de-sign or construction. A maximum noise level can be mea-sured easily enough, but not until the factory is in operation. It is easier (though not always wiser) to recommend exclud-ing the factory from the start.

Thus, while preferring performance statements, we may use form criteria when performance is difficult to pre-dict or specify or test for and when fixing the form alone is not likely to have serious side effects. Because of their simplic-ity, form standards may also be best when performance is easy to predict and is likely to be similar in all kinds of cir-cumstances. We state a minimum grade for parking lots, rather than citing the speed with which surface water should flow or the frequency with which a lot may be permitted to be flooded. (And yet, in an arid climate, an infrequently used lot might indeed be built dead flat!) Elsewhere, one relies on performance standards or at least habitually questions the connection of form to performance and the relevance of performance to the situation.

Many standards are thought universal and in fact depend on the social situation or the client. They would be more useful (and unhappily bulkier) if they stated the client and context to which they were relevant, as well as the purpose toward which they were aimed. Standards should be under constant test and revision, and therefore their underlying hypotheses should always be explicit somewhere. A little uneasiness about the pervasive influence of these declarations might be salutary.

# Chapter 11

# Design and Management
# of the Site

As a prelude to discussing the site-planning role, it is necessary first to describe the typical technical process in current practice. This will also explain how multiple issues are normally woven together. In the usual case a single client intends to construct a project on a specific piece of land in a relatively short time for some obvious purpose.

*Site analysis*
The design begins with the analysis of site and purpose. Site analysis, which may be preceded by site selection, starts with a general unoriented reconnaissance, continues through a spot check of customary data to test for its relevance, and then to a systematic inventory of the information that seems, at this beginning stage, to be significant. Emphasis is put on information that from experience is likely to have continued usefulness throughout the processes of design and implementation or is liable to change the course of those processes in some marked way: a topographic map, a description of the ecology, census data. But each problem has its own set of peculiarly relevant data, which will not be completely revealed until the design is complete. The initial site analysis ends with a concise statement of the site's essential character, how it maintains itself and is likely to respond to development, as well as its major problems and potentialities. In parallel, a statement of objectives and performance requirements is also prepared. These objectives and requirements should be stated as con-

cretely as possible without dictating any particular physical solution. An acceptable budget and schedule, consistent with site and purpose, must also be defined at this time.

Site and objectives cannot be studied independently but only in relation to each other — the purposes indicating what aspects of the site are relevant, the site analysis influencing the goals that are possible or desirable, and the budget defining what can be done. The statement of these three factors will be modified throughout the development of the design, since the design process is itself an exploration of site and goal possibilities. Despite this circularity the first-round analysis of situation and purpose is the beginning step.

*Site, purpose, and budget*

Site and purpose are always specific and particular, never standard. There are, however, certain general site factors that are almost always important, including such elements as subsurface condition, topography, climate, ecology, and the existing patterns of land use and circulation. Similarly, there are some basic human goals that very often appear in any statement of objectives: accessibility, adequacy, diversity, cost, health and safety, adaptability and stability, legibility. They will be supplemented by the direct technical objectives inherent in the original problem. These aims are stated as a total system for each significant group of users, since most goals and users are in some conflict with other goals and users.

*See Chapter 2*

*See pages 37–44*

Next a detailed program is prepared, springing from aims and resources and a knowledge of the actions and purposes of users, as influenced by the site and the technical possibilities. The program furnishes a quantitative schedule of behavior settings to be provided, their linkages, their desired qualitative characteristics, and the resources to be devoted to them. It is prepared with the client and reviewed by him. It will be modified as design proceeds. In fact, design has already begun. The resulting activity diagram, while not yet referring to any spatial distribution, has already taken spatial possibilities into account. It is the first bare, misarranged bones of a plan.

*Program*

*See pages 28–33*

It is customary at this point to review other site plans with similar objectives, not only in publications but especially in reality, to see how they have fitted plan to purpose and with what success. This is not done in the spirit of imitation, although there is no reason why good forms should not be imitated, but to prepare the mind for the work to come.

When both site and purpose are understood and the

246

*The design
process*

*See Chapters 3, 6,
and 9*

*Trial designs of
subsystems*

preliminary program is in hand, the site planner then proceeds to the heart of the matter, the design itself. Like any creative process, this is difficult to describe. It becomes particularly difficult in site planning, where the factors to be dealt with are so numerous.

The site plan deals in its essence with three fundamental patterns of location in space and time: the pattern of activity, the pattern of circulation, and the physical forms. These are the subject matter of first sketches and remain dominant themes throughout the work. Their nature has been explored in the preceding chapters. A site planner's stock-in-trade is his knowledge of a broad range of alternatives for these three patterns.

The planner is faced with a multitude of interlocking possibilities. The difficulty lies in treating as an interdependent whole a set of decisions that seem too numerous to grasp. So it is often useful to begin with a piecemeal attack, reserving final judgment until the problem can be seen as a whole. The planner may first study some possible alternatives of the activity pattern. Then he will drop these studies and go on to the analysis of circulation and then of form. He may look for suggestions in the site, defining focal points or areas difficult or easy to develop or key features to preserve. By alternating between these factors, he gains an insight into their possibilities and can begin to pick up points of conflict and support, until at last he is dealing, even if only in a very loose way, with the three elements simultaneously.

Alternatively, the planner will work with a single objective at a time: the cheapest plan possible or the most flexible, regardless of their implications for other valued ends. Here again, a partial analysis lays the groundwork for simultaneous study. Still another useful breakdown between part and whole is on an areal basis. The designer begins by making quick sketches for overall patterns of the whole, alternating with other sketches for the development of small units of the development. The alternating sketches at first proceed independently of each other and are gradually built into total systems.

These common approaches — unit analysis; plans for single objectives; isolated studies of use, form, site, or circulation — are design techniques leading up to the study of complex wholes. The alternation of attention from part to part, while judgment is reserved, prepares the mind for studies in which the significance of each partial decision is quickly understood in every important dimension. This si-

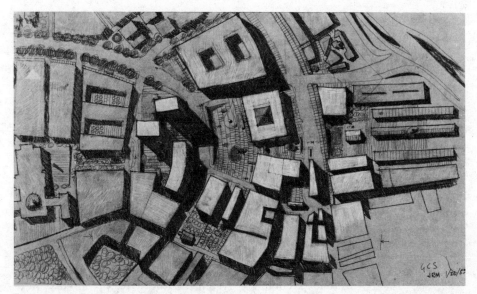

FIGURE 42 *An early study by John R. Myer for the Government Center, Boston. Building mass, open spaces, grades, circulation, paving, and detail are being developed together in the context of the existing city.*

multaneous mastery of the whole, which is essential to an integrated plan, takes time to achieve. When it is attained, it will seem that each trial modification of the developing plan immediately reacts on the remainder of the design in all its aspects. The designer will begin to imagine total systems, sharp and precise at the critical points, loose and unresolved where decisions have less significance for the whole. He will begin to weigh total systems against each other, rather than comparing fractional alternatives.

The studies themselves are carried out in various forms. Plans and sections are essential, and so are diagrams of behavior settings and circulation. Perspective sketches are helpful. Almost always it is advisable to make model studies since the designer is dealing with decisions in three dimensions. Unfortunately, models are not sufficient in themselves because they are imprecise, they falsify detail, they overemphasize static form, and they take time to build.

Studies proceed in the schizophrenic manner common to all design: the planner is at times relaxed and uncritical, allowing his subconscious mind to suggest new forms and connections, most of them completely fantastic and unwork-

*Reason and unreason*

able. At other times he looks sharply at these suggestions, consciously testing them for the way in which they apply to his purposes. Thus he is involved in another alternating process: a swing from almost automatic doodling, in which ideas and forms seem to develop "of themselves," to a sternly critical review of each new suggestion. Part of the skill of a designer lies in managing these two states of mind so that his critical powers do not inhibit creative suggestion, while his irrational processes do not prevent adequate analysis.

Large numbers of form possibilities must be produced in a state of mind free from prejudice and practicality. When one or two suggestions seem to have some possibility of use, they are then fully developed in sketch form. These sketches may be developed quickly in a loose free style, but they should be complete, fixing all major aspects. Alternatives should not be "worked over" by constant modification and erasure: they should be developed, set aside, and redrawn as complete systems. Otherwise, potentially valuable possibilities will be buried under layers of partial changes. A good designer knows where his sketch can be vague and where it must be precise — that is, where he can reserve judgment and neglect detail and where he must test the key decisions.

In this way a wide range of alternative possibilities is

FIGURE 43 *An early sketch by Sven Markelius for the Lincoln Center, New York City, in which he faces the buildings on an internal square, one level above the surrounding streets. Rapid and free, the sketch deals with the essentials in plan and section.*

developed. Certain alternatives will be rejected, others retained for further trial and development, and new ones suggested in the process. Criteria will be rethought, the site reanalyzed, the program modified, as these alternatives open up the potentialities. The designer will redraw feasible alternatives several times, modifying them to meet various objections. But he must know when to abandon them and when to reject some scheme that has been so overlaid with compromises as to lose all its original force. He will also be alert to catch a hint of some totally new arrangement appearing momentarily in this troubled shifting of forms, alert to extract it and start afresh. Final decisions on the basic scheme will be made as the alternatives and criteria narrow down, and as the designer begins to see the whole complex in all its significant dimensions simultaneously.

The design process should be kept as open and fluid as *Fluidity* possible until a wide range of alternatives has been developed and tested. All too often this process is cut short by a state of mind that is narrow and critical from the beginning, as though design were a logical process that proceeded from initial assumptions by rational steps to a unique solution. On the contrary, design is an irrational search, conducted over a ground previously prepared by experience, the study of principles, and the analysis of site and purpose. It is after this search has produced possibilities that rational criticism is brought to bear. Every plan should be preceded by great numbers of discarded sketch alternatives. Every designer should be haunted by the fear that he has left something untried. Even when a final alternative has been selected, it is wise to allow some time to elapse before confirming the choice. A designer has an emotional attachment to plans that arise in the heat of creation. Later, such plans may appear surprisingly weak.

Chapter 12 will describe various design methods in detail and indicate the new possibilities that are arising. We have here outlined the usual process today: a large number of sketch studies, which proceed gradually from partial aspects to a simultaneous treatment of the whole pattern in all its major dimensions and which typically alternate between bursts of unconscious suggestion and the rational development and criticism of feasible alternatives. These studies finally result in a preliminary general plan, dealing *The preliminary* primarily with the patterns of activity, circulation, and the *plan* physical environment. Normally, this sketch will show building location and form, the circulation on the surface, the expected activities in all outdoor and associated indoor

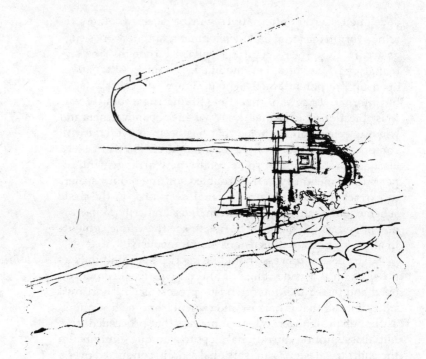

FIGURE 44  *Frank Lloyd Wright's sketch for the Coonley house. Inside and outside, as well as building and site, are dealt with as one. From Frank Lloyd Wright,* Drawings for a Living Architecture, *published for the Bear Run Foundation Inc. and the Edgar J. Kaufman Charitable Foundation by Horizon Press, 1959.*

areas, the general shape and treatment of the ground, the major landscaping, and any additional features that will affect the outdoor space. This decision will be expressed in plan, in section, in activity diagrams, in a sketch model, and often in perspective or isometric views. The plan may show only ultimate development, or it may indicate a series of stages by which this goal is to be reached, each stage being viable in itself and capable of enduring for some time. This schematic plan is usually accompanied by a duly revised program and budget. Plan, program, and budget are now formally reviewed with the client.

*Its technical development*

This preliminary plan is then developed in its technical dimension and in its details. The sketch will have left some aspects unresolved, and there will be many details to consider. Substantial technical development must also be carried forward. Its principal elements are the precise alignment and specification of the road and walk system, the location and design of utilities, and the grading plan. It

*See Chapters 7 and 8*

is only the detailed development of these features that is put off until this late period. In sketching the road system, the designer has already considered its technical demands. He has been aware of special problems he may have created in regard to utilities. He must already have evolved a general grading plan, since the shape of the ground is a key to the area's usefulness and appearance. It is unlikely that detailed technical development will cause any radical revision of the plans of an experienced designer. But technical development is certain to cause some modifications.

Practice differs in the extent to which technical development is carried out by the site planner. Ideally, the entire design process, down to the detailing of curbs and manholes, is pushed to completion in one office, which must then include a trained civil engineer. At the opposite extreme, the site planner may go no further than the schematic plan, leaving to an independent engineer the road and utility layout and the grading plan. But since these technical drawings are an essential part of the whole scheme, the site planner and the engineer must continue to make mutual adjustments; otherwise, the intent of the plan will be thwarted, and the engineer will be forced into awkward solutions.

*The professional division of labor*

A halfway position is fairly common: the site planner prepares the schematic plan, the overall road and utility layout, and the grading and landscape plans, leaving to the engineer the precise alignments for the surveyor, the utility systems in detail, the road and walk cross sections and specifications, and the computations of earth balance. Whatever division of duties is agreed upon, the site planner should prepare as a minimum the schematic plan, the landscape plan, and a freehand version of the grading plan.

Technical development usually begins with a precise layout of the structures and paths shown on the schematic plan, to the degree of accuracy required for their location on the site. This drawing involves reducing street layouts to circular curves and tangents and specifying the geometry of buildings and property lines with relation to bench marks and compass directions. Accepted standards for the horizontal alignment of roads are given in Chapter 7. The freehand sketch of the road center line is approximated as closely as possible by a succession of curves and tangents conforming to these standards, or minor modifications are made. Station points are marked on this precise center line.

*Precise layouts*

*See pages 141–145*

The vertical dimension of the plan is then detailed. This task usually begins with the design of the road profile,

*Road profiles*

*See pages 151–154*

a succession of straight grades and vertical curves, constructed over a plot of the existing surface, following the standards given in Chapter 7. On a separate sheet of cross-sectional paper, a continuous section through the ground at the center line is drawn along each road or consecutive run of station points. The horizontal scale is that of the road layout; the vertical scale is usually exaggerated ten times. The designer plots the existing surface along this line, as if this sinuous vertical section had been flattened out to a single plane. A new road profile is then approximated in several trials by drawing a series of straight tangents over the existing profile, usually adhering rather closely to it.

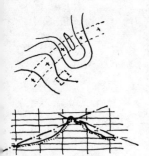

The designer searches for a line with grades neither too steep nor too flat, with positive drainage (no sag curves at points difficult to drain in the plan), and one that minimizes and balances the cut and fill. Once he has found such an arrangement, he draws the necessary vertical curves at the intersections of the tangents and readjusts the line where difficulties develop. He also checks the profile in relation to the horizontal layout to judge the shape of the road in three dimensions. The designer should be sure that the profile is self-closing — in other words, that elevations are the same on different profiles where they intersect with each other.

The relation of the profile to the grading plan is more difficult. The balance of cut and fill along the profile is sometimes a misleading indication of total earthwork. Since the profile tends to generate the detailed grading plan, this profile must permit a good shape for the ground surface as a whole. In drawing the profile, a skilled planner will usually be aware of how he is influencing the grading plan, but subsequent development of the grading plan will often force him to reconsider the profile.

Spot elevations at other critical points in the plan, such as the elevations of finished floor in the principal buildings or those at the base of existing trees to be saved, are set to conform with the sketch. These spot elevations are then transferred to a precise layout on which existing contours have also been shown. Since the profile of the road center line has now been established, tick marks showing where the new contours will cross this line in plan can also be put on the layout. And since the road cross section is known, these new contours can be drawn as far as the tops of curbs or the edge of the road shoulder.

*The grading plan*

The next step is the grading plan, which will specify the new shape that the ground is to have when development is complete. Standards for this plan are outlined in Chapter 8, and it is shown by drawing the contours of the new ground surface where it will differ from the existing surface. This new surface, as a minimum, will make the transition between any predetermined new surfaces (roads, the spaces close by new buildings) and the existing land to be left undisturbed. It respects any features to be retained, such as trees, outcrops, or existing roads and buildings. While the grading plan, if it is a simple one, may be indicated in final contract documents only by spot elevations at key points, it is essential to develop it as a contour drawing in order to control the landform as a whole. The grading plan is the most delicate and significant portion of the technical development. In fact, it may sometimes cause the basic plan itself to be modified. The skill with which it is laid out will have much to do with the technical adequacy of the plan and also with its visual and functional success. It therefore requires care and time for proper development.

253
See pages 160–163

It is most likely that the road profiles and the spot elevations of buildings will have to be revised to make good transitions possible. The most common difficulties that occur are excessive or unbalanced cut and fill, which is costly and damaging to the land and its cover; drainage pockets in the land, on the roads, or against the sides of buildings; the destruction of desirable stands of trees; steep grades that may be dangerous, cause erosion, or make use, maintenance, or access difficult; a poor visual or functional relation between a building or a road and its immediate surroundings; and visually awkward transitions between one ground surface and another. Checking for these problems and eliminating them will be slow work until the designer has become skillful in reading contours on paper as if they were actual forms in space. Their interspacing, linear quality, degree of parallelism, and general pattern all have distinct meanings. Chapter 4 discusses the nature of contour patterns.

This concept of the grading plan as simple adjustment between rigid structures and fluid ground is the normal one, and it is justifiable in many circumstances. On occasion, the designer may take a more active attitude, molding the ground into an abstract sculpture and attempting to accomplish more than just harmonious, trouble-free adjustment. But in any case the modeling of the ground surface should have been an integral part of the general plan from the beginning.

When the grading plan has been completed, the layout

*Utility layouts*

of utilities is made, usually beginning with storm drainage, which is the utility most likely to be significant. This step will include, as a minimum, the plan layout of utility lines. At this time the designer should check to see that no critical problems of elevations or sizing will occur. The engineering

*See pages 168–172*

of these utilities is discussed in Chapter 8. If the designer has been aware of their general implications, it is not likely that major revisions of the plan will be required, although they may sometimes be necessary. But it is quite possible that utility considerations will require changes in the precise layout or in the grading plan or will suggest economic or functional modifications.

The layout of all utilities may be shown on one sheet, or it may be more convenient for the storm drainage to be shown on the grading plan because it is so intimately related to topography. Depending on the extent to which engineering consultants will prepare construction drawings of their own, the utility plans will go beyond general layouts to show subsurface elevations and the sizing of conductors.

*Landscaping and details*

Finally, precise landscaping and site details are specified, including the utility fixtures, pavement construction and finish, and street furniture. Utility and road construction details and specifications, which are necessary contract documents, are likely to appear on the drawings of consultants, but they may be part of an integrated set of site drawings. Engineering services are usually required to prepare them except in the simplest cases.

*See pages 209–219*

The landscaping specifications, the finish of the ground plane, and the street furniture are too often ignored or given only cursory notice. "Tree stamps" are frequently applied to the drawings, in lines along the streets, or in random clumps, or to obscure the parking lots and service yards. Decisions as to plant materials, surface and wall textures, and the shape of minor structures and objects demand the conscious attention of the site designer. They may be shown on a landscape plan, supplemented by partial sections, plant lists, and by detailed drawings of special objects, such as fences, signs, utility poles, seats, steps, and fountains. Notes should also be made as to the level of maintenance implied by the plan.

When technical development is complete, it must be checked for internal consistency and for compliance with the basic plan, the program, and the budget. The plan may be evaluated once more in the light of these findings and readjusted. The developed design is now expressed in a series of final technical drawings, consisting most often of a precise surveying layout, a set of road profiles, a grading plan with spot elevations at key points, a utility layout, a landscape plan, and a sheet of details, which are the "working drawings" of a site plan. Together with a set of specifications for pavements, utilities, grading, landscaping, and site maintenance, they form the contract documents on which estimates and work can be based. These are the drawings needed to guide actual construction, but they may not cover all legal and administrative needs. For the latter purposes, requirements vary over the United States and include such items as plats for legal record, sketches for approval by public agencies, bidding procedures, the timing and interrelations of the trades, and the general and special conditions of the work. Many of these drawings and other documents will soon be developed, stored, and exhibited by computer graphics rather than by draftsmen and typists.

Important as these technical drawings are, they are not the essence of the site plan. The essence can be found in the sketch, which may be a drawing or a model and which sets forth the pattern in three dimensions of activity, circulation, and physical form. The correctness of this essential pattern will be tested by the way it conforms to purposes, resources, and the spirit of the site.

Particularly in larger projects the drawings will very often be accompanied by a written report that explains the reasoning behind the proposals and describes policies and features that are more easily put in words. The words need not describe the drawings, which should speak for themselves, or be a colorful gloss on them. Words and graphics are separate languages, both appropriate to convey different kinds of ideas. Designers will often look on a report as "mere words" added after the real work is done, while laymen will think of the drawings as "mere pictures" illustrating the report. Each group is prejudiced by its unfamiliarity with one of the languages. The written or spoken word is as necessary as a drawing to convey a design to client or contractor.

The product is not the report and the drawings but the reality on the ground. Words and sketches need do no more than express the intent as accurately as possible. Excessive "finish" will confuse the client, and even the designer, as to what the end result will be. Willful distortions of presenta-

*Words and pictures*

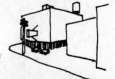

tion, such as suppressing the surroundings or falsifying light or viewpoint or using a salesman's language, are too easy.

This necessarily lengthy description of the process of site design may be summarized as the following series of steps in which plans are commonly prepared today and by which the client maintains control over the whole process:

1. A program phase, which concludes with an agreed-upon program, a total budget, a design and construction schedule, and a site analysis, all of which are judged to be consistent with one another.

2. A schematic phase, which concludes with a revised program and schedule, a schematic site plan at 1 inch = 100 feet or 40 feet, and a rough cost estimate. The general site plan will show structures, activity locations, circulation, major outdoor spaces, critical utility mains, plant massing, overall ground form, and general level of finish. Rough costs will be estimated from experience by the length or area of typical features at given levels of finish. The essential site design has now been fixed.

3. A design development phase that results in a complete layout and a specification of detail sufficient to assure the solution of all problems and to allow a detailed costing. This will normally include one or more site plans at 1 inch = 40 feet, which show buildings, all paved surfaces, all planted areas by type, old and new contours, the location of all utilities except laterals, and the location and nature of details. There will be sketch sections and studies of key detailed areas, as well as brief outline specifications. Costs will be estimated by elements. Program and schedule revisions will be stated. These drawings and calculations may be accompanied by a report outlining the governing policies and assumptions.

4. A contract documents phase, which produces the drawings and verbal documents on which the contract bidding is based. The drawings normally include a grading and layout plan at 1 inch = 40 feet, to which the utility layout is either added or shown as a separate sheet, a set of road and utility profiles, a planting plan, and a set of plans and sections of details (for example, walls, paving, plant boxes, outdoor furniture, lights, signs, inlets). These detail drawings are keyed to the layout or to the utility sheet. Drawings are accompanied by bid procedures, the general and special conditions of work, and the technical specifications for the constructions to be accomplished, usually broken down by

subcontract, such as clearing, grubbing, and demolition, and earthwork, utilities, paving, and planting and other landscape work. Bids may be asked for construction with and without certain marginal features in order to allow last-minute adjustment of contract price to estimated budget.

5. The last step is to supervise construction on the site, to ensure compliance but also to make detailed adjustments as unexpected problems and opportunities arise. Ideally, one studies and modifies a layout as it is staked out upon the ground or as it is under construction or, even better, when it is in use. This may be a rare opportunity but should certainly be practiced where possible. When users begin to design their own settings, it may become more common. Superintendence should be continuous whenever a development is long-range or takes time to mature. As an irreducible minimum, the designer is responsible for helping to make a smooth transition between site development and ongoing site management. Better, he continues to consult with the site managers, who were themselves involved in the site design. The continuing effect in reality is the arbiter of the plan.

Site planners normally deal with particular kinds of problems: medium- to large-scale residential areas under one management, university campuses, large medical centers, regional shopping centers, urban renewal projects, large resorts, world's fairs, large parks, and, much less frequently, the siting of small groups of houses. Except for the last, these are situations involving complex decisions, in which it is necessary to arrive at some definite allocation of site and circulation simply in order to coordinate investment and construction. Some site plans are just that: workable arrangements of buildings, streets, and territories, which resolve obvious conflicts and allow construction to proceed. Other plans serve broader interests.

We can imagine other situations — large-scale completely centralized site design or its opposite: site planning in which ultimate users design the setting for their own purposes. Alternatively, we can imagine the design of sites of constantly varying function, where the emphasis would be on rapid response, temporary situation, and continuous management; or "interior" sites, where all space is inside space; or other isolated or exotic environments. But the normal conditions illustrate the methods and nature of site planning and raise the issues inherent in its processes.

Site design is an episode in the continuous process of decision about the environment and its use and is subject to

**T**ypical Site-Planning Tasks

the form of that decision process. It is locked in with all the other factors of decision: clients, values, institutions, political and economic constraints, available information, predictions, actions, lines of influence and communication. Site problems are of the class of "open" problems, not easily bounded and never defined until the solution itself, with its relevant criteria and analyses, has been created. Site design is not hermetic or the monopoly of specially gifted individuals or *Values* concerned solely with appearance or with "higher values." It is certainly concerned with values, but what values or whose values is just what is meant by defining a problem. It is form-providing, not form-imposing. If site planning has any internal values of its own — other than the way of looking at problems inherent in its choice of methods and subject matter — they are those of sustaining life, facilitating individual development, and expressing concern for the voiceless client and the future state.

*Clients*     The relation to the client is one pervasive problem. The ultimate user usually plays no active part in site design. His needs are represented by vague intentions, by general restraining rules and standards, or by the indirect signals of a market oriented to effective economic demand. Site plans serve the interest of developers first — and the interests of those able to pay for their use second. Given the nature of the decision process today, this fact is hardly surprising.

The good intentions of the designer can sometimes ameliorate the situation or substitute other values in dimensions of the plan not critical to the interests of the dominant parties. But even in these areas of freedom the designer will just as often simply inject his own values. The mystique of the design process reinforces this. Sometimes, indeed, even the interests of a developer may be compromised as he wrestles with a designer's complex and apparently monolithic proposal. Difficulties of communication and control are magnified in the multiple-developer situation, where the ultimate users are diverse, to some degree transient, mostly without effective economic or political leverage, and always far from the drafting board. Setting the problem — which means deciding on the criteria, the active clients, the accepted restraints and bounds, the available information, and the class of solutions to be sought — depends on the initiators of the decision process, the type of professionals they call in, and their customary ways of looking at the world. Redefining the problem or changing the client is traumatic. These are pervasive issues of social decision making, and their resolution will not depend largely on the actions of site planners. But how could site planners work if those issues were resolved?

In the ideal case the user of a piece of ground would design it for himself, or it would be designed by a developer who was directly accountable to a small group holding the same values, clearly defined. In that case the site designer becomes a teacher, someone who helps the user to analyze his own needs and create his own possibilities. In that sense one function of this and similar books should be as sources of information for people who want to build their own places. The site designer still acts as a specialist in creating form possibilities, predicting their effects, and explaining how they can be technically accomplished, but his basic role is to disengage himself by communicating the necessary techniques of design and analysis and thus allowing the client to invent and build his own world. An ongoing process of user management is substituted for sporadic professional intervention. This ideal role depends on a radical decentralization of power, on the possibility of territories belonging to very small groups, and on a free choice of client and professional based on a mutual fit of ideas. But even here the professional is not self-effacing. He works to reveal hidden needs and possibilities. He speaks for the future and for clients not yet present, since all sites have long histories.

Although this role is rare today and appears only in the occasional planning of a garden or house for an affluent and interested client, it may someday become much more common if environmental control ever is placed largely in the hands of users. But even in a better society there will be many cases where the designer cannot play the ideal role but must remain a professional concerned for clients who are at some distance from himself. This will always be so where systems of large scale, broad use, or long life are being designed — large parks or central city plazas — where the clients are necessarily numerous and of conflicting values, or transient, or not yet present to be consulted. It also happens when the designer is planning sites and facilities that may be freely chosen by their users — that is, when sites are relatively small in relation to the total supply of areas and are being developed in advance of demand to attract a clientele to some new way of life. It also appears in caretaking situations — either voluntary, where needs are fairly clear but not crucial and the client is glad to leave decisions to a professional (for example, the design of a parking lot or an outdoor amphitheater), or the ethically more difficult cases of involuntary caretaking (for example, prisons, hospitals, or playgrounds for very small children). In all these cases the professional necessarily uses more formal methods of communication, of behavioral analysis, and of evaluation. He hopes that his direct client will be representative of the ultimate user, whether by intimate involvement, by political influence, by sensitivity to the market, or from accurate formal knowledge of the group to be served.

*Opening up the site design process*

Although most of the necessary changes in social decision making lie beyond the scope of a site-planning text, the professional can do a number of things to expand the frequency of direct user control or to improve the processes of indirect response. He will, wherever possible, try to reach out to the user and to teach him the techniques of site design and analysis. Similarly, he will try to see that professional site designers of diverse social background are trained in large numbers so that there is a better chance of there being a professional working directly for a group whose values he shares. He will attempt to push information about a problem out to a wider audience, in preparation for public discussion and for changes in the direct clients to make them more representative of the users. Making the design process explicit, open, and penetrable to nonprofessionals is one means of achieving this end. Preparing explicit and detailed programs, which refer to the expected actions and purposes of users, is another.

See page 28

The site designer will build behavioral and attitudinal research into his design process, in the expectation that it will reveal diverse and otherwise hidden requirements. He will look for ways to divide his site (in space or in time) into special territories that might be controlled by small groups. Whenever possible, he will support participatory action. In addition, he will advocate a flexible plan (which is easier to say than to do), as well as adaptive management, which can learn and can change its clientele. Finally, he will promote and monitor specific environmental experiments so that new possibilities are opened up for the user, who can then, by his response to the experiment, clarify his requirements both to himself and to others.

*Programming*

One neglected avenue for improving the response to need is the preparation of adequate programs. The normal program simply gives the quantities of space to be provided, by broad categories of standard function ("playgrounds," "commercial use"), and specifies their spatial linkages and their allowable costs. The quality of those spaces, the behavior expected to occur in them, and the purposes and attitudes of their users get very little attention. Moreover, the program is most often fixed before design begins, and thus the environment is unwittingly predesigned by financial and administrative considerations that have unforeseeable side effects and are limited to routine categories of form. Small wonder that we can fulfill an approved program and yet enrage the user!

If a program is properly made, it can overcome many of these difficulties. Rather than giving room counts or square feet of labeled space, it should begin by specifying what actions are expected to take place, by whom, and with what purposes. These action specifications spring from the analysis of objectives, clients, site, and context. Behavior settings for clusters of these actions are then proposed, with their required qualities, linkages, equipment, and quantities. Estimated costs for these provisions are budgeted, and the management and service support of the desired behavior are also given. The focus is on clusters of behavior and their appropriate settings and support rather than on customary physical form. Moreover, there is an explicit linkage through objectives, resources, and constraints, all the way to detailed settings with their costs and management. Plans can be evaluated directly against this program, and actual use can be monitored to learn if the environment or the program must later be modified.

Such a program is one that can be readily understood by the client. He can evaluate it and influence it before design begins. Resources can be allocated more efficiently, and the general findings of social science or a particular analysis of client behavior can be applied at a strategic point. The designer himself is guided more accurately and yet freed from unnecessary prescriptions of form. All participants are now able to learn from subsequent experience. The program itself must be open-ended, loose-leaf, since it will have to be modified continuously, first as design proceeds and new possibilities, new data, and new clients accrue, and second as the site goes into use and errors appear in cost estimates, in behavioral and form predictions, or even in basic criteria.

Programs of this kind cost time and money. They are appropriate where client control is indirect, where site development involves a large investment and lengthy maintenance, or where the developing agency can generalize over several projects or must learn to improve its future performance. Yet even in simpler cases a program of this type, if not of this precision, may be far preferable to the usual "2 acres of parks, 20 acres of single-family residence." It is true enough that a performance program may be resisted for other reasons than its cost — because its explicit linkage of purpose and form exposes a developer to visible instead of only hidden failure.

*Environmental
management*

We are beginning to look at sites as problems of continuing management, where form, activity, services, and administrative controls are modified continuously and interdependently in order to maintain some level of performance or even to achieve changing levels of performance. The performance of a parking lot, to take a simple example, will depend not only on its spatial form but also on the number and turnover of users, their driving skill and expectations, the regulations and charges imposed, and the maintenance and policing of the lot. Changing any one factor will affect the others as well as general performance. A parking lot design must take them all into account, whether by prediction or prescription. Most designs make careless and hidden assumptions about these factors, exposing performance to unaccountable fluctuations.

A once-and-for-all prescription for the spatial form of a place may sometimes be of little consequence relative to the impact of daily management. An on-the-spot manager, who is in close control and commands a high flow of current information, can respond to change and maintain performance in a rapid, effective way. On the other hand, he is limited to incremental changes and cannot easily break out of a worsening situation by any radical change in treatment. Moreover, performance of the setting may gradually "drift" in undesirable directions, without participants being directly aware of it.

Site designers have much to learn from observing the ongoing management of a place. Their designs and programs should include explicit management actions as well as spatial patterns. They must come to see their own intervention as only one episode in a continuous history of site development and management. They may find a new role for themselves in the continuous support of management: designing temporary patterns in response to newly apparent needs or making ongoing experiments from which management can learn. They will begin to see their design as an organization of events in time as well as in space. It will then express the fluctuation of function, the establishment of territories bounded by time, and the way events interact because they succeed or are contemporary with one another.

Site-form controls need not be permanent fixtures. General performance standards linked directly to desired outcomes allow many kinds of response according to a shifting situation. For example, if one purpose in a parking lot is safety, an increase in illumination may do more than an increase in turning radius if the lot begins to be used at night. Indirect incentives or the communication of design information or making design skills available to other agents may be more effective than negative controls. Zoning ordinances, as one example, are turning more and more to "unified development" provisions, where exact locations are not fixed as long as overall balances and ceilings are observed. Long-range site planning by stable institutions can go even further toward general performance statements, to be applied later according to current circumstances.

Behavior may fluctuate rapidly, and management must be able to respond to those fluctuations. There are two factors that are more permanent in their form and effect and thus tend to act as organizers and stabilizers of behavior. One is the spatial and temporal environment that has already been discussed. The other is the set of institutions that regularizes the relations between persons.

*Environments and institutions*

These two patterns, similar in their longevity and in some of their functional effect, are, not surprisingly, often interrelated. The relation is obvious when we consider those institutions directly concerned with the development or management of environment: planning agencies, private developers, community associations, school boards, highway authorities, and the like. Here the final quality of the setting may be due as much to the pattern of the decision process as to the pattern of spatial form: to the timing and clarity of decision, who participates in it, how criteria are evoked, how decisions are communicated and revised, or the continuity and responsiveness of management. Environments change in response to changes in underlying institutions, and their effectiveness changes even more markedly. Environmental change, for its part, will often have institutional side effects: stimulating the creation of new management forms or hastening the decay of old forms of association. The coupling is loose but sometimes substantial.

The site designer is not often able (or trained) to recommend institutional changes, but he must be aware of how the performance of his designs will be affected by probable institutional forms and what changes in management organization are required by his proposals. He should recognize the opportunities for new institutions that occur in creating a new environment. Houses or grounds can be cooperatively owned or maintained, schools can become part of community life, government can be decentralized, or health care can be put on a group basis. These issues are far beyond the scope of this book, but it is fair to point out that environment and institutions, both of them patterns of long life, have strategic effects on the whole quality of human life and that these effects are magnified if they are coordinated. Planning for the concurrent modification of these two patterns is a powerful social lever.

Managing
Designers

The design process itself poses problems of management, particularly when it is long, complex, and done by ⅼ team. Site planning for any but the smallest of projects is now carried on in large offices. A project manager is assigned to the particular design while it is in the office, and he draws on the services of a pool of specialists who are also part of the firm: landscape architects, architects, engineers, perhaps even lawyers, economists, or construction or management specialists. In addition, outside consultants will be drawn in, to provide either general advice or specific information. On occasion, the necessary team cannot be found in any one firm but is put together as a consortium of firms, organized solely for that particular task and usually under the lead of the office that initiated it.

Managing the design process means maintaining the flow of information, coordinating the work of all the actors, keeping the design open to all who are vitally concerned, choosing the best design strategy, and encouraging a cyclic return to the original problem without allowing the cycling to become a closed trap from which recommendations never emerge. All of these objectives require the design manager to evaluate process and product together — to estimate how much better a design will be produced by the application of how much more time and manpower and information. We have no rational means for making such evaluations, and the open-endedness of design may even preclude it. Design management decisions are made intuitively and are based on personal experience gained from many previous tries, within the constraint of a design interval that is usually set by custom.

Conventional
schedules and
organizations

For example, designing a complex site may be expected to require 18 months to reach the stage of construction drawings. This period is allocated to a standard sequence including such processes as survey, criteria formation, program, preliminaries, review, developed design, review, and construction drawings. Into this conventional interval the design manager will pack the manpower he estimates to be needed and will promise the outside reviews and consultations he thinks he can manage. Sometimes the beginning of this sequence — through preliminary design and review — is treated as being unpredictable, simply going on until an acceptable sketch design can be found. For this time, the manager makes no promises and asks for payment on a cost-plus basis. Once an acceptable general design is agreed upon, however, the process is considered to be determinate, producing detailed construction documents at the end of a predictable time at a predictable cost.

Team composition and hierarchy are set by rule; problems are defined the way they have always been defined by the professionals concerned. The strength of personality of the various team members determines many of the critical choices. Thus, in most cases, uncertainty and problem shift are banished; but when they are not, the site design process may break down internally under an overload of factors and interests to be resolved. The designer then falls back on arbitrary allocation, using standard lots and street plans to resolve the confusion. Thus he ends with no clear idea of the purposes to be served, whose purposes they are, or how his proposals address them. Construction can proceed, of course.

Defining the problem is the crucial and initial step, that is, deciding who the client is, what the criteria are, what resources can be used, what limits must be imposed, what type of solution is expected, and therefore who should develop it. Ideally, this question would be considered afresh and completely before any design begins. In fact, problems cannot be completely redefined at the beginning since all factors are interrelated and their comprehensive redefinition would require infinite time. Moreover, all problems have a previous history of speculation, experience, institutional involvement, and clientele, and are thus predefined by a long process of accumulation.

*Defining the problem*

The design manager can at least require that the problem be explicitly set, so that its dimensions are nowhere hidden. He will also seek to be involved as early as possible in that definition, so that his design is not later hedged about by unforeseen restrictions. Occasionally, he will play a decisive role in problem setting, by proposing new criteria and resources, by advocating the inclusion of a hidden client, by revealing unanticipated solution types, or even by creating a client to suit his proposals.

In any case, he will always ask if the problem is correctly stated: Is a site plan really required? Who will be the actual users, and what criteria are relevant to them? Has the client the resources to carry out what is proposed? Most important, the design manager will insist on a means for redefining the problem in the course of its solution, whether that redefinition is called for by information generated in the design process itself (as when a new possibility for site exploitation appears) or is required by external changes (new clients enter the process or a new criterion surfaces). He consciously directs the design process and the first steps of implementation to generate the kind of information that stimulates redefinition. Early designs are speculative tests, and site experiments are employed wherever possible.

We are a long distance from any systematic way of making a metadesign, or design for designing. We can, however, at least set out the whole procedure explicitly though intuitively: design method, time, manpower, client, ways of setting goals, gaining information, and predicting results, the limits on recycling or on the entrance of new actors, the use of external professionals. If the system is openly considered as a whole, then trade-offs can be made between its elements, and we can learn something for next time. Critical path analyses may uncover the bottlenecks, but only to the extent that time requirements are predictable. Better record keeping and good case studies of the actual design process are invaluable for developing our design management capability.

Combining the initiation, design, building, and management of a site in one single organization is therefore advantageous, since information flows more easily within a single agency, and trade-offs can be arranged. The designer learns from the troubles of the man who installs the sewers, and he is stimulated to suggest new possibilities for management as well as for form. The organization can consider lengthening the design period to allow a better fit between site and user or can gain the advantages of very rapid decision by applying more skilled manpower and a more compressed method. This fluid style affects the organization

*Design teams*

of the design team itself. Rather than a strict hierarchy, with explicit roles and a chain of command, the team must operate as a group of equals. Each member has some special skill but is able and expected to play the roles of other team members to some extent. The focus of decision shifts as the problem shifts, small subteams are formed and dissolved to perform particular tasks, conflicts are expected and openly resolved. Most often they will be resolved by consensus, although a formal arbiter will be required to break deadlocks and maintain the schedule.

The design process must be penetrable to clients and other participants. It should not be arcane — a back-room magic that blossoms into marvelous untouchable pictures. The relation to outside professional consultants, with their set tasks and set intervals for reporting, may be as difficult as managing client participation. Teams may therefore try to incorporate special skills within their own boundaries or put other professionals on a flexible retainer basis. Consultants may be used for purposes other than information, of course. They may be wanted to lend prestige to a process or to resolve conflicts. The formal report of carefully limited scope may therefore be preferred. In that case the timing of those reports and the tasks they are given to accomplish can be as critical as the quality of the report itself.

All of these are problems of internal and external communication which must be solved during the delicate process of search and evaluation. Making the design process viable and explicit by the use of systematic methods is one way of improving that communication.

The choice of technical language — the system of graphic symbols, numbers, and words — plays a neglected but not trivial role here. Ideally, design, data, predictions, evaluations, and controls would all be expressed in the same language, and this language would be comprehensible not only to oneself (as in that sketch stage of design which is essentially self-communication) but also to other professionals and to clients, users, and builders. Such communication requires simplicity, and yet the language must be rich enough to deal with the nuances of the spatial and temporal pattern of behavior and form. It must also be manipulable, rapid, and coherent.

*Technical language*

No one will be surprised that we do not possess such a masterly language, and it is even doubtful that we shall ever find one that will perform all these feats. But our customary languages are so deficient that we are forced to search for something better. Plans, sections, elevations, and models perform relatively well as descriptions and controls of physical form. Nevertheless, they do not express pattern or development in time; they fail to record behavior, institutions, or management; they are slow and costly to manipulate; they do not directly convey the sensuous experience of a place. Furthermore, they are difficult for laymen, and many professionals, to read. They are inaccurate communications and easy to falsify. Evaluation is difficult, short of experiencing the completed reality. Surprisingly few site designers realize what they are proposing until it is done.

See pages 286–288

The technical obstacle of language must be overcome by a whole series of innovations, using the entire range of iconic, diagrammatic, verbal, quantitative, and simulation modes. Languages expressive of process and dynamic form are particularly required. These are not hopeless tasks — a number of new languages are presently being developed and will be described in the chapter to follow.

**Required
Revisions**

The "current best practice" described at the beginning of this chapter must be revised in a number of ways. By enumerating them, we can summarize our discussion.

1. While continuing to be value-oriented, the purposes of a successful site design are properly those of the user, not those of the designer or even of his direct client. Most designers would object that they have always been concerned about the user. Yet if sites are to facilitate user purposes, there must be major changes in the process of environmental development and in the techniques of site design and analysis. The changes include the decentralization of power and a new role for the designer as teacher, student, and facilitator. Site designs cannot be wholly preoccupied with present vocal users, however, but must be particularly concerned for those absent or hidden.

2. Communication between participants in the site design process, as well as between them and clients, users, and builders must be greatly improved so that the process is penetrable to all parties and so it can handle with dispatch the required quantity of information. To improve communication there must be changes in the organization of the design team, a more explicit and systematic process, the use of behavioral programs, and the construction of new design languages.

3. Site design must become a learning process, cyclically returning to earlier phases, moving back and forth from initial problem definition to site occupation, management, and the feedback therefrom. This process is in contrast to site planning conceived of as a momentary task, which terminates after a detailed plan has been made to

meet a predetermined program. Institutionalizing feedback into the site design process is yet an unsolved problem, however.

4. In addition to specifying the form of exterior spaces and objects and their cost, site plans must also deal with performance, behavior, attitude, management, and environmental institutions. This approach is a new way of looking at site design.

5. While proposing the spatial pattern of certain elements, site plans must also consider their development, or their cyclical pattern, in time. Plans should specify temporal rhythm and process form. They are interventions in a very long term process, future oriented, directed toward change, and concerned with the client not yet present.

Together these changes add up to profound shifts in technique and role, shifts of which all environmental design stands in need. Some experiments and new departures of these kinds are already under way, but for the most part they lie in the future.

# Chapter 12

# Technique:
# Design Methods

Mysteries of
design

By common account, design is a mystery, a lightning flash. Men of genius receive these flashes, and they learn to receive them by following the example of other men of genius. After the revelation, there are details to develop and the work of carrying out the revealed solution. But these are separate problems, whether one thinks of them as grubby nuisances or as the overriding issues of practicality.

Common account is correct: there *is* a mystery in design, as there is in all human thought. But the account is otherwise wrong. Design is not restricted to genius, nor is it a uniform or simple process, nor is it distinct from practicality or detail. Practicing designers are aware of its convolutions, but they also half believe in the lightning flash. They are trained to design in one set way, which they apply to every occasion. The one way is often clumsy and wasteful. But most of the new systematic techniques now used for problem solving do not seem very useful either, since site planning is so open-ended a process.

If design is the imaginative creation of possible forms (of environment in this case), which are created to achieve certain purposes and are complete with the instructions for making them, then design is practiced by many people and in many different ways. Some ways are new, some quite old, and each is relevant to a particular situation. All of them include the generation and evaluation of new possibilities. Let

Inventory of
design methods

us begin with a descriptive inventory of the known methods of generating and selecting form possibilities:

*Incremental adaptation*: The great majority of environmental designs are incremental adaptations of solutions previously used, especially those that have been used often enough to become stereotypes. There are vast numbers of such stereotypes — the cul-de-sac, the backyard, foundation planting, the street tree, the park of trees and grass, the axial vista, the playground, the sidewalk café, to name only a random few in site planning. Our heads are full of such customary forms, as well as the situations, purposes, and types of behavior with which they are customarily associated. People who do not call themselves designers use them repeatedly to imagine and decide on environmental form, making minor adaptations to fit them to the current situation.

Avowed designers use the method just as frequently: they "review the literature" for previous solutions and follow the fashions of the day. Professionals and laymen are not wrong. Creating a new form possibility, complete with its detail, its purpose, its method of production, its fit with behavior, is an exhaustive undertaking. Repeated trials will be needed to test its usefulness and to adapt its details. In the complexities of environmental design, it is impossible to innovate most features or to do so continuously. We must fall back on previous achievements.

The finest site planning of the past has been a culmination of a long process of this kind — each designer copied a past solution but made a few adjustments to improve the functioning, so that late products are miracles of well-fitted form. Where appropriate stereotypes are widely diffused, magnificent regional landscapes develop — created by many minds, yet harmonious and visibly meshed with a way of life.

*The usefulness of incremental design*

Incremental adaptation is useful when changes in the external situation are slow relative to the pace of environmental decision — when objectives, behavior, technology, institutions, and physical settings are all stable. In addition, the available stereotypes must have some reasonable relation to the problem. It must be possible that a chain of small modifications can lead to a good solution. Forms that are the product of recent fashion or were developed in different circumstances may be radically inappropriate. The shallow-lot wide-front "ranch house" of current suburbia may not be worth gradual modification, since it is only a momentary way of providing visible status — a way that imposes severe costs in development and privacy. On the contrary, the underlying stereotype of a low-density, tree-planted suburbia of single dwelling units, which has a long history and fits many features of current living style and desire, is the kind of form that well deserves careful tuning.

Even the most innovative designers use stereotypes. In ordinary work, they appear everywhere, and fateful decisions are unconsciously made thereby. When bitter arguments arise over the exact alignment of an expressway, no one stops to wonder about the standardized model of the inner circumferential road on which that exact alignment is based. The plan for a new town in Ghana looks strangely like the product of an American school of planning. Stereotypes cannot be avoided — the danger lies in using them unthinkingly.

This assertion has several consequences. First, a designer must be aware of the ubiquity of stereotype forms and consciously review those that are applicable to his own problem. Second, he must have some understanding of the purposes and situations for which those types are useful. Third, he must be able to recognize the problems for which an adapted solution will do and those which call for innovation. The latter judgment is most difficult — it requires a knowledge of previous performance, an accurate estimate of the nature of the problem, and a rapid preview of the design process to come. The automatic use of previous solutions and the automatic worship of innovation (the ideal that most designers are trained to admire) are both irrational.

We ought to develop libraries of stereotypes — inventorying forms and their consequences and changing these data as experience accrues. The creation and evaluation of new stereotypes (or prototypes, to use a more genial word) becomes a task of influence and value, worthy of substantial public investment.

*Incremental computer programs*

Incremental improvement is not tied to traditional forms. It may be used in systematic optimization. There are computer programs that begin with any arbitrary diagram of room locations and a precise way of evaluating the linkages between them in terms of weighted access or conflict. Random incremental changes in single room locations are then made and retained whenever the "goodness" of the total system increases in any degree. The pattern therefore gradually "improves," until some stable pattern is achieved beyond which random modifications produce no further improvement. This is an optimum solution along that particular branch of development. Of course, a better solution might have been found had a "jump" been made or had the original classification of rooms or the evaluation procedure itself been revised. The technique is limited to simple problems, capable of incremental shift and precise evaluation, and requires a source of rapid calculation. No human being would work that way.

Incremental adaptation is particularly useful where it can be carried out in the field, making real modifications to an environment in use, observing the results, and then improving again. The feedback is rapid and accurate, and a close fit between form and purpose can be achieved. Although this procedure is rarely possible today because of the cost and scale of our operations, it might be used more frequently were decentralized management dealing with settings of small scale. Working directly with reality, rather than with simulations of form, is the privilege of the designers of paintings and pottery. Site planners manage more unwieldy material. Nevertheless, locations can be traced out on the actual site, full-scale mock-ups can be used, or decisions be deferred until use has begun.

*Optimizing the essential function*: While unconsciously relying on stereotypes, most designers advocate other techniques. A common one proceeds from general structure to details: first abstracting the "essential" function of an environment, then imagining a form that will satisfy this general function as well as possible, and finally adapting this form to satisfy other functions and constraints. If, for example, an area is to be used as an outdoor market, it will first be decided that the act of purchase is the essential behavior, and that the environment must make that act inviting. The designer — most often by introspection — considers how environment can be made inviting for purchasing, imagines an ideal form, and then finds ways to adapt the form to meet other problems such as cost, the delivery and protection of goods, the arrival of customers, and the form of the site. If he can do so without compromising his ideal too far, he wins.

The technique is analogous to linear programming, the optimization of a single function subject to constraints. Like linear programming, it is a powerful way of dealing with complexity, but it has serious limitations. First, it must be possible to discover a truly dominant function, whose satisfaction is far more important than any other factor. Designers will often falsify a many-sided problem in order to discover such a function. Even if the dominance is real, the "ideal" solution may be so compromised in the process of adaptation as to lose most of its force or, on the contrary, may be so fiercely defended from assault as to impose very difficult expedients on secondary functions. The correct balance between dominant and secondary functions is hard to maintain, and the recognition of the dominant one may be verbal sleight of hand. The dominant function of a university is pronounced to be "learning," and that function is then seen as a standard process requiring a standard condition. All the rich complexity of a real university is lost in the process. Concentration on one key aspect can lead to dramatic confrontations between designers, clients, and other actors in development. Sometimes drama is what is wanted, but more often a flexible attitude, with the possibility of making trade-offs between many issues, is more productive.

*Optimizing particular functions*

Optimizing is an extremely useful method, however, when it is used as part of a more general design strategy. In early stages of planning, one can learn about the requirements of a particular function by optimizing for it, while holding other requirements subordinate. By doing this in turn for each of the major functions, one gains insight into the complexity of the problem and its hidden conflicts. None of the "optimal" designs is likely to be more than an unworkable caricature, but among these designs, and particularly among combinations of them, will be the seeds of viable general alternatives. The technique is surely correct in pointing to the importance of purpose or function. It is a powerful way of getting at the heart of a complex problem wherever there is an obvious dominant function whose form requirements can be stated rather clearly, and whenever the restraints are equally clear but do not limit the possible form too severely. This situation may occur in the design of a storage yard or a bus terminal. Elsewhere, when used as the principal design approach, it can be dangerously misleading, resulting in forced and formal designs and reliance on verbal or graphic abstraction. Unfortunately, it is often effective in influencing decisions simply because of its apparent clarity.

*Problem structure*

*The structure of the problem*: Another way of approaching a design is to look for clues in the structure of the problem itself. In site planning it is common to begin by analyzing the possibilities inherent in the existing terrain. The planner may consider the ground piece by piece, imagining the potentialities of each location, or he may search for some more general structure latent in the land: a major division, a key pass, a focal point. The technique is not limited to the analysis of site, although it is perhaps most familiar there. The site planner can begin with other aspects of the problem: the difficulties and issues that have led to the demand for a new setting, the structure of political power and institutions which surrounds the decision process, the behavior settings that now inadequately fulfill the stated purposes.

By close attention to existing reality, and particularly to the difficulties or "misfits" that reality exhibits, the planner often finds that suggestions for design seem to rise immediately out of the problem. The design is not an alien solution. The rich diversity of reality comes through. We are much better at recognizing problems and misfits than we are at imagining ideal solutions. A habit of mind that converts bewildering difficulties into assets should be encouraged.

*Use of misfits*

This method is appropriate, then, wherever the existing situation is the crucial factor and is easily observable, where an adequate response to a misfit is the most important aim, where a partial solution is more likely to be appropriate than a radical reorganization of reality, and where it is possible to decide what aspect of existing reality is the key — whether it is the site, the organization of society, or the nature of behavior.

Designs do not actually "rise out of problems," however. What really happens is that the designer, observing reality, thinks of a form that will satisfy a perceived misfit. Often enough, the misfit is perceived because a possible solution is known. The contemplation of terrain suggests known ways of response to terrain. The designer looks for conditions he remembers as being susceptible of solution — steep grades, pockets, sweeping views — or he looks for restraints that may help to determine the solution for him — a shortage of good land, a severe climate.

The analysis of problems, while less risky than utopia, tends to neglect possibilities that could be achieved by radical innovations or could do more than solve present difficulties. Perhaps the terrain is not crucial or can be exploited in unheard-of ways, or perhaps a new terrain can be manufactured. To analyze the problem is surely an essential part of design. Often enough, the correct tactic is to begin with the problem structure, if one can be found. But what must be kept in mind is that solutions do not rise out of problems and indeed that recognition of a problem includes the recognition of the possibility and the nature of a solution.

*Disaggregation*: The two preceding techniques cope with complexity by choosing some one crucial aspect of a problem to manipulate first. Multiplicity can also be managed if it is divided into many parts. By solving each part separately and by combining the results, one can find a solution to the whole which responds to all the multiple aspects. How to divide the whole and then how to recombine the divisions are now the critical operations.

One traditional way of disaggregating a site plan is to divide it into smaller areas, each one small enough to be developed as a whole without unreasonable effort — preferably area units that can be repeated elsewhere in the plan.

*Modules*

These are called *modules*. But the area must be large enough to coincide with important issues of the plan: for example, spatial form or social grouping. Thus in a large housing development a module of one or two houses might miss the most important issues of interrelation, while a module of 500 houses would be inconvenient for studying the whole and would be too large to be repeated and adapted. In low-density housing ten or twenty dwelling units often provide a convenient module. The unit must have enough self-sufficiency so that many internal relations can be determined, independently of their effect on outside patterns.

Modular design is convenient if division is possible. It should not, however, be elevated from a design convenience to a design principle. Some sites are best planned as a series of repeated units because they have similar functions; others are not. Areal divisions need not be modular. They can refer to terrain compartments or to groups of residents of diverse characteristics. But the relative independence of the spatial units is essential.

*Design by behavior settings*

It may prove useful to divide the plan into behavior settings — relatively independent, stable patterns of customary behavior together with their appropriate physical settings — which are units in time as well as in space. These are more logical divisions than purely spatial ones since they follow the grain of the way a place is used and are often relatively independent of each other. They follow from the structure of a properly made program. Combining the individual settings may still be a puzzle. The principal danger is that a single-minded focus on them would lead to the neglect of larger relations: time overlaps, movement patterns, regional influences.

The plan may be broken down into general aspects, each of which covers the entire site. Activity pattern, circulation, and visible physical form have been the divisions used in presenting the material in this book. However convenient for purposes of analysis, these aspects are unfortunately highly interdependent. Separate consideration of such general entities is sometimes useful as a tactic for entering a problem or as a way of presenting results, but it will cause serious difficulties if maintained as a complete design process.

*Breakdown by criteria*

To consider separate criteria is another way of making nonspatial divisions — preparing ideal plans for each of a number of major purposes (access, diversity, cost, maintenance, and so on), while satisfying other criteria at reasonable levels. This is the same tactic used in optimizing a single function, but here a number of diverse optimums are prepared for a deeper understanding of the problem. Correspondences are sought and reinforced, and conflicts are avoided or compromised on some intuitive basis of weighting to give a solution that responds to many criteria at once. Relative independence between the solutions for such criteria is not to be expected. Therefore, this is also only a useful beginning tactic.

A complete method for disaggregated design, inclusive of a systematic means for resolving conflicts, has been proposed by Alexander. It also involves the development of forms appropriate to separate criteria, though only when the criteria are so finely divided that they are no longer verbal generalities but are operational statements about what characteristic of form is needed in a particular circumstance. Requirements are stated as thresholds. Instead of "a suitable environment for learning," we have "all pupils' seats to be movable."

*Christopher, Alexander:* Notes on the Synthesis of Form, *Harvard University Press,* 1964

Once these statements (verbal or graphic) have been prepared — and there will be hundreds or thousands of them for any normal problem — the probable mutual interferences between each pair of statements are compared. Then a treelike path of design is constructed in which each design decision considers the conflicting requirements of only two subdesigns, the more important conflicts being resolved as early as possible. The final result is a solution that reflects the whole branching chain of suboptimizations and compromises. Multiplicity is explicitly dealt with.

In practice, the method breaks down because of the time required to make all the separate statements and to consider their stepwise resolution. Moreover, it does not easily deal with system-wide considerations or allow for reconsidering the problem in a new light. Yet the requirements are only simple thresholds, which in themselves assume types of solutions. Nevertheless, the technique is instructive as a first attempt to rationalize the mysterious process of design. It reveals how the disaggregated method depends on one system for division and another for recombination. Recombination may be very hazardous, however, without rules for the design of the whole. An airplane made of correct parts might not fly. The technique makes it clear why optimizing, which is impossible for more than one variable even in theory, is in practice never used. Designs are accepted whenever they satisfy acceptable levels of various criteria, although designers may set rather high levels of acceptance in the early stage of a design and may raise or lower the levels as the design process reveals more or less room for maneuver. The method also makes evident how many criteria are actually involved in design and how badly they are stated — most of them commonly being unconsciously assumed, stated vaguely, or accepted as fixed "standards" incapable of adjustment.

*Means orientation*

*Focus on means*: Rather than concentrating on objectives or on problems, design may proceed from the opposite end. In such a case it will begin by assembling or imagining possible means to see what they are good for. Designers play with different forms — lines, circles, and checkerboards — to see how they fit a site. They manipulate these forms, watching them grow and change, alert for the appearance of something useful. Similarly, they might imagine what a new kind of machinery, a special structural technique, or a new law or an administrative program would accomplish. These are means in search of ends. The process may seem to epitomize all the worst in our society, the proliferation of senseless technique. But since design is a linking of ends and means, it is just as useful to begin one way as another, as long as the connection of the two is finally effectively made.

An open-minded investigation of the possible use of things is a good way to innovate. One may be led far from the original problem, however. The technique is best suited to long-term, free search and invention or to such problems as the best use of a given piece of land. Even in the normal case the method is valuable as a preliminary warm-up or for producing "well-spaced" alternatives for consideration.

A more formal and systematic application, the so-called "morphological" approach, looks for optimum solutions by outlining all the possible changes of major form variables, listing all the combinations thereof, discarding the impossibilities, and then selecting the best of the remainder. As a technique for the open-ended, multivariable process of site planning, the morphological method is an infinite waste of time because the possibilities are so vast. But it might be of use in more limited cases.

As another variant, the consequences of possible immediate actions may be tried out in some kind of simulation, since site planning is a staged process. The future consequences of first moves is projected forward not only to evaluate those moves but also to discover new future patterns so that one can consider what they might be good for. This can be done intuitively or preferably in some systematic model that abstractly simulates the development of a place. "If I put a road here, what happens in ten years, and how do I like it?" All such methods are risky since they may produce very small changes or suggest answers to someone else's problem. But they are paths to invention and, if successful, have their means of implementation built in.

*Improving subconscious suggestion*: There are groups of methods, both new and traditional, which aim at freeing the flow of subconscious suggestion. They may be used as complete methods themselves or as supporting techniques. Form possibilities may be suggested by natural forms or by chance happenings in the human environment. A very fertile source is the surprising associations that well up from the memory store of the designer, the "flashes" that have invested the design process with such mysterious splendor. Actually, these flashes are experienced by everyone, but training can increase their frequency and their novelty. We are taught early to suppress "inappropriate" or "irrational" ideas, and creative training is concerned largely with undoing this previous education and finding ways to outwit our built-in censor.

One cluster of techniques relies on the shift of context to confuse the censor and suggest new connections. Thus the designer imagines the worst possible setting, which may be devilishly easy for him to do, and from this he can suggest new actions in reverse. A jump in time or size scale can be used, designing the site in the palm of the hand or as if actions were to take centuries. The external context can be jarred, by inquiring how the site might be designed under socialism or at the equator or upside-down. Solutions from other contexts, particularly the rich diversity of forms in nature, can be searched for illuminating analogies. The designer can project himself into the form, pretending that he is a playground and wondering how he might help the children to play on him. A method of graphic analogy has been developed by Robert Schwartz, in which a group confronts a large collection of random but interesting visual images, and participants "unthinkingly" point out the pictures that seem to them to have some connection with the problem. When they go on to describe that connection, they bring to light unsuspected new associations.

These are children's games. Designers must sometimes be childish. Once the mental censor is prevented from interfering, we tap new possibilities. Most suggestions are indeed unworkable, but there is abundant raw material for choice. Experienced designers have just that ability for childlike observation and suggestion, free of obvious or proper association.

*Brainstorming and competitions*    Groups of people may be used to increase the flow by the way in which members stimulate one another to disregard conventions. This is "brainstorming," which relies on a set of group rules to discourage criticism and self-censorship. Groups are also used in a more public way in design competitions, where the ideas of many participants are harvested and innovation is specifically encouraged. Design teams will do the same, more informally, by asking their members to produce their own initial suggestions for solution, as a way of beginning team design.

All of these methods are useful for encouraging innovation and are particularly useful in the early stages. They can be only temporary since a design must also be carefully evaluated in the light of criteria and resources and must be developed in detail. Moreover, there is a danger that such techniques will encourage innovation for its own sake, which is as irrational as an unthinking attachment to custom. A good designer will know how to swing gracefully between invention and criticism.

*Design probes*    *Probing*: Design is a learning process that gradually uncovers limits, possibilities, and criteria. One technique of design attempts to do this explicitly, rapidly creating some first solution, to begin the learning as soon as possible. This may be done before much information is available and even before the initial objectives and issues are clearly formulated. By proposing an action, the designer is face to face with what information is needed and with what the issues are. The design is made rapidly but still worked out in some detail to probe the various levels of the issues. Such a design is made to be thrown away; the designer must not become attached to it. The probing design is often a variant of some likely stereotype. It may also be given certain outrageous features in some area that is guessed to be sensitive: for example, densities will be doubled if it is judged that the load on facilities might become crucial, or resident populations are mixed haphazardly if issues of group conflict are suspected. The solution is meant to be revealing rather than reasonable. The evaluation of the probe uncovers new criteria ("Why do we dislike this?"), as well as data needs ("How would we know if this works?"). Like most of the context reversals described earlier, this is a useful entering wedge rather than a complete technique.

Probing may also be carried out in reality. Initial actions will be temporary experiments, planned to explore the problem: novel house types, a new bicycle path, a small gathering place built to see what happens there. As in any experiment, actions must be preceded by a prediction of what the response will be and include some means for observing the results. Since they are trials affecting real users, they will be more conservative than design probes. The risk of failure will be more serious; yet failure is the way to learn. Both user and developer must be protected against the risk — by prior explanation, by free choice, by making the experiment relatively independent of other actions. Often enough, actions that must be taken early in any case, such as the location of a bridge or of a construction camp, may also be designed so that monitoring their use will clarify other aspects of the problem.

*Experiments*

All the preceding techniques involve ways of generating possible solutions, and not the total strategy of a design. There are also choices between strategies. Those most common in site planning are the so-called "rational" ones, where the problem is thought to be explicit, predictable, and concerned with a stable product that will appear after a relatively brief period of planning and construction. The supremely rational method would generate an optimum solution, given the specific situation and precise, weighted criteria. I have argued that this is impossible. Generating and developing several alternatives and then using criteria to choose among them are more often advocated. The traditional sequence is to gather the necessary data, clarify the issues and objectives, generate and develop a number of so-

Design
Strategies

*Generating a
limited set of
alternatives*

lutions by any of the foregoing techniques, evaluate them, choose one, fill out its technical detail, and build it. Because of our limited ability to generate and choose, only three or four alternatives are customarily made up, although use of the computer may increase this number. An attempt is made to produce a set of reasonable and desirable possibilities, which are "well spaced" along the major variable dimensions.

The system is open to abuse. Designers will often try to manipulate their clients by giving them an illusory choice between one favored design and two or three unworkable dummy solutions. Even if the system is used honestly, it is often difficult to choose a solution without seeing all its detailed implications, while it is too time-consuming to develop all the alternatives in such detail.

*Generating sequential alternatives*

According to a different strategy, we develop one reasonable possibility at a time, beginning with the most likely one. Each possibility is developed far enough so that it can safely be accepted or rejected; if rejected, the process recycles to seek a new solution, carrying with it the lessons previously learned. The single alternative may be drawn up by any of the techniques we have cited earlier. The choice is informed by its detailed consequences and becomes a simple yes or no. The process is economical if a good first try has been made and very wasteful if not.

*Typical compromises*

Actual design practice tends to compromise these two approaches: first a broad search is made to expose "well-spaced" basic alternatives, of which one is tentatively chosen for full development and evaluation, with the option of falling back on another solution in case of failure. Many of the real choices are made not simply in considering the general alternatives but continuously in the course of design as modifications occur and are considered. The client may play a role in this string of choices but more often is excluded, having only the power to say no at the end of the process. For this reason the first system of multiple alternatives, producing an array of possibilities for client consideration at some formal stage, may be preferable. But the alternatives must be honest ones and sufficiently developed to allow a real choice. This system is expensive in time and effort, and not responsive to the actual fluidity of decision and events. Fateful choices may be made on superficial grounds. It may be a formal necessity, however, or be used to give the client a "stake" in the outcome. It can be worth the cost when it is necessary to make decisions about large systems whose features are not expected to change rapidly.

It can be argued that this "rational" strategy should be applied only to questions of general site pattern so that necessary long-term decisions can be made (such as for a main sewer, a large park, or a general density) and so that a framework is available to coordinate small-scale decisions. Within this fixed framework of general activity and density pattern or of major infrastructure or of landscape, local site plans are treated as an incremental sequence, spread out over time. Plans are made for each part as needed, according to the limits and demands of the time. Each new decision must take account of the framework and of accumulated past decisions. Plans are flexible, diverse, and attuned to actual circumstances.

*Incremental strategies*

More radically, even the framework may be dispensed with, and no decision is made until it must be. The total site plan is an accumulation of small choices, which are responsive to immediate real conditions. Thus the client can more easily join in them. This method will work particularly well if there is a dominant existing situation (a powerful landscape or a built region being rehabilitated), which will automatically furnish a context for the small decisions. It also works well where the client is the designer, acting in his own domain for his own inarticulate purposes. So a fine garden may grow, or a small traditional community may arise. The danger lies in being boxed in by previous decisions, which may happen if circumstances change rapidly or if early moves are likely to have long-range or large-scale effects.

Real situations are mixtures between local and extensive decisions, between cataclysmic periods of construction and streams of continuous modification. The critical judgment is to distinguish one situation from the other and to modify design strategy accordingly. The strategy required is usually a recycling one, which begins with probes and with broad searches of possibilities. It distinguishes long-term and short-term decisions, making the former where it must and reserving the latter where it can. It also uses the process of design and necessary initial actions as experiments by which to learn about the problem. Information and criteria are periodically revised, and new possibilities are developed as the situation changes. This approach does not imply that decisions are endlessly deferred. The cycling process results in detailed recommendations on aspects of development as they are required. But it does mean that design and evaluation are continuous, and not sporadic, events.

*Recycling*

Very little site planning is done as a recycling process.

Our habits of construction, of investment management, and of design itself are all shaped by the attitude of "build and pass on." Only the reality of site use points in the direction of recycling.

Meanwhile, until we adjust to this reality, a conscious choice of design strategy must be made, and mix of design generation methods must also be chosen. Strategy and methods will depend on the time available, the talents of the team, the limits in the external situation, the criteria to be achieved, and the resources to be used. No single method should be followed, any more than a single form can be applied on every occasion. But an explicit plan for the design process should be made from the beginning.

**New Directions for Design**

Substantial research is under way on the process of design, some of it originally stimulated by Alexander's monograph. Little of this has yet proved applicable to site design, although it has been used in more determinate problems such as the design of structural members and the allotment of standard offices within a given building envelope. Attempts have focused on systematic decomposition, following Alexander's original suggestion, or on the generation of random changes with a view toward incremental improvement, or on inclusive search through all logical combinations as in "morphological" design, or on optimization under restraint as in linear programming. None of these, however, has become an established site-planning method.

*See reference on page 277*

The old technique of analyzing a locality by overlaying many maps, each of which shows the areas that are undesirable because of some single factor, has been systematized in a useful way. But the current new look at design will surely improve what has up to now been a hidden, intuitive process. Decision theory has much to say about the rational evaluation of complicated alternatives. Some of its techniques, such as looking at decision as a competitive game or quantifying complex results by a single measure that takes account of diverse values and diverse clients, do not help us very much. But it does advise us about how these alternatives should be presented for explicit, if ultimately intuitive, decision.

**The generation and testing of prototypes**

One new effort that should prove useful is the collection of prototype environmental forms, with lucid descriptions of their proper context and purpose. Developing prototypes might indeed become the task of special teams, supported by research funds. Designing and testing would run together. Once a probable solution to some problem or potentiality, complete with hypotheses as to results, had been generated by normal design techniques, it would be tried out in reality. Some of the original designers might themselves be subjects of the experiment. As performance information accumulated, the real form and its attendant hypotheses would be modified until a satisfactory state was reached or there was a clear failure without an apparent escape. This is more like design method objectified than it is like classic research. Proofs of causation would be shaky, but this could be a fertile way of disclosing new alternatives and their results.

The computer is beginning to show its power in the design process. It is already used for storing design information — on program, site, client, or financing — and for displaying those data on call, either verbally or graphically. Computer maps of spatially located characteristics are now a useful adjunct in large-scale site planning. The computer can also be used for performing some routine functions: calculating strength or earthwork or cost or revenue; estimating traffic flow; quantifying the space, activity, composition, users, or parking demands of a plan; composing accurate sections, plans, and perspectives from a sketch; or even outlining movies of the visual experience of an approach. All these possibilities, for which programs now exist, liberate creative design by eliminating the need to make the routine studies that are constantly required in the development of a plan.

Information storage and the diverse routines for evaluating or developing a plan may someday be brought together in a general capability that could be used rapidly and flexibly. In that case, a site design might be generated by a copartnership of machine and designer in communication with each other. The man would generate criteria and solutions and supply information. The machine would respond with precise layouts and programs and display the detailed consequences of any solution suggested (its cost, its demand, its quantities, its capacity, its timing, its appearance), or perform routine evaluations (warning of criteria that have been disregarded or computing the relative advantage of various solutions). The interchange could be continuous throughout the period of design, as possible solutions grow and change. Such a partnership not only would permit more effective design but should allow a creative man to explore many more possibilities than he now has time for. General programs of this kind are now being developed. But they

*Computer-aided design*

have some distance to go before they will be sufficiently comprehensive, flexible, and clear to be of general use.

All of these techniques use the computer to support and extend the traditional design operation. However, the new resource might actually cause design to be done differently. For example, computer design procedures have been developed for rather determinate problems. The performance of one aspect of a solution is optimized, subject to constraints imposed on all the other variables: costs not to be exceeded, minimum design standards that are mandatory, a total capacity to be met, and a type of solution to be used with all its appropriate elements and features. Given these restraints, the computer is asked to indicate, for example, a highway layout of minimum length, or minimum capital cost, or having a minimum impact on existing housing. The problem must be straightforward, the criteria and solution type well defined, and one criterion must be of compelling interest, relative to the others. The method is therefore only marginally useful in site design.

Other new techniques may develop in time. For one thing, the computer may allow us to design, display, and evaluate streams of events rather than a restricted set of frozen "stages." Then we can propose solutions that take account of the process of construction, the daily cycle of activity, and the gradual secular development. All these aspects largely escape us today. That they do so is not for lack of computing ability but for lack of understanding. Working on new computer techniques may help us to gain that understanding.

*Design languages*  Developing adequate design languages is a related technical task. Our inherited languages are the architectural ones of model, plan, section, elevation, and perspective, which show the static physical form, to which we add verbal schedules of specifications and a quantitative program. These modes neglect behavioral patterns as well as time. They vacillate between vagueness and extreme specificity, and it is often difficult to decide whether a solution expressed in their terms meets the quality desired. Nonprofessionals are usually quite at a loss to understand them. The three-dimensional model is easier to read, but it is also timeless and empty of people. Its miniature scale is dangerously seductive, and its construction time-consuming. It is more often used for "selling" than for design.

Languages must be developed that, on the one hand, are compelling simulations of the actual experience of a place, or, on the other hand, compress the essence of a site, including its behavior and its growth over time, into a simple symbolic diagram rapidly made and easily modified. These requirements point in two different directions: one toward computer or motion picture simulations, or games that bring all kinds of observers close to the real experience of a place, and the other one toward simple graphic or three-dimensional diagrams of behavior, form, and growth, designed for professional manipulation. If these languages are to be useful, it should be possible actually to design with them, so that they are not reserved merely for catchy presentations. They must convey accurate information about consequences, as many of our slick drawings, glittering models, and engaging "word pictures" do not. Such design languages are only beginning to appear.

Indeed, we find that a large component of effective site design consists of the continuous communication of solutions, criteria, site data, and other information between designers, clients, consultants, users, and those who will carry out the plan. The timing, content, and accuracy of that communication are critical. The early preparation of behavioral programs, described in Chapter 3, is a key element in this interchange. Programs can interrelate behavior, form, purpose, quantity, and cost and are comprehensible to most of the interested parties.

Good communication is essential to relate predictive models to designs, although this relation is awkward and punishing today. Both model and design must use the same data, be expressed in the same language, respond to the same criteria. Only then can they relate to each other so that the tentative findings of a location or a traffic model become early guides to the design, and the possibilities of design as quickly become presuppositions of the model. Most commonly, designs and the predictive models run down separate tracks, colliding at some ultimate switching point.

Two normative assertions can be made about design method: first, that it should become a cyclical process, allowing successive returns to the original problem, which is the interrelated concept of situation, purpose, and solution type; second, that the design should be penetrable by nondesigners. Clients and other actors, with their own information and values, must be able to watch the process and to intervene in it. Program statements and diagrams are modes that make participation in design possible for nonprofessionals. Computer graphics may be another. Interactive com-

*Continuous communication in the design process*

*See pages 28–31*

*Designs and predictive models*

*Client communication*

puter displays could allow various people to study and question alternative solutions. They could ask, for example, how much a certain change would cost or how many steps must be climbed between supermarket and apartment door. They might even see what would have to be done to improve some feature they criticize.

Manipulable three-dimensional physical models are another, somewhat more proved device. They must be simply made so that they can be taken apart without dismay. Models of this kind can be carried directly to the site and to its users. Rearranging the elements of the model can be a focus for a lively interchange of information and solutions. Successive states can be illustrated by successive changes in the model, and a series of photographs can be taken to record ideas or sequences of site form. They would be even more useful if we could symbolize types of behavior, as well as physical objects. Perhaps this representation could be managed with scale figures or by three-dimensional symbols. The study model is a far more important device than the expensive presentation showpiece.

*Chapter* 13

# *Technique:*
# Costs

It is dangerous to give cost data, since they will be out of date before they are published and even at best are applicable to only one area. Reliable cost estimates require detailed calculations, based on familiarity with current costs in a given place and the use of a given level of technology. On the other hand, two kinds of knowledge about costs can be useful to a site planner: a sense of what the critical elements are and the rough figures that help him to make preliminary estimates or to judge between alternatives.

Variations in site construction costs are caused by fluctuations in the costs of labor and materials, in the skill of construction management, and changes in technology. But variations are also caused by the nature of the site and the type and skill of the design. Unfavorable site conditions may increase total development costs by over 100 percent. Variations in design may shave unit costs by as much as 20 percent or inflate them by as much as 30 percent. These differences may depend on skill of the layout but even more on the intensity and level of finish of the site development. Extensive paving or storm drainage, fine materials, and the use of parking structures are typical cost boosters.

To illustrate these effects, assume that one was designing a housing area and had no other thought in mind than to make it as cheap as possible, within the limits of tolerance. How would it be laid out? First, it would be put on a

*Cost variations*

*Reducing first
cost*

site that was neither steep nor dead level, and one that was free of peat, new fill, or rock close to the surface. It would have a compact shape, with adequate utilities at its borders.

Buildings would be grouped compactly, using the highest density allowable for the particular building type. Structures and streets would be regularly arranged, so that there were no fragmentary open or waste areas. Common facilities and public open space would be omitted or kept to the allowable minimum. All open spaces, particularly the publicly maintained ones, would be as concentrated and as regularly shaped as possible. There would be no landscaping other than grass, no hard surfacing except on the roads, and no fences or retaining walls.

The streets would use a regular pattern with a minimum number of intersections; that is, blocks would be rectangular and very large. Buildings and streets would be arranged to minimize the street length per dwelling unit, by occupying all frontages solidly and by using such devices as double and triple building lines or rows end-on to the street. The roads would follow the topography closely, having long-radius curves and gentle (but not flat) gradients. The design would allow the separation of roads by function into major, feeder, and minor streets, and the pavements would then be made as narrow and light as possible. They would be gravel, or stabilized earth, if standards would allow it. Parking space would be reduced and would be provided in double-loaded, perpendicular, off-street bays. Garages or parking structures would not be used. There would be no street curbs, no sidewalks.

Utility lines would have a minimum length per dwelling unit, and there would be no storm sewer system and no street lighting. The sanitary sewer system would also be omitted if densities allowed the installation of septic tanks. Electricity and telephone lines would be carried on poles overhead or strung from building to building. Underground utilities would lie at minimum depth. No roof drains would be attached to the sewers, and all utilities would be sized exactly to present loads. Electricity and water would be distributed in a branching rather than in a loop pattern. There would be a minimum number of manholes, cleanouts, valves, hydrants, poles, transformers, and other such fixtures. Cleanouts would be used in place of manholes wherever possible.

Dwelling units themselves would have a minimum floor area. They would occupy narrow, deep, two-story row houses, or compact three- and four-story walk-ups. There would be a minimum number of building types, arranged in a regular pattern. Buildings would be sited close to existing ground level and would not be placed on fill. They would have no breaks, offsets, or projections in plan or section. They would have low ceiling heights and be surfaced in inexpensive materials. They would be set close to each other and to the street, in long, attached structures with minimum setbacks and end spacings. (In general, each extra foot that a house is set back from the street costs almost twice as much as each foot added to the depth of rear yard or block interior, and each extra foot of street frontage costs almost five times as much as that same extra foot of rear yard).

Costs are also reduced if the layout permits an efficient site organization of the construction process. This is particularly true at high densities where work space is limited, in staged or renewal work, where normal site functions must go on in the midst of construction, where heavy machinery will be used with its special demands, or where systems building is being employed. In all these cases the process of construction must be simulated when evaluating the plan — to see that phasing can proceed smoothly, that temporary access will work, that there is space to stockpile material and to fabricate parts that cranes and other machines can move efficiently.

Obviously, this is not the best way to design a residential area, but this caricature exposes most of the design factors affecting the first cost. It is the first cost that is most visible when a design is reviewed, but maintenance costs over the life of the project will often be more significant, even when properly discounted. Many of the features just recommended — particularly those that call for inexpensive materials, light pavements, and conservatively sized utilities — are likely to inflate future running costs.

*Reducing maintenance cost*

In general, maintenance costs are also minimized by compact, regular forms, by the concentration of public open space, and by a simplicity, even a barrenness, of landscaping. But durable material is now called for: heavy road pavements, curbs, paved walks, a more expensive surfacing of the houses. While compact densities are still desirable, to keep down the lengths of road and utilities to be repaired, there should nevertheless be ample room for growth and change in the form of wide street rights-of-way, oversized utilities, and space about the dwellings, particularly in deep rear yards. The new ecological system should be a self-maintaining one, as far as possible, which requires densities below the carrying capacity of the land, "rough" natural landscaping, gentle slopes, and no disturbance to the existing drainage system. Most important of all, perhaps, the environment and its associated institutions should encourage caretaking by local users and discourage vandalism. To achieve this end, a large proportion of the open space should be private and attached to dwelling units, and even public open space should be divided into territories easily controlled by groups of dwellings. The dwellings themselves should be single-family houses, or at least so designed as to appear to be separate units, and should be capable of being repaired by simple means. The users should have a responsible part in creating the environment and in maintaining it.

Cost is an allocating device, and it is hardly surprising that there would be conflicts between construction and maintenance costs or between these costs and other, more intangible community costs. Some of the problems in allocating these costs in our present system have been mentioned in Chapter 3. In any case, these economizing rules reflect costs only in the United States, with present technology, subject to our present custom as to what is the tolerable minimum.

See pages 39- 43

**I**tem Costs
for Cost
Comparisons

Modified from "Unit Price Ranges for Budget Estimates: Site Development Items" for State University Construction Fund, State of New York, by Clarke and Rapuano Inc., Jan. 1968

To provide a basis for making rough first cost comparisons between alternative plans, the following generalized item costs are given. They do not include professional fees or the general contractor's profit and overhead. They do include the subcontractor's profit and overhead, however. They are based on average New York State prices in 1969. They will never be accurate for any particular job. They must at least be inflated by the average rise in construction prices since the base date, and they are not reliable in an area whose climate or building industry is significantly different from that of the northeastern United States. Even then, they are best used for comparisons because the relative cost of items is more stable than their absolute cost. Such comparative figures will be usable for a few years, until significant changes in building organization or technology upset the balance between items:

*Site preparation and earthwork*

| | |
|---|---:|
| Clearing and grubbing, per acre | $400.00 |
| Demolition of structures, per cubic foot | $0.05 |
| Removing pavement, per square foot | $0.25 |
| Removing tree and stump, per inch of diameter | $7.00 |

| | |
|---|---|
| Excavating and replacing earth, 500- to 1500-foot haul, per cubic yard | $0.80 |
| Excavating unsuitable earth and removing it from site, per cubic yard | $1.90 |
| Excavating rock, drilling and blasting, per cubic yard | $5.75 |
| Borrow fill in place, per cubic yard | $1.80 |
| Stripping, piling, and replacing topsoil, per cubic yard | $2.70 |
| Topsoil furnished and placed, per cubic yard | $5.75 |

*Roads, walks, and paving*

| | |
|---|---|
| Asphalt parking pavement, light duty, per square foot | $0.35 |
| Asphalt road, light duty, per square foot | $0.40 |
| Asphalt road, heavy duty, per square foot | $0.60 |
| Concrete road, light duty, per square foot | $0.75 |
| Concrete road, heavy duty, per square foot | $1.10 |
| Concrete curb and gutter, per linear foot | $4.00 |
| Gravel walk, per square foot | $0.20 |
| Asphalt walk, per square foot | $0.30 |
| Concrete walk, per square foot | $1.00 |
| Loose gravel or crushed stone surface, 4 inches deep, per square foot | $0.10 |
| Brick or asphalt block pavement, per square foot | $2.00 |
| Granite block pavement, per square foot | $3.00 |
| Snow-melting system, electric mats, per square foot | $3.00 |
| Concrete steps, 5 feet wide, with handrails, per square foot | $20.00 |

*Utilities*

| | |
|---|---|
| Concrete storm drains, in place, all fittings, 6-foot average depth, per linear foot of main: | |
| 12-inch diameter | $16.00 |
| 18-inch diameter | $19.50 |
| 30-inch diameter | $29.00 |
| Clay sanitary drains, in place, all fittings, 7-foot average depth, per linear foot of main: | |
| 8-inch diameter | $15.00 |
| 12-inch diameter | $18.00 |

| | |
|---|---:|
| Underdrain lines, in place, 6-inch diameter, 3-foot average depth, per linear foot | $6.00 |
| Six-inch water pipe, in place, all fittings, 5-foot average depth, per linear foot of main | $12.00 |
| Four-inch gas mains, in place, all fittings, 4½-foot average depth, per linear foot of main | $12.50 |
| For each foot of extra depth of a utility, add per linear foot | $2.00 |
| For trenching in rock, 5-foot average depth, add per linear foot | $22.00 |
| Overhead electric power, including poles and transformers, per linear foot of cable | $5.00 |
| Underground electric power in fiber duct, including above-ground transformers, per linear foot of cable | $15.00 |
| Lighting roads, per linear foot of road | $12.00 |
| Lighting walks, per linear foot of walk | $14.50 |
| Lighting park areas, per acre | $6000.00 |

*Landscaping and site structures*

| | |
|---|---:|
| Hydroseeding of secondary areas, per acre | $500.00 |
| Playfield, seeding and fine grading, using on-site topsoil, per square foot | $0.10 |
| New trees, in place, standard varieties, including two-year maintenance, per inch of caliper squared | $10.00 |
| Sodded swale, 3 feet wide, under 3 percent slope, per linear foot | $1.30 |
| Asphalt gutter, 4 feet wide, per linear foot | $3.50 |
| Concrete gutter, 3 feet wide, per linear foot | $5.00 |
| Concrete culvert, per linear foot times clear span in feet | $18.00 |
| Concrete retaining wall, per square foot of wall face | $14.00 |
| Freestanding brick screen wall, per square foot of wall face | $7.50 |
| Chain-link fence, 6 feet high, per linear foot | $6.00 |
| All-weather tennis court, each | $9500.00 |
| All-weather basketball court, each | $11,500.00 |

| | |
|---|---|
| Outdoor swimming pool, including perimeter walks and equipment but no building, per square foot of pool | $17.50 |
| Eight-foot wooden bench, concrete supports, each | $100.00 |

For extremely rough first guesses, not to be used for comparisons, costs may be summarized as *acreage costs* (land price, clearing and grubbing, general earthwork, landscaping), plus *linear costs* of the road system (fine grading, pavement and base, walks, curbs, sewer, water, electricity, lights, trees and culverts), plus *percentage costs* (profit, contingency, overhead, fees). From experience, general figures of this kind may be kept in mind for work of a certain type and quality of finish at a given time and place, or they may be calculated from quickly sketched type layouts for unit areas. These rules of thumb can then be rapidly applied to preliminary designs or proposals.

*Preliminary estimates*

*Chapter* **14**

# Housing

*References 47,*
*49, 55*

**S**ince it is the most common and fundamental kind of development, site planning for housing will be considered in some detail. As the discussion becomes more concrete, it will apply less and less generally. Much of the material in this chapter is a reflection of American practice.

Based on the pattern normal to our culture — the allocation of one family or one person to each dwelling unit, or independent living quarters including cooking and bathing *Common* facilities — there are a number of common residential *housing types* building types. Should the nuclear family lose its dominant position, this classification would no longer be relevant, but these common types today include:

1. *The single-family house*: each dwelling unit in its own isolated structure, movable or fixed in place.

2. *The two-family house*: two units attached side by side.

3. *The row house*: three or more units attached side by side in a row. Now often called a "town house" for promotional reasons.

4. *The flat or walk-up apartment*: single-story units stacked one above the other to a height of two, three, or, rarely, four or more stories, and accessible by common stairs. The apartments may be paired side by side, with stairs between, or be grouped in threes, fours, or even more, around a central stair. These pairs or clusters may stand alone or be

connected in lines. Alternatively, the apartments may open off a central corridor or an external gallery.

5. *Elevator apartments*: units stacked to greater heights and served by mechanical lifts, typically either of the slow-speed type, resulting in heights of about six to seven stories; or the high-speed type, allowing heights of twelve or more stories. Like walk-ups, elevator structures are most often either in a tower form ("point houses"), with three to six units clustered about a central elevator shaft, or in slab form, with units disposed along continuous central or external corridors. The slabs may either be in straight lines or be arranged in X, L, Y, or Z forms. The towers may be square in plan, or form X's or Y's. The X's or Y's can themselves be interlinked to form more complicated shapes.

These normal types have been listed in order of increasing density and the decreasing directness of access to street and ground. The first three allow for individual yards and independent access to each unit from the outside. Families with children between the ages of two and ten will usually prefer them.

The advantages of the conventional one- or two-story single-family house are well known: it has adequate light and air and room for gardening, play, parking, and other outdoor uses. It enjoys direct access to the street and to its own private ground; it can be shielded from noise and view. It can be built, maintained, remodeled, bought, and sold independently. It symbolizes the individual family. It can be constructed at reasonable cost, although it is not the least expensive type of housing. In many parts of the world it is popularly considered to be the ideal house. It imposes low densities, which may entail problems of city sprawl, poor transportation, sparse community services, and the loss of rural land. Only where land costs are low is it economical. If single-family houses must be used at net densities higher than 5 or 6 families per acre, then many of their advantages of space, privacy, individuality, and noise control begin to disappear. It is more difficult to arrange small houses to make a coherent visual scene than it is to group larger units. Nevertheless, the largest share of new housing in the United States continues to be of this type, since it corresponds most closely to popular desire and to the capabilities of the house-building industry.

*Single-family houses*

The prefabrication of houses as a solution to the housing problem was long heralded by experts. It arrived, not from

*Mobile homes*

the quarter toward which most people were straining their eyes but by way of the little house trailer, originally intended for summer camping or for migratory workmen. Free of the normal restrictions of codes and financing, the trailer industry has shifted from 8-by-40-foot units to 12-by-60-foot units and to "expandables" and "double-wides." Of the new housing units produced in this country, 20 percent are now these "mobile homes." The selling price of such units, complete with furniture and fittings, has been kept close to $10 per square foot, and they are almost the only new dwellings available at less than $15,000. They have substantial advantages for the small new family or the retiree: they are inexpensive, they are easy to buy (though not so easy to resell), the buyer knows exactly what he is getting, they are compact and easy to maintain, and they are fully equipped and furnished. They have the glamour of newness, and some of the social camaraderie of camping lingers in the trailer parks. Although few can now be drawn behind the family car, and the mobile home family moves no more frequently than the average family, the units are mobile by means of special carriers and can follow the displacements of a family if they are of moderate range. As the wheels come off and the sizes of the units rise to 800 or even 1500 square feet, the old trailer has become the leading moderately priced prefabricated single-family house, and we must face the problems of siting and regulating it.

*Two-family houses*    The two-family house, usually two stories high, is frequently used in parts of the eastern United States and in England. It is cheaper than the single house, can be built at higher densities, and provides opportunities either for individual ownership or for small-scale investment and management, one unit being owner-occupied and the other unit rented out. Meanwhile, it retains many of the advantages of light and air, access, privacy, individual yards, and even some sense of individuality. Esthetically, it is no easier to handle than the single unit and is likely to produce a similar dentelated effect at close densities. Another variant follows the pattern that has developed by individual effort in many older areas: detached houses that contain a small separate apartment. The apartment may be rented out for extra income or may house older parents or other members of the extended family, while preserving the independence of the nuclear family.

*Row houses*    The row house provides the most space at the lowest cost and is the cheapest to maintain and heat. It will provide greater privacy than the single or two-family house on small lots and makes more efficient use of the land that would otherwise be lost in the narrow side yards. Each unit generally occupies about 25 to 35 feet of frontage and may be one or more, but usually two, stories high. It may be planned at densities at which adequate public transportation and community facilities can be provided. It is much easier to achieve coherent visual spaces with these continuous units, and long rows of them, particularly if curving or bent to follow terrain or enclose an area, can be very dramatic.

All these benefits are achieved at some sacrifice of individuality, although independent access and the private yard are retained. Noise control may be a problem; thus the party walls must be acoustically insulated. Access to the rear yards from the street is troublesome and must be provided by through passages (perhaps incorporating carports) or by rear alleys or short footways coming from the street or service yards. For this reason, it is now customary to put the kitchen and service entrance on the street side of the unit, combined with the principal entrance. A neat service enclosure must then be incorporated with the front facade or waste storage allowed for within the house. For economy, a row contains an even number of dwellings — usually four, six, or eight together. Given its advantages, it is fortunate that the row house is beginning to shake off its undeservedly poor reputation.

The walk-up apartment was at one time the cheapest kind of housing available. It would still be so today if the fire laws had not banned nonfireproof construction in apartment buildings and if walk-up dwellings above the third floor were not now considered undesirable. Even the three-story walk-up is not so often built today except where there are pressures for economy or high density or where a public agency believes that subsidized units should be less than desirable so that poor families will not loiter there. But within the last decade the two-story walk-up has been built more frequently than ever, since it provides the convenience and freedom of apartment living at low densities and an intimate visual scale. It is appearing throughout the suburban regions and the inner ring of metropolitan areas, catering to the needs of small families, single people, and transients. Thirty-five percent of all new housing is now in apartment dwellings. Some units may still have private yards if desired. Moreover, parking and access are still manageable. Units can be grouped about the stairs so that each one has

*Walk-up apartments*

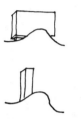

good light and cross ventilation. By increasing the ground coverage, relatively high densities and a special intimate and intense "urban" character can be achieved.

But the elevator apartment, rather than the crowded four-story walk-up, is now the normal response to the pressure for high densities. The tower block provides better light and air and is a visually handsomer unit; the slab often has unpleasant proportions and may block the view, cast deep shadows, or adjust clumsily to terrain. The central corridor prevents cross ventilation in the units of a slab building, while a system of exterior gallery access raises problems of privacy, danger to children, and exposure to weather. The elevator apartment is the most costly type of housing to build, and the tower form is more costly than the slab.

The tall apartment has advantages besides its usefulness at high densities. Tenants are not responsible for maintaining buildings or grounds, they acquire some anonymity and social freedom; and they may be lifted up high enough to enjoy fine views. The buildings themselves provide dramatic accents at the urban scale: they can compose well within large spaces and relate to strong natural landscapes. Moreover, it is possible to supply special services at these densities: catering, nurseries, convenience stores in the building, social rooms, and special recreation facilities.

FIGURE 45  *Apartment towers accent a rocky site at Danviksklippan in Stockholm, Sweden.*

Thus for some families without small children the tall apartment may be a preferred living style and need not be confined to central areas. Its problems are the access to ground, as well as the ground-level congestion of circulation, parking, unit storage, and recreation. It is usually preferable to furnish some outdoor sitting space close to the unit by means of private balconies. Play space can be provided on the roof, or even at intermediate levels, at a cost. Stores and special facilities may be put on upper floors, but it is usual to have these on the ground so that they can serve more than one building. Ground-floor dwelling units are at a disadvantage because of the adjacent activity, and it will be necessary to screen them or eliminate ground-level units entirely. It is fashionable to lift the entire building off the ground on stilts, but this procedure is expensive and may cause unpleasant winds underneath. Furthermore, it neglects many common functions that are logically located at ground level. With slab apartments, special care must be taken to prevent uncomfortable winds, shadows, or reflections of radiation or noise.

These prevalent building types by no means exhaust the possibilities. Other types remain to be developed, or to be tried out on a significant scale. One of the most important contributions that building designers can make is to refine the known types and to create new ones, since the bulk of residential building will follow such type patterns. Some of these new possibilities are:

*The courtyard house*: Single-family units can be packed side by side and back to back if their open space is within their walls rather than outside them. This derives from an old Mediterranean prototype. It allows the privacy, control, and directness of access of single-family houses to be provided at much higher densities.

*The combination of row housing with walk-up flats*: "Garden apartment" is now a euphemism for a two- or three-story walk-up, but the term originally applied to two-story row housing, of which some portion, particularly on the ends, was devoted to small flats, that is, to single-story units stacked one above another. It is also possible, especially on sloping terrain, to put a two-story row house over a one-story flat. Or two two-story rows may be placed one above the other, to give the effect of a three-story walk-up in a four-story building. These hybrids provide a variety of accommodation and allow higher densities while still providing individual yards and direct access to many or all units.

**New Housing Types**

*Elevator apartment variants:* Two-story units may be stacked vertically, each having access to a common balcony that occurs every second floor. This is more economical than the usual apartment type, allows cross ventilation without loss of privacy, and gives some feeling of individuality to the unit. Many other variations may be made upon the slab apartment, including the use of access balconies, skip-stop elevators with corridors every third floor and stairs internal to units, interlocking and through units, and so on. All these attempt to improve the privacy, economy, ventilation, or sense of individuality in the standard central-corridor slab. Apartments are now being built of prefabricated elements or even prefabricated units. Such techniques have been more fully developed in Europe and in the Soviet Union. A few experiments have been made with mobile units, plugged into multistory permanent frameworks.

*"Habitats":* This complex type is named for the famous residential demonstration at the Montreal Exposition, in which units were stacked vertically but the whole was so interconnected with bridging footways at all levels that each unit seemed to have direct access to an open public street. Private outdoor space was provided on balconies or on the roofs of units below. The total structure had an irregular, piled-up form. Some of the values of single-family units and the conveniences of apartments were combined with the qualities of living in a dense and lively village. The type is expensive, but it drew the applause of many visitors.

*Patterns of tenure:* Much of the living quality of a residence arises from the nature of its ownership. The previous discussion has assumed one of the two standard types of tenure in this country: individual ownership of the unit in fee or its rental from some other owner, public or private. But other patterns of tenure are possible, including housing cooperatives (in which tenants buy shares in the company that owns and maintains a group of units, and in return have the right to occupy a unit) and condominiums (in which the "insides" of units are owned by the resident, while the "outsides" and the grounds are owned by a cooperative or other association that maintains them for a fee). Such patterns of ownership affect not only the economic and social aspects of a plan but also its technical and physical nature. Under a cooperative arrangement, for example, all units need not have direct access to a public way, and various common spaces and facilities can be provided and maintained.

The ground in a residential area must provide for more

than the coverage of buildings. Typical uses include circulation (foot and vehicle), parking, play, sitting areas, gardening, laundry drying, outdoor work areas, disposal facilities, storage areas, utilities, landscape settings, and barriers to sight, sound, sun, or wind. These uses may be provided for individually, as in private yards, or communally, as in allotment gardens, public playgrounds, or group drying yards. Until recently, communal provision has been relatively neglected in this country in favor either of the individual lot or of services for larger areas installed by local government. But intimate community management and ownership are proving to be an attractive and efficient alternative.

A space of about 40 by 40 feet is likely to be the minimum if it is to be usable for sitting, playing, and raising a few flowers. A simple "outdoor room," used only for sitting, might be as small as 20 by 20 feet. In any case this space should be intimately related to the unit, with a suitable slope and a good orientation. On steep ground it may be necessary to build open decks or do massive grading. The yard size can be varied for different units, and clusters of allotment gardens allow for more extensive cultivation. In low apartment housing a private yard for the ground floor units may often be arranged. At all but the lowest densities at least some part of the yard should be given visual privacy by a fence or hedges. Fences and hedges should be provided from the start.

Tall buildings at high density do not miraculously free the uncovered ground space. The requirements for use at the ground go up with the increase in density, and at the upper range of density the "free" ground area is likely to be largely paved and devoted to circulation, parking, and intensively used play areas. Private balconies can to some extent substitute for the private yard, however.

The spacing between buildings has an important effect not only on the ground left over for outdoor use but also on the livability of the interior rooms. If structures are too close to each other, especially if they surround a space, noises will resonate within them. Every room should have adequate light and air: a substantial piece of sky should be visible through the windows from normal standing positions in the room to ensure good daylight and prevent claustrophobia. A minimum standard may be that from each window, in principal rooms, the major part of the forward 60-degree cone of vision should be unobstructed by anything that is more than

*The space between buildings*

*References 35, 53, 54*

*Private outdoor space*

*Daylight*

half as high above the sill as its distance from the window. This minimum is assured by spacing buildings at more than twice their height, but other, denser arrangements will also pass this test.

Even where this rule is observed, it is unpleasant to look directly into facing windows that are close enough to destroy visual or acoustic privacy. Therefore it is well to avoid any layout in which one eye-level window faces another more closely than 75 feet away. Units may have blank walls or high windows where they face on the private areas or facades of other units. Similarly, no principal window should be closer than 20 feet from any public way, unless that way is well below the sill.

There are proposals for experiments with windowless apartments, which seem repugnant but would have advantages of cost, upkeep, security, and density. If fire safety, health, and ventilation can be provided for, it may indeed be possible for some rooms to be windowless, but for visual and psychological relief at least some windows of a dwelling should command a long, free view. All the views from principal rooms should be studied in relation to the time of day in which they are used. It is preferable that the different rooms have a variety of views.

Handbooks on site design and official subdivision and building regulations frequently cite standards for building spacings, setbacks, and lot sizes. The standards attempt to ensure adequate light, privacy, fire safety, and "amenity," using mechanical rules that can be repeatedly applied. But the rules result in inflexible layouts and the waste of land. For example, in single-family areas, a minimum lot width at the street of 50 feet is usually given. But this is based on the average small-house design, with 10-foot side yards. It is indeed important to keep separate structures far enough apart that fire equipment may be brought between them. Yet if the unit is different, or if it is built to the lot line with a fireproof wall (as it can be, without loss of safety or amenity), 50 feet is too much. Elsewhere, regulations will require 75-foot, or larger, lots to accommodate the one-story ranch house with generous side yards. This puts up a good show along the street, where breadth of unused front lawn is proportional to apparent social status, but it also raises the price of the house and brings about a shallow back yard without any privacy. Minimum lot sizes, minimum front, side, and rear setbacks are obstacles to efficient and commodious design. Sometimes they are deliberate devices for zoning out low-cost housing. Official rules and guides should be in the form of performance standards, setting desired qualities such as light, privacy, outdoor space, noise transmission, fire safety, and access, along with allowable average densities and use mixtures applicable to entire development areas. If rules are explicitly tied to results, then site plans can be both efficient and diverse.

The orientation of buildings with respect to sun and wind is also important. It was once fashionable to align all structures in some "ideal" orientation. But under ordinary circumstances in the temperate zone, properly spaced single- and two-family structures can adjust to many orientations. So can row houses, point towers, and gallery access slabs, in which each dwelling has more than one open side. Interior plans in the latter types must often be varied to adapt to the different orientations, however, and some alignments may be better than others. When the buildings are tall or long, shading and wind effects on the remainder of the site are significant.

The orientation of the tall, central-corridor slab is the most difficult problem. Not only does it have a serious external influence on wind and sun shadow, but each of its dwelling units has only one orientation. In the higher latitudes an east-west axis must be avoided to prevent sunless dwellings and ground areas in winter. A north-south axis, while preferable, is not ideal, since it exposes some dwellings to the hot western sun of summer. In the tropics such an alignment may be extremely uncomfortable. Thus the local climate, with regard to this one awkward type, may indicate a preferable alignment. In the Boston area this might be a slab running north-northwest to south-southeast, a compromise between the demands for winter sunlight and summer breezes.

Vandalism and assault are common dangers in many housing areas. To deal with them effectively is to deal with their social causes. But where such dangers exist, the layout of exterior space can make a place more or less secure. The key techniques are surveillance and giving local residents a sense of control and responsibility over the locality. Thus one arranges doors, external pathways, and building corridors so that they are always visible from a number of windows and from the street. Electronic and optical devices can also be used to supplement the unaided eye. Paths are laid out so that the pedestrian sees his route open well ahead of him, without nearby hiding places. Grounds are well lighted and made easy for police to patrol in some rapid and systematic way. Territorial concern is defined so that spaces are either clearly part of the public street or as clearly attached to dwellings or groups of dwellings, and thus subject to residents' control if they choose to exercise it. Governance of the housing area is organized to put responsibility in the hands of local groups. Walls, locked doors, fences, and other barriers are useful only if they can be monitored. Their greatest value is in defining territory and making the potential trespasser visible. Trained police and changes in the organization of society are more effective ways of dealing with human aggression. But in troubled times the nature of external space is relevant to the security that can be achieved. Many of these security techniques conflict with privacy, on the one hand, and with a sense of openness and warmth in the landscape, on the other. But until there is social peace, a defensive stance is necessary in the major public areas, and those areas must be clearly defined.

*Storing the car*

Storing the car consumes space. Inevitably it is a troublesome feature in housing areas. In wintry climates most people prefer to use a garage to protect the car from rain and snow and to shield it from the lowest temperatures. A carport is only a substitute for this, and open parking, while workable, is third best. Placement of the garage has never been satisfactorily solved, except in low-density single-family areas. The traditional location at the rear of the lot entails a long driveway and reduces the size of the private

*Reference 51*

yard. A position near the street masks front entrances and destroys the street space while reducing pedestrian safety. Placement in or under the units themselves is likely to be expensive, since the dwelling must then be made fireproof. Location alongside the dwelling, on the same building line, is often the best technique if there is sufficient space between units. Garages can be paired in this case. Arranging the garages in large compounds makes them inconvenient to the houses. Sometimes it is possible to group two to six garages together, between or behind the units, or in small courts, so that they are both convenient and not visually disruptive. At higher densities garages are large multilevel structures, which are part of the total architectural composition. The cost of such structures makes it difficult to provide for more than a fraction of the total parking need in this way. If garaging is placed underneath the apartments, it will be even more expensive.

In warmer climates and in colder areas when economy

dictates, the car will be stored in the open. And even where garages are provided, it is necessary to allow for the parking of visitors. It is now customary in the United States to provide one and a half to two parking or garaging spaces per dwelling unit, and this ratio is rising. One car space per unit is considered a reasonable minimum in housing of moderately high density. In central-city housing of very high density, the parking ratio may drop to as low as one-half space per unit, although this is certain to result in congestion. Providing surface space for parking at high densities begins to eat up all available ground; yet garaging may be economically impossible. One compromise is to park one level of cars on a pavement that is a half story below grade and a second level on a light open deck above them.

At low densities surface parking is a simpler matter, being provided at the curb or in small one-or two-car parking stubs beside the unit. At moderate densities it may become necessary to group cars in small off-street bays, since the alternative is to allow solid ranks of head-in parking at the curb, which is dangerous for children and those crossing the street, disrupts traffic, and restricts the street view to an endless wall of cars. Solid curb parking can be ameliorated by occasional projections of the planting strip to break the line of cars and to provide a safe launching pad for crossing the street. Curb parking must also be kept away from intersections. Parking on the street is expensive since it devotes highly accessible and heavily paved space to a low-value use. Even where cars are grouped into off-street parking lots, it is preferable to keep these lots no larger than six to ten spaces, since larger lots will be remote from the units and visually depressing. This rule is abandoned only at higher densities.

It is also possible to improve the look of small or medium-sized parking lots or stubs by dropping them a few feet below pedestrian grade so that the normal line of sight passes over the cars. This also makes it easier to screen the lots with planting or low walls. Trees may be planted throughout large parking lots to provide shade and visual relief. But substantial open space must be allowed at the base of each tree, so that air and water can reach the roots.

Thus the automobile, so much a part of our way of life and so necessary in most suburban areas, constantly bedevils the conscientious site planner. Wherever one uses other modes of transport — walking, bicycling, bus travel — residential areas are more pleasant, economical, and com-

*Divorcing the car*

modious, as well as freer from pollution and danger. But the designer is mistaken if he thinks that most Americans are easily divorced from their car. It provides too many other satisfactions and meshes with too many other aspects of their lives. Divorce may be wise, but it will be brought about only by fundamental changes in the pattern of living and in the technology and ownership of the means of transport. For example, it would require living at compact densities again, plus a renewed and efficient public transit system, clustered services, and a loss of freedom in vacation travel. Alternatively, private city travel would have to be restricted to some new small, low-powered vehicle, while large cars were stored on the periphery and perhaps rented or communally owned. Or living at moderately low densities might be coupled with a diffuse microbus system, routed on call, plus special paths for bicycles, horses, and electric carts, while large private vehicles would be restricted to infrequent use by means of permits or charges. Each solution requires a coordinated set of rather large-scale actions, and to be successful it must satisfy all the many reasons for which the automobile is preferred today.

### Residential Modules

The arrangement of individual buildings may first be studied at the level of a "module," or small group of structures considered as a repeatable unit. Residential buildings are, in fact, often repeated in series, and, in any case, their fundamental interrelations can be analyzed in such groups. Since it is the pattern of buildings and circulation, rather than the lot or landscape pattern, that is primary to a site plan, modules of paths and building units are the most useful ones to know. Modules are only schematic: while worthy of study in the first stages of a site plan, they should not be applied by mechanical repetition. But a knowledge of the common modules or residential grouping is very useful.

### Street-front units

The street-front pattern is the most common module, in which the building units — houses, rows, or apartment towers — line both sides of the street. Access and orientation are easy, and there is little ambiguity in the plan. Although sometimes visually monotonous, the corridor space can be strong or richly varied by path alignment, building setback, and landscaping.

### End-on units

For reasons of economy, a second type has been developed in which rows of units are disposed end-on to the street. The street frontage per unit, a reliable index of site development cost, is thereby sharply reduced. Units are removed from the noise and danger of the street but also removed from

FIGURE 46  *In Persson's romantic Open Air City in Malmo, Sweden, row houses are located end-on to the street, and their front entrances alternate from one face to the other of the same row. The effect is charming, but parking is difficult.*

its convenience. Successive rows of units may face toward each other on common entrance pathways or may turn their backs on each other to enjoy some favorable orientation. Rows may run through from one street to the next to form a continuous path system at right angles to the street system.

A third and highly favored module is the court arrangement, in which groups of units face inward on a common open space. This is done primarily for social and visual reasons: to promote neighborly relations, to exclude outsiders, to provide a pleasant enclosed space. Vehicular circulation may be allowed to enter the court, perhaps as a narrow one-way loop, or may pass through it in some indirect fashion, as in the square, or may be excluded from it, as in the English "close." The court with its circulation may shrink to the width of a cul-de-sac. The internal space of the court or cul-de-sac may be open to the street, forming an inlet of the major street space, or the entrance may be narrowed or even formalized with a gateway so as to produce an independent space, secure and well identified. The land outside the courts may be committed to public open space, to private yards, or to service access. In all these types, land in the block interiors is relatively inexpensive, since it adds little to the street frontage costs. If raw land is cheap, then reasonably large parks, gardens, or allotments may be provided at relatively little additional cost.

Court systems are economical of expensive street frontage, except where loops are brought into the court, and are

*Courts*

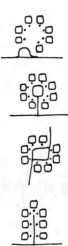

FIGURE 47 *Sunnyside was built in Queens, New York, in 1924–1928 by the City Housing Corporation on land already divided into narrow blocks. Modest row houses were put around quiet courts, and today this is still a favored residential area. Contrast the tenements put up on the same land by the speculative builders — the trees in the distance mark the location of Sunnyside.*

favorable (sometimes too favorable) to neighborly intercourse. They may, however, complicate the street system, lengthen the journey for service vehicles, and make units difficult for the stranger to locate. The courts tend to look best on fairly flat ground or when sloping uphill from the observer. Marked cross slopes destroy the visual unity of the space, and a court or cul-de-sac lying downhill from the approach gives the terminal buildings a peculiar sense of inferiority and instability, in addition to raising practical problems of surface drainage and the flow of utilities.

A fourth general module is the cluster, in which units are concentrated and surrounded by open space. The street may pass alongside or penetrate this cluster. The module produces a strong visual effect of mass, the opposite of the spatial focus of the court type. Access may be complicated, but a sense of group unity can be achieved without forcing social intercourse. There are significant savings on roads and utilities, and overall density can be maintained even while preserving substantial open space. A number of recent successful developments have used this principle to conserve a handsome piece of landscape. The most difficult problem is likely to be the interrelations between individual buildings, in terms of privacy and the use of adjacent land.

*Clusters*

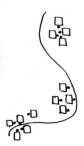

These modular layouts apply to all types of residential units, whether they are single-family houses, mobile homes, rows, or slab or tower apartments. Differences in scale between these types will of course markedly change the effect. Innovative modules are always possible.

There is an extensive literature on desirable standards for nonresidential facilities in residential areas. The usual warning must be made that these standards refer to the urban United States, to the present day, and to the completely average situation. In those cases they have some value as quick first checks.

For example, about two-thirds of an acre per 1000 inhabitants is cited as being required for neighborhood convenience shopping. This is exclusive of community and central stopping but includes such facilities as supermarkets, drugstores, laundries, beauty parlors, barbershops, shoe repair shops, and filling stations. This acreage provides for the stores, their access, and customer parking at a ratio of 2 square feet of parking for each square foot of selling space. It takes a market area of at least 5000 people to support a center of any strength, and a market of 10,000 is preferred. There is much to be said for scattered convenience stores

*Standards for Providing Shopping*

within the housing area itself. And what of the offices, restaurants, clinics, libraries, meeting rooms, motels, and other common facilities that the community needs? What if storekeepers take on other functions than selling or stores are cooperatively owned or goods are not distributed by retailers selling for profit?

*Recreation standards*

One and a quarter acres per 1000 people is a quoted standard for playgrounds serving the age group from six to twelve. These should be within half a mile of their users, or preferably a quarter of a mile, with a minimum size of 3 acres. The elementary schools are commonly combined with the playgrounds, and these schools demand approximately half an acre per 1000 pupils for the building site, the setting, access, and expansion room. The minimum size for a combined elementary school and playground is 5 acres. If the school is separate from the playground, then additional play space must be added to the school site itself. Where there are no private yards, additional play lots must be included in the plan, close to the dwellings, at a scale of about 50 square feet per child between two and six years of age.

These standards do not provide for parks, whose standards are more variable, or for schools of other types. They represent only the bare minimum, local, formal requirements for the education and organized outdoor recreation of children up to twelve years of age. They are not based on studies of where and how children actually play and learn but are only a summary of the kinds of provisions we are officially accustomed to make for those purposes. They are not relevant to other age groups. Is this why our playgrounds all look alike?

Schools and playgrounds, which look so good on a plan, may be nuisances for the immediately adjacent dwellings because of the noise and activity they generate. For this reason, and because of their large size, they do not fit easily into housing areas. It is advisable to locate tall apartments near them, to turn low dwellings at right angles to their boundaries, to screen them, or to place them next to nonresidential uses. A pleasant but expensive solution is to bound play areas with roads on which housing faces from across the street. Location next to shopping and other community facilities is of mutual benefit if the large play areas do not dilute the necessary concentration and accessibility of the center.

Recreation is a broad function, being both organized and unorganized, indoor and outdoor, daily and intermittent, local and distant. Sidewalks, for example, are a more important recreation facility than playgrounds and should be designed with that use in mind. Particularly important for the child is the chance for adventure and for play of his own invention in woods, swamps, back alleys, junkyards, and vacant lots. For the adult, the important recreation facilities may be special sports fields, commercial entertainment, access to natural scenery, city promenades, or the private garden. Many special recreational facilities may be needed: swimming pools, boat landings, parks, allotment gardens, golf courses, skating rinks, walking and riding trails, and picnic grounds. It is becoming more and more common for small housing developments to provide some of these facilities privately and locally on a cooperative basis. Properly organized, they are very successful. As we grow more dubious about recreational space standards, we turn to the actual diversity of recreational place and activity and think of providing for this complex diversity according to the particular people we house.

Many other types of community facilities are needed in relation to residential areas: clinics, fire and police stations, and churches. Most of these facilities do not make large demands on gross land area at the scale we are considering, except perhaps for churches and community centers, which generate substantial traffic and parking and should be sited at accessible points where they will not disturb residential uses. With their heavy off-peak parking requirements, they are often successfully related to commercial parking lots. Fire stations, on the other hand, must be near several major roads, close to the center of the area served, yet not at any point that is likely to be jammed with traffic, such as on a major intersection or near a large parking lot.

*Other community facilities*

Facilities and the institutions that will use and maintain them should be planned together. Neighborhood associations that manage a local park and swimming pool are already commonplace. In many trailer parks and apartment developments, the local management provides and maintains pools, playgrounds, laundries, meeting rooms, and restaurants. But institutions need not be confined to the support of conventional activities. Providing shopping or recreation is an opportunity for creating new ways of distributing goods or of integrating work and play. If teen-age youths form their own associations for recreation and learning and have the territory and resources to support it, we shall see new kinds of facilities. A school can use local residents as teachers and can be completely dispersed in the residential living space.

Conventional forms and conventional institutions are mutual brakes upon each other. Planning a new environment is an opportunity to plan the two together in a way that supports innovation in each.

*Use segregation*

Customarily, we separate residential and nonresidential activities by exclusive zoning, by planning specialized buildings, and by the spacing rules contained in subdivision regulations. Even domestic animals may be excluded. This kind of regulation enhances the conceptual order of a place, increases the security of property owners, and prevents certain conflicts of noise or congestion. Inflexibility, poor access, isolation, and a periodic emptiness in the environment are the corresponding prices to be paid. Human activities normally overlap and succeed one another in space, with some friction, yet in doing so they make efficient use of that space to their mutual enrichment. We could plan more lively and flexible places, offering a greater range of services close at hand, if nonresidential uses were allowed to occur in housing areas, subject only to density rules and to performance standards for such things as noise, traffic flow, or air pollution. Where the timing of activity can be controlled, we can attain much greater space efficiencies. The problem is to create the performance standards that are effective and are also easy and practical to administer. It is when continuous monitoring is required that there is the greatest difficulty. Thus it is possible to allow institutional, commercial, and industrial uses in housing areas if they are restricted in their size and density of structure and in numbers of patrons and employees and also subject to strict limits on parking, truck access, and sources of noise, light, and fumes. A large church or school can be a far greater nuisance than a small factory.

*Variations in the definition of density*

The housing type, its occupancy, its arrangement on the ground, and the facilities provided with it all result in a certain density of population. Density is associated with significant effects, and it is a useful concept in project planning. Unfortunately, the definitions of the various units of measurement are ambiguous and subject to manipulation. As a general guide to the site planner, the densities shown in Table 6 are considered reasonable for the normal building types listed.

*References 46, 52, 54*

Net density refers only to the land that is in the house site, exclusive of the street. "Neighborhood" density is the average for an extensive area, which contains all streets and local facilities as well as housing. These are not magic figures but represent reasonable densities in normal practice, according to accepted standards for circulation, open space, and community facilities. The composite net density

of a mixed development is easily computed by adding the separate "pure" densities after they have been weighted by the percentage of the net area allotted to each such density.

TABLE 6. DENSITIES BY RESIDENTIAL TYPE

| Type of unit | Floor area ratio | Families per net res. acre | Families per neighborhood acre |
|---|---|---|---|
| Single-family | Up to 0.2 | Up to 8 | 5 |
| Two-family | 0.3 | 10–12 | 7 |
| Row | 0.5 | 16–20 | 12 |
| Combined flats and row | 0.75 | 25–30 | 16 |
| Three-story walk-up | 1.0 | 40–45 | 20 |
| Six-story elevator | 1.4 | 65–75 | 28 |
| Thirteen-story elevator | 1.8 | 85–95 | 31 |

Skilled designers can move densities upward a little; abandonment of standards, especially for parking or play space, can move them upward markedly. Any type can be built at lower densities than those given, although the justification for the type may be questioned when figures drop much lower, and it may be difficult to maintain community facilities and services at very low densities. Single-family houses are commonly built at significantly lower densities, going down to 1 or 2 families per net acre in some developments or lower in the outer suburbs. Although the floor area ratio and the families per acre are the common units of measure in this country, different units are used in other countries, such as population or habitable rooms per acre or hectare. These measures may be more sensitive ones in cases of wide variation in family size.

With our present technology it seems that in urbanized areas there is a broad range of density outside which we should not go. The limits might perhaps be set at 1 to 120 families per net acre. Anything of lower density produces expensive, scattered development. It may be pleasant in itself, but it leads to excessive city sprawl and a costly transport system. Furthermore, community facilities become less accessible.

Areas of a density higher than 120 families per acre can be built but only with a loss of open space that results in substandard living conditions. These limits may change, however, as transportation and utility techniques develop, as living habits shift, or as we become able to build needed open spaces into buildings at upper levels. Twenty-story apartment developments are now being built, for example, at floor area ratios of 2.3 and net densities of 150 families per acre. These provide adequate light and air but supply parking for only half the units and inadequate outdoor park and play space. In the American situation they may be tolerable only for special families in special central locations. As an example of what is technically possible, however, refugee housing has been built in Hong Kong at nearly 500 families per acre, and some slum areas exceed this by a good margin.

Even as it stands, 1 to 120 families per net acre is an extremely broad range, although it is significantly narrower when translated into neighborhood densities. It can perhaps be said that families with children between two and ten years old should be housed at densities below 20 families per acre so that each family may have direct access to the ground. On the other hand, some recently married or childless couples, the aged, the unmarried, or those who have no sympathy for the joys and sorrows of house repair may prefer apartment living at higher densities. New building types or ways of living may shift these preferred ranges.

*Density thresholds*  Each building type has its own appropriate density, and the choice of density (if it is not fixed by city-wide considerations) should therefore depend upon the building type or types that are most appropriate to the situation. Some very general thresholds, where the character of development is likely to shift, may be identified within the overall range. At a density of about 12 families to the acre problems of noise control and privacy develop. Below this density it is more difficult to provide common maintenance of grounds or group facilities such as clubrooms, nurseries, or laundries within very close range of the units. About 20 families to the acre seems to be near the point of maximum economy today, and above this density it becomes increasingly difficult to provide outdoor space, direct access from all units to the ground, easy surface parking, and external identification of units. At a density of about 45 families to the acre one is likely to lose most of the sense of visual intimacy or "human scale."

At 80 families to the acre, shortage of space for parking, for landscaping, and for recreation begins to develop. At the same time, certain "urban" characteristics have appeared which may be highly desirable, such as a wide variety of accessible activities and facilities. Above 100 families to the acre, the pressure for space becomes severe enough to affect the size of the dwelling units themselves and to make circulation congested. The upper ranges above 80 are suitable only for special family types living in central urban locations, who will accept limitations on their facilities for recreation and movement in return for that location. In sum, there is no one ideal, but the density variations have important implications.

Single- and two-family houses at moderate to high densities are difficult to arrange without an appearance of restless repetition. This arises from their small scale in proportion both to the size of a continuous housing area and to the scale of the car and its associated right-of-way. This is especially true of the modern one-story or one-and-a-half-story small house and is intensified where each building is isolated and yet close to the next one. Where houses can be clustered, or related across a footway or pedestrian space, the proportions can be much more pleasant, and the ground surface can be designed to unify the whole. In the ordinary case any reduction in street width and the depth of front yard helps in a similar way.

A number of devices can be used to give unity to small structures. Individual houses may be linked with screen walls, planting, garages, or porches. Garages may be paired or grouped in compounds to improve their proportions. House spacing and setback may be varied to create visual groups or to modulate the street space. Tall forest trees may take over the role of space enclosure, contrasting with the low roofs of the houses and providing a larger-scale structure. The individual houses may use similar roof slopes, wall materials, or proportions of window openings. Low-density houses suffer from particular discontinuities at the crossing of roads. In fact, spatial gaps appear just where strong enclosure is most desired. This annoyance can be avoided by the use of screen walls, special house groups, or corner units.

Tracts of standardized units, such as mobile homes, reveal the problem in its most acute form. The units are small and numerous, they sit lightly on the ground, and they are made of shiny, hard new materials. The unit size puts a premium on privacy and usable outdoor space, yet the long, narrow boxes look directly into one another, even when set on the customary diagonal. There is only a patch of concrete before the door. The siting and even the unit itself must be redesigned so each element can live with its neighbors. The mobile home is in uneasy transition from trailer to perma-

**Visual Qualities of Small Houses**

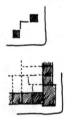

*Standardized units and mobile homes*

nent prefabricated house, which is never moved or moved only occasionally, when it is sold or when the owner changes his permanent residence. "Foundation planting" or sheets of fake masonry make a pretense of a solidly rooted house. Why not set them down off their wheels or, better, express the new connection in some direct and elegant way? Mobile home parks are laid out at 4 to 9 families per net acre, quite like normal single-family subdivisions of high to moderate density. Could they not be made equally attractive or even be erected in conventional housing areas? Could they be designed to be attachable in rows and clusters in order to pool usable open space?

Diminuitive scale is not by itself unpleasant: the tiny wooden houses in Oak Bluffs, on the island of Martha's Vineyard, Massachusetts, are packed together along the pedestrian ways of a former tenting ground, and the effect is charming. Mobile homes might be grouped in clusters or attached in rows or lines, with landscaping used for private enclosures, and even the car might be sited to create space instead of destroying it. In a mature grove of trees, each small rise and fall of ground could determine where a unit should sit, while narrow car tracks could wind among the tree stems. In open areas the homes might be put within a

FIGURE 48    *A mobile-home development in Florida. Mature planting and an irregular layout contribute to an interesting setting. The houses themselves have almost disappeared behind the skirtings and porches that have been added.*

labryinth of shrubbery, walls, or berms of earth. As the compact standard unit becomes a more frequent element in the landscape, the responsibility for organizing that landscape falls more heavily on the site planner. Siting defenseless small houses requires considerable skill.

Row houses and walk-up apartments may enclose space in a much more continuous and flexible manner than single houses, although they still suffer from low height relative to street width. They may be set back to form an emphatic space at an intersection or a curve, or they may be used in step fashion in plan and (on a slope) in vertical section. They may make sweeping curves, as do the crescents at Bath. They may form continuous enclosures, as in Hampstead Gardens, or be grouped in looser rectangular layouts. The development of continuously modulated street spaces by the use of row housing is perhaps best illustrated in contemporary English work.

Greater spatial variety and freedom of siting can be achieved with tall elevator structures because of their commanding scale, their lack of "front" or "back," and their flexibility of entrance location. Slabs may enclose large spaces, towers may be grouped in fluid lines or clusters, but they may also overpower the human being or generate a wasteland of access and service at their base.

A development need not be made up of one pure building type or density. Objectives may best be met by some mixture that will increase the choice of dwelling for the resident and add visual interest. But similar building types should be clustered in large enough areas to achieve their own typical environment. The transitions between types must be studied. For example, tall apartments may overlook the roofs and gardens of row houses or clog their streets with parking.

One particular concept of residential organization is the doctrine that houses should be grouped into "neighborhoods," units of from 2000 to 10,000 people, insulated from through traffic, bounded by greenbelts or other barriers, and self-contained with regard to all daily facilities except the workplace. This concept usually centers about the elementary school and includes such devices as superblocks, neighborhood centers, and the separation of motor and foot traffic. The idea is based on a presumed unit of social organization and has been applied and expanded in many different situations throughout the world.

Although the idea of neighborhood units developed in

FIGURE 49 *Row houses, tower blocks, and four-story duplex walk-ups serving different clients are well related in the handsome Roehampton Lane project of the London County Council. The mature trees of the original setting and the views over London and Richmond Park are skillfully exploited. A marked increase in car ownership since 1959 has put some pressure on this plan, however.*

the urban United States, it does not often apply there. Most city dwellers are not organized socially in such units, and their life does not center about the elementary school. Nor would they desire to be confined to such self-contained areas, with all their implications of local isolation and lack of choice. The attempt to fit all services into the same unit size is basically inefficient, a typical product of the professional weakness for solutions in which components are neatly separated and grouped. In urban America, at least, the neighborhood unit seems to be a fiction.

Nevertheless, it has been a convenient fiction. It contains some valuable ideas and has attached itself to other valuable ideas. The concept worth saving is that local facilities should be distributed so as to be easily accessible to dwellings and that when some facilities are associated in common centers, they have special convenience. It is not necessary for all functions to occur at the same center, however, nor need their service areas coincide. A resident should have a choice as to his school or store or playground.

Areas need not be neatly packaged, single centered, or of a magical size. It will still be important to keep through traffic out of residential streets and to see that small chil-

dren do not have to cross such busy streets on their way to
school. The superblock is a useful device, and so is the separation of foot and motor traffic, where the flow becomes intense
enough to justify it. But major arteries need not surround an
inward-looking cell. Local shopping, for example, may best
be placed along major streets rather than inside the area
those streets delimit.

It may be desirable to group some dwellings to encourage the formation of true neighborhoods, that is, areas within
which people are on friendly terms partly because they live
close to one another. Such neighborhoods are much more
likely to be of the scale of 10 to 40 families rather than the
1500 families of the conventional unit. Physical arrangement may aid neighborhood formation, especially if the population is socially homogeneous, but factors such as class or
personality are likely to be even more influential. Our urban
areas are far too complex to be ordered by such a simply cellular device as the traditional neighborhood unit.

Having said this, I may calmly contradict myself
whenever the social situation is altered. If true communities
exist or are realistically intended, where residents hold vital
interests of work or worship or family life in common, then
their spatial expression and support makes good sense. Such
units may be found in village economies, among religious or
socialist utopians, in special ethnic groups, and in temporary special-interest camps. But in these cases the spatial
unit would be logically far more thoroughly integrated than
in the conventional neighborhood unit. Political, social, and
economic organization is relevant to the organization of the
living space.

Since social organization, values, and technology may
change within the life expectancy of the dwelling and especially of the site plan, which tends to have a life measured
in centuries, it is sensible to make that site plan as adaptable as possible. Adaptability may be enhanced by using low
densities, especially by providing reserves of unbuilt land.
A good circulation system is most useful, since persons and
activities may then revise their linkages without shifting
their locations. Putting dwelling units in separate structures permits the typical decision unit — the family — to
make changes without impinging on its neighbors. Mobile
units such as trailers can be added to, exchanged, or discarded with less difficulty than permanent units, but only
if lot sizes, utilities, and access are adequate to take a fluctuation in demand.

Sometimes it is possible to predict the nature of a com-

True
Neighborhoods

ing change, such as a more informal living style, new means of transportation to displace the car, the advent of mass-produced but consumer-responsive housing, or even a loosening of the nuclear family. In such a case, provision for the predicted future change may be made explicitly. In general, however, we find that the problem of adaptability has been more acute in nonresidential areas. Since the use of houses has never changed suddenly, housing has rarely become obsolete within the last century by reason of its physical form, provided that it was well built in the beginning and had sufficient space and unit independence to make adaptations easy. The proviso is critical. Housing obsolescence has often occurred as the result of social or geographical shifts, of crowded conditions, or of initial poor design. Designing low-cost housing that can be contiuously upgraded and therefore will not quickly become obsolete is not a trivial problem.

*Adaptability*

The house trailer has grown into the mobile home, which will soon become the customary, mass-produced single-family unit, to be sited permanently in residential subdivisions. But the need for truly mobile housing persists, whether for vacationing, for migratory occupations, or for sudden surges in the housing demand, such as around new colleges, after disasters, or for temporary encampments. The wheeled trailer is therefore still being built and used, and the "camper" truck has appeared as a popular vacation dwelling. Summer tent camping has boomed in popularity.

*Temporary housing*

Trailers and campers are looked upon as nuisances and either banned or swept into some corner. Camp layouts are normally as dreary as parking lots. They have all the features of the mobile home parks discussed earlier, but in exaggerated form. Yet they provide highly valued recreation for large sectors of the population and essential temporary housing for some. For all their crowdedness and cluttered look, they are often pervaded with a spirit of instant comradeship that many people find very attractive.

*Trailer courts and camp-grounds*

Permanent residential areas that will be occupied by transient units — trailer courts or campgrounds — require careful layout and extensive common facilities. There must be a standing for the tent or trailer, with road access to it, a private outdoor area, parking space, toilets, bathing and laundry facilities, sewerage, water supply, electricity, storage areas, recreation space, a waste disposal system, and continuous vigilant management. The simplest tenting grounds use earth roads, cleared tent sites, and a modest

*Reference 50*

central structure housing utilities, toilets, showers, and laundry tubs. Trailer courts, which may be occupied for substantial periods by residents wanting full services, provide hard standings for the trailer, paved and lighted roads, and paved setting areas. Water, electricity, and sewer connections are at the standing, and perhaps telephone and television connections as well. There are laundry-drying areas, lockable storage spaces for each trailer, a management building, swimming pools and sports grounds, a hall for meetings, recreation, or a nursery. A substantial part of the site is recreational open space.

Densities are set by the load on public facilities and by the spacing of units, which is itself governed by requirements for fire protection, light and air, access to the unit, but, above all, privacy. The protection of the outdoor setting area, the control of noise, and the views from tent or trailer windows are key considerations. Densities of up to 8 to 10 units per net acre in trailer courts can be achieved by skillful design (F.H.A. regulations allow even 12 or 13), but lower densities are better, and most courts are quite unimaginatively laid out. Campgrounds, too, usually suffer a lack of privacy, even though the costs of a more extended and sheltered plan are in this case rather small.

It is clear that temporary housing must be kept from overrunning the more sensitive and handsome landscape regions: the lakeshores or mountain valleys. There is probably good reason for concentrating it in special areas, where the special services and the like-minded residents can be found, and where it will not interfere with more permanent activities. But banning it altogether means social exclusion and the denial of a legitimate demand, and to relegate it to industrial areas or to the edges of highways is only a way of creating new slums. Good management and siting can make these temporary camps into pleasant and novel places to live.

Most of these temporary houses have a shape and a skin that is new in the world. They contrast sharply with the forms of landscape and of traditional building. This sense of visual novelty and its clash with the existing landscape lie at the root of much of the adverse public reaction to the trailer. On the other hand, it is the very notion of mobility and contrast that attracts many users. Even when the unit may actually be fixed in place for a substantial time, there is still a sense of impermanence. Impermanence, real or fancied, raises problems of taxation, social relations, ser-

*Mobility and visual novelty*

vices, and participation that are beyond the scope of this text. The psychological and esthetic feeling of impermanence, however pleasant to some, and perhaps in part to all of us, inhibits the sense of history and of place, the emotional ties to objects or locations which develop with long association. It may retard the formation of friendships not based on family or occupation and can be particularly difficult for the young child.

But the trailer park and the camping ground reflect the actual mobility of the American family. It would be a mistake to react by make-believe: to camouflage the trailer as an ancient feature of the site. Many human societies have been nomadic, yet their communities have been strong. The park designer can encourage neighborly association by his layout. He may also use landscape elements to express the permanence of the earth to which the units are momentarily attached. Impermanence has pleasures of its own. Increasingly we shall have to deal with mobility and temporary gathering. It will repay the investment of substantial design talent.

Much of the world's housing is built by the resident himself, particularly in rural areas and in the "squatter" settlements associated with most great cities. Little of it is built now in the United States (although it was a common feature of the nineteenth century), but isolated self-help communities of young people are beginning to appear — a way of life now explicitly chosen rather than one imposed by poverty. Both kinds of communities are built by the users, in isolation from the processes and technology of large-scale development. Because material resources are scarce, the means must be as cheap and simple as possible; but labor may be plentiful.

These are hopeful places: the settlers are building for the future. To the outsider, the settlements appear chaotic and ugly, and they have obvious problems of sanitation, mud, dust, confusion, and discomfort. Yet in their lively activity and their powerful sense of personal care and expression, they are often much more visually engaging than the professionally designed suburb. At first glance, site-planning techniques seem wildly inappropriate to these self-help settlements: too expensive, too complex, too authoritarian, or concerned with the wrong ends. But if the new priorities are understood and if the techniques can be transmitted to the resident himself, then site-planning skill turns out to be as appropriate as ever.

*Tenure*

Security of land tenure is usually one of the most impor-

FIGURE 50  *Dwellings are in different stages of construction in a self-help settlement in Lima, Peru. The walls enclosing the lots are erected first.*

tant requirements, and the framework of the settlement, primitive at first, must allow for progressive future improvement. Thus the layout of the site — the quality of the survey, the pattern of the rights-of-way, the lotting, the provision of space for future growth, the easements — will be an extremely critical aspect of the design. All the techniques of subdivision layout may be brought to bear, and they can easily be taught to the settler, along with elementary surveying.

Access is paramount, yet expensive roads cannot be built. If the pattern of roads has been attended to, the next priority is to deal with surface drainage, keeping the tracks shaped and drained to be passable in all weather. Gravel, corduroy, and the use of binders as in soil-cement are all inexpensive ways of maintaining roads. Mud and rain are the most pervasive and dispiriting of all physical discomforts, as many campers have learned to their sorrow.

Large and lightly used open spaces should be avoided,

*Access*

unless they can be left in a natural self-maintaining condition or be actively maintained as a by-product of agriculture or some other self-motivating function. Sophisticated utilities can be dispensed with, but pure water is essential. If it is not piped in, there must at least be a protected source. Electric power is a great convenience and often not difficult to tap into a developing area. But self-help settlements benefit most from relatively simple and decentralized technologies of the kind that are now only part of our tradition in the United States: privies, dug wells, trash dumps, kerosene lamps, wooden fuel. A socially useful area for technical research is the development of those decentralized low-cost technologies which are also sophisticated and efficient: solar heaters, small water or disposal systems, stabilized earth roads and walls.

*Design quality in low-resource housing*

Although the buildings may be small and primitive, they need not therefore be uncomfortable or ugly. Pressed-earth blocks stabilized with cement, for example, are a very serviceable and beautiful building material. The technique of manufacturing and laying them can be easily taught. By providing design services, the natural expressiveness of the self-built house can be enhanced. The owner can learn how to site it in accord with the accidents of the local terrain. Plants, paint, and other inexpensive ingredients can be used to make it handsome and comfortable. Careful attention to the local ecology — the nature of the soil, the plants, the animals, the movement of water — will not only avoid expensive adaptations but conserve the detailed natural landscape in a way that large-scale development can rarely do. Thus an understanding of site and site planning may be even more essential to the self-help builder than to his professional counterpart.

Trailer camps and squatter settlements are considered the poorest kind of housing, to be strictly regulated and if possible abolished. Regarded more carefully, they are responses to important needs and worthy of much better design. Out of them may come new ways of living.

*Chapter* 15

# Special Types of Site Planning

The location of a shopping center depends on analyses of market and accessibility. The market analysis considers the distribution of population, its buying power, the location of competing centers, the means of access to the site and its capacity, the time distances involved, and the customary routes of travel for other purposes. Centers are typically located along major arteries, and it is desirable to have more than one line of access. But a position at a major intersection or close to a freeway ramp may make access complicated, and a position along a highway already flowing full and used primarily by fast through traffic may discourage customers. Good visibility from the main lines of travel is desirable. The area to be developed should be level and fairly compact in shape, with no surrounding development that is ugly, competing, or of nuisance character.

A common rule of thumb divides shopping centers into three types: the neighborhood center, dominated by a supermarket, containing about 40,000 square feet of selling area and serving perhaps 10,000 people; the community center, featuring a variety or junior department store, having from 100,000 to 300,000 square feet, and serving 20,000 to 100,000 people; and the regional center, with one to four major department stores and serving a very large urban area. Such generalizations are useful only as first guesses, however, and must be developed by detailed analyses. Area requirements vary, but a 50-acre site is a normal minimum for a regional center, while 75 acres will allow for expansion to three or four department stores. A 125-acre site is desirable since it allows for commercial development of the residual land.

The composition of a center in regard to the types and sizes of stores can only judged be on completion of market and financial analyses, with the balance between kinds of tenants being quite significant. Large centers now have other facilities in addition to retail stores, including theaters, offices, banks, post offices, and even hotels, clinics, and cultural facilities. In this way the shopping center begins to resemble the older central district, except for its isolation from its immediate surroundings and the lack of residential facilities or of commercial activities using space of marginal quality. It is this local isolation and this narrowness of function that remain the most serious disadvantages of the new centers.

When a shopping center is being planned by a public agency as a part of a larger area, it is possible to correct some of these faults. Community facilities can then be introduced as a matter of policy, and shopping can be connected to surrounding residences and supporting services and commercial activity. Leading developers themselves now look for sites in the 500-acre range, with the intention of building "total communities" that include substantial housing, employment, and public services. They thereby assure that

FIGURE 51   *Stonestown Shopping Center, San Francisco, California. A typical new center with its central mall and large external parking lots. Note the added housing and office buildings on the periphery, and yet the lack of fit with the surroundings.*

some part of their market will be held close to their stores, even though outer suburbia expands and new centers are built farther out. The connection with surrounding development and particularly the provision of space for economically marginal activities when all structures are new and occupy valuable land remain a difficulty. Some experiments are being made with providing low-rent space in basements or in parking decks or with subsidizing special tenants by manipulating rentals. Churches, community centers, libraries, and other "approved" facilities can thus be provided. Can places also be found for secondhand stores, cheap restaurants, studio lofts, and coffeehouses? Or facilities run by teen-agers at their own times and in their own way?

Shopping centers normally consist of one-or two-story structures, 100 to 200 feet deep. Individual stores within these large structures may run the full depth, or they may be as small as 40 feet deep with a 20-foot frontage. Centers typically take one of several general forms. They may be arranged in the traditional pattern, as a strip along the street, or the strip may be bent into a U or L shape, set back from the artery it faces, with landscaping or, more likely, car parking occupying the forecourt. The stores may surround a hollow square, occupied by service entrances and surface or decked parking, while the stores front outward to pedestrians and streets. This is a compact type, suitable for central shopping, but there is liable to be insufficient space for parking. More commonly in the United States the stores will be arranged with buildings facing inward toward a square, parking and access being on the outside and a landscaped pedestrian court within. Usually this inner court is narrowed and lengthened to form a pedestrian shopping street, or "mall."

Finally, the stores may be clustered together compactly, with parking and access outside and an interior web of pedestrian ways on which the stores front, so that some stores, particularly the major magnets, are completely within the pedestrian zone. These general forms may be further varied by using two levels instead of one, by allowing vehicles to penetrate the interior spaces, by making stores double-fronted, or by roofing over the pedestrian ways. In high-density areas the stores may even be sandwiched, in one large structure, between layers of parking above and below, with walk-in access at the street level. The main structure is owned by the developer of the center, while the interior fittings of the stores belong to the commercial ten-

*Typical shopping center layouts*

ants. Parking areas and the sites for outlying structures may be either leased or sold under tight restrictions.

The location of the various types of stores is critical. The basic principle of location is to expose storefronts to the maximum foot traffic, keeping this traffic in concentrated channels and at the same time well distributed over the center as a whole. Rather than allow the customer to enter his destination directly and to leave it as quickly, paths are located to bring him past the remainder of the center.

Certain stores are considered to be primary attractions that draw customers to the center by their own power. Such are the department or junior department stores, large specialty and fashion stores, and, in smaller centers, variety stores and supermarkets. These activities not only draw people to the center itself but can be located to pull buyers past other stores and distribute traffic evenly. Secondary attractions, such as banks, post offices, quality restaurants, clusters of apparel stores, and groups of service outlets (barber, beauty shop, shoe repair, cleaner) can also be used to cause people to move about the center. Other stores are presumed to subsist from the distributed foot traffic so generated, while supporting the primary stores by the variety of goods and service they afford. On the other hand, the parking and service requirements of activities that may pull in large crowds, but whose patrons are not likely to shop in other stores (such as moviegoers or people buying a week's groceries), must not be allowed to interfere with other movements in the center.

Normal practice in store location, therefore, is to put the primary attraction in the center, or as a pair of opposed magnets if there are two, or at three or four ends of a set of converging malls. Secondary activities are distributed to encourage balanced pedestrian flow throughout the area, the service outlets being put at the farther margins or on a lower level. Other stores are grouped by similar types and prices of goods to facilitate comparison shopping: food, women's wear, family wear, housewares, and so on. Or if certain facilities stay open at night, such as theaters, restaurants, and drugstores, they will be kept together. Goods usually bought on impulse, such as candy, pastry, gifts, tobacco, and cards, are sprinkled individually among the clusters, usually at intersections in pedestrian traffic. Cinemas, car accessory sales (TBA's), and supermarkets are placed in separate, freestanding buildings, or in "backwater" areas that do not preempt mall frontage and can be reached directly from parking. The details of pedestrian layout are significant: the entrances from the parking lot and the bus terminal, the stairways, elevators, and escalators. The problem is similar in principle to the internal layout of a large department store.

The objective behind these arrangements is to maximize sales, and it is interesting to see that this objective sometimes coincides with the customer's objectives, as when it facilitates comparison shopping, for example, and sometimes does not, as when it forces extended movement throughout the center to maximize impulse sales. Furthermore, since the objective is to maximize total rather than individual sales, neither does the pattern correspond to that of an unplanned business center. The pattern is based on a highly sophisticated negotiation between shopping center developer and commercial tenant, usually a large retail chain. Whenever a shopping center would be built for service rather than for distributor's profit, we should expect to see fundamental changes in some of these locational criteria.

*Circulation*

The relations between the circulation of cars, service trucks, and shoppers on foot are a standard problem. Generous parking, a short walking distance, easy service, and a pleasant pedestrian environment are all desired, and they are in conflict. The traditional arrangement was to put service access on one side of the strip of stores and shopper parking on the other, with a pedestrian walk along the storefronts at the edge of the parking area. This is still a good technique for smaller centers, where shoppers move in and out quickly and the parking load is light. Storefronts and parking are visible from the first moment of entry, service is screened, and the shopper can park close to the store he wants to patronize. But this system results in an ugly view of parking lots from the main road, and it prevents the development of a special pedestrian environment. At larger sizes it becomes difficult to get parking within a reasonable distance of the stores.

More recently, vehicular access has been put on one side of the stores and pedestrians on the other. Store service occurs along the "backs" of the stores, preferably in bays screened off from customer parking, or even in basement tunnels. But truck tunnels are extremely expensive and usually avoided. This pattern creates a pedestrian world along the fronts of stores, and if the shops are arranged in a closed court, more parking spaces may be provided within a given distance of the shopping area. The view from the street on entering may be no handsomer, however, since the parking lot is still dominant. It may even be uglier, since the stores now turn their backs to the entrance side. A recurrent problem is the entrance of shoppers into the inner court. How do they cross the service zone? How do they sense the quality of the inside area or know where to go to reach the store they want? Some of these problems may be mitigated by screening the service areas, by using prominent signs, by designing special entrances, or by giving the stores double frontage.

The visual experience of approach and departure still leaves much to be desired, and so does the physical effort of carrying purchases back to the car. Subdivision of the parking area into smaller compartments, opening a view of the inner area to the outside, extension of fingers of landscaping or shopping into the parking, mechanical devices for the carriage of packages out into the parking lots, and the integration of inner and outer circulation into one clear system are all helpful.

It is unfortunate that shopping centers are usually designed only for people arriving by private car. It is unnerving to walk into one from the outside, and they are rarely tied to any system of public transit. Like any highly specialized device, these centers may have a short life. A few of the earliest centers are now showing the first signs of obsolescence. Some centers are now providing bus terminals as an integral part of the design and receiving substantial patronage from them. Location on a subway or railway line might also be possible, as in Place Ville Marie, in Montreal, Canada.

*Parking rules*      Various rules are given for the amount of car parking to

FIGURE 52 *Asphalt wilderness, the pedestrian approach to a modern shopping center (Park Forest, Illinois).*

be provided. The simplest standards relate the number of parking spaces to the total area of selling space. Thus an older urban center, built at high density and drawing trade from transit passengers, may be contented with as little as three parking spaces per 1000 square feet of selling area. A regional shopping center, depending on automobile trade drawn from a wide area and liable to peak loads, will require five and a half spaces per 1000 square feet, which will satisfy the demands of all but the ten hours of highest parking load per year. This allows for the peak shopping of certain holidays such as Christmas, but the reserve areas, so often empty, further complicate access to the center and degrade its appearance. Reserve parking of this kind is often put outside the access road that rings the main parking lot. On the other hand, certain facilities, such as churches, create off-peak parking demands and can use the parking areas assigned to stores. Some sharing with office buildings is also possible. One rule is that office space up to 20 percent of the selling area may be added without providing additional parking.

The farthest parking spaces should be no more than 600 feet from the selling area, and these will be used only at peak sales periods. Everyday parking works best if placed within 300 feet of the selling area. It should be possible to have a general view of the lot on entrance and to move through it systematically while locating a parking space. Where land is cramped or costly, in order to minimize the car-to-store distance, or to distribute shoppers to a two-level center, multilevel deck parking may be used. It may also be possible to depress the levels of parking lots by a few feet so as to reduce their visual dominance.

Since parking turnover is rapid and customers are often entering cars with bulky packages, parking spaces should be generously sized. As much as 400 square feet per car may be provided for lots, exclusive of main circulation, in preliminary layouts. For the parking maneuver, 45- or 60-degree parking is easiest, but it requires a confusing and unenforceable one-way flow system that 90-degree parking avoids. Parking lots should be divided into areas of no more than 800 cars, each identifiable and lighted to 1½ to 2 footcandles. There should be walkways, and these walkways and the aisles should point toward the center. Drivers will want to get near their point of first purchase or to pick up heavy packages. Parking areas visually "opposite" stores (in distinction to corner areas that *seem* remote) will be favored despite actual longer walking distances. Surface parking will be preferred to the mysteries and confined maneuvers of decks and garages, and so the deck entrance ramps may be designed to lead a driver in unwittingly. There will be considerable circulation within the lots. For this purpose, ring roads are put at the outer edge and also through the middle or at the inner edge of the lots. The pattern works best if they occur at the inner edge, but they form a major barrier for the pedestrian to cross, a dilemma as yet unsolved. Food markets require concentrated parking near them, as well as pickup stations.

The circulatory system must take traffic of the public roads into the lots and have sufficient length so that traffic can slow down gradually and not back up onto the highway itself. The peak loads are higher at exit than at entrance, and at closing time employees and shoppers may leave within one-half hour, although store closings can be staggered to spread it out over a full hour. Exit and feeder roads must be sized to take the impact of the expected peak emptying rate. Discharge of the lot onto more than one road is a distinct advantage, but shoppers prefer to enter and exit at the same place. Service traffic should branch away from passenger traffic as far from the center proper as possible. A shopping center may have one truck per day for every 4000 square feet of selling area, and more in the case of supermarkets. As much as 10 to 20 percent of the daily truck volume may accumulate at any one time. To strengthen visual identity from the highway, the designer will use stacks, water towers, signs, flagpoles, and tall buildings for landmarks. The character of the skyline from the road, including the intrusion of structures on the roof, must be controlled. The intervening sea of parking is played down as much as possible.

*Environmental detail*

The designer of a shopping center usually has some scope for adornment, since the center is normally under unified control, the locational values created are concentrated and high, and there is a strong economic motive for display and for a handsome environment. Special landscaping and paving can be justified, as well as careful attention to outdoor furniture and other detail, the use of color, sculpture, fountains, and special displays, and the inclusion of facilities such as outdoor restaurants, kiosks, resting places, auditoriums, meeting rooms, exhibit space, libraries, and nurseries or play areas for children. Signs are carefully coordinated for harmony and legibility so that they also become orna-

FIGURE 53 *The Merceria, Venice. Congested but dramatic, the display windows are at arm's reach.*

mental. An orderly architectural framework for the individual storefronts is created.

The sequence of interior spaces is proportioned to give a sense of intimacy, contrast, and activity. Covering the shopping mall not only permits an equable climate — warm in winter and cool in summer — and the use of special plants, birds, sounds, and odors but allows stores and their goods to open directly onto the pedestrian street. The center is thereby further isolated from its context, however. Storefronts should not be too far apart. Their contents ought to be visible in detail on both sides of any pedestrian way, except where an open space is inserted which is itself to be the center of attention. On the other hand, depending on the num-

*Interior malls*

ber of shoppers, spaces should not be so tight as to feel congested or oppressive. A pedestrian street 35 to 45 feet wide is likely to be about right. The shopping mall should not be so long as to discourage movement from one end to the other, and in large centers it will be preferable to use "side streets" and other devices to keep the selling area compact. Two-level shopping streets are sometimes used to bring the stores closer together. The two levels may be put a half level above and below the parking grade to minimize the climb or descent, and escalators may be employed. Because it is difficult to induce shoppers to change level, one level may be favored and the other one "dead." For this reason, parking may also be split into two levels, with no more than 60 percent being assigned to one level, and that to the level potentially the most inactive. Shopping magnets will also be distributed to even out the foot traffic.

*Future growth*    The plan should allow for future growth, but not by leaving gaps at the center. Primary stores, fixed in location, will probably grow vertically. Other stores will be added at the periphery. Locations may be left for adding new cross malls, with new primary stores at their ends. Structures and utilities must be sized for this expansion. Rights-of-way below ground and in the air may be reserved to permit a future circulation system in three dimensions; levels and modular spacings can be coordinated to permit easy remodeling. Surface parking areas are designed and held to permit gradual development of their air rights for parking decks and further structures. But a large expansion may be met more efficiently by building another center, rather than by continuous addition to the original unit. The development must be able to operate as a compact whole from the beginning, without depending on future additions. Similarly, each future stage must be a workable unit.

The regional shopping center is a highly sophisticated device for selling goods with convenience and profit. Given the motives, the site planning for these centers is as advanced and as solidly based on behavior as any done in the United States today. The central malls of the newest centers are marvels of comfort and delight, though also somewhat unreal and even oppressive in their material display. Built for selling, these centers are also becoming the social focuses for large suburban regions. Conscientious developers are trying to adapt them to this new role, but it is still uncertain if they can be successfully so modified within the institutional setting that created them.

The older central shopping and business districts, hampered by fragmented ownership, a scarcity of space, complex existing structures and high land values, but with some advantages of traditional dominance, use mixture, transit accessibility, and historic association, are desperately seeking to use some of the same devices as the new regional centers. At substantial expense, the old centers are being rebuilt with public plazas, enclosed malls, arcades, escalators, upper-level pedestrian connections, and integrated parking structures. The resulting site plans are complex, yet often rather barren and formal in character. The best examples retain the mixture of uses and a sense of the past, and they capitalize on the human vitality of an established downtown. They fit walkways, subways, corridors, elevators, and escalators into one integrated movement system. They make walking a pleasure, using seats, arcades, radiant heat, displays, and proximity to lively activity. There are some rather simple rules, for example, to ensure that a central public open space will be actively used and enjoyed. It must have a good microclimate and be a comfortable place to sit and talk. It must be close to heavy pedestrian flow and commercial activity, that is, be at the very edge of the action; yet it must convey a sense of a protected and intimate territory. Most downtown plans are sophisticated in their management of traffic or the placing of buildings for profit or prestige. They are more inept, however, in providing for the active use of their decorative open spaces.

Another type of commercial development is as important as the new shopping center but is universally condemned: the highway commercial strip. In its gaudy confusion, it seems to symbolize the worst of our material culture. Critics always save room for a photograph of it in their books and articles. Undoubtedly, it is ugly, visually domineering, an extended traffic hazard. Local governments and highway authorities work hard to prevent or confine it. Yet it continues to flourish, for it has an important function. It is the preferred location for those automobile-oriented, special commercial functions that need cheap space and must be easy to find: the drive-ins, the repair garages, the car sales, and all the rest. They want vivid legibility and direct access from the highway, parking at the door, low-cost land and buildings, and the ability to change and grow quickly. For the consumer, they are a great convenience, and their gaudy signs have a spirit often lacking in more controlled development. But their instant access disrupts through traf-

*Older shopping districts*

*Reference 63*

*Commercial strips*

fic, and their visual chaos defeats their own goal of quick recognition. By the aggressive way in which they urge themselves on all passersby, they set the dominant tone for the landscape.

Like the trailer camp, here is another important use that needs site-planning attention. One thinks of special bypass routes or loops particularly devoted to these road-hugging activities, of ways of designing those roads to permit frequent access without disruption, of the use of signs to increase the legibility and the gaiety of the scene, that is, of a design based on the actual behavior of the driver as he seeks, locates, drives in, parks, and enters the commercial premises. Lighting, supergraphics, artifical topography, and planting can all be employed in new ways to make this act a pleasant one. By consistently neglecting the commonplace environment, site planning relegates itself to the occasional place: the campus, the downtown plaza, or the "cultural center."

Industrial
Districts

References 62, 64

Like the regional shopping center, the organized industrial district is a relatively new type of development. Industries of moderate size now prefer to cluster together for reasons of access and service, for protection, for prestige, to avoid complaint, or to obtain adequate sites. But there has been less refinement of the technique of siting industrial uses. Yet industrial layouts affect the efficiency of the economic base, the daily environment of a substantial percentage of the population, and the appearance of the city as a whole.

Industrial districts require substantial areas of moderately flat and inexpensive land that can support heavy loads. Housing for employees should be within commuting range, but the district itself should lie to the leeward of nearby housing areas and in such a position that the traffic it will generate will not disturb those areas. Districts range upward in size from 50 acres, with an average near 400 or 500 acres. Oversize districts may be difficult to relate to other uses, while districts that are too small may be uneconomical to serve efficiently. There is no reason, from a planning viewpoint, why light industry may not be mixed more intimately with other uses, given adequate controls over noise and other emissions and sufficient separate access. Yet homeowners are traditionally averse to industry located nearby, and industry prefers to be separate to avoid the possibility of residential complaints. Thus the environment becomes increasingly segregated and visually more sterile.

Good access is the primary requirement for industry, particularly in the United States for trucks and for workers coming by private car. Although most small and medium-sized industries today make little use of rail service and many districts are now oriented only to highways, it is still desirable to locate a district on a rail line to preserve flexibility of service for future tenants. Some estates are located next to airports, in response to the growing importance of air freight. In at least one district, the factories are served directly by airport runways. Districts are often far from public transportation, although bus lines may later be routed near them. But the tendency of industry to become more and more dependent on the truck and the private automobile may in the end prove shortsighted. In some localities, particularly abroad, workers may come primarily on foot, on bicycles, or by public transport.

*District layout*

Industrial districts are typically laid out with a gridiron of roads that enclose large blocks 1000 to 2000 feet long and 500 to 1000 feet deep. If there is rail service, the tracks usually run through the mid-block, parallel to the long axis. Thus individual plots can have a street in front and a rail line behind. The plots should be from 200 to 500 feet deep, with grades not exceeding 4 or 5 percent. Where rail spurs are provided, they should be given a 40-foot right-of-way, have a maximum grade of 1 or 2 percent, and a curvature with no greater than a 400-foot radius. Spurs typically diverge at small angles. In the road system, lanes must be of ample size, rights-of-way broad (80 to 100 feet for major roads, and 60 feet for secondary ones), and docks and turns must accommodate the large tractor trailers. It is desirable to separate truck circulation from the general circulation of passenger cars as much as possible within the district. Crossings with the rail lines should be minimized. Separate cycle paths should be laid out if this is a significant mode of employee transport.

If legally possible, the frontage is assigned only to individual tenants at the time of sale or lease. The lots may range in size from a half acre to 40 or 50 acres. Where possible, factories are grouped together if they have similar space requirements, or similar locational demands (railroad or canal access), or special utility needs, or if they emit particular nuisances. Special loads are likely to be imposed on the utility system, and the rules of thumb for residential areas cannot be used. Power, water, and sewage disposal of high capacity will probably be required. These are the priority services, whose demand is variable and difficult to estimate. Provisions for waste disposal or recycling will become more demanding as environmental standards rise, as they must. Other special utilities — gas, steam, compressed air — may also be wanted.

Some general-purpose factory buildings may be erected before tenants are found, to provide for small or growing firms unable to plan for, or invest in, their own plant. Such speculative buildings are typically simple, high-ceilinged, one-story structures, made up of 30- to 40-foot square bays, designed for high floor loads and light roof loads. Planning, financing, and maintenance or supply services may be extended to all plants in the estate.

*Density of industrial areas*

Most industries want to assure themselves of room for future growth and will buy plots substantially larger than immediately needed. There are also large open-land uses, such as storage and car parking. Buildings are generally one-story high to allow easy horizontal movement of materials. Thus industrial estates tend to be wasteful of land, and where land is scarce, or where development costs are high, governments and estate managements try to prevent underbuilding. Expansion land may be reserved, for a group of factories, for example, rather than for each one singly. But floor area ratios tend to be low, ranging from 0.1 to 0.3, with 0.2 as a likely average. Density of employees per acre will also be low in these new industrial areas, ranging from 10 to 30 workers per acre. These are United States norms; in other situations where there is greater pressure on the land, for example, in England or in central urban areas, floor area ratios may come closer to 0.5, and employee density to 50 to 75 workers per acre, while total estate size may lie in the 50- to 150-acre range.

*Parking*

Extensive parking space will be needed for workers' cars. Considering some doubling up, it is perhaps enough to allow one car space for every 1.2 workers, but some planners prefer the more generous figure of one space for each worker. Since one shift arrives before another leaves, spaces must unfortunately be adequate for two shifts of employees at one time. The problem of exit congestion at shift time will be serious, and the capacity of interchanges and exits must be checked to see that they will permit this flow. A network of secondary roads which permits quick dispersion of the concentrated load is preferable to a single high-capacity highway. Staggering of shift hours will also help. These peak flows of workers' cars have become the principal conflict between industrial and residential uses, in place of the traditional nuisances of noise, smoke, and dirt.

Since almost all drivers are destined for one particular location well known to them, parking places may be more dispersed than in a shopping center and more closely related to the actual point of work. Daylong parkers can also be asked to walk farther to their cars than short-term parkers. The maximum distance from car to plant may be near 1000 feet rather than the maximum of 300 to 600 feet for a shopping center. Despite all this, internal circulation in the district should have a simple and understandable form so that traffic disperses quickly to its destination and visitors are not confused. Clear visual identity for district exits and entrances is important and can be accomplished through large-scale landscaping or vertical features. The ability to control or check movement at these gates may also be significant.

As a daily environment for employees, these working areas suffer from isolation. They are large and sealed in; there are no independent local facilities to serve employees, or to give some relief from the factory routine. It is not unusual now to provide services useful to the industries themselves, such as banks, post offices, industrial advisory services, repair shops, and fire stations. It would also be possible to introduce stores, restaurants, bars, parks, schools, crèches,

*Employee services*

FIGURE 54 *A typical industrial estate: New England Industrial Center, Needham, Massachusetts. Low, bulky buildings on flat land in an irregular gridiron, visible from the expressway but disassociated from their surroundings.*

Cabot, Cabot and Forbes

FIGURE 55    *A more recent industrial area in the new town of Columbia, Maryland. A few of the trees are preserved, but otherwise the featureless buildings are surrounded by grass and asphalt parking lots.*

libraries, medical clinics, hospitals, bus terminals, or places of recreation. The grounds should be attractive places in which to walk and spend lunch hours or other leisure periods. Parks or recreation grounds must be planned to resist the inevitable pressure for subsequent industrial expansion.

*Visual quality in working areas*

Visually the contemporary industrial district is characterless, even though the individual buildings may be competently designed and cosmetic landscaping has been applied. The low structures are dotted over a flat, empty landscape, surrounded by parked cars. Grass, asphalt, and chain-link fencing are the predominant materials. Since the interesting industrial processes are invisible, one new factory looks much like another. The grounds are for show or storage rather than for active use. While the view from the bordering roads is considered to be important, both for its advertising and its scenic value, the problem is usually handled by the use of large signs. It would be more effective to open up the plants visually or otherwise to make them more expressive of their internal activity. Approaches can be made legible, and structures can even be grouped for visual effect. Storage and parking can be screened. Moreover, grounds can be developed for active use and pleasure rather than being thought of as empty land to be made decent with grass. A planned landscape structure and character can be introduced. Most industries are indeed anxious that design controls be exercised over their surroundings. Up to the present these controls have been rather negative ones, dealing with setbacks, coverage, planting, and building material.

Industrial areas, like roads, are not simply unpleasant necessities to be kept as neat and reticent as possible. Roads, dams, bridges, pylons, cooling towers, stacks, quarries, even spoil heaps, are magnificent objects if well shaped. They are big enough and meaningful enough to take their place in large landscapes. They explain the industrial basis of our civilization; they contrast handsomely with hills, trees, and lakes. As Fairbrother advocates for the British landscape, they could well be interwoven with the extensive recreational open spaces we so urgently need on the urban fringe. Visually complementary, and making joint use of parking lots and services, this close weaving would also allow employees to enjoy their moments of leisure.

*Reference 1*

Institutions are extremely diverse, yet a few comments can be made about site planning for the larger ones: colleges, universities, hospitals, governmental units, and cultural centers. Such activities are normally long-lived as well as complex and extensive, and with this continuity it is possible to achieve environments of great richness and strong character. For the most part the grounds of American institutions stand in sharp contrast to this possibility. It is astonishing how little the popular and romantic conception of a campus corresponds to its actual harshness and disarray. Yet we are in a period of rapid institutional growth. Campuses and hospitals are often the fastest-growing activities in their area. Hundreds of new institutions are being built from scratch, allowing us, if we will, to break clear of many traditional forms of site and function.

Institutions

*Reference 57*

The elements of an institutional site are highly individual. Rather than a repeated series of factories, stores, or houses, there is a juxtaposition of classrooms, public meeting places, offices, libraries, clinics, residences, wards, laboratories, museums, ceremonial rooms, studies, and research areas — a collection of singularities, even though repressive monumental design can reduce all this to bleak monotony. Each structure requires particular services and a particular situation.

*Diversity of institutional elements*

The diversity of use makes it difficult to isolate basic

University of Virginia

FIGURE 56    *One of the rare examples of a serene and ordered American campus: the Lawn of the University of Virginia, designed by Thomas Jefferson.*

FIGURE 57    *A part of the University Circle area in Cleveland. This is the normal condition of an urban institution: a chaotic collection of buildings besieged by cars and with little room for growth and change.*

Ed Nano

objectives that bear on physical arrangement. Administrators respond with vague generalities, convinced that there is no vital link between the site plan and their essential purposes, other than the obvious requirements for shelter and access. Or they may hold a conflicting set of objectives, happily concealed under the heading of "flexibility" or "balance." University proposals rarely connect planning to learning, nor do hospitals link environment to health. Many persons vitally concerned — students, patients, nurses, secretaries, visitors — are customarily excluded from the site-planning decisions. Yet the institutional case is preeminently the one in which long-term purpose and policy can be made by those who are involved in its consequences, and where these policies can be applied most nicely to the planning of the physical shell. Therefore the planner must raise such issues as intended behavior, staff interaction, patient and student requirements, flexibility, image, privacy, access, stimulus, climate, community relations, and a host of others. He can inflame and inform the debate at the beginning by presenting physical alternatives that have direct and startling consequences for those policies.

*Institutional linkages*

The individual structures of the institution contain a fluid and shifting set of activities, with many complex linkages throughout the institutional group and the community beyond. At present it is difficult to isolate more than a few of the most obvious of these links, but in the future the interconnections may be studied as a total system. For now the planner can make only a first approximation of the activity arrangement that will optimize such linkages for his given purpose. He is understandably prone to group activities along traditional lines, as by university department or medical specialty. Closer study may show that these standard patterns ignore sensitive spontaneous linkages, such as those between research workers in different fields. Careful analysis of linkage is likely to be very important in institutional work.

Time distances between probable pairs of communicating activities become critical. Movement is typically on foot or in slow public vehicles such as elevators or escalators. In the future, we may see the use of special vehicles, or belt conveyors, to connect an extended site. Face-to-face interactions, spontaneous or planned, are important. When walking times exceed certain limits, the institution begins to operate in sectors rather than as a unit. Students may be unable to move from class to class unless curricula are compartmented; staff will not meet those from other branches without special provisions for clubs or other meeting grounds.

The problem is an interrelated one of total size, of density, of the disposition of paths and foci, and of grain, or the relative size and mix of specialized units. A typical problem of grain in a university, for example, is whether student housing should be in one place or several, separate from or integrated with other housing, in close contact with the teaching facilities or not. The size and density of the school, its purposes, and the rhythm of student life will determine a unique solution.

There are four general ways of organizing an institution in space. One is to group it by administrative unit, locating the department of physics in one place, the dormitories for women in another, the geriatric unit in a third. This arrangement will fit management convenience and prestige, correspond to the boundaries of maintenance and control, and reinforce internal communications within the administrative unit. It may, however, discourage cross-connections within the institution as a whole and decrease flexibility. But since most planning decisions are made by administrators, this is the most common method of allocation. Plans which begin with other premises will often shake down to this.

A second way is to group spaces by their physical type or requirement. Thus the libraries would be clustered, as well as the classrooms, the laboratories, the operating theaters, the service functions, the parking lots. This makes sense in terms of functional requirements and can better respond to shifting loads. But it not only denies the administrative unit but may thwart desirable interactions as well. In large systems it may produce an inhuman scale of specialization in activity and form. But for some particular function — an incinerator or a stadium, for example — a separate location may be the only efficient solution.

Other institutions will mix functions while clustering them in modular units corresponding to some social community. Thus many universities have used a "college" system, in which residences, seminar rooms, libraries, dining halls, and offices are grouped in a unit intended to act as a learning community. The spatial unit corresponds to a social unit that is diverse and held together by informal as well as formal ties. Where such a unit actually functions and will have a stable existence, this is an excellent system. But in many institutions the social unit is doubtful or will shift radically in time.

Finally, the spatial distribution may take on a more "urban" character, with wide dispersal and mixing of functions, held together by a good transportation and communications system. This arrangement is meant to favor diverse interactions and continuous shifts in the functional network. To be workable, spaces must be made usable for diverse purposes, communications must be excellent, and the growth, interactions, and displacement of units must be centrally monitored and controlled on a continuous basis. On occasion, activities may even be juxtaposed which have little formal connection but between which new interactions are desired.

In most cases, the real spatial organization of institutions will be a mix of all of these methods but primarily one based on administrative lines, as blurred by the accidents and compromises of historic growth. The plea here is for a reexamination of this common pattern, a search for the real interactions that lie behind the table of organization, the communities that actually exist. Moreover, where chance meetings are an important part of the communications network of an institution, as is so often the case, the location, capacity, and form of lobbies, corridors, and central spaces may be more important than unit divisions or the form of the headquarters office or the main auditorium.

Similar problems must be studied in relation to the world outside the institution. There will be activities to which it must be closely linked: clinics, private offices, shopping, restaurants, laboratories. It will require good access to its supporting population of citizens, patients, or students. It will typically have to provide many types of entrance without chaos or interference for staff, visitors, clients, and suppliers. All of these problems relate to multiform linkage, and in this way the large institution is much like a city in miniature. *Relation to external context*

Quite often a large institution is seen as an alien intrusion by its surrounding neighbors. It performs no service for them, draws its clientele from a wider sphere, and at the same time exerts severe pressure on local housing, traffic, and protective services. Since the institution is long-lived, its surroundings may have utterly changed since its original founding. That most institutions are tax-exempt and in urban areas are often used by people of distinctly different social class only add to the hostility. The institution reacts by drawing a sharp boundary, with controlled entrances.

The underlying issues are ones of social and economic policy, but they are reflected in site planning as questions about the nature of the institutional boundary, the location of common facilities or access ways within the grounds, the provision of institutional "outposts," and even, in some cases, whether the institution might better be spatially dispersed rather than located in a territorial enclave. The location of housing for students and young staff is always a thorny question. A mix of local and institutional housing or a campus that is open to community use may be socially desirable but difficult to achieve because of habitual mental boundaries. Certainly, no institution should be planned without consideration of the heavy demand it will make on its surroundings, a demand sometimes tantamount to requiring the facilities of a new town.

*Change is
frequent*

Internal links not only are complex but shift unpredictably. In a hospital, for example, a rapid connection between a single ward and a certain therapy unit may suddenly become important. Activities move in and out of a given building, expanding and contracting. Functions change in unforeseen ways. Long-term growth may be certain, but its rate is not easy to manage or predict. Therefore a high premium must be put on flexibility: on adaptable space, a physical shell that is easy to add to, on a good communication system that favors new connections. Elaborate design methods are currently used to optimize particular relations between activities when those relations will surely be transformed within a few years. It would be more sensible to plan for a dense network of access and services and a mix of room or bay sizes, which have proved in the past to be highly reusable.

*Symbolic form*

At the same time, most institutions have symbolic importance and will want a visual setting that creates a certain mood, whether of awe or serenity or stimulus. The unity and expressiveness of the environment are essential. The designer has the problem of producing a strong overall form and character that can also house complex functions and survive major change and that will have some quality even in the early stages of occupation. He turns to the techniques

*See pages 232–237*

of long-range site planning described in Chapter 10. Landscaping, lighting, and the form of the path systems may be of great interest to him. Important natural features can be used as visual anchors or as the basis for consistent long-range form. He will take advantage of the continuous control and management that are available. Certainly he will recommend the establishment of a continuing planning staff.

The prediction of future growth and change, as well as

its translation into future program requirements, is a normal part of the work. Immediate space demands are usually calculated by summing up the short-range needs of the various units of the institution and arranging them in a consistent priority order. Longer-range growth is more likely to be gauged by an estimate of the future growth of the base population: employees, patients, professionals, or students. To these estimates of population change are applied ratios of space per person for various kinds of facilities, such as libraries, classrooms, wards, clinics, laboratories, and offices. These ratios are derived from past experience and are modified by speculation as to future change. Typically, most institutions will underestimate future space demands and will lcok upon the next building program as the last. The planner must correct for this habit of mind.

Future requirements for land area are then computed from the floor space requirements by fixing a set of desired structural densities or floor area ratios. These will vary from

FIGURE 58 *Air view of Scarborough College, Toronto, Canada. Diverse functions are put in a single building of complex form and arranged along a sinuous corridor system.*

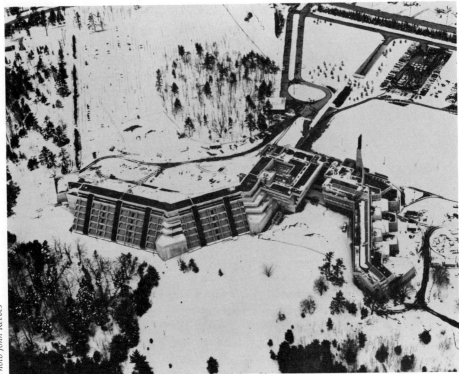

institution to institution. A college of open plan may stay below a ratio of 0.5 or even 0.3, while an urban university may commonly go up to 2.0, and a large city hospital on expensive land, which needs close contact between its working parts, may aim for a ratio as high as 2.5. In large hospitals, except those dealing with chronic or convalescent cases, the high-rise structure may be preferable simply because of the reduction of time distances between activities. Land costs, the tax losses, and human displacements that expansion brings on, all encourage dense, highly integrated institutional complexes in center city areas. Columbia University, for example, already at a floor area ratio of 3.0, now plans a doubling of its floor space without further land acquisition. Such densities are costly. They make possible the creation of a powerful and intricate architectural order. However, they are just as likely to produce a sterile and oppressive environment. The general pattern of structural density is an important feature of any institutional plan, since it will tend to determine site acquisition, service load, linkage between parts, future flexibility, and general visual character. There will be a continuous struggle to retain open space, whether for visual amenity, recreation, or future growth.

FIGURE 59    *The campus becomes a parking lot: Case Institute of Technology, Cleveland.*

Ed Nano

Parking is a problem for institutions as for any activity, but it is likely to be more difficult because of the conflict of the large parking lot with intensive development and with the symbolic meaning of the institution. Most professional and many nonprofessional staff members now drive to work; so do visitors, and even most students if they can. A "drive-in" campus may provide a parking space for each of its members, but more commonly the ratio might be one to four. In order to preserve a quiet setting, the institution may have to take an extreme measure, such as severe administrative regulation, underground garages, or distant fringe parking served by shuttle bus. In the institutional case it may be possible to impose a longer walking distance from car to destination. On the other hand, there are likely to be key personnel — doctors, professors, or research directors — on whose quality the institution depends and who will use all their power to secure convenient parking for themselves regardless of the cost to the whole institution. Thus the institutional parking solution is likely to differentiate among users and require a full-fledged control system. Controls favoring small cars or cars carrying more than one person may also be employed. Public transit and bicycles can be favored; even hitchhiking might be officially exploited. Parking charges may be used to defray part of the cost of the garages.

Designing public open spaces has become an important branch of site planning, as a result of the intense demand for outdoor recreation and the growing realization of the need for conservation. Parks are heavily used. Some are so loaded that their plant cover is breaking down and the natural character that made them attractive is disappearing. Sharp jumps in the use of vacation areas were predicted, and these predictions now seem to be overfulfilled. At present, the outstanding popular activities are pleasure driving and all the water sports, but the traditional rural pleasures of hiking, picnicking, camping, hunting, and fishing are enjoyed by wider and wider segments of our population as general incomes rise and minority groups come to share in dominant middle-class ways of life. Providing the space needed for these activities, particularly within a day's drive of the great metropolitan regions, has become an urgent necessity.

Supplying ample rural space is not sufficient, however. There are great differences in recreational demand between different groups in society. Certain groups are not

Open Space

References 59, 60

served at all: single women, teen-agers, the elderly, and the impoverished minorities most blatantly. Even within a family group, the various members should be able to follow their own diverse interests.

Large recreational areas should therefore contain a great variety of facilities and atmospheres, suitable for all kinds of special-interest groups: challenging and autonomous places for the teens; serene rural quiet; or crowded and active areas for those who want stimulus and companionship. Recreational areas could do more than simply help one to reestablish contact with nature. They might be places where one learns new skills and hobbies, feels out a new career, or experiences past or future or different ways of life. They can be a way of meeting strangers or of trying out new roles and relationships in a situation where the pressure is off and the social fabric not so vulnerable to lasting damage. Making this possible requires new ways of managing public open space and also of designing it.

*Origins of open space design*    Much of the skill in designing public areas for outdoor recreation developed in this country, particularly in the National Park Service, in the park departments of large cities, and within the profession of landscape architecture. The accomplishments have been substantial. Broader concepts of park planning need not abandon what has already been achieved. Past designs have been based on a strong appreciation for natural landscapes of particular kinds — forest, beach, glade, and mountain — and on a settled view of what wholesome outdoor recreation is and of its graded degrees of superiority. Small-group backpacking and nature observation are rated very highly, while trailer camps or fun fairs are deprecated. Indeed, the attitude is closely linked to that love of nature which is the emotional basis for much of our scientific knowledge about natural systems. The problem is to see how it may be reconciled with the changing ways in which open space is being used by ever larger numbers of people.

*"Openness"*    The "openness" of open space is not so much a matter of how few buildings stand upon it but rather of how open it is to the freely chosen actions of its users. Openness is a product of physical character but also of access, ownership, management and of the rules and expectations that govern activity. An open area need not be a natural one, in the sense of being untouched by man (there are very few of these anyway), and indeed in special cases the open space might be heavily occupied by man-made structures or even be a large interior volume. This is a behavioral definition: a space is

open if it allows people to act freely within it. This is not the case with most urban spaces, of course, interior or exterior, or with commercial farms, single-purpose rural reservations, playfields, or even with certain carefully tended woods and parks.

*Variety of demand*

We have a better idea today of the great variety of people who may want to use an open space and of the variety of things they may want to do there. Our list of open-space prototypes — picnic ground, playground, meadow, beach, wood with trails — is too restricted, and so is our focus on space standards or on the recreational demands of the "average family." We are beginning to ask by whom the space will actually be used, what their specific demands are, and how those demands will be communicated to the park designers and management. We are also less certain about how to sort out "good" recreational activities from "bad" ones.

Finally, while the motive of conserving nature is as strong as ever, or even stronger, we also begin to see man and his works as part of that nature and to realize that all ecological systems are changing and cannot be immobilized. Considering men and other organisms together leads us to attempts to change both of them in orderly ways.

*Dual criteria for open space design*

We then come to a double set of criteria for design. On the one hand, we are concerned with the quality of human experience in the open space: the free choice of activity; the release from the intense stimuli of close urban living; the chance to become actively engaged, to exhibit mastery; the opportunity to learn about the nonhuman world; the ability to meet new people or experiment with new ways of living. These gains are to a large extent psychological, and they are not achieved by strict conservation of the preexisting state of nature. On the other hand, we are also concerned with the ecological balance of the site so that it can continue to renew itself under the new pressures that will be put on it. This aim should be for some new "natural" balance of which men and their activities are an integral part. The solution must satisfy both sets of criteria: psychological "openness" and ecological self-renewal. The analyses that precede the plan, therefore, start with both the client group and the natural site.

*Carrying capacity*

A concept carried over from range management is that of "carrying capacity," or the number of people or intensity of activity that a place can support without losing its ability to renew itself naturally: for the ground cover to hold, the trees to succeed themselves, or the water to purify itself. But carrying capacity also refers to the quality of human experience desired, whether it is that of wilderness or of companionship. So the carrying capacity depends on the ecology of the place (a hayfield and a grassy dune are very different in their response to crowds), as well as on how intensively it will be managed, what kind of outdoor experience is desired, and what the expectations of its users are. One man may feel that his pack trip is spoiled if he meets anyone in the course of two weeks, while another will be frightened when he is out of sight of his fellows for more than fifteen minutes. Two thousand persons per mile of beach will seem pleasantly open to a city dweller and unhappily crowded to one used to rural solitude. For this reason it is difficult to set general density standards for areas of different types. It is more useful to provide a diversity of densites — bustling campgrounds and lonely shelters — and to use management and constant monitoring to ensure ecological renewal. Areas may be rotated through a resting period, for example, or access may be regulated by controlled entrance permits, or an ecology may be modified by introducing "weeds" or other sturdy plants.

*Gradation of access*

Large open spaces, which will serve varied populations, are usually organized on a principle of graded access so that diverse activities that would conflict with each other are spread out in space. High-capacity roads come up to some edge or focal point, where are located the centralized facilities, the dense camping areas, the intensive activities. From this point or edge, the intensity of activity and the capacity of the access system grade outward together, until regions are reached that can be penetrated only on foot with some difficulty, in which there are no man-made structures, in which the human occupation will be low and sporadic. A whole national park may be organized in this way, with a ring of highways, campgrounds, and picnic groves, surrounding a core "wilderness," approachable only by difficult pack trails. An ocean beach can be planned to have one section — complete with parking lots, restaurants, toilets, and lifeguards — which is meant for heavy use, as well as areas that will be lonely because one must walk a mile to reach them. The preferences of two different, potentially conflicting groups are met, and facilities are efficiently centralized. Areas that will sustain a heavy load can be designed and managed to take the shock, and other areas that may be peculiarly fragile can be protected from heavy intrusion.

In a similar way, large recreational areas need not be "pure," that is, devoid of any commercial concessions, motels, or trailer parks. They can include teen-age camps, self-built summer housing, conservation work camps, or centers for temporary education. They may contain productive activities as well: lumbering, mining, and grazing are traditional elements in the national forests. But open space may also have enclaves of industrial use if the plants are regulated to prevent environmental pollution. As another example, operating farms are now successfully being integrated with holiday accommodation.

See page 342

Since the experience of openness and freedom is a psychological one, it can be preserved, even when large numbers are using a place, by an organization of the space into small territories, each of which is shielded from sight and sound of the other. Natural masks of cover and terrain can be used or artificial ones created. Shielding the different access routes from each other is a part of the strategy. At the same time, it is useful to locate diverse areas close to one another so that different members of the same group can enjoy their preferences or move easily from one kind of action to another. Close juxtaposition can even add to the sense of diversity, as when a leafy glen close to an active amusement area seems by contrast all the more secluded.

*Diversity of territory*

At the same time, since many users of an open space will be strangers to it, as well as unaccustomed to rural landscape forms or accompanied by children liable to wander off, it is important that the area as a whole be clearly organized, at least in the more actively used parts. Here the general structure must be easy to picture in the mind; approaches should be direct, sequences clear. Legible maps and signs will supplement this purpose.

Thus the distribution of users can be controlled by the location of access and facilities. In addition, people take pleasure in motion itself, and much of the delight of a place lies in how one gets to it. The design of the access system is therefore a key decision in park planning. One deals with the whole network: highways, forest tracks, bus schedules, cycle paths, riding stables, waterways, foot trails. Routes can be masked one from the other and still interlace closely in the same territory. Each one can have a memorable visual sequence, suited to its own mode of motion. Each one can be given glimpses of the larger terrain and make an understandable approach to its destination. What is seen by the

*Design for motion*

wayside can convey a knowledge of the geology or ecology of the place. Certain localities can be made remote by virtue of a difficulty or break in transportation: a ferry or a tortuous defile. The degree of use can be regulated by the capacity of the access system. Delight in motion is now a common taste, abetted by the new machines that open up previously impassable terrains: beach buggies, snowmobiles, underwater tractors. Facilities must be made for these new kinds of movement, and other regions must be defended against them.

Considering this very strong interest in motion — pleasure driving, in particular, but also cycling, boating, and hiking — we come to the need for creating a continuous recreational network, penetrating the metropolitan regions and their hinterlands. This means not only rural roads with frequent wayside picnic and swimming areas but also a coherent network of bicycle paths, of suburban and rural walking trails, even of public bridle paths or canoeing routes. These badly needed trails will usually be quite inexpensive to construct and maintain. The principal problem will be to secure the public right-of-way.

Other than motion, water is the strongest attraction: people will gravitate toward the lakes, ponds, streams, and ocean shores. Water provides the most attractive recreational activities and at the same time will be most vulnerable to overuse. Control and management is usually required. The natural tendency is for all structures and access to be drawn to the water's edge, resulting in a mutilated shore and a neglected interior. It is better to put buildings and roads back out of sight, keeping the water edge unencumbered and its use spread out.

*The principle of occupying the margin*

This is one instance of a more general strategy: the most attractive and fragile features of a landscape should never be permanently occupied since occupation often destroys what is most valued. Permanent structures are put on the less attractive land but should look toward and be accessible to the best areas. Meanwhile, the new structures can enhance what is otherwise a relatively featureless terrain. Thus, on a recreational island, settlements are best put in the interior, leaving the ocean beaches open and free. Houses are set, not in the middle of a meadow, but at the edge of the woods, looking over the grassy expanse. A mask of undisturbed trees is left around the shores of a pond. Buildings are set, not on the very top of a hill, but on the brow, or lower down on the upper slopes, where they enjoy the view without demeaning the natural feature that affords it. An essen-

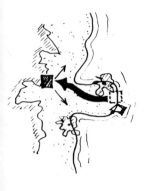

tial part of the analysis of an open space is the identification of valuable features to be left unencumbered but accessible.

Open spaces can provide for that kind of direct action and accomplishment which is increasingly denied us in a highly organized society. People can learn new sports, plant gardens, build summer homes, hunt, camp, learn new skills. Parks should be designed for this kind of active participation far more than they are today. They can be places for meeting challenges in ways that are socially acceptable and personally satisfying: rock-climbing, backpacking, even mock warfare. Some dangerous ground can be preserved and made accessible by special permit. Parks can also be places for learning not only about natural history but also about society and about oneself. They can be both familiar and strange — places where one feels at ease and relaxed and yet where, within a short distance, one can move off into unknown territory.

It is not enough to provide the space for recreation: people must be taught the new skills. Undoubtedly, the current popularity of camping in the national parks is due to what was learned in summer camps a generation ago. Not only should traditional pleasures be taught, but new activities should be developed and communicated: skin diving, orienteering, gliding, sky diving, and water-skiing are all recent inventions. Iceboating, spelunking, cross-country skiing, or rock-climbing are older skills but are just now being taught to a general public. We can even design new recreational landscapes, which use light and sound and three-dimensional depth: caves, mazes, aerial runways, underwater jungles, changeable terrains, do-it-yourself construction yards, man-made boating marshes. This is a further way of providing for diverse demand.

*Learning new recreation skills*

Urban renewal is one aspect of a more general process in which an existing environment is rebuilt and rehabilitated by group effort to satisfy new purposes or new standards. Urban renewal as a formal process in the United States has been much criticized for its social disruption, its authoritarian style, and its economic inefficiency. A thorough discussion of this process lies far beyond the scope of this book, but it is clear enough that a substantial amount of site planning will occur, and has occurred, as a result of the systematic rebuilding of the environment, whether it is carried out under this program or in some socially less destructive way. While renewal has traditionally been associated with central city areas, we can expect suburban renewal to

Renewal

Reference 61

become a major issue within the decade. Site planning in a renewal situation may be done for many purposes and thus has affinities with many particular types of site organization. But a few general comments particular to renewal sites may also be made.

The outstanding fact, of course, is that the area is already occupied — there are residents, workers, and users who have a substantial stake in it. If the area is to be reused by the existing residents, then they should be involved in its site planning from the beginning — setting goals and criteria, analyzing requirements and situation, devising and choosing alternatives, evaluating the changes as they occur, maintaining and controlling the rehabilitated environment. The participatory techniques discussed elsewhere in this book find their greatest usefulness in this kind of situation. Physical change can be an opportunity for social renewal. Even if the area will be reused by others, and not by the existing residents, the latter will still have an important voice in the process of renewal — in the staging and character of displacement and relocation.

*Existing assets in a renewal area*

In renewal, we work over ground occupied by many human and physical assets, all entangled in the urban spider web. Dealing with those assets demands a sympathy for city life and for the way in which it develops. Designers who perform brilliantly on clear sites will raise havoc in renewal areas, to which many of our inhuman redevelopment projects mutely testify. The area is likely to be studded with structures and activities that still have social and economic utility. The impulse of a designer trained to order and pattern is to sweep them aside or, if their retention is forced upon him, to seal them off like lumps of foreign matter. But many human associations have gathered about the old buildings; they accommodate activities economically marginal but socially useful. They will provide a contrast to newer structures and maintain continuity with the past. Existing types of behavior may be renewed and made visible, not suppressed; an order can be found which will embrace the new and old together. Much of the meaning and vitality of urban life rises from just such a sense of complex association, of the layers of historical development made visible. A shopping center in an old chocolate factory or a neighborhood community center in the home of a brilliant nineteenth-century feminist have rich overtones for the present.

The search for order contends with the fact that rebuilding must be done piecemeal, as the community acquires the power to carry out the plan. Formal order is unlikely to be successful: a flexible and multiform pattern is required. The designer resigns himself to the sad or glorious fact that the fabric will be inhabited by a succession of activities. He need not find a permanent shell within which they can all be confined but may look for a general principle to which successive activities may attach themselves and from which they will grow and elaborate. An open space system or a circulation system can be a more important contribution than a pattern of building shapes. Or the critical contribution may be just the opposite of a general ordering system; it may lie in the detailed treatment of existing waste and public spaces that can be modified at small cost, with minimum disturbance of existing structures and with little threat to the existing pattern of psychological and social territories. So we look to a new form for an old park to encourage new behavior or think of face-lifting a street so that it supports what people want to do in the street and is a focus of community pride and identification. By creating strategic effects with minimum site effort the designer achieves his greatest value.

Renewal design is fractionated, rather like a subdivision, if not so seriously. It is a special case of the "multiple-developer" situation described in Chapter 10. A general site plan, fixing use, density, circulation, public facilities, perhaps even building mass, is prepared by the community or a public agency. Other public and private developers carry out this plan for their own purposes: public or private housing, shops, factories, offices, clinics, schools, highways, transit lines. These developers may have been in close liaison with the original planners, or they may be late arrivals. The original agency must anticipate developer requirements, judge how detailed its own plan should be, and devise controls that will carry out its intent while allowing adjustment to the unforeseen future. The developer makes his own plan in the spirit of the original and yet must know when to break away from that original because of a new idea or a new situation. Ideally, each actor will penetrate the other's function, the developer influencing the original program, the initiating agency making a detailed illustrative plan as a test of its ideas. From this plan the needed controls are extracted, detailed at critical points, and left quite general elsewhere. But this separation in planning, required by the lapse of time, political conflict, competitive bidding, or

*Incremental
order*

*The fragmenta-
tion of renewal
design*

*See pages 237 and
238*

administrative partitioning, is a chasm not easily bridged. The problems of coordination make it all too tempting to use a single developer, thus squeezing out mixed uses and small agents, regardless of the resulting social loss.

Renewal sites merge into their settings. Structures flank neighboring ones, streets run into contiguous streets, activities are part of a city-wide network. Most redevelopment plans deny these connections (as do shopping centers, institutions, and so many other new creations of ours). The plans focus inward, turn their parking lots outward, emphasize their distinctiveness. Designers and inhabitants call them "projects" or "islands." Design habits are reinforced by the administrative procedures that divide the rebuilding process into actions located in areas with sharp boundaries. Renewal actions that focused on functional systems, or on time periods, or on networks rather than bounded areas might overcome some of this tendency. We cannot deal here with these issues or with the issue of form at the city scale. Lacking some better public directive, the site planner cannot contribute directly to connections at this comprehensive level. But he can at least make sure of the local fit of his design. He can think of approach or the outward view, of boundaries and the tendency of human activity to overrun them, of harmonies of scale and form between site and setting.

What has been said here is only an elaboration of the more general themes of this text. Yet these issues are so commonly forgotten in site planning for renewal that it seems necessary to point out their special application in that context. We can expect more and more of our urban development to become a renewal process, and surely we must learn how to do it in a rich and humane way.

# Selected Bibliography

1. Fairbrother, Nan. *New Lives, New Landscapes.*
   New York: Knopf, 1970.

   Good sense, sharp observation, and useful ideas on the relation between environmental setting and contemporary changes in ways of life.

2. Goodman, Paul and Percival. *Communitas.*
   New York: Vintage (paper), 1960 (orig. ed., 1947).

   The connections between environment and ways of life.

3. Lynch, Kevin. "Environmental Adaptability."
   *American Institute of Planners Journal*, Vol. 24, No. 1 (1958), pp. 16–24.

   A theoretical discussion about providing adaptability in physical layouts.

4. Ministry of Housing and Local Government, Great Britain. *Design in Town and Village.*
   London: H.M.S.O., 1953.

   Three essays on urban design in villages, urban residential areas, and city centers. Standard English good practice.

5. Neutra, Richard. *Survival through Design.*
   New York: Oxford (paper), 1969 (orig. ed., 1954).

   Much good sense and sensitivity about the impact of built environment on the human being.

6. Princeton University, Research Center for Urban and Environmental Planning. *Planning and Design, Workbook for Community Participation.*
   Princeton, N.J.: Princeton University Press, 1969.

   An attempt to lay out explicit choices and procedures for client design of housing areas. Tedious and mechanical, but much useful material.

*General*
*References*

7. Sitte, Camillo. *City Planning According to Artistic Principles.*
Translated by G. R. and C. C. Collins. New York: Random House, 1965 (orig. ed., 1889).

The foundation for the romantic approach to open space design and the massing of buildings.

8. Stein, Clarence S. *Toward New Towns for America.*
Cambridge, Mass.: M.I.T. Press (paper), 1966.

A full and honest description of the site planning and community development of Stein and Henry Wright, which comprised most of the forward work in the United States in the twenties, thirties, and forties: Sunnyside, Chatham Village, Radburn, Baldwin Hills, etc.

*Social and Psychological Aspects*

9. Alexander, Christopher. "Major Changes in Environmental Forms Required by Social and Psychological Demands."
*Ekistics*, Vol. 28, No. 165 (August 1969), pp. 78–85.

An interesting and sensible, though speculative, discussion of the connection between spatial form and social needs.

10. Barker, Roger. "On the Nature of the Environment."
*Journal of Social Issues*, Vol. 19, No. 4 (1963), pp. 17–38.

A presentation of his concept of behavior settings.

11. Carr, Stephen. "The City of the Mind."
In W. Ewald, ed., *Environment for Man.* Bloomington: Indiana University Press, 1967.

A good compact summary of the psychological implications of environment.

12. Cooper, Clare C. *Some Social Implications of House and Site Plan Design at Easter Hill Village: A Case Study.*
Berkeley: Center for Planning and Development Research, University of California, 1965 (mimeographed).

Detailed study of the physical attributes of a low-density public housing project in their relation to the kinds of behavior and preferences of occupants.

13. Festinger, Leon, S. Shachter, and Kurt Back. *Social Pressures in Informal Groups.*
Stanford, Calif.: Stanford University Press, 1963.

Among other issues, discusses the spatial ecology of a student housing area.

14. Gans, Herbert J. "Planning and Social Life" and "Homogeneity or Heterogeneity in Residential Areas?"
*American Institute of Planners Journal*, Vol. 27, Nos. 2 and 3 (May and August 1961), pp. 134–140 and 176–184.

An urban sociologist on the connection, and lack of connection, between environment and behavior.

15. Grey, A. L., D. L. Bonsteel, G. H. Winkel, and R. A. Parker. *People and Downtown: Use, Attitudes, Settings.*
Seattle: College of Architecture and Urban Planning, University of Washington, September 1970.
An excellent study of the actual use of the public physical setting in downtown Seattle.

16. Gutman, Robert. "Site Planning and Social Behavior." *Journal of Social Issues*, Vol. 22, No. 4 (1966), pp. 103–115.
A good review of the then current knowledge of the relation between these two. Focused on typical sociological themes, such as social linkage; tends to neglect the more obvious impacts of site plans.

17. Jacobs, Jane. *The Death and Life of Great American Cities.*
New York: Random House, 1961.
Keen observations on the street life of central city bohemian neighborhoods, inflated to general planning principles.

18. Perin, Constance. *With Man in Mind: An Interdisciplinary Prospectus for Environmental Design.*
Cambridge, Mass.: M.I.T. Press, 1970.
Linking spatial design and behavior by the use of behavioral programs.

19. Schorr, Alvin. *Slums and Social Insecurity.*
Washington, D.C.: U.S. Department of Health, Education and Welfare, Social Security Administration, Research Report #1, 1963.
An excellent discussion of the physical and social aspects of poverty housing.

20. Sommer, Robert. *Personal Space: The Behavioral Basis of Design.*
Englewood Cliffs, N.J.: Prentice-Hall, 1969.
A solid though repetitive exposition of recent work in small-scale environmental psychology. Sane and humane, not profound.

21. Suttles, Gerald. *The Social Order of the Slum.*
Chicago: University of Chicago Press, 1970.
A fine account of individuals, social structure, and place, all operating as a total system.

22. Crowe, Sylvia. *Garden Design.*
New York: Hearthside, 1958.
A good modern handbook.

23. Flawn, Peter T. *Environmental Geology: Conservation, Land Use Planning and Resource Management.*
New York: Harper & Row, 1970.
A practical reference on geology, soil, and water, for use in land planning.

*Land and Ecology*

364

24. Hubbard, Henry V., and Theodora Kimball. *An Introduction to the Study of Landscape Design.*
New York: Macmillan, 1917.

A classic text, useful even today.

25. McHarg, Ian. *Design with Nature.*
Garden City, N.Y.: Natural History Press, 1969.

A propaganda piece for ecology as the basis for landscape design.

26. Odum, Eugene P. *Ecology.*
Modern Biology Series. New York: Holt, Rinehart & Winston, 1963.

An excellent brief summary of ecological theory.

27. Repton, Humphry. *Landscape Gardening and Landscape Architecture*, J. C. Loudon, ed.
London: Longmans, 1840.

Valuable ideas on the design of extensive landscapes.

28. Simonds, John O. *Landscape Architecture: The Shaping of Man's Natural Environment.*
New York: McGraw-Hill, 1961.

Sometimes verbose, but still an excellent manual on landscape design. Particularly interesting in regard to pedestrian movement.

29. Smith, W. H. "Trees in the City."
*American Institute of Planners Journal*, Vol. 36, No. 6 (November 1970), p. 429.

A sober review of current knowledge as to the effects of city trees on noise, air pollution, microclimate, water supply, and runoff.

30. Twiss, Robert H. *Natural Resources Study for the Santa Cruz Campus of the University of California.*
Prepared for the Office of Physical Planning and Construction, University of California, Santa Cruz, October 1966.

A good example of ecological analysis as a basis for site development.

31. Wyman, Donald. *Trees for American Gardens.*
New York: Macmillan, 1965.

The best compilation on the subject.

32. Zion, Robert L. *Trees for Architecture and Landscape.*
New York: Reinhold, 1968.

Detailed data on most of the principal ornamental tree species and their use in site planning. Magnificent illustrations.

*Technical Data*

33. Avery, T. Eugene. *Forester's Guide to Aerial Photo Interpretation.*
U.S. Department of Agriculture Handbook #308. Washington, D.C.: Government Printing Office, December 1969.

Excellent brief handbook on the use of aerial photos, plus specialized material on forestry interpretation.

34. Baerwald, John E. *Traffic Engineering Handbook.*
Third Edition. Washington, D.C.: Institute of Traffic
Engineers, 1965.
A basic general text.

35. Beazley, Elizabeth. *Design and Detail of the Space Between Buildings.*
London: Architectural Press, 1960.
Detailed, thorough, and very useful, particularly in regard to the "hard" elements of landscape design at
high to moderate densities.

36. Committee on Land Subdivision, City Planning Division, American Society of Civil Engineers. *Land Subdivision, Manual of Engineering Practice.*
No. 16. New York, 1952.
An old monograph that to date has no direct replace-
ment.

37. Geiger, Rudolf. *The Climate near the Ground.*
Translated by Scripta Technica, Inc. Cambridge, Mass.:
Harvard University Press, 1950.
An old book, not easy to read, and focused primarily
on agricultural microclimates; but it covers the essen-
tial principles and has no recent rival.

38. Highway Research Board. *Highway Capacity Manual.*
Washington, D.C.: Highway Research Board, 1965.
Detailed analysis of those characteristics of roads that
affect capacity.

39. Newville, Jack. *New Engineering Concepts in Com-
munity Development.*
Technical Bulletin #59. Washington, D.C.: Urban
Landscape Institute, 1967.
New techniques in clearing, grading, drainage, streets,
sewerage, and utilities.

40. Parker, Harry, and John W. MacGuire. *Simplified Site
Engineering for Architects and Builders.*
New York: Wiley, 1954.
Prosaic, old, but useful material on grading, utilities,
road design, etc.

41. Peterson, J. T. *The Climate of Cities: A Survey of Re-
cent Literature.*
Washington, D.C.: U.S. Department of Health, Edu-
cation, and Welfare, National Air Pollution Control
Administration, October 1969.
A useful brief summary of current knowledge.

42. Seelye, E. E. *Data Book for Civil Engineers*, Vol. 1:
*Design.*
New York: Wiley, 1960.
A good source for the details of various site engineer-
ing structures.

43. Way, Douglas. *Air Photo Interpretation for Land Planning.*
Cambridge, Mass.: Department of Landscape Architecture, Harvard University, 1969.

Reading geology, topography, and vegetation type from vertical air photos. Useful and systematic written material, poorly reproduced photographs.

44. Weddle, A. E., ed. *Techniques of Landscape Architecture.*
New York: American Elsevier, 1967.

An uneven technical symposium, with several very informative essays on landscape construction methods.

45. Working Group, Ministry of Transport, Great Britain. *Traffic in Towns.*
London: H.M.S.O., 1963.

A thorough and practical discussion of vehicular traffic in urban areas that puts the emphasis on the environment served by it. Many examples. Focused on English problems and the city-planning scale, however.

*Residential Site Planning*

46. American Public Health Association, Committee on the Hygiene of Housing. *Planning the Neighborhood: Standards for Healthful Housing.*
Chicago: Public Administration Service, 1948.

Out of date and obsessed with precise standards but still a useful and comprehensive background.

47. Central Mortgage and Housing Commission. *Site Planning Handbook.*
Ottawa, 1966.

An excellent condensed manual on residential site planning. Many detailed standards.

48. Kennedy, Robert Woods. *The House and the Art of Its Design.*
Chapters 9 and 10. New York: Reinhold, 1953.

Sensitive discussion of the siting of small middle-class houses.

49. McKeever, J. R., ed. *The Community Builders Handbook.*
Washington, D.C.: Urban Land Institute, 1968.

A lengthy and practical treatise on large residential developments from the builder's point of view.

50. Ministry of Housing and Local Government, Great Britain. *Caravan Parks.*
London: H.M.S.O., 1962.

Good general manual on the layout of trailer parks.

51. Ministry of Housing and Local Government, Great Britain. *Cars in Housing / 1.*
London: H.M.S.O., 1966.

Good examples of the diagrammatic possibilities of relating houses of parking, open space, and pedestrian ways.

52. Ministry of Housing and Local Government, Great Britain. *The Density of Residential Areas.*
London: H.M.S.O., 1952.
Density measures and their consequences.

53. Ministry of Housing and Local Government, Great Britain. *Landscaping for Flats.*
London: H.M.S.O., 1967.
An excellent practical, detailed, but not very imaginative guide.

54. Royal Institute of British Architects. *Family Life in High Density Housing, with Particular Reference to the Design of Space about Buildings.*
London: The Institute, 1957.
The title explains itself.

55. United States Federal Public Housing Authority. *Public Housing Design.*
Washington, D.C.: National Housing Agency, 1946.
An old handbook on housing project site planning, of substantial value today.

56. Appleyard, Donald, Kevin Lynch, and John R. Myer. *The View from the Road.*
Cambridge, Mass.: M.I.T. Press, 1964.
An early attempt to analyze the moving view.

57. Brawne, Michael, ed. *University Planning and Design.*
London: Lund, Humphries, 1967.
A general discussion of new university planning by administrators and architects, plus a dozen cases of new university plans.

58. Gruen, Victor D., and Larry Smith. *Shopping Towns U.S.A.*
New York: Reinhold, 1960.
A thorough and well-illustrated coverage, now somewhat outdated.

59. Hole, Vere. *Children's Play on Housing Estates.*
Ministry of Technology, Building Research Station, Research Paper #39. London: H.M.S.O., 1966.
Good observation of how preteen playgrounds are actually used, although limited to traditional kinds of playgrounds and without a theoretical basis.

60. Lynch, Kevin. "The Openness of Open Space."
In Marcou, O'Leary and Associates, *Open Space for Human Needs.* Washington, D.C.: The National Urban Coalition, 1970.
Some of the behavioral possibilities in open space design.

*Site Planning for Other Uses*

61. Montgomery, Roger. "Improving the Design Process in Urban Renewal."
    *American Institute of Planners Journal*, Vol. 31 (February 1965), pp. 7–20.

    Analysis of the problems of design control, based on renewal experience.

62. Pasma, Theodore K. *Organized Industrial Districts.*
    Washington, D.C.: U.S. Department of Commerce, Office of Technical Services, Area Development Division, 1954.

    An old and somewhat sketchy discussion.

63. Pushkarev, Boris S., and J. M. Zupan. *The Pedestrian and the City.*
    Cambridge, Mass.: M.I.T. Press, forthcoming.

    An excellent detailed technical manual on calculating pedestrian capacity and demand in midtown Manhattan.

64. United Nations, Department of Economic and Social Affairs. *The Physical Planning of Industrial Estates.*
    New York: United Nations, 1962.

    A thorough discussion, primarily for use in the developing countries.

*Pictorial*
*References and*
*Examples*

65. Bardi, P. M. *The Tropical Gardens of Burle Marx.*
    New York: Reinhold, 1964.

    Well-illustrated catalog of the work of a master landscape artist.

66. Caminos, Horacio, John F. C. Turner, and John A. Steffian. *Urban Dwelling Environments: An Elementary Survey of Settlements for the Study of Design Determinants.*
    Cambridge, Mass.: M.I.T. Press, 1969.

    A comparative graphic description of sixteen urban residential neighborhoods, eight in Boston, Mass., and eight in four Latin American cities.

67. Eaton, Leonard K. *Landscape Artist in America: The Life and Work of Jens Jensen.*
    Chicago: University of Chicago Press, 1964.

    The fine natural landscapes that Jens Jensen created in the Middle West.

68. Eden, William A. "Hampstead Garden Suburb: 1907–57."
    *Royal Institute of British Architects Journal*, Vol. 64 (October 1957), p. 489.

    A description of the classic "garden city" and of its evolution.

69. Harada, Jiro. *Gardens of Japan.*
    London: Studio, 1928.

    A good picture book and exposition of the basic principles of these gardens.

70. Hegemann, Werner, and Elbert Peets. *The American Vitruvius: An Architect's Handbook of Civic Art.*
New York: Architectural Book Publishing, 1922.

A fine picture book of the accomplishments of early civic design, though the pictures are too small. Surprisingly enough, the text is also thoughtful and informed. Peets became one of the most skilled U.S. site planners of his day.

71. Hyams, Edward. *The English Garden.*
New York: Abrams (paper), 1966.

A good historical summary of the great English gardens.

72. Katz, R. D. *Design of the Housing Site.*
Urbana, Ill.: University of Illinois, 1966.

Numerous informative plans and illustrations of current residential site planning, though the text is weak.

73. Masson, Georgina. *Italian Gardens.*
New York: Abrams (paper), 1961.

A good historical summary of the Italian garden.

74. Rasmussen, Steen Eiler. *Towns and Buildings.*
Cambridge, Mass.: Harvard University Press, 1951.

A delightful and very observant description of various fine towns and building groups, with handsome marginal drawings.

75. Siren, Osvald. *Gardens of China.*
New York: Ronald Press, 1949.

Still the best book on the subject.

# Index*

*Italic page numbers refer to illustrations.